Praise for *The Iran Nuclear Deal*

"Dennis Jett has provided startlingly clear, well-documented background to the campaign in the United States against and in favor of American approval of the deal to limit Iran's nuclear capacity in return for international sanctions relief. He also makes it clear that the American political conflict over the agreement is not over, identifying the players and the resources at their disposal clearly."
—Dan Simpson, *Editor of* Pittsburgh Post-Gazette *and Retired US Ambassador*

"Ambassador Dennis Jett offers a fresh and insightful analysis of how American foreign policy is actually made. He leaves aside traditional academic and theoretical explanations as incomplete and misleading. Focusing on the Iran Nuclear Treaty, Jett argues instead that American foreign policy is created through the dynamic interaction of powerful forces—money, technology, truth, partisanship, and globalization. This is a highly readable, learned, and unique perspective offering clarity in the making of our foreign policy."
—Richard K. Scher, *Professor Emeritus of Political Science, University of Florida, USA*

"To understand what's happening to America, don't waste time analyzing the Trump phenomenon—a symptomatic singularity only—but look closely at developments regarding the nuclear agreement with Iran. This stellar diplomatic achievement and fundamental move toward peace in the Middle East is being undermined systematically by almost the entire Republican Party and key members of the Democratic Party. In *The Iran Nuclear Deal*, Ambassador Dennis Jett tells us why: money, war, Israel, and money."
—Lawrence Wilkerson, *Visiting Professor of Government and Public Policy, College of William and Mary, USA, and former chief of staff to Secretary of State Colin Powell*

"Ambassador Jett provides a fascinating, if concerning, look into how negotiations work in today's complex world. His insight into the influence of dark money, social media, and raw politics is a must read for anyone who wants to understand how Washington works—or does not work—today."
—Nancy Soderberg, *former Deputy National Security Advisor and Ambassador to the UN*

"Dennis Jett's analysis of the forging of the agreement to curb Iran's nuclear weapons ambitions is outstanding. The private money poured into supporting and opposing the agreement is breathtaking. It raises deeply disturbing questions about exactly how policy on crucial issues is determined in democracies. This book is essential reading."

—Richard Butler, *former UN Chief Weapons Inspector in Iraq and Australian Ambassador to Thailand*

The Iran Nuclear Deal

Dennis C. Jett

The Iran Nuclear Deal

Bombs, Bureaucrats, and Billionaires

Dennis C. Jett
Pennsylvania State University
University Park, Pennsylvania, USA

ISBN 978-3-319-59821-5   ISBN 978-3-319-59822-2 (eBook)
https://doi.org/10.1007/978-3-319-59822-2

Library of Congress Control Number: 2017953557

© The Editor(s) (if applicable) and The Author(s) 2018
This work is subject to copyright. All rights are solely and exclusively licensed by the Publisher, whether the whole or part of the material is concerned, specifically the rights of translation, reprinting, reuse of illustrations, recitation, broadcasting, reproduction on microfilms or in any other physical way, and transmission or information storage and retrieval, electronic adaptation, computer software, or by similar or dissimilar methodology now known or hereafter developed.
The use of general descriptive names, registered names, trademarks, service marks, etc. in this publication does not imply, even in the absence of a specific statement, that such names are exempt from the relevant protective laws and regulations and therefore free for general use.
The publisher, the authors and the editors are safe to assume that the advice and information in this book are believed to be true and accurate at the date of publication. Neither the publisher nor the authors or the editors give a warranty, express or implied, with respect to the material contained herein or for any errors or omissions that may have been made. The publisher remains neutral with regard to jurisdictional claims in published maps and institutional affiliations.

Cover design by Fatima Jamadar.

Printed on acid-free paper

This Palgrave Macmillan imprint is published by Springer Nature
The registered company is Springer International Publishing AG
The registered company address is: Gewerbestrasse 11, 6330 Cham, Switzerland

To Helen and Clifton who made all that their sons accomplished possible.

Foreword

At the start of each class that I teach at Penn State, I tell the students there are two things that they should know about me. First, that I grew up in New Mexico. Second, that I spent 28 years in the State Department before spending the last 17 as an academic.

I then explain the significance of those two facts. First, that there is nothing bad they can say about Texas that I won't believe. Second, that as a professor of social science at a large, public, northeastern university and a former career bureaucrat, the chances that I am politically liberal and believe there is an important role for government are both in the neighborhood of 99 percent.

I tell my students these two facts because I always urge them to begin reading any book by first looking at the description of the author since it will often indicate how that person's background might affect what is written. Because this book has nothing to do with the southwestern United States, the first fact is not relevant. The readers of this book, like my students, should be aware of the second however. I am not one to pretend that my experience and political beliefs do not affect how I approach a subject or that I can present an issue in a way that all sides will think is unbiased.

This book is about the debate over the Iran nuclear agreement and the efforts of groups outside of government to influence it. The book is not about the 20 months of negotiations that were required or about the agreement itself, which runs to over 31,000 words. Both the negotiating history and the features of the agreement will be discussed, but not in depth since that is not the purpose of the book.

The book is instead about those people and organizations outside of government who attempted to influence the outcome of the negotiations and who continue their efforts to see the agreement succeed or fail. There were an incredibly large number of actors who supported the deal and who opposed it. How the two camps are labeled tells something about the view of the person doing the labeling. Are the supporters pro-diplomacy or pro-Iran? Are the opponents pro-sanctions or pro-war, even though few of them would admit that their position would lead to military conflict?

My view toward which camp has the better argument, as with everyone's position on controversial topics, is affected by my experience. In the case of the Iran deal, there are three incidents that come to mind as having a bearing.

The first was in A-100 class, which is a six-week boot camp for bureaucrats that I took in 1972. In that course, the State Department attempts to educate newly minted Foreign Service Officers about the government they are going overseas to represent. There was but one brief lecture on how to conduct negotiations, but I still remember it. The speaker asked us what should be the outcome of a successful negotiation. We offered a number of responses, all of them wrong from his point of view. He then explained that a successful outcome is when the other side has something it can take back to its capital and defend. If the other side cannot do that, he added, the agreement reached will never last.

The second incident was from the Liberian civil war in 1990. While I did see some fighting while in uniform during the Vietnam War, it was in a bar in Honolulu. There were other conflicts and their effects that I witnessed earlier as a diplomat, but Liberia would provide an object lesson of what happens to a country at war. The war started at the end of 1989 as a minor border incident. By mid-1990, it had engulfed the entire country and the government controlled little more than a few square blocks of downtown Monrovia.

It was a drive through those streets that brought home the impact of war as I had the driver stop to take a look at what lay by the side of the road. The memory is still vivid because it included the smell, as well as the sight, of a stack of bodies decaying under a tropical sun. They were dumped in a heap on a street a couple blocks from the embassy and the presidential mansion. The dead were men in civilian clothes and it was impossible to tell whether they were rebels without uniforms or innocent civilians. It was estimated that war would go on to kill some 200,000 Liberians, though that is just a guess as no one has any idea of what the real death toll was.

The final incident was considerably more upbeat. It happened in Brasilia when I went to witness the presidents of Peru and Ecuador sign a treaty that ended a border dispute between the two countries. A US military plane in the late 1940s was helping demarcate the border in a particularly remote region and discovered a river that had never been previously mapped. The resulting uncertainty over where the border lay had flared up periodically over the years in short military confrontations with casualties on both sides. The territory in dispute was a trackless jungle, but it had become the object of national pride for both countries. An innovative solution was finally found, with the help of mediators from the United States, Argentina, Brazil and Chile, that allowed both sides to claim victory. The resulting agreement that was negotiated put to rest this long-standing source of conflict that had held back the economic and political development of both countries for many years.

The takeaway lessons of those three experiences for me were first that negotiations were not about one side winning but about both sides being able to say they won. Second, that war is best avoided as a way of solving disputes. And third, that diplomacy can succeed with a lot of hard work and creativity.

As a result, I fall into the pro-deal camp on the Iran nuclear accord and that will be reflected in what I write even though I will attempt to describe the other side and its arguments accurately. While I believe that diplomacy did work in this case, I am not writing to argue the merits of the agreement that was reached. Instead, it is to describe the enormous number of actors outside of government that were involved in the debate and the methods they used to try to influence the outcome.

The purpose of the book is also to more generally portray how the influence of money, technology, partisan politics, a growing disregard for truth and globalization has complicated the making of foreign policy, especially when the issue is controversial. It leaves me to wonder how much these factors have all diminished the chances for diplomacy to succeed, for negotiations to reach lasting agreements and for war to be avoided. It also raises the question as to whether these changes have made a foreign policy based on the national interest possible. Or whether policy on each issue will be forged by the victor in a battle between special interests. While it is hard to be optimistic about the outcome, each reader can reach his or her own conclusions and just considering the questions may make a somewhat better result possible.

Preface

The nineteenth-century Prussian statesman, Otto von Bismarck, once said, "Laws are like sausages, it is better not to see them made." Or, maybe he didn't. As with many quotes that are often repeated over the years, historical accuracy is less important than a good turn of a phrase.

There is no definitive evidence that Bismarck actually uttered those words.[1] The reason the quote, accurate or not, has had such a long life is that is true. When governments make laws, the process has always been messy. And it can be just as messy for other decisions that governments make. That is especially true for domestic policy decisions as those affected by such actions recognize their impact and work to influence them.

In the past, when it came to foreign policy, the process seemed a little neater. During the Cold War, for instance, before use of the word "globalization" became commonplace, the impact of international issues seemed remote to most Americans. There was the threat of nuclear war with the Soviet Union, but dealing with that possibility was left to the military planners and strategic thinkers. With fewer people feeling they needed to have a say in the decision making, and given that the issues were complicated and somewhat arcane, foreign policy was largely left to the experts in government.

The process of making foreign policy has gotten much messier in recent years, however. This book will use the debate over the Iran nuclear agreement to describe how that has happened, what new factors have come into play and why the policy that results from such a process may be incoherent, inconsistent and have little to do with the nation's interests. It won't attempt to describe either the negotiations or the deal itself in great detail. Both were very long and complicated and the focus will instead be on individuals and groups outside of government and how they attempted to influence the outcome.

The debate over the nuclear deal also demonstrates that there are a number of things that affect foreign policy more profoundly today than in the past. Those factors are money, technology, truth, partisan politics and globalization. None of these influences are new, as they have always been a part of politics and, therefore, have had an effect on government deliberations. But they have greater weight on foreign policy today than they used to, in part because of their interaction with each other.

Before beginning to describe the case of the Iran nuclear agreement, it is necessary to consider how each of these factors has changed the sausage-making process. That will be followed by a discussion of why the traditional theories of international relations do not take those factors sufficiently into account. Because of that, while grand theories can be constructed, they offer little real insight into how foreign policy is made today, especially when contentious and high-profile issues are involved. This chapter will then end with a brief outline of the remainder of the book.

What's Changed: Money for Starters

Money has always played a significant role in American politics and elections. Thanks to the 2010 Citizens United case and other decisions by the conservative majority on the Supreme Court, however, there is now no effective limit on how much a wealthy individual can give to political campaigns. As National Public Radio's Supreme Court reporter, Nina Totenberg, noted the decision "essentially undid about a century's worth of understandings about regulation of campaign money and at least three decades of specific decisions" and "opened the floodgates to enormous—millions and millions—probably hundreds of millions of dollars in campaign cash."[2]

The cost of congressional and presidential elections had been growing steadily even before the Citizens United decision (Table P.1). The Center for Responsive Politics has charted how elections have mushroomed into a multibillion-dollar industry.[3]

Table P.1 Cost of presidential and congressional elections

Cycle	Total cost of election	Congressional	Presidential
2016*	$6,917,636,161	$4,266,514,050	$2,651,122,110
2014	$3,921,590,197	$3,921,590,197	N/A
2012*	$6,609,557,743	$3,853,016,288	$2,756,541,454
2010	$4,020,984,328	$4,020,984,328	N/A
2008*	$5,927,046,595	$2,787,598,803	$3,139,447,791
2006	$3,416,234,314	$3,416,234,314	N/A
2004*	$5,300,543,183	$2,859,135,182	$2,441,408,000
2002	$2,927,842,804	$2,927,842,804	N/A
2000*	$4,321,482,961	$2,340,275,009	$1,981,207,952
1998	$2,397,891,231	$2,397,891,231	N/A

*Presidential election year. All dollar amounts adjusted for inflation

In the Citizens United case, the Supreme Court, by a 5 to 4 vote, removed any practical limit on the amount that corporations and labor unions could spend to support or oppose political candidates. Declaring that political spending was protected under the First Amendment's free speech provision, the Court equated corporations, and other entities like labor unions, with individuals, entitling them to the same free speech protections.

Because labor unions favor Democrats in their spending and corporations give more to Republicans, it could be argued that this ruling would not have that much effect on the balance of power between the two political parties. Union membership has been falling nationwide, however, and at the same time corporate giving via political action committees (PACs) has increased dramatically. A paper by the Brookings Institution describes the change:

> In 1978, congressional campaign contributions made by labor PACs actually surpassed corporate contributions slightly at a difference of $35.9 to $34.5 million (in 2014 inflation-adjusted dollars). But that relationship flipped in 1980, when corporate giving increased by $20.7 million to $55.2 million total while labor giving only increased $2 million. That difference only grew as time went on, resulting in a discrepancy of $178.1 million in corporate PAC giving compared to just $50.7 million labor PAC contributions to congressional campaigns in 2014.[4]

So, while political spending by unions grew about 41 percent from 1978 to 2014, spending by corporations quadrupled over the same time period. Corporations were not the only ones who saw opportunity in being able to buy political influence through increased campaign thanks to the Supreme Court's decision. Harvesting such contributions has become a big business and the superrich have become eager customers. The creation of an unlimited number of PACs has made possible, and they are dedicated to collecting unlimited amounts of money from billionaires and others who want to have an impact on policy.

As US News put it in a 2015 article on the decision: "As a result, a small group of wealthy donors has gained even more influence on elections, and are able to maintain that influence once candidates take office. Of the $1 billion spent in federal elections by super PACs since 2010, nearly 60 percent of the money came from just 195 individuals and their spouses, according to the Brennan Center report. Thanks to Citizens United, supporters can make the maximum $5200 donation directly to a candidate, then make unlimited contributions to single-candidate super PACs."[5]

And the mega-donors are not giving just because they want the best candidate to win. As one woman, whose father and husband were both billionaires, and who has given over $5 million to political campaigns since 2011, put it: "I have decided to stop taking offense at the suggestion that we are buying influence. Now I simply concede the point. They are right. We do expect something in return. We expect to foster a conservative governing philosophy consisting of limited government and respect for traditional American virtues. We expect a return on our investment."[6]

The woman who wrote that in a 1997 opinion piece in Roll Call is Betsy DeVos. She was confirmed by the narrowest margin possible when the Senate voted on her nomination by President Trump as his Secretary of Education. She was thought by many to be the least prepared and least qualified nominee for a cabinet position in many years. But she was very good at spreading her money around among the right politicians. Seventeen of the senators voting on her nomination had received donations from her.⁷ While having no previous experience in education of any significance, DeVos can now limit government and promote respect for her kind of virtue in ways that will affect school children throughout the country.

While the Supreme Court did make clear its support for transparency in the decision, the reality is big donors wishing to hide their identity can easily do so. Corporate CEOs, for instance, can use their company's money to support candidates without any fear of a backlash from shareholders or customers simply by concealing their actions from the public. That can be accomplished by giving to 501(c) organizations that don't have to reveal the source of the money.

Or it can be done through entities like Donors Trust, a nonprofit that was created to "support charities and sponsor programs which alleviate, through education, research and private initiatives, society's most pervasive and radical needs, including those relating to social welfare, health, environment, economics, governance, foreign relations and arts and culture."⁸ Donors Trust says it is dedicated to "safeguarding the charitable intentions of donors who are committed to promoting a free society."⁹ In other words, it is dedicated to hiding the identity of those who wish to use their charitable giving to promote a society free of taxes and government regulation.

Founded in 1999, Donors Trust took in $83 million in 2015 and has steered hundreds of millions of dollars to organizations like the Heritage Foundation, Grover Norquist's Americans for Tax Reform, the National Rifle Association's foundation, the Cato Institute, the American Enterprise Institute, the Federalist Society, and the Americans for Prosperity Foundation. Those groups were then able to work to undermine labor unions, prevent action on climate change, block efforts at gun control and mount opposition to foreign policy initiatives that the far-right objects to like the Iran nuclear agreement.[10]

In this way, Citizens United has helped drive hundreds of millions of dollars into nonprofit political organizations where it is possible to hide the source of the money.[11] Trevor Potter, a former chairman of the Federal Election Commission, described the situation in a *New Yorker* article this way: "A single billionaire can write an eight-figure check and put not just their thumb but their whole hand on the scale—and we often have no idea who they are. Suddenly, a random billionaire can change politics and public policy—to sweep everything else off the table—even if they don't speak publicly, and even if there's almost no public awareness of his or her views."[12]

As with the spending by labor unions and corporations, the two political parties are not affected equally. The billionaires have a very clear preference for one party over the other. According to a study done by the Campaign Finance Institute, a nonpartisan think tank associated with George Washington University, the Democrats had only 35 donors who contributed more than $100,000, which amounted to 21 percent of what the party collected. The Republicans, on the other hand, had 441 such mega-donors, and they accounted for 64 percent of what that party took in.[13]

It should, therefore, be no surprise that whenever Republicans talk about tax reform, the plan includes massive reductions for the rich, chump change for the middle class and no benefit to the working poor.[14] Their reform proposals also include doing away with the "death tax," which when framed less negatively is known as the inheritance tax. The tax is one that 99.8 percent of Americans will never pay since it does not kick in until an estate exceeds $5.5 million.[15] Any legislation to eliminate it should be called the Plutocrats

Protection Act since, without it, billionaires will be able to pass on all that they have accumulated to their offspring.

One example of this kind of "reform" was the tax plan put forth by President Trump in April 2017. It was a bare bones proposal that would not fill the back of a cocktail napkin but it amounted to "a multitrillion-dollar shift from federal coffers to America's richest families and their heirs," according to a *New York Times* analysis.[16] Even when Republicans are not reforming taxes, who they hope to help most is clear. The health care reform proposal that a group of 13 Republican senators crafted in secret in June 2017 would have given the poorest 20 percent of American households a tax cut or $280 while those in the top 0.1 percent, who make $5 million or more a year, would receive $250,000.[17]

Even without "tax reform," the wealthy have the opportunity to influence elections to a greater extent than ever before. Given the importance of money in today's elections, the American system of democracy has become one where it is more like "one dollar, one vote" than "one person, one vote." And that money does not go to educate the voters about policy choices but instead is designed mainly to appeal to their fears. What is best for the country's interests and even what most would consider as facts is, at best, secondary.

The Partially True, the Wholly Untrue and Nothing but Untruth

Another feature of today's political process that deserves mention is the remarkable disregard for facts. There has always been a tendency on the part of politicians to ignore or deny evidence that they do not like or that threatens the interests of their key constituents or financial supporters. But that proclivity had not risen to the point that it could prompt them to ignore consequences that could be as grave as affecting the habitability of the earth.

Despite the overwhelming consensus among some 97 percent of scientists that the earth's climate is changing and that human activity is a major contributor to that change, there are many politicians who will deny that fact in return for campaign contributions from energy companies. When Scott Pruitt was Attorney General in Oklahoma, he had two political action committees supporting him that collected three quarters of a million dollars in 2015 and 2016. Of that amount, 27 percent came from the energy industry.[18] Pruitt was named by Trump as the head of the Environmental Protection Agency, which should probably now be renamed the Energy Industry Protection Agency. Pruitt has said repeatedly he does not believe carbon dioxide is the main driver of climate change even though the agency he heads is on record saying it is.[19]

Pruitt was not the only politician who denies climate change. According to one study, there are 142 congressmen and 38 senators, all Republicans, that would agree.[20] To the extent there are scientists who argue the climate is not changing because of human activity, they are also probably on the payroll of the oil companies or the billionaire Koch brothers. According to one article in the *Proceedings of the National Academy of Sciences*, corporate funding has swayed public opinion on the issue, polarized the politics around it and prevented an effective policy response.[21] One analysis by the Center for American Progress Action Fund found that the 180 climate change deniers in Congress had received more than $82 million in campaign contributions from the fossil fuels industry.[22]

While spending by fossil fuel companies has bought politicians and swayed public opinion, it has also generated some pushback. On Earth Day in April 2017, demonstrators held marches in Washington and 600 other places around the world in support of science.[23] Thousands of people felt compelled to march in support of the facts that scientific inquiry produces. This was their reaction to President Trump's repeated assertion that climate change is a hoax and the fear that his policies will not only fail to address it but make it far worse.[24]

It is not just people in the street who are concerned about climate change. A September 2016 report by agencies of the American intelligence community concluded that "Long-term changes in climate will produce more extreme weather events and put greater stress on critical Earth systems like oceans, freshwater, and biodiversity. These, in turn, will almost certainly have significant effects, both direct and indirect, across social, economic, political, and security realms during the next 20 years."[25] Yet, despite these obvious risks to national security, Congress has remained largely indifferent and done nothing to address the problem.

The Impact of Technology

One development that even Congress could agree has changed is the impact of technology on every aspect of life including politics. A remarkable story in the January 18, 2017, *New York Times* described that fact by demonstrating how untruth has become an industry thanks to technology.[26] It was about a 23-year-old, recent college graduate named Cameron Harris who had an intense interest in politics and a need for some income. Early in the fall of 2016, as the presidential election was heating up, Harris came up with a way to satisfy both.

Harris, an aspiring Republican political strategist, sat down at his kitchen table and made up a fake news story about an electrician in Ohio, which is always a crucial swing state in presidential elections. The gist of the story was that the electrician had found boxes full of ballots already marked for Hillary Clinton. To give the story more credibility, Harris included a photo that he found on the Internet of a man in work clothes standing next to some ballot boxes.

The story was a total fabrication, but as Harris told the *Times*: "Given the severe distrust of the media among Trump supporters, anything that parroted Trump's talking points people would click. Trump was saying 'rigged election, rigged election.' People were predisposed to believe Hillary Clinton could not win except by cheating."[27]

Harris put the article he invented on his website, ChristianTimesNewspaper.com, an abandoned domain name he had bought for $5. The story went viral and was eventually seen by an estimated 6 million people. At one point, the website was earning $1000 an hour in ad revenue and had an estimated value of over $100,000. Unfortunately for Harris, he did not sell the site at that point.

Once Ohio officials investigated and announced that the story was entirely false, the ads dried up and the website became worthless even faster than it had become valuable. Harris did manage to collect 24,000 e-mail addresses, however, of people who signed up to find out how "Hillary intends to steal the election." Those can no doubt be sold to someone looking for a gullible audience predisposed to believe any negative story about Clinton.

There appears to be no limit to that gullibility thanks to a hyper-partisan political atmosphere where anything bad said about one side will be believed by many on the other. One good example of this partisan divide is another story that made its way around the Internet. It was a report that Comet Ping Pong, a Northwest Washington DC pizzeria, was the headquarters of a satanic child pornography ring that involved high-level Democratic Party officials.

The story was spread by a number of websites including one called Infowars. Run by Alex Jones, a right-wing radio talk show host, the site traffics in conspiracy theories including claims that the 9/11 terrorist attacks were an inside job carried out by the US Government and that the 2012 killings at Sandy Hook elementary school were a hoax invented by gun control advocates.[28]

The pizzeria story was believed by one man from South Carolina who became so enraged that he drove to Washington with an AR-15 assault rifle, went into the restaurant and fired multiple rounds into the ceiling as he searched for evidence of the pornography ring. He was arrested, tried and sentenced to four years in prison for the attack. In an interview with the *New York Times* explaining his actions, he uttered a line that ought to go down with "alternative facts" as symptomatic of the current age. He said: "The intel on this wasn't 100 percent," but he still refused to admit the online articles were wrong and conceded only that there were no children inside that particular building.[29]

The spread of the Internet, social media and other technology has done more than just provide fake news to people willing to believe negative stories about political opponents. It has provided a route to wealth for those interested in engaging their proliferation. President Trump's chief policy advisor, Steve Bannon, is one such person. Trump thinks so highly of Bannon that he elevated him to a seat on the National Security Council (NSC).[30] Putting a political strategist formally on the NSC was without precedent and generated so much criticism that less than 10 weeks later, the decision was reversed.[31] Even though Bannon was taken off the NSC, there is little doubt that his influence on the president continued.

Financial disclosure forms revealed Bannon made millions trading on his association with a billionaire hedge fund manager, Robert Mercer and his daughter Rebekah.[32] Mercer bankrolled Breitbart News, which Bannon ran. While the website is called alt-right, that hardly does justice to describing its white supremacist, racist, often anti-Semitic content, and its far-right conspiracy theories. It may have been an article from Breitbart that prompted Trump's tweet falsely accusing President Obama of wiretapping Trump Tower. Trump admitted his only evidence was a couple of news reports and said more information would come out soon proving him right, but as with so many of Trump's claims, nothing was ever produced.[33]

Social media and the Internet provide opportunities for the like-minded to share information and opinions, often without benefit of any real facts. It can provide validation to any opinion or worldview regardless of how extreme. And it can encourage acts of violence like the one carried out by the man who shot up Comet Ping Pong. Social media platforms, like Facebook, were the source of at least some news for 62 percent of US adults according to a 2016 poll, and nearly a third of them consumed news that way frequently.[34]

With the capacity of technology to spread misinformation and disinformation with such speed, and the financial benefits of doing so, it has made the growing partisan divide between Americans and their elected representatives even deeper.

Can Politics Get Any More Partisan?

One reason stories like the one about Comet Ping Pong are credible is the willingness of many conservatives to believe the worst about liberals. And many liberals are as ready to hold equally low opinions of conservatives. Welcome to the more-polarized-than-ever America.

The willingness of people to believe fake news is not distributed evenly over the political spectrum, however. It is much more prevalent on right than on the left despite the articles that talk about an increase in progressive fake news.[35] Some studies show liberals think more critically than conservatives making them somewhat less susceptible to stories that are obviously false.[36] In addition, a number of studies have shown the viewers of Fox News to be the least well informed and more likely to believe only what they learn from that source.[37]

Technology, the disregard for the truth and the increasingly partisan view combine and interact to amplify the effect of all three. For example, Fox News reported in May 2017 what it claimed to be sensational developments in the case of Seth Rich, a Democratic National Committee staff member, who was murdered on the streets of Washington the previous July in what the police believe was a botched robbery attempt. The Fox story claimed Rich had provided tens of thousands of DNC e-mails to WikiLeaks. This was Fox's way of attempting to validate President Trump's claim that the Russians were not responsible for those leaks despite the fact that the entire American intelligence community had concluded they were. It then quoted one of its own contributors who claimed "someone with the D.C. government, Democratic Nation Committee or Clinton team is blocking the murder investigations from going forward."[38]

Buzzfeed, a liberal news website, and other media outlets quickly debunked every one of those claims.[39] Rich's parents wrote an opinion piece for the *Washington Post* imploring conservative news outlets and commentators to stop politicizing the death of their son and denying he had any contact with WikiLeaks.[40]

When asked by a reporter from CNN about Rich's alleged connection to WikiLeaks, the investigator who was the source for the Fox story said he had no proof and that he was just repeating what the Fox reporter had told him.[41] Fox then retracted the story and removed it from its website saying in a statement that it had not gone through "the high degree of editorial scrutiny we require for all our stories."[42] That degree of scrutiny did not constrain Fox personality Sean Hannity, however. After promoting the story constantly, when faced with the truth he said he retracted nothing. After advertisers began to abandon his show, he claimed they were doing so because of a liberal plot, but he added he would drop the story "for now" out of respect for the parents' feelings.[43] He also said his search for the truth would continue.

Even when confronted with the lack of truth in his story, Hannity, not unlike President Trump, just doubled down and kept on asserting he will be shown to be right someday. The lack of regard for even the most basic facts about a story is not as important as providing his viewers a narrative that they want to hear. The result is the consumers of right-wing news and progressive news live in parallel universes and their distrust of each other is amplified and justified by the media from which they choose to get their information. Thanks to technology and the partisan segmentation of the media market, they can select whatever source that reinforces their beliefs and worldview. It also amplifies partisan differences and makes a rational discussion of policy all the more difficult.

The result of these parallel universes is that the middle ground for American voters seems to have slipped away to the point that, instead of a bell-shaped curve, there is a bimodal distribution among the electorate. According to a Pew Survey, "ideological overlap between the two parties has diminished: Today, 92% of Republicans are to the right of the median Democrat, and 94% of Democrats are to the left of the median Republican."[44]

Partisan politics is also reinforced by the way the members of the House of Representatives are elected. Gerrymandering, the drawing of congressional districts to favor one party, is often attributed as a source of polarization.[45] Although some studies claim its effect is minor,[46] others credit gerrymandering with being responsible for growing polarization in Congress as exemplified by the creation of the Freedom Caucus. It is a collection of about three dozen, all male, far-right Republicans who appear to be beyond the control of even their party's leaders and President Trump.[47]

Because gerrymandering predetermines the outcome of the general election by favoring one party or the other, the only thing many congressmen fear is a challenge in the primary election by someone even more extreme than they are. Because only the most partisan, politically active voters take part in primary elections, the more extreme candidate usually wins. And so it is a race to the right in Republican primaries and to the left in Democratic ones.

Another theory explaining the growing partisan divide is a growing tendency of people to live in communities that tend to think alike. A journalist and a sociologist teamed up to write a book titled *The Big Sort*, which described what they saw happening:

> Living in politically like-minded groups has had its consequences. People living in homogenous communities grow both more extreme and more certain in their beliefs. Locally, therefore, governments backed by large majorities are tackling every conceivable issue. Nationally, however, Congress has lost most of its moderate members and is mired in conflict.[48]

This partisan divergence among Americans, regardless of its cause, has implications for the ability of their government to construct policy solutions to any problem, foreign or domestic. It has also led to a tendency to even reject the idea that there is a problem and to have no faith in those who claim so. A Pew poll found that "Clinton and Trump supporters have widely diverging views of scientists who study climate change. About half of Clinton supporters (51%) say climate scientists understand very well whether or not climate change is occurring while only 17% of Trump supporters do. Clinton and Trump backers were similarly divided over whether climate scientists understand the causes of climate change: 41% of Clinton supporters say climate scientists understand this very well compared with 15% of Trump supporters."[49]

The distrust of experts extends beyond climate change to all areas of government. According to one poll, a slight majority of Americans think "Everyday Americans understand what the government should do better than so-called experts." Among those who voted for Trump, 71 percent agreed with that statement.[50]

There have been a number of books over recent decades written about the anti-intellectual tendency of Americans. A recent one, titled *The Death of Expertise—The Campaign Against Knowledge and Why It Matters*, was reviewed in the *New York Times* by Michiko Kakutani.[51] She commented that "Citizens of all political persuasions (not to mention members of the Trump administration) can increasingly live in their own news media bubbles, consuming only views similar to their own. When confronted with hard evidence that they are wrong, many will simply double down on their original assertions. 'This is the 'backfire effect,' in which people redouble their efforts to keep their own internal narrative consistent, no matter how clear the indications that they're wrong. As a result, extreme views are amplified online, just as fake news and propaganda easily go viral."

Clearly, Sean Hannity is the poster boy for the backfire effect. Thanks to the disregard for the truth and expertise, technology, political partisanship and the money to be made, fake news and propaganda can easily go viral and affect policy making as well as elections. It can even be used by one country to attack another country in ways that may not be as direct but can be just as destructive.

WAR BY OTHER MEANS

Social media and other technological innovations have enabled a country to attack other nations in an attempt to destabilize their political systems, undermine their elections and disrupt their economies without ever firing a shot. One name for such cyber activities is active measures. The Federation of American Scientists described the term in the following way:

> Active measures were clandestine operations designed to further Soviet foreign policy goals and to extend Soviet influence throughout the world. This type of activity had long been employed by the Soviet Union abroad, but it became more widespread and more effective in the late 1960s. Among these covert techniques was disinformation: leaking of false information and rumors to foreign media or planting forgeries in an attempt to deceive the public or the political elite in a given country or countries. The United States was the prime target of disinformation, in particular forgery operations, which were designed to damage foreign and defense policies of the United States in a variety of ways.[52]

This definition is accurate but misleading because of its use of the past tense. The end of the Cold War did not bring an end to active measures. Russia has not only continued but expanded the use of such tactics under Vladimir Putin's leadership. Putin was a career KGB intelligence officer before he became a politician and was well acquainted with the use and power of such tactics. They were employed extensively in the Russian efforts to interfere in the American presidential elections in 2016 and elections in other countries. And the obsession of Sean Hannity with the Seth Rich case was little more than an attempt to shift the responsibility from the Russians to someone within the Democratic Party itself. Hannity probably did it because it fit into his never-ending negative ranting about liberals, but he was certainly doing something that Moscow welcomed.

A cyber warfare expert, testifying at a March 2017 Senate Select Committee on Intelligence hearing on Russian active measures put the blame for them where it belonged. He identified four general themes to the propaganda messages put out by the Russians[53]:

1. Political messages—Designed to tarnish democratic leaders and undermine democratic institutions.
2. Financial propaganda—Created to weaken confidence in financial markets, capitalist economies and Western companies.
3. Social unrest—Crafted to amplify divisions amongst democratic populaces to undermine citizen trust and the fabric of society.
4. Global calamity—Pushed to incite fear of global demise such as nuclear war or catastrophic climate change.

Those kinds of propaganda messages were just part of the Russian efforts at disruption aimed at the United States. A report by the intelligence community, representing the opinion of all 17 agencies, concluded the following about Russian activities and intentions during the 2016 elections[54]:

- Russian President Vladimir Putin's efforts to influence the 2016 election were a significant escalation in directness, level of activity, and scope compared to previous operations.

- Russia's goals were to undermine public faith in the democratic process, hurt the electability and potential presidency of Clinton and help the chances of Trump.
- Moscow's messaging strategy blended covert intelligence operations—such as cyber activity—with overt efforts by Russian state-funded media, third-party intermediaries, and paid social media users or "trolls."
- Russian military intelligence used the Guccifer 2.0 persona and DCLeaks.com to release data obtained in cyber operations publicly and in exclusives to media outlets and to WikiLeaks.
- Moscow will apply lessons learned from its campaign to future influence efforts worldwide, including against US allies and their election processes.

Whether those efforts changed the outcome of the presidential election is something that will be debated for years to come but is impossible to prove one way or the other. That they are having an impact on public perceptions is not in doubt, however. A Pew Research Center poll found that 64 percent of Americans thought that fake news has created a great deal of confusion about the basic facts of current events, 24 percent feel it has caused some confusion and only 11 percent believe it has caused little or no confusion.[55] Some 23 percent of the respondents also admitted to having shared a made-up news story.

Russian propaganda and Trump's relentless attacks on the media, where any story he does not like is labeled fake news, have combined to sow this confusion and undermine faith in traditional sources of information. In fact, many of the things Trump has done seem to be straight from the active measures playbook. According to an April 2017 Washington Post-ABC News poll, 52 percent of Americans think mainstream news organizations regularly produce false stories while 44 percent do not.[56] The same poll found 59 percent believe the Trump administration regularly makes false claims, while 35 percent do not.

The Russian active measures were made possible by the enormous resources Putin devoted to them. Technology amplified them and made them far more effective, allowing the Russians to undermine democracy wherever they choose to intervene. In essence, Russia has been able to wage war simply by using Internet and social media technology as a weapon.

What's Globalization Got to Do with It

Another factor that is not new but has had a growing impact on a country's foreign policy is globalization. An ever-increasing number of books address the many aspects of globalization and the term appears in newspapers on a daily basis. But when asked to define it in a single sentence, few people can come up with a coherent or comprehensive answer. Put most simply, such a definition would look like this: Globalization is people, things and ideas crossing national boundaries with greater speed, frequency, impact and reach; usually driven by technological change, it is neither new nor reversible.

Because globalization makes the crossing of borders much easier and more frequent, it weakens what borders constrain and makes any entity that can ignore them more powerful. Multinational corporations, drug cartels and international organizations are among those that benefit. Labor unions and national governments are among those that see their power diminished. One reason there is so much debate about the effect of globalization is because it creates winners and losers.

The losers protest its impact and stress its negative aspects, while the winners defend it and point out the positive benefits. And both sides use moral arguments to support their point of view by focusing on the people who lose or gain.

National governments are among the losers because their sovereignty and ability to act are weakened by more porous borders that offer less effective limits on the movement of people, ideas and things. That diminished control makes it more difficult to formulate a nation's foreign policy even for the world's only super power. And it creates more and graver challenges that no one nation can address alone.

Some people would like to ignore the impacts of globalization that challenge their policy prescriptions. Opponents of the Iran nuclear deal, for instance, often assert Iran was given too many concessions and that all that needs to be done is to increase economic sanctions. They argue that once Iran is brought to its knees, it will be forced to dismantle its entire nuclear program, including energy production and research, thus ensuring there is no chance it would ever develop nuclear weapons.

That argument ignores the fact that the deal was not a bilateral agreement. There were six countries on the American side of the table, and it is unlikely that any of the others will be willing to not only reimpose sanctions, but increase them, just because the United States wants to take that course of action. In addition, economic sanctions are never airtight and usually just raise the cost of doing business.

With wide support, they can provide a significant effect, but cannot dissuade a country determined to pursue a particular course of action. Without the support of other major countries, the main economic damage they do is to the nation imposing them. Even if they are effective, sanctions hurt the economy of the country imposing them as well as the economy of the country to which they are applied. A study published by the National Iranian American Council estimated that between 1995 and 2014, the sanctions against Iran cost the American economy between $203 and $272 billion and perhaps hundreds of thousands of jobs.[57]

The limitations on the effectiveness of sanctions is but one example of why globalization and its effects are major contributors to making the formulation of foreign policy more difficult. Along with the impact of technology, partisan politics, fake news generated at home and abroad, and the corrupting influence of money on politics, that process is far more difficult to accomplish coherently than in the past. Those factors also make reliance on a theory of international relations to explain the sausage making more problematic. Theories can simplify the world but in doing so they will fail to accurately describe it.

Why a Theory Won't Explain It

When textbooks talk about how governments take decisions, they tend to leave out the messy parts of the sausage making. This is especially true for foreign policy issues where the process depicted is usually one where high government officials make sober, dispassionate assessments of the national interest and act accordingly. In other words, the descriptions often sound as if the nineteenth-century world of diplomacy where elderly white men in conservative suits conferring with each other behind closed doors is alive and well. Politics hardly gets mentioned in the textbook descriptions and any discussion of the influence of groups outside of government is rare.

The world is simplified in that way because those who work in social sciences would like to be able, like those in the hard sciences, to put forth a theory that explains the way nations relate to each other as simply as a theory for how molecules do. Chemists and physicists have a great advantage over economists and political scientists since they can control the variables in an experiment and explain how the natural world works. And that explanation is generally accepted until a new paradigm comes along based on new data that forces a revision.

A political scientist or an economist, on the other hand, faces a challenge that cannot be easily overcome. To attempt construct a general theory that can capture all aspects of international relations, in a parsimonious and widely applicable way, is to offer an illusion.

The theories fail the simplicity test because not all foreign policy issues have equal weight. There are decisions that get made at the highest level by elected leaders. There are decisions made at the next level by people appointed to the position by the president. And then there are the more routine decisions made by lower level officials with little to no publicity or public debate. As one *Washington Post* article put it:

> Paradoxically, as the president's powers have grown, the presidency has become less about policy and more about politics. Presidents generally make the final call on policy decisions, and, for better or worse, their names are the ones that go down in history. But the day-to-day business of government flows not through the Oval Office, but through the offices of Cabinet secretaries, deputy and assistant secretaries, chief financial officers, general counsels, agency heads, ambassadors and others.[58]

The theories do no better when it comes to being widely applicable. In order for a theory to be universal, it would imply that the personality and management style of the country's leader is unimportant. That is like saying the recent history of Iraq would be the same regardless of whether Al Gore or George W. Bush had won the presidential election in 2000.

It also assumes away any importance of culture, history, geography and the system of government of a country. To take these features into account when considering how foreign policy is made would make a simple and universal theory impossible.[59]

Nevertheless, textbooks invariably cover the two most prominent theories—realism and liberalism—and usually consider others as well. There are at least a dozen theories that can be examined and many of them have subdivisions within a particular theoretical school.

The fact that there are at least a dozen competing international relations theories demonstrates the difference between social science and natural science. In social science, the variables cannot be controlled, and in many cases, cannot even be identified. Even those factors that are known are somewhere between difficult and impossible to measure with any accuracy. And there will be disagreement about what factors matter and what do not.

That is also what makes government different from the corporate world. In the latter, the only factor that matters is next quarter's bottom line, which can be determined to the penny. In the former, something a secretary of state will never be able to say is that this year's foreign policy is 14.5 percent better than last year's. Even whether the foreign policy of an administration has made things better or worse will be up for debate. The formulators of the policy will always claim their efforts produced a more prosperous and secure world, while their critics will always argue that they could have done better.

One example of the difference between the two worlds not being taken into account is the argument that because Rex Tillerson was a successful CEO of Exxon, he will succeed as Secretary of State. The goals are much more complex, and often conflicting, and the measures of performance are not the same however. His main preoccupation in his first few months on the job seems to be how to dismantle much of the State Department through proposed draconian budget cuts of 30 percent. That prompted one of his predecessors, Colin Powell, to write in the *New York Times* that such a budget "signals an American retreat, leaving a vacuum that would make America far less safe and prosperous."[60] It will take years to determine what history's verdict on Tillerson's performance as secretary will be, but his first few months give no indication that it will be a positive one.

While the lack of objective and precise measurements will pose a challenge to Tillerson, it allows all the different theories to flourish. It can be argued that they all add value to the discussion and give some insight even if each one only provides a narrow view. Graham Allison, in his classic work *The Essence of Decision*, analyzes the Cuban missile crisis from three different theoretical perspectives. And in all three, he comes up with a plausible scenario for what happened and why.

The same could have been done taking each theory and looking at the crisis through the lens each of those perspectives provide. Since it would be hard to name a woman that was involved in the decision making in the Cuban missile crisis, proponents of feminism as an IR theory would probably have a lot to say. All of the theories might contribute some understanding of the crisis, but none of them would have been "the" explanation for what happened. That is because foreign policy is inherently political, complex and comprised of a vast range of issues of unequal importance.

It is political because government officials, who have gotten to their positions by successfully navigating the world of politics, make the decisions that collectively become foreign policy. The politics can be of three different types—electoral, relational or bureaucratic. At the elected level of politics, and at the top of the pecking order, are the elected politicians. In the case of the United States, that obviously means the president and vice president who are the only ones elected at the national level. After that are the senators and congressmen, who are chosen by each state and congressional district.

At the next level are the appointed politicians who owe their jobs to the president who has named them to their positions. They often received their jobs because of their contribution to getting him elected whether it is campaign contributions, policy advice or political connections. That kind of contribution weighs more than their own individual expertise. While the theories do not account for these kinds of personal relationships, they matter as much in foreign policy as they do everywhere else.

Cordell Hull was Franklin Roosevelt's secretary of state and the person who has held the position longer than anyone else. Yet Roosevelt routinely ignored him and relied on other, often unofficial, envoys like Sumner Welles, William "Wild Bill" Donovan, Harry Hopkins, Averell Harriman, and Wendell Willkie when it came to advice on issues about which Roosevelt cared the most.[61] As the State Department's historian politely put it in a summary of Hull's career, his role in US foreign policymaking was "greatly circumscribed by President Roosevelt."[62]

At an even greater distance from the president are those in the third group—the career civil servants who have worked their way up through the ranks during various successive administrations and achieved their status because of their ability and their success at politics at a bureaucratic level. This group might also be described as the "deep state," a term that has become popular recently with some at the political level as a way of justifying their agenda by questioning the ability, expertise and loyalty of career bureaucrats who might disagree with it.

While issues get decided at all three levels, only a few are made at the presidential or congressional level. Many are made by appointed politicians, but the vast majority are routine decisions that are left to the career people. To assume there is a theory that explains the motivations and decisions of all three groups is to believe there is no difference between any of them and how they think.

The theories fail the universality test because not all governments act the same and not all presidents do either. A president's top priority in his first term is reelection. In his second term, it is ensuring the best possible place in history. In dictatorships, the man in charge makes the decisions and those decisions are usually made on the basis of what is good for him. A 2004 CIA study about Saddam Hussein, which tried to figure out the failure of the agency to understand why he would not admit he had no weapons of mass destruction, demonstrated the agency's inability to understand his thinking. It concluded that he "so dominated the Iraqi Regime that its strategic intent was his alone."[63] And that intent was never anything more than ensuring his own grip on power remained firm.

American presidents lack the ability to dominate their government's decision making given that there are three coequal branches that can be involved. For those in Congress, the future never stretches beyond their next election. They always have to constantly consider what impression the positions they take have on key constituencies and financial backers. Thanks to the gerrymandering of congressional districts, the most important constituencies are the base voters of whichever political party has been engineered to dominate in that district.

The appointed politicians only have to worry about pleasing the president who appointed them and not offending other elected politicians who take a strong interest in a particular foreign policy issue. Career civil servants do not make the same calculations as politicians, however. They usually think in terms of the national interest, or at least their assessment of it, as well as how they think the vague policy guidance they have received from above should be translated and implemented on the ground.

The failure to reflect reality does not seem to diminish the academic attachment to theory. That is particularly true of realism, which is said to be the most commonly held IR theory. As James Lee Ray, the author of one IR textbook, points out, realism is "the most important, most widely adopted theoretical approach to foreign policies and international politics."[64] This worldview rests on the assumption that a state of anarchy always prevails in international relations because there is no supranational body forcing countries to play by a set of rules. The theory, therefore, assumes that because the international community lacks any adult supervision, the world is in a constant state of anarchy and every country always tries to maximize its power in order to protect its national security.

Those who were against the Iran nuclear deal reflected a realist approach by arguing that Iran was relentlessly pursuing a nuclear weapons program and could never be trusted despite any promises made by the Iranian government or binding agreements. For that reason, they saw the use of force as the only option. They asserted that the economic sanctions could be made even tougher to bring Iran to its knees and prevent any nuclear program.

And if it failed to do so, the hawks were ready, and at times seemed eager, to use military force to destroy Iranian nuclear facilities. They were not deterred that the UN Security Council would not approve a resolution allowing member states to use "all necessary means" to eliminate Iran's nuclear program.

The lack of such a resolution did not deter George W. Bush from ordering the invasion of Iraq, however. The UN, created in the wake of World War II to help promote international peace and security, does not declare war on anyone and a Security Council resolution with the phrase "all necessary means" is as close at it ever comes. But it would take far more than simple American dislike of the nuclear deal for the Council to authorize such a step against Iran.

While it is clear that North Korea's development and testing of nuclear weapons is a threat to international peace and security, the UN response has been various sanctions but not a resolution giving a green light for military action. It did when Iraq invaded Kuwait and President George H.W. Bush organized Operation Desert Storm. It did not when President George W. Bush ordered the invasion of Iraq. Many of those who supported invading Iraq in 2003 now argue for using military force against Iran. Their enthusiasm for military operations is undiminished even though, 14 years later, the United States still has soldiers fighting in Iraq long after their combat role supposedly ended. That Iran has four times the land area and three times the population of Iraq also does not deter the advocates of using force in the least.

The realists also assume that the state is the main player and a unitary and rational actor. If the realists really believe that the American government is unitary and rational, they have apparently never visited Washington.

That air of unreality is often acknowledged by those who adhere to or try to explain realism. While acknowledging that, they generally argue that it does not really matter if the theory is not consistent with the way policies made within the Beltway emerge. For instance, an explanation of realist thinking from a popular IR textbook that is in its fifth edition contains the following passage: "The image of a unified, rational state is truly an assumption, not a description of the actual world.

Realists who embrace positivism use such assumptions to build theories not describe reality."[65]

Since positivism is a philosophical system that holds that every rationally justifiable assertion can be scientifically verified or is capable of logical or mathematical proof, the second sentence of the quote is nonsense on steroids. If an unrealistic assumption can be scientifically verified, does that prove it to be true despite it being disconnected from reality? That is the same as arguing that any correlation can be used to prove causality.

And what use is a theory about how nations interact if it is not intended to describe how those interactions take place? If the purpose of constructing a theory is to help understand the past and anticipate the future, then it should begin with assumptions that reflect reality. Otherwise, it is like speculating about how many angels can dance on the head of a pin—an interesting exercise, but one devoid of significance.

In his book, Ray argues that "the world is too complicated to be understood without some degree of simplification. Theories reduce the world to basic essentials to make it intelligible; ideally, they are based on streamlined assumptions that are sufficiently valid to make the world more comprehensible than it would otherwise be, even though they do not provide an accurate or complete description of the world, or the events on which they focus."[66]

But to what extent should the world be simplified if the process of making it understandable also makes it an unrealistic and unreliable predictor of how nations act? The longing of social sciences to be like the natural sciences exists in a world where immutable laws are possible and causal relationships are clear cut should not trump making theories that actually explain the real world.

Ray does not claim to be a realist, but instead says he is most sympathetic to what he calls rational political ambition theory. That theory holds that political leaders want to stay in power and have to deal with both internal and external competitors. For that reason, the domestic and foreign policies those leaders select depends on the structure of their domestic political systems. Or as one writer quoted by Ray put it: "the president will normally give primacy to his domestic calculus, if a choice must be made" as the president plays a two-level game. The two levels are the international one, the president's counterparts in other states, and the domestic one, where the president's political supporters and competitors in the domestic political arena are the other players.

Both levels of the game certainly came into play in the Iran nuclear agreement. The United States had to negotiate with Iran but also had to first forge a common position with the other countries on its side of the table—Russia, France, the United Kingdom, Germany and China. In other words, all five permanent members of the UN Security Council plus Germany. This grouping was called the P5 plus one, or as the Europeans preferred to describe it, the EU three plus three.

Given the difficult relationship between the Western powers and Russia, and the usual lack of enthusiasm on the part of the Chinese for putting outside pressure on any country to change its policies, it was no small feat that the group was able to forge and maintain a common position. At the same time, the domestic calculus, at least in the United States, was an even bigger challenge for the Obama administration, as the rest of this book will be devoted to explaining why.

This book is therefore not about IR theory. It is about how foreign policy is made in the real world and why there is no theory that explains how that process unfolds. It will do that in the case of the Iran nuclear agreement by describing how groups outside of government attempted to influence the outcome of the negotiations and continued to do so even after an agreement had been successfully concluded.

Those groups fell into two broad camps—those who supported the deal and argued for its acceptance and those who opposed it and pushed for Congress to reject it, or to at least force the Obama administration to renegotiate it and make it much tougher. Both sides promoted their point of view vigorously in a way that IR theorists would never recognize. Therefore, examining the maneuvering behind the Iran nuclear negotiations will be useful to those who want to understand how foreign policy is really made.

WHAT'S NEXT

The next two chapters will set the scene and discuss some of the history and politics surrounding the Iran nuclear agreement. The chapter after that will consider the actors in the debate, describing some of the organizations outside of government that formed the two sides of the debate, their motivations and finances and the individuals who fund them. They include think tanks, nongovernmental and nonprofit organizations, religious groups, the media, and groups invented solely to participate in the debate. And they will reflect the impact of technology, partisan politics, globalization and the diminishing role of truth in the debate.

The techniques used by the actors to increase their visibility and influence will be considered in the following chapter. Those techniques include the use of social media, grass-roots organizing, lobbying Congress, the use of validators, messaging and outreach to the media and the public.

The final chapter will address how and whether all these activities by all the various actors affected the outcome and influenced policymakers and politicians. And it will discuss how the battle over the agreement continues in 2017 even though it was concluded in the middle of 2015.

Notes

1. Luxenberg, Steven. 2005, April 17. "A Likely Story … and That's Precisely the Problem." *The Washington Post*. http://www.washingtonpost.com/wpdyn/content/article/2005/04/16/AR2005041600154.html Accessed on (5/22/2017).
2. Totenberg, Nina. 2017, March 21. "Senators Grill Supreme Court Nominee Gorsuch on His Judicial Philosophy." *NPR*. http://www.npr.org/2017/03/21/520996059/senators-grill-supreme-court-nominee-gorsuch-on-his-judicial-philosophy Accessed on (5/22/2017).
3. "Open Secrets." Cost of Election. https://www.opensecrets.org/overview/cost.php?display=T&infl=Y
4. Kramer, Curtlyn. 2017, March 31. "Vital Stats: The Widening Gap Between Corporate and Labor PAC Spending." *The Brookings Institute*. https://www.brookings.edu/blog/fixgov/2017/03/31/vital-stats-corporate-and-labor-pac-spending/?utm_campaign=Governance%20Studies&utm_source=hs_email&utm_medium=email&utm_content=49901363 Accessed on (5/22/2017).
5. Levy, Gabrielle. 2015, January 21. "How Citizens United Has Changed Politics in 5 Years." *US News*. https://www.usnews.com/news/articles/2015/01/21/5-years-later-citizens-united-has-remade-us-politics Accessed on (5/22/2017).
6. Altman Alex and Haley Sweetland Edwards. 2017, February 7. "Betsy DeVos' Confirmation Signals Dark Times for Democrats." *Time*. http://time.com/4662853/betsy-devos-confirmation-democrats/ Accessed on (5/22/2017).
7. Stratford, Michael. 2016, December 20. "DeVos Heads into Confirmation Hearings with a Megadonor's Advantage." *Politico*. http://www.politico.com/story/2016/12/betsy-devos-donor-senators-232792 Accessed on (5/25/2017).
8. From Donors Trust's form 990 which can be found on the ProPublica website.

9. http://www.donorstrust.org/impact/
10. Kroll, Andy. 2013, February 5. "Exposed: The Dark-Money ATM of the Conservative Movement." *Mother Jones.* http://www.motherjones.com/politics/2013/02/donors-trust-donor-capital-fund-dark-money-koch-bradley-devos Accessed on (5/22/2017).
11. Cillizza, Chris. 2014, January 22. "How Citizens United Changed Politics, in 7 Charts." *The Washington Post.* https://www.washingtonpost.com/news/the-fix/wp/2014/01/21/how-citizens-united-changed-politics-in-6-charts/?utm_term=.91a75b82cd26 Accessed on (5/22/2017).
12. Mayer, Jane. 2017, March 27. "The Reclusive Hedge-Fund Tycoon Behind the Trump Presidency." *The New Yorker.* http://www.newyorker.com/magazine/2017/03/27/the-reclusive-hedge-fund-tycoon-behind-the-trump-presidency Accessed on (5/22/2017).
13. Robert Mutch. 2016. "*Campaign Finance—What Everyone Needs to Know.*" Oxford University Press, p. 90.
14. Norquist, Grover. 2017, February 6. "Everything You Need to Know About the Trump-GOP Tax Reform Plan." *The Hill.* http://thehill.com/blogs/pundits-blog/economy-budget/318088-everything-you-need-to-know-about-the-trump-gop-tax-plan Accessed on (5/22/2017).
15. Craig, Tracey. 2016, March 28. "4 Things You Probably Don't Understand About Estate Taxes." *Time.com.* http://time.com/money/4272083/estate-taxes-who-pays/ Accessed on (6/20/2017).
16. Davis, Julie Hirschfeld and Patricia Cohen. 2017, April 27. "Trump Tax Plan Would Shift Trillions from U.S. Coffers to the Richest." *New York Times.* https://www.nytimes.com/2017/04/27/us/politics/individual-business-tax-wealth.html Accessed on (5/23/2017).
17. Gleckman, Howard. 2017, June 26. "The Senate Leadership's Health Bill Is a Big Tax Cut, Especially for the Top One Percent." *Tax Policy Center.* http://www.taxpolicycenter.

org/taxvox/senate-leaderships-health-bill-big-tax-cut-especially-top-one-percent Accessed on (6/28/2017).
18. Adcock, Clifton. 2106, December 8. "Energy Sector Gave Nearly Half of Donations to Pruitt PAC." *Oklahoma Watch.* http://oklahomawatch.org/2016/12/08/nearly-half-of-donations-to-pruitt-pac-came-from-energy-sector/ Accessed on (6/17/2017).
19. Rott, Nathan. 2017, March 9. "EPA Head Scott Pruitt Doubts Basic Consensus on Climate Change." *NPR.* http://www.npr.org/2017/03/09/519499975/epa-head-scott-pruitt-doubts-basic-consensus-on-climate-change Accessed on (6/18/2017).
20. Koronowski, Ryan. 2017, April 28. "The Climate Denier Caucus in Trump's Washington." *Think Progress.* https://thinkprogress.org/115th-congress-climate-denier-caucus-65fb825b3963 Accessed on (5/22/2017).
21. Farrell, Justin. "Corporate Funding and Ideological Polarization About Climate Change." *Proceedings of the National Academy of Sciences* 113, no. 1 (2016): 92–97.
22. Koronowski, Ryan. 2017, April 28. "The Climate Denier Caucus in Trump's Washington." *Think Progress.*
23. Smith-Spark Laura and Jason Hanna. 2017, April 22. "March for Science: Protesters Gather Worldwide to Support 'Evidence.' " *CNN.* http://www.cnn.com/2017/04/22/health/global-march-for-science/ Accessed on (5/22, 2017).
24. St. Fleur, Nicholas. 2017, April 22. "Scientists, Feeling Under Siege, March Against Trump Policies." *The New York Times.* https://www.nytimes.com/2017/04/22/science/march-for-science.html Accessed on (5/22/2017).
25. Office of the Director of National Intelligence. 2016, September 21. "Implications for US National Security of Anticipated Climate Change." https://www.dni.gov/files/documents/Newsroom/Reports%20and%20Pubs/Implications_for_US_National_Security_of_Anticipated_Climate_Change.pdf Accessed on (5/22/2017).

26. Shane, Scott. 2017, January 18. "From Headline to Photograph, a Fake News Masterpiece." *The New York Times*. https://www.nytimes.com/2017/01/18/us/fake-news-hillary-clinton-cameron-harris.html?emc=eta1&_r=1 Accessed on (5/22/2017).
27. Ibid.
28. Eli, Rosenberg. 2017, March 25. "Alex Jones Apologizes for Promoting 'Pizzagate' Hoax." *The New York Times*. https://www.nytimes.com/2017/03/25/business/alex-jones-pizzagate-apology-comet-ping-pong.html?emc=eta1 Accessed on (5/22/2017).
29. Haag, Matthew. 2017, June 22. "Gunman in 'Pizzagate' Shooting Is Sentence to 4 Years in Prison." *New York Times*. https://www.nytimes.com/2017/06/22/us/pizzagate-attack-sentence.html Accessed on (6/22/2017).
30. Montanaro, Domenico. 2017, January 30. "FACT CHECK: Spin Aside, Trump's National Security Council Has a Very Big Change." *NPR*. http://www.npr.org/2017/01/30/512489785/fact-check-spin-aside-trumps-national-security-council-has-a-very-big-change Accessed on (5/22/2017).
31. Goldmacher, Shane, Josh Dawsey, Tara Palmeri and Bryan Bender. 2017, April 5. "Bannon Ousted from National Security Council." *Politico*. http://www.politico.com/story/2017/04/bannon-ousted-from-national-security-council-236908 Accessed on (5/22/2017).
32. Goldstein Matthew, Steve Eder, Kate Kelly, Alexandra Stevenson and Ben Protess. 2017, March 31. "Bannon Made Millions in Shaping Right-Wing Thought." *New York Times*. https://www.nytimes.com/2017/03/31/business/dealbook/how-some-top-trump-aides-made-their-fortunes.html?ref=politics Accessed on (5/22/2017).
33. Rucker, Philip. 2017, March 15. "Trump Says Wiretapping Accusations Based on News Reports." https://www.washingtonpost.com/news/post-politics/wp/2017/03/15/trump-defends-obama-wiretapping-charges-predicts-very-in-

teresting-items-to-be-revealed/?utm_term=.138e110833cd Accessed on (5/22/2017).
34. Gottfried, Jeffrey and Elisa Shearer. 2016, May 26. "News Use Across Social Media Platforms 2016." *Pew Research Center.* http://www.journalism.org/2016/05/26/news-use-across-social-media-platforms-2016/ Accessed on (5/22/2017).
35. Cherry, Tyler. 2017, February 9. "Yes, Fake News Exists on the Left—But It's Being Overblown." *Media Matters for America.* https://mediamatters.org/blog/2017/02/09/yes-fake-news-exists-left-its-being-overblown/215273 Accessed on (5/22/2017).
36. Ingraham, Christopher. 2016, December 7. "Why Conservatives Might Be More Likely to Fall for Fake News." *The Washington Post.* https://www.washingtonpost.com/news/wonk/wp/2016/12/07/why-conservatives-might-be-more-likely-to-fall-for-fake-news/?utm_term=.34fb6d076622 Accessed on (5/22/2017).
37. Bartlett, Bruce. 2015. "How Fox News Changed American Media and Political Dynamics." *Social Science Research Network Working Paper.* https://poseidon01.ssrn.com/delivery.php?ID=035082020017064119026108031099079073062005049007084090076020118111095079090087096072053057049122058038019122014094067024111064016009043022084022123122090081126109005052011095071116076098119124110117019119022068008010013093004003087028110112120070000&EXT=pdf Accessed on (5/22/2017).
38. http://www.foxnews.com/politics/2017/05/16/slain-dnc-staffer-had-contact-with-wikileaks-investigator-says.html
39. Campbell, Alex. 2017, May 16. "The Family of a Murdered DNC Staffer Has Rejected a Report Linking His Death to WikiLeaks." *Buzzfeed.* https://www.buzzfeed.com/alex-campbell/seth-rich-family-refutes-report?utm_term=.kgzXAklGb5#.ny88yVmW06 Accessed on (5/22/2017).

40. Rich, Mary and Joel. 2017, May 23. "We're Seth Rich's Parents. Stop Politicizing Our Son's Murder." *Washington Post.* https://www.washingtonpost.com/opinions/were-seth-richs-parents-stop-politicizing-our-sons-murder/2017/05/23/164cf4dc-3fee-11e7-9869- bac8b446820a_story.html?tid=ss_mail&utm_term=.8ad2ab694807 Accessed on (5/24/2017).
41. Rutenberg, Jim. 2017, May 24. "Sean Hannity, a Murder and Why Fake News Endures." *New York Times.* https://www.nytimes.com/2017/05/24/business/media/seth-rich-fox-news-sean-hannity.html?emc=eta1 Accessed on (5/24/2017).
42. Ibid.
43. Ibid.
44. Pew Research Center. 2014, June 12. "Political Polarization in the American Public." http://www.people-press.org/2014/06/12/political-polarization-in-the-american-public/ Accessed on (5/22/2017).
45. McCarty, Nolan. 2012, October 26. "Hate Our Polarized Politics? Why You Can't Blame Gerrymandering." *The Washington Post.* https://www.washingtonpost.com/opinions/hate-our-polarized-politics-why-you-cant-blame-gerrymandering/2012/10/26/c2794552-1d80-11e2-9cd5-b55c38388962_story.html?utm_term=.b25382ac0209 Accessed on (5/22/2017).
46. Ibid.
47. Daley, David. 2017, March 29. "Trump Can't Stop the Freedom Caucus. He Has GOP Gerrymandering to Blame." *The Washington Post.* https://www.washingtonpost.com/posteverything/wp/2017/03/29/trump-cant-stop-the-freedom-caucus-he-has-gop-gerrymandering-to-blame/?utm_term=.80b11fb9dbd9 Accessed on (5/22/2017).
48. The Big Sort. "The Book." http://www.thebigsort.com/book.php Accessed on (5/22/2017).
49. Kennedy, Brian. 2016, October 10. "Clinton, Trump Supporters Worlds Apart on Views of Climate Change and Its Scientists." *Pew Research Center.* http://www.pewre-

search.org/fact-tank/2016/10/10/clinton-trump-supporters-worlds-apart-on-views-of-climate-change-and-its-scientists/ Accessed on (5/22/2017).
50. Edwards-Levy, Ariel. 2016, December 12. "Americans Don't Think the Government Needs 'Experts'." *Huffington Post.* http://www.huffingtonpost.com/entry/poll-civil-service-experts_us_5849d515e4b04c8e2baeede9 Accessed on (5/22/2017).
51. Kakutani, Michiko. 2017, Match 21. " 'The Death of Expertise' Explores How Ignorance Became a Virtue." *The New York Times.* https://www.nytimes.com/2017/03/21/books/the-death-of-expertise-explores-how-ignorance-became-a-virtue.html Accessed on (5/22/2017).
52. Foundation of American Scientists. 1989 May. "Active Measure." https://fas.org/irp/world/russia/kgb/su0523.htm Accessed on (5/22/2017).
53. Watts, Clint. 2017, March 30. "Statement Prepared for the U.S. Senate Select Committee on Intelligence Hearing: 'Disinformation: A Primer in Russian Active Measures and Influence Campaigns.' ". https://www.intelligence.senate.gov/sites/default/files/documents/os-cwatts-033017.pdf Accessed on (5/22/2017).
54. National Intelligence Council. 2017, January 6 "Background to 'Assessing Russian Activities and Intentions in Recent US Elections': The Analytic Process and Cyber Incident Attribution." https://www.intelligence.senate.gov/sites/default/files/documents/ICA_2017_01.pdf Accessed on (5/22/2017).
55. Barthel, Michael, Amy Mitchell and Jesse Holcomb. 2016, December 16. "Many Americans Believe Fake News Is Sowing Confusion." *Pew Research Center.* http://www.journalism.org/2016/12/15/many-americans-believe-fake-news-is-sowing-confusion/ Accessed on (5/22/2017).
56. The Washington Post. 2017, April 27 "Americas Say Media and Trump Regularly Spread Falsehoods." https://www.washingtonpost.com/page/2010-2019/WashingtonPost/

2017/04/27/National-Politics/Polling/release_469. xml?tid=a_inl Accessed on (5/22/2017).
57. "Report: Iran Sanctions Cost US Economy up to $272 Billion." 2016, December 13. https://www.niacouncil.org/report-iran-sanctions-cost-us-economy-272-billion/ Accessed on (6/19/2017).
58. Sazak, Selim and Lauren Sukin. 2017, April 4. "Presidential Appointees Decide Our Futures. We Should Be Able to Vote for Them." *The Washington Post*. https://www.washingtonpost.com/posteverything/wp/2017/04/04/presidential-appointees-decide-our-futures-we-should-be-able-to-vote-for-them/?tid=ss_mail&utm_term=.155eae7797b0#comments Accessed on (5/22/2017).
59. The attachment to theory remains a particularly strong feature of social scientists even when the real world cannot be reduced to a parsimonious and universal description. And articles based on theory are what are most acceptable to scholarly journals. Here is one personal example. A colleague and I wrote a paper about the appointment of ambassadors and submitted it to several peer-reviewed academic journals for publication. The paper made the case that the selling of certain ambassadorships, mainly in Western Europe is a thinly veiled form of corruption that is a time-honored Washington tradition. It went on to demonstrate how the price, in terms of campaign contributions, goes up as the size of the economy of a country and the number of tourists it receives increases. So, London costs more than Lisbon and Libreville gets reserved for the career ambassadors.

The working draft of the paper attracted attention from journalists and the subject of articles in the *New York Times*, the *Washington Post*, the *London Sunday Times* and several other magazines and newspapers. It was nonetheless rejected by a number of academic journals before finally being accepted for publication. The most common reason given for rejection was that it lacked a theory.

The "theory" was that this is how government works in this limited area. It was an explanation of why people with no significant international experience, but large bank accounts and a desire to burnish their resumes with an impressive title, wind up as ambassadors of the USA in some of the most important capitals in the world. But that was insufficient for academic journals that wanted something grander even though it would wind up being an explanation that had no relationship to reality.

60. Powell, Colin. 2017, May 25. "American Leadership—We Can't Do It for Free." *New York Times*. https://www.nytimes.com/2017/05/24/opinion/colin-powell-trump-budget-state-department.html?ref=opinion&_r=0 Accessed on (5/25/2017).
61. Fullilove, Michael. 2014. *Rendezvous with Destiny: How Franklin D. Roosevelt and Five Extraordinary Men Took America Into the War and Into the World*. Penguin. https://www.amazon.com/Rendezvous-Destiny-Franklin-Roosevelt-Extraordinary/dp/0143125621/ref=sr_1_2?s=books&ie=UTF8&qid=1468083358&sr=1-2&keywords=franklin+roosevelt%2C+harry+hopkins%2C+harriman
62. Department of State. "Biographies of the Secretaries of State: Cordell Hull (1871–1955)." https://history.state.gov/departmenthistory/people/hull-cordell Accessed (5/25/2017).
63. Central Intelligence Agency. 2004. "Regime Strategic Intent." General Reports: Iraq WMD. https://www.cia.gov/library/reports/general-reports-1/iraq_wmd_2004/chap1.html Accessed on (5/22/2017).
64. James Lee Ray. 2014. *American Foreign Policy and Political Ambition*. CQ Press, p. 15.
65. Paul R. Viotti and Mark V. Kauppi. 2012. *International Relations Theory*. Fifth edition. Pearson, p. 41.
66. Ray, p. 17.

Contents

1 Introduction   1

2 A Bit of History   25

3 Who Was Involved   47

4 The Tactics Used   123

5 The Results and the Future   167

Acknowledgments   193

Appendices   195

Index   465

List of Tables

Table 1.1 Opposition of Republican Senators to Arms
           Control Treaties   9
Table 3.1 Number, average staff and revenue of think tanks   70

CHAPTER 1

Introduction

In July 2015, the United States and five other countries concluded an agreement with Iran concerning that country's nuclear program. The negotiations were difficult and the deal that was reached was complex, but it was based on a simple tradeoff. Iran would get relief from economic sanctions and, in return, it would dismantle parts of its nuclear infrastructure and place limitations on the rest. The goal was to provide the world assurances that the program would not be used to construct nuclear weapons.

With seven countries participating in the negotiations and a long history of mistrust between some of them, especially the United States and Iran, it was a miracle the talks finally produced an accord. Their successful conclusion was hailed by some as the greatest foreign policy victory of the Obama administration.[1]

Those who opposed the deal could not condemn it strongly enough, however. Opposition among Republicans in Congress even took the form of what some thought was a criminal act. In March 2015, Senator Tom Cotton of Arkansas drafted a letter about the agreement that 47 of the 54

Republican senators signed.² It was remarkable that so many of Cotton's colleagues were ready to follow his leadership given that he had, at that point, been in the Senate for less than ten weeks. Neither his lack of experience nor his penchant for conspiracy theories deterred them. For instance, he believes that Iraq was involved in 9/11, that ISIS and Mexican drug cartels will inevitably form a partnership, and that signing up for Obamacare will get one's identity stolen by Russian hackers. None of that diminished the enthusiasm of his colleagues for adding their names to his letter.³

Cotton lost no time once he took office, in becoming in a matter of weeks "one of the most aggressive national security hawks in the Senate, audaciously challenging Obama's foreign policy with harsh rhetoric and confrontational tactics."⁴ The purpose of the "open" letter, which was addressed to "the leaders of the Islamic Republic of Iran,"⁵ was to undermine the negotiations by pointing out that the next American president could reverse any agreement with the stroke of a pen.⁶ The letter supposedly sought to instruct Iranian leaders on this point since they "may not fully understand our constitutional system."

Cotton made clear his objective in a speech at the rightwing Heritage Foundation, when he said "the end of these negotiations isn't an unintended consequence of congressional action, it is very much an intended consequence." Cotton asserted that Iran is "not a rational or peaceful actor; it is a radical, Islamist tyranny whose constitution explicitly calls for jihad."⁷

The focus and intensity of Senator Cotton's attempts to derail the Iran nuclear deal just might be linked to the fact that he received millions of dollars from fervently pro-Israel billionaires. A *New York Times* article by Eric Lipton described some of the money trail connecting Cotton and other opponents of the deal:

> The Emergency Committee for Israel, led by William Kristol, editor of the conservative Weekly Standard, spent $960,000 to support Mr. Cotton. In that same race, Paul Singer, a hedge fund billionaire from New York and a leading donor to pro-Israel causes, contributed $250,000 to Arkansas Horizon, another independent expenditure group supporting Mr. Cotton. Seth Klarman, a Boston-based pro-Israel billionaire, contributed $100,000. The political action committee run by John Bolton, the United Nations ambassador under President George W. Bush and an outspoken supporter of Israel, spent at least $825,000 to support Mr. Cotton.[8]

Whether motivated by money or ideology, Cotton's intervention in foreign affairs was labeled by some as unprecedented, illegal and even treasonous.[9] Editorial writers in newspapers from coast to coast expressed their outrage and most condemned the attempt to sabotage the diplomatic process.[10] In an editorial titled "Republican Idiocy on Iran," the *New York Times* said the letter was a disgraceful and irresponsible attempt to scare Iranians from making any deal.[11]

The outrage was not limited to newspaper editors. Over 320,000 people signed a petition to the White House asking that those who sent the letter be tried for violation of the Logan Act.[12] The White House ignored the petition and declined to order the Justice Department to even consider prosecution.

The origins and history of the Logan Act illustrate the evolution of political speech in America. As explained by University of Texas law professor Steve Vladeck in an article in the *Atlantic*:

> The law dates back to 1799, and it was enacted at a very different moment in American history. We were much more into punishing partisan political differences as crimes at that moment. This was the same Congress that passed the notorious Alien and Sedition Acts. The Logan Act was basically a response to an effort by a Philadelphia Quaker named George Logan to try to negotiate directly with the French government. This was a big scandal at the time in foreign affairs because Logan—a Democratic-Republican—was trying to thwart the policy of the Federalists, who controlled both houses of Congress and the White House. It was a controversy back at home, and Congress took none too kindly to this effort to circumvent them or President Adams on a question of diplomatic relations.
>
> It wasn't until the 20th century that the Supreme Court really breathed life into the First and Fifth Amendments when it comes to prosecuting individuals for their speech or their conduct. At the Founding, there was much more tolerance for the idea that someone could be sent to jail for nasty speech, for libelous speech, for partisan political opposition. The partisan politics of that day were often unbound by what we today think of as obvious constitutional constraints, just because the Supreme Court had not recognized them yet. At that time, Congress thought more capaciously about its power to punish speech, in ways that we would never think a contemporary Congress would act because of the intervening development of our modern First and Fifth Amendment jurisprudence.[13]

While the Logan Act has been law for over 200 years, no one has ever been successfully prosecuted for violating it, not even George Logan. Since he was already engaged in his attempt at diplomacy with the French when the law was passed, he could not have been convicted of violating it retroactively.

In addition to possible violations of the Logan Act by Cotton and his colleagues, Republican rhetoric seemed to have no limits when it came to denigrating the agreement. Almost all of the candidates for the 2016 Republican presidential nomination seemed to be in a competition to say who would tear the agreement up faster once they took office.[14]

Donald Trump labeled it "the worst deal ever." During the campaign, he repeatedly asserted he would "walk away from the 2015 accord, or renegotiate it, or enforce it so rigorously that it might collapse."[15] He also said he would have "doubled and tripled up the sanctions very easily."[16]

Other Republican leaders were as extreme in their criticism as the deal was being considered. They made references to Chamberlain's appeasement of Hitler, the Holocaust and any other historical analogy they could think of to discredit the deal:

> Governor Scott Walker: "Instead of making the world safer, this deal will likely lead to a nuclear arms race in the world's most dangerous region."[17]

> Senator Marco Rubio: "President Obama has consistently negotiated from a position of weakness, giving concession after concession to a regime that has American blood on its hands, holds Americans hostage, and has consistently violated every agreement it ever signed."[18]

> Former Governor Jeb Bush: "This isn't diplomacy—it is appeasement."[19]

> Former Governor Mike Huckabee: "Shame on the Obama administration for agreeing to a deal that empowers an evil Iranian regime to carry out its threat to 'wipe Israel off the

map' and bring 'death to America'."[20] And, in what must win the prize for the most extreme rhetoric, he claimed that by trusting the Iranians, President Obama "will take the Israelis to the door of the oven."[21]

Senator Ted Cruz: "It is a fundamental betrayal of the security of the United States and of our closest allies, first and foremost Israel."[22]

Speaker of the House John Boehner: "The deal will only embolden Iran" and is "likely to fuel a nuclear arms race around the world."[23]

Senator Lindsey Graham: "This will be a death sentence to Israel if they don't push back."[24]

Ben Carson: "This is not a good deal, but a recipe for disaster, and the first fateful step toward a frenzied nuclear arms race in the Middle East."[25]

Former governor George Pataki: The agreement would "deepen the distrust of America with our allies."[26] "Reject this deal and send a message to President Obama, Secretary Clinton the UN and leaders throughout the globe that America does not reward terror."[27]

Senate Majority Leader Mitch McConnell was a bit more measured, but made clear what he thought the goal should be. According to him, the deal did not advance national interests, but instead was "reaching the best deal acceptable to Iran."[28] He insisted that the point was to end the nuclear program and not just manage it, and that he and other congressional opponents of it would "do everything we can to stop it."[29]

Senator Rand Paul was among the mildest of all the Republican critics: "While I continue to believe that negotiations are preferable to war, I would prefer to keep the interim agreement in place instead of accepting a bad deal."[30]

Some Republicans suggested it was just a simple question of turning up the economic pressure. The assumption seemed to be that all our negotiating partners would follow the American insistence on harsher sanctions and this would bring Iran to its knees and force it to capitulate or prompt regime change that would bring into power a new government that they assumed would capitulate.

> Former Senator Rick Santorum: The administration should have "ratcheted up those sanctions"[31] and that, if he were president, he "would have continued to put pressure on this regime to capitulate".[32]

> Governor John Kasich: He would impose more sanctions to "crush them economically until they change"[33] and the agreement was "bogus" and a "bad, bad deal."[34]

Others offered negotiating advice suggesting that all that was required for the negotiations to succeed was to abandon them:

> Carly Fiorina: "There is a lot of reason to be suspicious here."[35] "If you want a good deal, you've got to walk away sometimes."[36]

> Governor Chris Christie in reference to President Obama: "He should have walked away."[37]

And some could not pass up the opportunity to criticize Hillary Clinton, the presumptive Democratic presidential nominee, even though she left the Obama administration years earlier.

Former Governor Rick Perry: Hillary Clinton "played a significant role in initiating these negotiations with Iran, and will have to justify to the American people why she supports allowing a known state sponsor of terrorism to move toward obtaining a nuclear weapon."[38]

Governor Bobby Jindal: "While Secretary Clinton has been the architect of President Obama's foreign policy, she can do the right thing and prevent Iran from obtaining a nuclear weapon and oppose this deal."[39]

The Republican members of Congress reacted as negatively to the deal as the contenders for the party's presidential nomination did. John Isaacs, a Senior Fellow at the Center for Arms Control and Non-Proliferation, pointed out in an article in *The Hill*: "Most GOP members did not even wait for the ink to dry on the agreement to vigorously oppose the deal presented to Congress on September 14. They did not bother to read the 120-page document, study the details, wait for hearings or consult with experts."[40]

Looking at the history of Republican votes on nuclear agreements, Isaacs concluded: "The overwhelming Republican vote expected against the agreement to stem Iran's nuclear arms program sits securely with this history of partisan Republican votes on arms agreements. It is not the content that is important; it is the president."

Isaacs backed up that conclusion by compiling the following historical record, which demonstrates how Republicans consistently oppose arms agreements if they are negotiated by a Democratic administration (Table 1.1):

If nothing else, this record demonstrates that partisan politics has been a feature of nuclear agreements for as long as they have been negotiated.

Table 1.1 Opposition of Republican Senators to Arms Control Treaties

Year	Treaty	President	Senate GOP position
1972	ABM	GOP	1 independent conservative against
1978	SALT II	Dem	Shelved
1988	INF	GOP	4 against
1991	START	GOP	5 against
1977	CWC	GOP & Dem	26 against
1997	CTBT	Dem	51 against
2002	SORT	GOP	0 against
2012	New START	Dem	26 against
2015	Iran	Dem	54 against

The rejection of diplomacy in favor of confrontation seems to be an ingrained part of the psyche of some conservatives that dates back at least to the Yalta conference at the end of World War II. At that meeting, conservatives felt that President Roosevelt and Prime Minister Churchill had sold out the "captive nations" of Eastern Europe by recognizing Soviet hegemony over them since the Soviets were untrustworthy. The same kind of rhetoric appears today in the criticism of Iran and the nuclear agreement with accusations that Iran cannot be trusted and that signing the deal is selling out Israel.

In reviewing the antipathy of conservatives toward diplomatic agreements and the controversy over the nuclear agreement, two researchers at the University of Sydney noted: "In hurling brickbats at the president, the modern-day inheritors of the hardline tradition—from the Republican leadership to Democratic Senator Chuck Schumer—are simply reminding Americans of earlier episodes of right-wing rejectionism. Today, those past backlashes against important diplomatic overtures appear discredited and foolish."[41]

If the Iran nuclear deal survives and succeeds in ensuring Iran's nuclear program does not develop weapons, the criticism of it may one day be considered foolish. It faces an uncertain future under the Trump administration, however, as the controversy over it did not end with its signing.

Members of Congress continue to look for ways to pass legislation designed to limit the benefits to Iran from the agreement and to make its implementation more difficult.[42] Some of those efforts were directed at imposing sanctions for Iran's ballistic missile program. Others aimed to prevent U.S. funds from buying Iran's heavy water, which seems strange given that doing so would remove one of the basic components in a nuclear weapons program. The intent of those initiatives was clear—to take measures against Iran that would undermine the nuclear agreement by diminishing the benefits from it.

While the Iran nuclear issue marked a new low in relations between the Republican majorities in Congress and the Obama administration, it also prompted a remarkable, perhaps unprecedented, level of involvement by groups outside of government. Think tanks, political advocacy organizations, pro-Israel and religious groups, nonprofit associations, veterans' groups, media outlets, arms control organizations and others weighed in on both sides of the debate in an attempt to influence the outcome. It was a foreign affairs food fight with positions both for and against the agreement argued with great passion and intensity.

In an open letter to Congress in April 2015, over 70 national organizations implored the congressmen and senators to support the Iran nuclear deal.[43] Three months later, just after the deal was signed, a large rally was held by dozens of other organizations in New York City, to argue the opposite. Thousands of people showed up to urge Congress to vote it down. The turnout at the rally was large because the organizers used social media and other means to support the effort, advertising that a number of prominent former politicians, retired generals, media personalities and others would be there to rail against the deal.[44]

Those organizations also used the event to raise money for themselves and to cover the cost of the rally. One of the groups, Americans for a Safe Israel, used a picture in its online ad campaign to publicize the rally that showed a large gathering of people.[45] The picture was actually of a 2013 demonstration protesting the acquittal of George Zimmerman on murder charges stemming from his killing of an African-American teenager, Trayvon Martin.

How much the deceptive advertising worked is unclear, but the event did draw a large crowd. Its magnitude depended on who was doing the estimate however. The Israel News Agency put the number at 15,000,[46] the Jewish Press website reported that 12,000[47] had showed up, while the local CBS station said some 10,000 came to the rally.[48]

Regardless of the exact size of the crowd or truth in advertising, it was a formidable display of opposition to the agreement. And the number of organizations pushing for the deal's defeat by holding the rally was almost equal in number to those supporting it in the open letter to Congress.

That so many organizations and individuals were involved in supporting and opposing the deal demonstrates that, in some cases, foreign policy is not limited to diplomats and other government officials holding quiet discussions behind closed doors. Today anyone can attempt to influence it and when it comes to a high-profile and contentious issue, like the Iran nuclear deal, many will try.

In the past, trying to influence policy usually meant an individual decision who to vote for or to whose election campaign to contribute to. Acting collectively was more difficult. Not any longer, however, thanks to technology. Today, using social media and the Internet, connecting with like-minded people is only a few keystrokes away.

When the Founding Fathers wrote the Constitution, they knew that in a republic it was important for citizens to have the opportunity to express their opinions, air their complaints and try to influence government policy. They provided for that in the first amendment of the Constitution, which prohibits Congress from making any law that abridges the right of the people to petition their government for a redress of grievances.

Apparently, the Founding Fathers did not anticipate the creation of the Internet and the spread of social media. Not to mention the tens of thousands of lobbyists engaged in that multibillion-dollar industry and the thousands of nongovernmental, nonprofit and religious organizations, think tanks and business associations that have also set up shop in Washington in order to have an impact on government policy.

The drafters of the Constitution set up a system where only the vaguest references were made as to who in government gets to determine the country's foreign policy. The president is the commander in chief of the armed forces and can appoint ambassadors. Congress gets to determine the budget, approve laws and declare war. Beyond that the Constitution is, as one historian put it, an invitation to struggle.

The executive, legislative and judicial branches of government are the active participants in that struggle as all three can have a direct impact on foreign policy. But anyone else can indirectly affect it by trying to influence the decisions of policymakers. Members of Congress have limited power given that there are 100 senators and 435 congressmen. However, if an individual senator or congressman takes a strong interest in an issue and knows how to navigate the congressional system skillfully, that individual can have a significant impact.

What One Congressman Can Do

A good example of a single member of Congress having an impact on foreign policy would be Charlie Wilson.[49] He was a 12-term Democratic representative from Texas and an ardent anti-Communist who became obsessed with helping the rebels in Afghanistan defeat the Soviet army in the 1980s. He used his seat on Defense Appropriations Subcommittee to help provide the rebels with money, missiles and even mules to carry on their fight and enabled them to eventually defeat the Russians. The position also made him a favorite of defense contractors and lobbyists and at the top of their lists when it came to campaign contributions.[50] His subcommittee position allowed him to help steer defense contracts to the districts of other congressmen, building up a stock of IOU's that he could cash when he needed support.

The billions of dollars he had allocated to the rebels were far more than the amount the Reagan administration had wanted to give them. That desire may have been an attempt to keep the costs down rather than the fear of creating something that might become a threat to the United States. In any event, that is what happened. One of the insurgents who got training in military and terrorist tactics through his experience during this era in Afghanistan was Osama bin Laden.

Despite that bit of history, Wilson still defended what he had accomplished. He asserted that Washington was to blame for the rise of Bin Laden since it essentially abandoned Afghanistan after the Soviet's defeat and thereby allowed it to become a haven for terrorists. There was no congressman who championed providing economic aid to the Afghans with the same enthusiasm and effectiveness that Wilson had in arming them. Even if there has been someone to take up the cause, the results would probably not have been enough to change where Afghanistan is today. If nothing else, the experience demonstrates that the lobby for the military-industrial complex is far more effective than the one for development aid.

Wilson's exploits, both in supporting the rebels and in scandalous behavior[51] involving a variety of drugs and women, were so legendary a best-selling book was written about them[52] and turned into a movie starring Tom Hanks.[53] One thing can be said for Wilson is that he was no hypocrite. He seemed to enjoy, and never denied, his reputation for being a playboy.

Congressman can also become interested in issues that are far more mundane than aiding insurgents to kill Russian soldiers. The revelation of Hillary Clinton's e-mails by WikiLeaks provided one such example. A Republican Illinois congressman, Dan Manzullo, took up the cause of gefilte fish as a foreign policy problem and raised it to the level of the Secretary of State.[54] He had a constituent with 400,000 pounds of frozen carp, the basic ingredient of that Jewish delicacy, that had been shipped to Israel only to be hit with a 120 percent import duty.

Manzullo e-mailed Clinton asking for her to intercede on behalf of his constituent. After much high-level negotiation, the fish were allowed into Israel without paying the duty[55] and this foreign policy dilemma ended without any unintended consequences like providing billions of dollars to the people who became Al Qaida. Although it was a one-time exemption to the duty, the Illinois fish farmer was able to find new markets for his product, averting any further problem.[56]

While foreign policy can cover an array of issues from Afghan rebels to frozen carp, most of the decisions are made at a fairly low level and are implemented with little notice. When the media does seize on an issue, it gets pushed up the bureaucratic hierarchy and can involve the secretary of state, Congress and even the president if he becomes interested in the problem.

When Public Opinion Matters

The attention of the media to an issue can elevate a routine affair to the presidential level and force a change in policy even after a decision has already been made. One such example of was when a contract to manage security at six seaports in the United States was granted to a company controlled by the United Arab Emirates in 2006. Although the UAE is a close ally and cooperates in combatting terrorism, congressional and public opinion, once made aware of the decision by coverage in the media, was overwhelmingly negative.

In the wake of 9/11 and the national insecurity that resulted, there were few who would listen to the suggestion that not all Arabs were a threat. As Congress began to come up with legislation[57] to kill the deal, the company, Dubai Ports World, transferred its interest in management of the ports to a US-based company.[58]

The move by the company averted the possibility of a confrontation between the Bush administration and Congress over the issue, but the incident shows how routine foreign policy issues can take on a completely different hue once they are politicized and publicized and can end up being shelved or reversed. The media's temporary obsession with the issue brought it to the public's attention. The popular outcry that resulted prompted Congress to act, converting what had been a low-level, routine bureaucratic decision to a problem for elected officials, compelling them to take a stand.

When it comes to foreign policy decisions, Washington is a place where media attention, money and partisan politics can drive the agenda and the intensity of the debate on an issue. While most congressmen and senators do not matter that much, as Charlie Wilson demonstrated, even one can if that person cares enough about a policy and knows how to play the game. Even the smallest issue can become a subject of congressional interest and any group can attempt to influence the process. And, thanks to technology, a group can be created solely to take on a single issue in an attempt to give the appearance of widespread grassroots support.

In discussions of public diplomacy and digital diplomacy, it often seems as if the entire world is using social media and other technologies to such an extent that foreign policy decisions are now the result of electronic referendums.

It would be premature to say that traditional diplomacy is dead, however, because there are few matters that rise to a level where there is a great deal of public interest and activism in social media or via alternative means. Nevertheless, as the Iran nuclear deal demonstrates, there are some issues that do capture the attention of the broader public and, in a democracy, any individual or group that seeks to influence the outcome can weigh in and push their point of view.

When a policy attains a high enough profile that it attracts the attention of a broad range of actors, the debate about what direction to take can be vigorous. Those kinds of debates are usually orchestrated by the Washington establishment—those who live in and around the nation's capital and who are in government or the business of influencing it. But occasionally, as the general public becomes aware of and concerned about a foreign policy, any number of individuals can join the process. That is easier to do today, with e-mail, the Internet, social media and other technologies enabling those who want to broaden participation in the debate to do so. And all those means came into play in the making of the Iran nuclear agreement.

To describe that process, the next chapter will provide a brief history of the nuclear issue with Iran and the negotiations that led to the recent agreement. It will also talk about how the relationship between the United States and Iran continues to be affected by events in the past. And it will untangle the views of the other parties to the process—the other permanent members of the UN Security Council (Russia, China, France and Great Britain) plus Germany and Iran—and will discuss how their interests may diverge from those of the United States.

Notes

1. Zengerle, Patricia. 2015. "Last Bid to Kill Iran Nuclear Deal Blocked in Senate." Reuters. http://www.reuters.com/article/us-iran-nuclear-congress-idUSKCN0RF2VX20150917 Accessed on (5/25/2017).
2. Tom Cotton. 2015. "Cotton and 46 Fellow Senators to Send Open Letter to the Leaders of the Islamic Republic of Iran." https://www.cotton.senate.gov/?p=press_release&id=120 Accessed on (5/25/2017).
3. Lund, Jeb. 2015. "None Dare Call It Treason: Tom Cotton, Iran and Old GOP Ideas." *Rolling Stone.* http://www.rollingstone.com/politics/news/none-dare-call-it-treason-tom-cotton-iran-and-old-gop-ideas-20150316 Accessed on (5/25/2017).
4. Sullivan, Sean. 2015. "With Iran Letter, Tom Cotton Emerges as Leading GOP National Security Hawk." *The Washington Post.* https://www.washingtonpost.com/politics/with-iran-letter-tom-cotton-emerges-as-leading-gop-national-security-hawk/2015/03/11/4ce05a4e-c74f-11e4-a199-6cb5e63819d2_story.html?utm_term=.e623812202a5 Accessed on (5/25/2017).

5. Baker, Peter. 2015. "G.O.P. Senators' Letter to Iran About Nuclear Deal Angers White House." *The New York Times*. https://www.nytimes.com/2015/03/10/world/asia/white-house-faults-gop-senators-letter-to-irans-leaders.html Accessed on (5/25/2017).
6. Ibid.
7. Cotton, Tom. 2015. "As the Iranian Nuclear Talks Drag On, Congress Must Act." *The Wall Street Journal*. https://www.wsj.com/articles/tom-cotton-as-the-iranian-nuclear-talks-drag-on-congress-must-act-1422577455 Accessed on (5/25/2017).
8. Lipton, Eric. 2015. "G.O.P's Israel Support Deepens as Political Contributions Shift." *The New York Times*. https://www.nytimes.com/2015/04/05/us/politics/gops-israel-support-deepens-as-political-contributions-shift.html Accessed on (5/25/2017).
9. Marmon, Katelyn. 2015. "Iran Letter: 165,000+ Sign Petition to Prosecute GOP Senators for Treason." ABC News. http://abcnews.go.com/Politics/iran-letter-165000-sign-petition-prosecute-gop-senators/story?id=29564985 Accessed on (5/25/2017).
10. Rethink Defense. 2015. "Senate Letter on Iran Derided Coast to Coast as a "Political Abomination."https://storify.com/ReThinkDefense/senate-letter-on-iran-derided-coast-to-coast Accessed on (5/25/2017).
11. The Editorial Board. 2015. "Republican Idiocy on Iran." *The New York Times*. https://www.nytimes.com/2015/03/12/opinion/republican-idiocy-on-iran.html?ref=todayspaper&_r=0 Accessed on (5/25/2017).
12. The petition was not acted upon and has been removed from the White House website. It was at https://petitions.whitehouse.gov/petition/file-charges-against-47-us-senators-violation-logan-act-attempting-undermine-nuclear-agreement
13. Foran, Clare. 2017. "What Is the Logan Act and What Does It Have to Do With Flynn?" *The Atlantic*. https://www.theatlantic.com/politics/archive/2017/02/logan-act-michael-flynn-trump-russia/516774/ Accessed on (5/25/2017).

14. Slavin, Barbara. 2015. "Will the Next US President Scrap the Iran Deal?" Al-Monitor. http://www.al-monitor.com/pulse/originals/2015/12/presidential-elections-candidates-iran-stances-hawkish.html Accessed on (5/25/2017).
15. Morello, Carol. 2017. "Iran Nuclear Deal Is in the Crosshairs and May Not Survive a Trump Administration." *The Washington Post.* https://www.washingtonpost.com/world/national-security/iran-nuclear-deal-is-in-the-crosshairs-and-may-not-survive-a-trump-administration/2017/01/11/b56313d4-d744-11e6-9f9f-5cdb4b7f8dd7_story.html?utm_term=.f8b3c632a6e8 Accessed on (5/25/2017).
16. Sherfinski, David. 2015. "Donald Trump on Iran: 'If I Were President, You'd Have Those Prisoners.' " *The Washington Times.* http://www.washingtontimes.com/news/2015/jul/16/donald-trump-iran-if-i-were-president-youd-have-th/ Accessed on (5/25/2017).
17. Walker, Scott. 2015. "Governor Walker Statement on Iranian Nuclear Deal." https://www.scottwalker.com/news/governor-walker-statement-iranian-nuclear-deal Accessed on (5/25/2017).
18. Rubio, Marco. 2015. "Marco Rubio Statement on Obama's Dangerous Iran Deal." https://marcorubio.com/news/marco-rubio-statement-on-obamas-dangerous-iran-deal/ Accessed on (5/25/2017).
19. Bush, Jeb. 2015. "Jeb Bush on the Obama Administration's Nuclear Deal with Iran." https://jeb2016.com/statementdealwithiran/?lang=en Accessed on (5/25/2017).
20. Huckabee, Mike. 2015. "Huckabee Blasts Iran Deal, Calls to Topple the Iranian Regime." http://www.mikehuckabee.com/blogs?ID=85CC1EA9-F7F8-42CC-9B8F-2F3A3E4270E9 Accessed on (5/25/2017).
21. Wilde, Robert. 2015. "Huckabee: Obama Marching Israelis to 'Door of Oven'." Breitbart. http://www.breitbart.com/big-government/2015/07/25/huckabee-obama-marching-israelis-to-door-of-oven/ Accessed on (5/25/2017).

22. Wollner, Adam. 2015. "Now the 2016 Presidential Candidates Are Reacting to the Iran Deal." *National Journal.* http://www.nationaljournal.com/2016-elections/iran-deal-republican-presidential-candidates-20150714 Accessed on (5/25/2017).
23. Boehner, John. 2015, July 14. "Speaker Boehner Statement on Iran Nuclear Agreement." http://www.speaker.gov/press-release/speaker-boehner-statement-iran-nuclear-agreement Accessed on (6/17/17).
24. Ibid.
25. VOA News. 2015. "US Presidential Candidates React to Iran Deal." http://www.voanews.com/content/us-presidential-candidates-on-iran/2860693.html Accessed on (5/25/2017).
26. Pataki, George. 2015. "Governor Pataki Statement on Iran Nuclear Deal." http://georgepataki.com/news/campaign-news/governor-pataki-statement-iran-nuclear-deal/ Accessed on (5/25/2017).
27. Ibid.
28. Lewis, Paul, Sabrina Siddiqui, and Ben Jacobs. 2015. "Republicans Fume Over Iran Nuclear Deal But Hope of Undermining Accord is Slim." *The Guardian.* http://www.theguardian.com/world/2015/jul/14/republicans-iran-nuclear-deal-reaction Accessed on (5/25/2017).
29. Ibid.
30. Ibid.
31. Adam Wollner. 2016, July 14. "How the 2016 Presidential Candidates Are Reacting to the Iran Deal." *The Atlantic.* https://www.theatlantic.com/politics/archive/2015/07/how-the-2016-presidential-candidates-are-reacting-to-the-iran-deal/436686 Accessed on (5/25/2017).
32. Ibid.
33. Darrel, Rowland. 2015. "Kasich Calls Iran Deal 'Bogus'." *The Columbus Dispatch.* http://www.dispatch.com/content/stories/local/2015/07/23/john-kasich-new-hampshire-iran-deal.html Accessed on (5/25/2017).

34. Ibid.
35. Kaplan, Rebecca. 2015. "Carly Fiorina: U.S. Broke Every Rule in Iran Negotiations." CBS News. http://www.cbsnews.com/news/carly-fiorina-u-s-broke-every-rule-in-iran-negotiations/ Accessed on (5/25/2017).
36. Ibid.
37. Giambusso, David. 2015. "Top NJ Lawmakers Express Unease Over Iran Deal." *Politico.* http://www.politico.com/story/2015/07/top-nj-lawmakers-express-unease-over-iran-deal-120104.html Accessed on (5/25/2017).
38. Perry, Rick. 2015. "Statement by Gov. Perry on Iran Nuclear Deal." https://rickperry.org/statement-by-gov-perry-on-iran-nuclear-deal Accessed on (5/25/2017).
39. Wollner. Op.cit.
40. Issacs, John. 2015. "GOP on Nuke Treaties: Love 'em, When Republican Is President." *The Hill.* http://thehill.com/blogs/congress-blog/foreign-policy/253273-gop-on-nuke-treaties-love-em-when-republican-is-president Accessed on (5/25/2017).
41. Hemmer, Nicole and Tom Switzer. 2015. "Why Republicans Reject the Iran Deal—and All Diplomacy." *The New York Times.* https://www.nytimes.com/2015/08/26/opinion/why-republicans-reject-the-iran-deal-and-all-diplomacy.html?emc=eta1 Accessed on (5/25/2017).
42. Riechmann, Deb. 2015. "Iran Nuclear Deal Is Done, But Debate in Congress Isn't Over." PBS. http://www.pbs.org/newshour/rundown/iran-nuclear-deal-done-debate-congress-isnt/ Accessed on (5/25/2017). And Siegel, Josh. 2016. "Nearly a Year Since Nuclear Deal, Tom Cotton Alarmed by 'Empowerment of Iran'." *The Daily Signal.* http://dailysignal.com/2016/06/08/nearly-1-year-since-nuclear-deal-tom-cotton-alarmed-by-empowerment-of-iran/ Accessed on (5/25/2017).
43. No War with Iran. 2015. "Open Letter Urges Congress to Take Path of Diplomacy, Not War." http://nowarwithiran.

org/organizational-letter-iran/ Accessed on (5/25/2017). The list of organizations can be found in Appendix E.
44. Robly. 2015. "Stop Iran Now: Rally Through Strength." https://www.robly.com/archive?id=73efa9179d5d19c78ecb45d7306f7147 Accessed on (5/25/2017).
45. B'Ayin, Zayin. 2015. "Why Is This 'Stop Iran Rally' Website Using a Picture From a Trayvon Martin Protest on Their 'Donate' Page?" Heeb. http://heebmagazine.com/why-is-this-stop-iran-rally-website-using-a-picture-from-a-trayvon-martin-protest-on-their-donate-page/55147 Accessed on (5/25/2017).
46. Leyden, Joel. 2015. "15,000 at New York Protest Say No Deal to Iran Nuclear Terror." Israel News Agency. http://israelnewsagency.com/15000-new-york-protest-no-deal-iran-nuclear-terrorism-jihad-israel-jewish/ Accessed on (5/25/2017).
47. Marcus, Lori Lowenthal. 2015. "Stop Iran Rally Draws 12,000 to Times Square (Photo Essay)." Jewish Press. http://www.jewishpress.com/news/breaking-news/stop-iran-rally-draws-12000-to-times-square-photo-essay/2015/07/23/ Accessed on (5/25/2017).
48. CBS. 2015. "Thousands of Protesters Rally in Times Square Against Iran Nuclear Deal." http://newyork.cbslocal.com/2015/07/22/iran-nuclear-deal-protest/ Accessed on (5/25/2017).
49. Martin, Douglas. "Charlie Wilson, Texas Congressman Linked to Foreign Intrigue, Dies at 76." *The New York Times*. http://www.nytimes.com/2010/02/11/us/politics/11wilson.html Accessed on (5/25/2017).
50. Crile, George. 2007. *Charlie Wilson's War: The Extraordinary Story of How the Wildest Man in Congress and a Rogue CIA Agent Changed the History of Our Times.* Grove Press.
51. McKinnon, Mark. 2010. "How to Survive a Scandal." *The Daily Beast.* http://www.thedailybeast.com/articles/2010/03/09/how-to-survive-a-scandal.html Accessed on (5/25/2017).

52. Crile, George. 2007. *Charlie Wilson's War: The Extraordinary Story of How the Wildest Man in Congress and a Rogue CIA Agent Changed the History of Our Times.* Grove Press.
53. Wilson traveled frequently overseas and liked to visit Israel. It was there on two occasions that I, being posted to the American embassy in Tel Aviv at the time, got to be his control officer. A control officer is supposed to orchestrate the schedule of the visiting dignitary and escort the visitor to make sure all goes smoothly. "Control" wasn't quite the right word in Wilson's case as he always had his own thoughts on how to spend his time. Tom Hanks, in the movie, was a nicer Charlie Wilson than Charlie Wilson was in real life. But at least Wilson was no family-values-professing philanderer and was always an interesting visitor.
54. Ferdman, Roberto A. 2015. "The Story Behind the Funniest E-mail Hillary Clinton Has Ever Sent." *The Washington Post.* https://www.washingtonpost.com/news/wonk/wp/2015/09/01/the-story-behind-the-funniest-e-mail-hilary-clinton-has-ever-sent/?utm_term=.b9b0aa614a48 Accessed on (5/25/2017).
55. NPR. 2010. "Israeli Tariff Burdens Supplier of Gefilte Fish Listen Queue." http://www.npr.org/templates/story/story.php?storyId=124459181 Accessed on (5/25/2017).
56. Kelly, Amita. 2015. "Hillary Clinton's Fight for Gefilte Fish Listen·3:36." NPR. http://www.npr.org/sections/itsallpolitics/2015/09/02/436935051/hillary-clintons-fight-for-gefilte-fish Accessed on (5/25/2017).
57. CNN. 2006. "Congress Declares War on Ports Deal." http://edition.cnn.com/2006/POLITICS/03/08/port.security/index.html?iref=newssearch Accessed on (5/25/2017).
58. Alfano, Sean. 2006. "Dubai Company Gives Up on Ports Deal." CBS. http://www.cbsnews.com/news/dubai-company-gives-up-on-ports-deal/ Accessed on (5/25/2017).

CHAPTER 2

A Bit of History

Given the relations between the United States and Iran, it is remarkable that any kind of agreement could have been reached over the nuclear program. It is a relationship with a long and troubled history with each country having its own view about who is responsible for the problems.

History is what a nation collectively chooses to remember and how it likes to think of itself more than it is what an objective observer would say actually happened. History is also another weapon used extensively by opponents of the nuclear deal in both Tehran and Washington.

Americans opposed to the deal often cite Iran's record of supporting terrorist organizations, missile testing and abuse of human rights. They argue that the deal should not have been struck because Iran cannot be trusted. Iranian hard-liners also assert that the United States will not uphold its part of the bargain.

For Americans, the most prominent episode in the history of the relationship is the takeover of the American embassy in Tehran by a mob in 1979. The recent movie *Argo* refreshed memories of that period as it told the story of how a handful of embassy employees escaped being taken captive with the help of Canadian diplomats when a mob overran the embassy.

Older Americans recall firsthand the frustration of the time when the 52, who did not escape, were held as hostages for 444 days, and the American government seemed powerless to end the crisis. Even the State Department's history of the event describes it as a time when "Carter's foreign policy team often seemed weak and vacillating."[1]

The fact that the hostages were released immediately upon Reagan's inauguration was taken by the right as proof of the impact a candidate who portrayed himself as a strong and forceful president could have. Some on the left had a different view. They suspected that Reagan supporters had made a deal with Iran to delay the release of the hostages in order to avoid giving Carter a boost in the midst of his attempt to get reelected.[2] The subsequent revelation, years later, of the sale of weapons to Iran during the Iran-Contra scandal only seemed to confirm liberal suspicions.

Iranians have their own version of history. For them, it starts with the CIA's support for the overthrow of a democratically elected prime minister, Mohammad Mossadegh, in 1953. When he attempted to nationalize the Iranian oil industry, the United States and Britain decided Iran was in danger of being taken over by the Soviet Union and they engineered a coup to oust him. While the US role had long been discussed, it was 60 years before the CIA released the documents that acknowledged its part in the overthrow.[3]

Once the Shah of Iran was installed, he was seen as America's indispensable ally in the region. The United States limited contacts with any other political forces and ignored his repression of opponents and human rights abuses. The failure to appreciate the unpopularity of the Shah led to the failure to anticipate the embassy takeover.

Another incident long forgotten by Americans, but not by Iranians, was the shooting down of an Iran Air Flight 665, a scheduled commercial flight, which resulted in the death of 290 passengers and crew members, including 66 children. An Aegis radar system on the guided missile cruiser, the *USS Vincennes*, detected the aircraft on July 3, 1988, at a particularly tense time in the Persian Gulf. While the system was supposedly very advanced, it was relatively untested. The information it provided the crew was interpreted to mean the plane was a fighter descending rapidly and headed toward the ship in what appeared to be an attack. In response, the captain of the ship ordered an antiaircraft missile to be launched, bringing the Airbus down and killing all onboard.

Almost nothing that the radar system supposedly showed or that the American government claimed in the immediate aftermath of the incident was true.[4] The passenger jet was gaining altitude and heading away from the *Vincennes*, which had entered Iranian territorial waters.

Seven weeks later, the Pentagon issued a 53-page report that did admit the mistakes made, but it nonetheless concluded that the officers and crew had acted properly. Two years after that, the captain of the ship received a medal for "exceptionally meritorious conduct in the performance of outstanding service" during his time in charge of the vessel.[5]

George H.W. Bush, who was running for president in order to succeed Reagan as president at that time, did nothing to help Iranian feelings about this tragic incident. While campaigning, he declared, "I will never apologize for the United States. I don't care what the facts are."[6]

There are also more recent events that add to the Iranian distrust of the United States in the form of direct assaults on its nuclear program. A computer virus called Stuxnet was launched that caused the centrifuges in Iranian nuclear facilities that were used to enrich uranium to destroy themselves. According to former National Security Agency contractor Edward Snowden, the virus was created by the United States and Israel working together.[7]

Another series of attacks came in the form of the assassination of Iranian nuclear scientists on at least five occasions. When asked about one such incident, the State Department spokesperson initially gave a somewhat evasive answer in the January 11, 2012, noon press briefing. The transcript was subsequently annotated to include a footnote that stated: "The United States strongly condemns this act of violence and categorically denies any involvement in the killing."[8]

In an August 2015 *Jerusalem Post* article, the Israeli defense minister was reported to have hinted the country's intelligence services were behind the killings.[9] He then reiterated his view that the negotiations on the Iran nuclear program were "a historic mistake." The article also claimed the Obama administration had pressured Israel to stop the assassinations.

The chapter in the history of the relationship between the Iran and the United States that bothers Iran the most is one which resulted in the death of over one million Iranians, partially because of American actions. In 1984, the Reagan administration was working to improve relations with Saddam Hussein by giving Iraq financial aid and military intelligence. As the *New York Times* reported in 2003, a key player in that effort was a special envoy named Donald Rumsfeld[10]:

> As a special envoy for the Reagan administration in 1984, Donald H. Rumsfeld, now the defense secretary, traveled to Iraq to persuade officials there that the United States was eager to improve ties with President Saddam Hussein despite his use of chemical weapons, newly declassified documents show.

Mr. Rumsfeld, who ran a pharmaceutical company at the time, was tapped by Secretary of State George P. Shultz to reinforce a message that a recent move to condemn Iraq's use of chemical weapons was strictly in principle and that America's priority was to prevent an Iranian victory in the Iran-Iraq war and to improve bilateral ties.

During that war, the United States secretly provided Iraq with combat planning assistance, even after Mr. Hussein's use of chemical weapons was widely known. The highly classified program involved more than 60 officers of the Defense Intelligence Agency, who shared intelligence on Iranian deployments, bomb-damage assessments and other crucial information with Iraq.

The assistance to Iraq that the United States provided included helping that country develop its chemical, biological and nuclear weapons programs even after Hussein had used chemical weapons on Kurdish civilians.[11] Rumsfeld is, of course, the same person who, as secretary of defense under George W. Bush's administration, was one of the key architects of the 2003 invasion of Iraq. That attack was justified mainly on the basis of repeated assertions by administration officials that Iraq had programs to produce weapons of mass destruction. The culmination of that effort to make the case for war with Iraq was the speech that Secretary of State Powell gave on February 5, 2003, to the United Nations General Assembly only weeks before the invasion took place.

Virtually, all the information and conclusions on which Powell rested his case turned out to be false and ever since Powell, Rumsfeld, CIA Director George Tenet and others have blamed each other for the intelligence failure. Powell spoke with great assurance that day, however, in part because Rumsfeld kept from him an assessment that showed just how great the gaps in intelligence were and Tenet and his deputy, John McLaughlin, repeatedly assured him the information was reliable.[12]

The war between Iran and Iraq that the Reagan administration did so much to encourage resulted in an estimated one million Iranian deaths and a quarter to a half that many Iraqis.[13] Because of that fact and the other incidents, it is therefore unsurprising that there is considerable mistrust and ill will on the part of Iranian officials toward the United States.

The differences in what historical events mattered to the United States and Iran were not the only baggage brought to the table in the effort to reach an agreement over the nuclear program. All six of the countries that negotiated with Iran did not want to see Iran acquire nuclear weapons or another military conflict in the Middle East. But the P5+1 (for the five permanent members of the UN Security Council), or as the Europeans preferred to call them, the EU3+3, did not have identical interests beyond those two general objectives.

Russian interests were probably the most complex. On the one hand, increased oil production by Iran could drive down Russian oil revenues. Moreover, any rapprochement with the other countries at the table could result in growing Western influence and connections, which the Russians did not want to see happen. On the other hand, Iran would become a potential customer for more Russian weapons, and such a relationship could be a way to prevent further expansion of NATO. While Russia made the negotiations more complicated at several points, it did not torpedo them however. President Obama even called President Putin to thank him for not being a spoiler or vetoing sanctions.[14]

Ultimately, Russia was perhaps most influenced by China. Beijing's main goal was gaining greater access to the world's fourth largest oil reserves and it stood ready to undertake major gas and oil projects in Iran. While this would work against Russia by adding to world oil supplies, Russia has become dependent on China as an economic outlet due to its strained relations with the West and the economic sanctions applied against Russia.[15]

Commercial interests were also important to Germany and France, who saw billions in business deals that could be done with Iran once an agreement was reached and the sanctions eased. The German economy minister was the first high-ranking Western official to visit Tehran after it was signed.[16]

France was one of the hardest bargainers at the table and was more skeptical than the others as to whether Iran would be willing to abide by the agreement.[17] Once struck, it became a defender of the accord; and in January 2017, its foreign minister went to Tehran to provide assurances that it would hold up despite the rhetoric coming out of Washington.[18] It also moved rapidly to take advantage of any commercial opportunities. Several major French companies quickly signed deals with Tehran including Airbus, Total, Peugeot and Renault.

Britain's history with Iran is marked by some of the problems that the United States has had. The British aided and encouraged the CIA in engineering the coup against Mossadegh. In 2011, demonstrators overran the British embassy in Tehran, leading to a break in diplomatic relations and the closure of the Iranian embassy in London.[19] Relations were restored to normal and embassies in each capital reopened in 2014.

A further sign of the repaired relationship between the UK and Iran was a report issued in May 2017 by the chairman of the International Relations Committee of the House of Lords.[20] The report asserted that Britain could no longer rely on US leadership in the Middle East and should work closely with its European allies to ensure the nuclear agreement is sustained. It added that, as Britain exits the European Union, it should make increasing trade and banking links with Iran a top priority.

The House of Lords report[21] went on to make a number of other important points about the nuclear deal:

- That its endurance is not a foregone conclusion, in part because hard-liners in Tehran are arguing that the West is reneging on it and Iran is not seeing the benefits it was supposed to have delivered.
- Because of that perceived lack of benefit, the UK needs to ensure the Iranians get more than they have so far received.
- The major impediment to Iran having received more has been the significant US sanctions that remain in place. American individuals and companies continue to be broadly prohibited from engaging in transactions or dealings with Iran.
- As a consequence, US banks, or any international banks with US connections, have been deterred from providing services to Iran.
- Even with an Obama administration "actively lobbying banks to ease up on lending to Iran," the deal struggled to deliver. With a Trump administration and a Republican Congress opposed to the deal, the agreement is under real threat. President Trump is unlikely to renege on the deal, but his actions and those of Congress could undermine it in a number of ways.

Like Britain, the views of the other P5+1 countries are at odds with the somewhat contradictory American stance on the deal. Many American critics of the deal have pointed to Iran's continuing support for terrorist organizations, ballistic missile tests and the role it is playing in conflicts in Syria and Yemen as reasons for increasing rather than easing sanctions.

In April 2017, Secretary of State Tillerson described the accord as a failure just hours after the Department of State certified that Iran was in compliance with its provisions.

While the Trump administration is unsatisfied, Britain, France and Germany remain committed to the agreement. In September 2015, the leaders of the three nations wrote in an opinion piece in the *Washington Post*:

> We did not reach the nuclear deal in the expectation that Iran's external policy would change any time soon. But it does address the threat from Iran's nuclear program and may open the way to recognition by Iran that collaboration with its neighbors is better than confrontation: Although we may not have the same interests as Iran, we do face some common challenges, including the threat from ISIL. We are confident that the agreement provides the foundation for resolving the conflict on Iran's nuclear program permanently. This is why we now want to embark on the full implementation of the Joint Comprehensive Plan of Action, once all national procedures are complete.[22]

There was no indication by mid-2017, despite the leaders of France and Britain having changed, that the governments of those three countries had altered that position. As long as Iran seems to be following the terms of the agreement, there will be no enthusiasm for undoing the agreement especially after the long and complicated history involved in getting it concluded.

One could begin the recounting of that story of that history as early as 1956 when Iran first became interested in nuclear energy. The following year, the Shah's government signed an agreement with the Eisenhower administration dealing with the nonmilitary use of nuclear energy. The United States was not the only country among the P5+1 to have engaged in nuclear cooperation with Iran in the past. All of them except Britain did at various points.

Here is the very short version of the negotiations that culminated in the nuclear accord. The final agreement is contained in Appendix A at the end of the book. A detailed timeline is contained in Appendix B, which was put together by the Arms Control Association, a think tank that has worked since 1971 to advance and secure major arms control and nonproliferation agreements.[23]

> The first direct talks between Iran and the P5+1 began in April 2012. In September, Israeli Prime Minister Netanyahu used his annual speech to the UN General Assembly to warn of the Iranian threat and to declare that his red line was 250 kilograms of 20 percent enriched uranium, enough if further refined to make one bomb.

> In August 2013 Hasan Rouhani was inaugurated president of Iran. Three months later, Iran and the P5+1 signed a preliminary agreement. Implementation of the interim agreement, called the Joint Plan of Action, began in January 2014. The International Atomic Energy Agency certified that Iran is complying with the agreement, which required it to halt enrichment of uranium to 20 percent, dilute half the stockpile of 20 percent enriched uranium on hand to 3.5 percent, and stop work on a heavy water reactor. The IAEA also started to conduct more intrusive and frequent inspections. At the same time, the United States and the European Union took steps to ease sanctions and release Iranian oil money held up in the other countries.

> The following month in February 2014, talks got underway to arrive at a final agreement, which is known as the Joint Comprehensive Plan of Action (JCPOA). After a year of difficult negotiations, the seven countries seemed to be getting close. At that point, Republican congressional leaders, without bothering to inform the White House, invited Prime

Minister Netanyahu to give a speech to a joint session of Congress. In the speech, he asserted that an agreement would guarantee that Iran obtained nuclear weapons. Less than a week later, on March 9, 2015, Senator Cotton and his Republican colleagues sent their open letter to Iranian leaders.

On May 7, 2014 the senate in a 98-1 vote passed a resolution calling for a congressional review of the agreement. On July 14, conclusion of the deal was announced and on the 19th it was sent to congress, which started a 60-day review period. The following day, the UN Security Council approved the agreement.

By early September, 42 Democratic senators had announced support for the agreement, which meant that a presidential veto of any resolution to block the deal could not be overridden by congress. On September 10th, a vote in the Senate to end debate on a resolution of disapproval failed, which meant it could not come to a vote. The next day, the House rejected a resolution of approval by 269-162 with 25 Democrats joining all the Republicans. Less than a week later, the congressional review period ended.

On October 14, 2015, Iran concluded ratification of the agreement and four days later, Iran and P5+1 countries formally adopted it.

The politics around the deal was as intense as the vitriol between the two sides. Elizabeth Drew writing in the *New York Review of Books* described the struggle:

> Once the nuclear deal was presented to Congress in July, there was little question that it would fall into the deep crevasse that had developed between the two political parties. Ever since Barack Obama took office in 2009, the Republicans have opposed everything he wanted to do. In keeping with this

strategy, within days of the deal's being announced, numerous Republicans, without bothering to read the agreement or consider it seriously, jumped to oppose it. The debate on the deal throughout was only ostensibly on its merits. The Republicans' contempt for Obama—as a Democrat, as a black person, as, in the view of many of them, an illegitimate president—was clear to any close observer. For the first time in US history, the opposition party thumbed its nose at the president by inviting the head of another nation—Netanyahu—to address Congress to urge rejection of an international measure the president supported.[24]

Republicans were not the only ones seen by observers to have contempt for Obama because he is black. One opponent of the deal accused Susan Rice, Obama's national security advisor, of failing to keep Netanyahu briefed on the negotiations: "Instead, Rice, reflecting her generally more combative mindset, would say to Abe Foxman, national director of the Anti-Defamation League, that in reacting to the Joint Plan of Action, Netanyahu's posture was outrageous. In her view, the Israeli leader did everything but use 'the N-word' in describing the president."[25]

While Netanyahu may have been restrained enough to not use the N-word in this case, he hasn't been above playing the race card at home. When he ran for reelection in March 2015, he encouraged his supporters to go to the polls by telling them that Arab Israelis were voting "in droves."[26]

Keeping Netanyahu briefed would not have tempered his attitude. His inserting himself into the debate over the deal without even informing the White House that he was coming to Washington was as insulting as it was outrageous. His ambassador, Ron Dermer, also had no qualms about intervening into the internal political affairs of the country to which he is accredited. Dermer was an American citizen born in Florida and a Republican Party operative before he moved to Israel and became a political advisor to Netanyahu. Dermer intensively lobbied dozens of congressmen imploring them to defeat the deal and hinting that failing to do so would cost them Jewish votes in their next election.[27]

When as a presidential contender, Donald Trump went to address the AIPAC convention in April 2016, Dermer provided points for Jared Kushner, Trump's son-in-law, who wrote the speech.[28] As a result, according to a reporter from the Israeli newspaper *Haaretz*, "Large portions of the speech, especially those having to do with Iran and the Palestinians, sounded like they were taken verbatim from Prime Minister Benjamin Netanyahu's talking point sheet."

For two countries that are supposedly close allies, the actions of Netanyahu and Dermer were as remarkable for their aggressiveness as they were for their lack of diplomacy. If Susan Rice did display a combative mind-set, she was not the only one. That attitude and the antics of Israel officials were among the most significant milestones on the long road to the Iran nuclear agreement.

The road was so long because the Iran deal is a very complicated agreement. But it is one with a simple premise—Iran would agree to restrictions on its nuclear program in return for the lifting of crippling economic sanctions that had been imposed by the international community. It is commonly accepted that any country has a right to a nuclear program for medical research or generating electricity. The challenge was to structure constraints that would preclude Iran from being able to use its nuclear program to develop the ability to make weapons and verify that Iran was complying with those constraints.

A nuclear weapon can be made from either uranium or plutonium. The agreement was designed to prevent a uranium-based weapon by limiting the number of centrifuges and the amount of low-enriched uranium that would both be necessary to refine it further to the level of purity required for a bomb. The agreement also required a deeply buried nuclear plant at Fordo to be turned into a research center. Another facility at Natanz has to be reduced in capacity by cutting in half the number of centrifuges operating there. The agreement also places limits on the level of enrichment and the stockpile of low-enriched uranium is to be kept at a level insufficient for a bomb for 15 years.

Preventing a weapon using plutonium requires ensuring that the kind of reactor that produces it as a by-product has sufficient restrictions that it cannot be used for that purpose. To prevent that route to a bomb from being pursued, the agreement stipulates that the Arak reactor will be changed to ensure that it cannot be used to produce plutonium and that no new heavy water reactors will be built in the next 15 years.

To verify compliance with the accord, more intrusive inspections than in the past are required and the International Atomic Energy Agency, the UN agency that monitors nuclear activities, is given greater access to the entire nuclear program. Iran must also reduce its stockpile of low-enriched uranium by 98 percent, limit its research and development and enrichment capacity for 15 years and allow some inspections and other measures to ensure transparency for 25 years. The net result of the agreement is to extend the amount of time it would take Iran to produce enough material for a bomb to a minimum of one year.[29]

Once the deal was concluded, a *New York Times* editorial entitled "An Iran Deal That Reduces the Chance of War" summarized its view of what had been accomplished:

> The final deal with Iran announced by the United States and other major world powers does what no amount of political

posturing and vague threats of military action had managed to do before. It puts strong, verifiable limits on Iran's ability to develop a nuclear weapon for at least the next 10 to 15 years and is potentially one of the most consequential accords in recent diplomatic history, with the ability not just to keep Iran from obtaining a nuclear weapon but also to reshape Middle East politics. The deal, the product of 20 arduous months of negotiations, would obviously have provided more cause for celebration if Iran had agreed to completely dismantle all of its nuclear facilities. But the chances of that happening were effectively zero.[30]

Opponents of the deal nonetheless had serious reservations. They asserted that:

- A better deal was possible since Iran's economy was on the brink of collapse.
- The better deal could be brought about by the threat of even harsher sanctions and that the other members of the P5+1 group would go along with such measures and follow American leadership.
- The deal leaves Iran with a reinvigorated economy and on the threshold of acquiring nuclear weapons and will prompt a race to acquire nuclear weapons by countries in the region.
- Killing the deal would not lead to war as all the parties in the Middle East and elsewhere wish to avoid one. Iran will simply be forced to return to the negotiating table.
- Iran will never allow sufficient access to all its sites and cannot be trusted. Implantation of the agreement cannot therefore be verified with certainty.
- If the sanctions are eased, Iran will become more aggressive in the region and deterring it in the future will be more difficult if it is on the nuclear threshold.

While a majority of both houses of Congress appeared to agree with the deal's opponents it nonetheless survived. It did so for two reasons. First, and foremost, President Obama saw it as one of his most important accomplishments and was determined to invest the time and effort to ensure it withstood the assaults of its critics. And second, while many congressmen and senators could not think of enough bad things to say about the agreement, none of them, with the possible exception of Tom Cotton, wanted to take the responsibility for seeing it fail. Even they knew that killing it would open up a number of different scenarios for what would happen next. And most of them would not be good outcomes for the United States.

Those legislators were less reluctant to undermine the deal if the responsibility for its failure could be shifted elsewhere. For that reason, the opponents of the deal did not let its successful conclusion terminate their efforts to derail it. They continue to oppose it and look for ways to limit the benefits the Iranians obtain from it thereby creating doubt about how long it will last. Like Bismarck, the baseball player Yogi Berra is remembered for the quotable things he is reported to have said. One of them was "the future ain't what it used to be."[31]

It is hard to predict how the Iran nuclear agreement will fare, especially under the Trump administration. According to a *New York Times* report in early June 2017, the CIA officer who conducted the hunt for Osama bin Laden, and the campaign of drone strikes that killed thousands of militants and hundreds of civilians, was put in charge of operations aimed at Iran.[32] This was taken as an indication that the hard line against Iran that Trump took during the election campaign was being put into practice. Another sign that was not positive, as noted earlier, was the State Department certifying that

Iran was abiding by the agreement and a few hours later the secretary of state calling it a failure.

If this review of history demonstrates anything, however, it is that if the United States rejects the accord none of the P5+1 countries will follow if there is no solid proof that Iran violated it. Given the experience of the intelligence used to justify the invasion of Iraq in 2003, and the tendency of the Trump administration to frequently create what one of his closest advisors called alternative facts, any assertion by the United States that Iran has cheated is more likely to be regarded as fake news than the truth. As with the US departure from the Paris climate agreement and Britain's withdrawal from the European Union, the other signatories to the accord are not going to be eager to renegotiate it just because one of the parties has decided to back out.

That will not stop the opponents of the agreement from using history to make the case that the United States should nevertheless do just that. The next chapter will describe some of scores of individuals and organizations that opposed the deal. It will also talk about those on the other side of the debate as the argument continued over whether it was a repeat of Neville Chamberlain's agreement with Hitler at Munich or more akin to the Camp David accords that brought peace between two long-time enemies.

Notes

1. Department of State. 2017. "A Short History of the Department of State: The Iranian Hostage Crisis." https://history.state.gov/departmenthistory/short-history/iranian-crises Accessed on (5/29/2017).
2. http://www.nytimes.com/1991/04/15/world/new-reports-say-1980-reagan-campaign-tried-to-delay-hostage-release.html

3. Merica, Dan and Jason Hanna. 2013. "In declassified document, CIA acknowledges role in '53 Iran coup." CNN. http://www.cnn.com/2013/08/19/politics/cia-iran-1953-coup/ Accessed on (5/29/2017).
4. Kaplan, Fred. 2014. "America's Flight 17." Slate. http://www.slate.com/articles/news_and_politics/war_stories/2014/07/the_vincennes_downing_of_iran_air_flight_655_the_united_states_tried_to.html Accessed on (5/29/2017).
5. Ibid.
6. Ibid.
7. Jewish Telegraphic Agency. 2013. "Snowden Says Israel, U.S. Created Stuxnet Virus That Attacked Iran." *Haaretz.* http://www.haaretz.com/israel-news/1.534728 Accessed on (5/29/2017).
8. Nuland, Victoria. 2012. "Daily Press Briefing—January 11, 2012." U.S. Department of State. https://2009-2017.state.gov/r/pa/prs/dpb/2012/01/180454.htm Accessed on (5/29/2017).
9. JPOST Staff. 2015. "Israel Behind Assassinations of Iran Nuclear Scientists, Ya'alon Hints." *The Jerusalem Post.* http://www.jpost.com/Middle-East/Iran/Israel-behind-assassinations-of-Iran-nuclear-scientists-Yaalon-hints-411473 Accessed on (5/29/2017).
10. Marquis, Christopher. 2003. "The Struggle for Iraq: Document; Rumsfeld Made Iraq Overture in '84 Despite Chemical Raids." *The New York Times.* http://www.nytimes.com/2003/12/23/world/struggle-for-iraq-documents-rumsfeld-made-iraq-overture-84-despite-chemical.html Accessed on (5/29/2017).
11. Dixon, Norm. 2004. "How Regan Armed Saddam with Chemical Weapons." Counter Punch. http://www.counterpunch.org/2004/06/17/how-reagan-armed-saddam-with-chemical-weapons/ Accessed on (5/29/2017).
12. Walcott, John. 2016. "What Donald Rumsfeld Knew We Didn't Know About Iraq." *Politico Magazine.* http://www.politico.com/magazine/story/2016/01/iraq-war-wmds-

donald-rumsfeld-new-report-213530 Accessed on (5/29/2017).
13. Black, Ian. 2010. "Iran and Iraq Remember War That Cost More Than a Million Lives." *The Guardian*. https://www.theguardian.com/world/2010/sep/23/iran-iraq-war-anniversary Accessed on (5/29/2017).
14. Bernstein, Jonas. 2015. "Russia's Stake in Iran Nuclear Deal." Vox. http://www.voanews.com/a/russias-stake-in-iran-nuclear-deal/2867710.html Accessed on (5/29/2017).
15. Baev, Pavel K. 2015. "The China Factor in Russian Support for the Iran Deal." The Brookings Institute. https://www.brookings.edu/blog/order-from-chaos/2015/07/21/the-china-factor-in-russian-support-for-the-iran-deal/ Accessed on (5/29/2017).
16. Uniyal, Vijeta. 2017. "German Business Goals Played Key-role in Iran Nuclear Deal." Legal Insurrection. http://legalinsurrection.com/2015/07/german-business-goals-played-key-role-in-iran-nuclear-deal/ Accessed on (5/29/2017).
17. Collinson, Stephen. 2015. "How Did France Become More Hawkish on Iran Than the U.S.?" CNN. http://www.cnn.com/2015/04/01/politics/france-iran-nuclear-deal-hawks/ Accessed on (5/29/2017).
18. Irish, John. 2017. "France, Worried by Trump, Promises to Defend Iran Nuclear Deal." Reuters. http://www.reuters.com/article/us-france-iran-idUSKBN15E29Q Accessed on (5/29/2017).
19. BBC. 2011. "Iran Protesters Storm UK Embassy in Tehran." http://www.bbc.com/news/world-middle-east-15936213 Accessed on (5/29/2017).
20. Radio Free Europe. 2017. "Britain Can't Depend On U.S. Leadership in Middle East, Lawmakers Say." http://www.rferl.org/a/britain-no-longer-follow-us-on-iran-nuclear-deal-arab-israeli-conflict-lawmakers-say/28462887.html Accessed on (5/29/2017).

21. UK Parliament. 2017. "Chapter 6: Evolution of Middle East States." https://www.publications.parliament.uk/pa/ld201617/ldselect/ldintrel/159/15909.htm#_idTextAnchor096 Accessed on (5/29/2017).
22. Cameron, David, François Hollande and Angela Merkel. 2015. "Cameron, Hollande and Merkel: Why We Support the Iran Deal." https://www.washingtonpost.com/opinions/cameron-hollande-and-merkel-why-we-support-the-iran-deal/2015/09/10/a1ce6610-5735-11e5-b8c9-944725fcd3b9_story.html?utm_term=.73ffd7b64ed8 Accessed on (5/29/2017).
23. Davenport, Kelsey. 2016. "Timeline of Nuclear Diplomacy with Iran." Arms Control Association. https://www.armscontrol.org/factsheet/Timeline-of-Nuclear-Diplomacy-With-Iran Accessed on (5/29/2017).
24. Drew, Elizabeth. 2015, October 22. "How They Failed to Block the Iran Deal." *New York Review of Books.* http://www.nybooks.com/articles/2015/10/22/how-they-failed-block-iran-deal/ Accessed on (6/17/17).
25. Ross, Dennis. 2015, October 8. "How Obama Got to Yes on Iran: The Inside Story." *Politico.* http://www.politico.com/magazine/story/2015/10/iran-deal-susan-rice-israel-213227 Accessed (6/17/17).
26. Tharoor, Ishaan. 2107, March 3. "On Israeli Election Day, Netanyahu Warns of Arabs Voting 'in Droves'." *Washington Post.* https://www.washingtonpost.com/news/worldviews/wp/2015/03/17/on-israeli-election-day-netanyahu-warns-of-arabs-voting-in-droves/?utm_term=.627895737935 Accessed on (6/17/17).
27. Sherman, Jake. 2015, July 27. "Israeli Ambassador Dermer to Address GOP Whip Team on Monday." *Politico.* http://www.politico.com/story/2015/07/israeli-ambassador-ron-dermer-address-gop-iran-nuclear-deal-120659 Accessed on (6/17/17).
28. Ravid, Barak. 2016, April 17. "Israeli Ambassador Briefed Trump's Son-in-law Ahead of AIPAC Speech." *Haaretz.*

http://www.haaretz.com/israel-news/.premium-1.714796 Accessed on (6/17/17).
29. https://www.nytimes.com/interactive/2015/03/31/world/middleeast/simple-guide-nuclear-talks-iran-us.html?_r=0
30. Editorial Board. 2015, July 14. "An Iran Deal That Reduces the Chance of War." *New York Times.* https://www.nytimes.com/2015/07/15/opinion/an-iran-nuclear-deal-that-reduces-the-chance-of-war.html Accessed on (6/17/17).
31. Scott, Nate. 2015, September 23 "The 50 greatest Yogi Berra quotes." *USA Today.* http://ftw.usatoday.com/2015/09/the-50-greatest-yogi-berra-quotes Accessed on (8/10/17).
32. Rosenberg, Matthew. 2017, June 2. "CIA Names New Iran Chief in a Sign of Trump's Hard Line." *New York Times.* https://www.nytimes.com/2017/06/02/world/middleeast/cia-iran-dark-prince-michael-dandrea.html Accessed on (8/10/17).

CHAPTER 3

Who Was Involved

There were so many organizations and individuals involved in the debate over the Iran nuclear agreement that it would be impossible to describe them all or even sort them out in a systematic way. This chapter will look at a few of the most prominent actors including foundations, organizations and individuals. Appendix B presents and describes a much longer list containing dozens of organizations. It is worth reading in order to understand how interconnected many of them are, either financially or because of the people involved in them.

A couple of things do become evident from analyzing groups on both sides of the debate. First, organizations opposed to the Iran agreement raised much more money than those that supported it. One organization alone is estimated to have spent at least $20 million in the effort.

Second, those opposed to the deal were far less transparent when it came to revealing from where all their money was coming. The laws regarding taxes and Internal Revenue Service regulations have done a great deal to enable this anonymity. Contributions to these organizations were, in many cases, tax deductible and there is no requirement to reveal the identity of donors. Whether money given to an organization was deductible depended on the definitions of what is "social welfare" and "political activity." Those are both vague and enforcement of them is lax.

That is not the fault of the Internal Revenue Service. It has been given an impossible job thanks to the way Congress has written the laws and provided loopholes for any special interest with an effective lobbyist. That does not deter politicians from unloading on the IRS whenever a controversy arises. The harsh criticism the IRS faced from the right after it targeted Tea Party groups for particular scrutiny helped diminish what little enforcement efforts there were.[1] Lost in that controversy is the fact that those groups were applying for nonprofit status on the basis that they were not created mainly for political purposes, when that is exactly why they were established.

According to the IRS rules, 501(c)(3) organizations are charities that are required to avoid activities that involve participation in political campaigns or on behalf of or against a candidate. On the other hand, 501(c)(4) groups can lobby and engage in campaigns and elections as long as it does not account for more than half of their activity. The majority of their time is supposed to be spent on "social welfare" activities. Contributions to the former are tax deductible but not to the latter. Both are considered nonprofit associations and neither of them has to reveal their donors.[2]

Deep Throat, the most important anonymous source in the Watergate Scandal that brought down the Nixon administration, turned out to be the acting head of the FBI. He is remembered for having said, "follow the money." That is still good advice. In addition to looking at that factor in this chapter, the other influences—technology, partisan politics, truth and globalization—that make policy formulation increasingly difficult today will also be considered.

THE BILLIONAIRE BUYERS CLUB

The impact of money can be best described by looking at those individuals and institutions who use it, like Betsy DeVos unapologetically admitted, to buy influence on government policy. The money trail can be hard to trace because of the lack of any disclosure requirements for contributions to 501(c) organizations and super PACs. In addition, there are other ways to hide the source by using organizations like Donors Trust, which has been called "the right wing's dark-money ATM."[3] In her book *Dark Money*, Jane Mayer did a brilliant job of tracking how the Koch brothers organized a network of fellow billionaires who wanted to use their fortunes to affect public policy. But few of the billionaires in the club, besides the Kochs, have received any real scrutiny.

The activities of these billionaires clearly demonstrate one thing. There are more mega-wealthy people trying to influence policy more frequently in more ways than ever before. A 2016 article in *The Nation* explained what has changed from the past:

> One difference now, though, is that America's donor class is far wealthier than ever before—so they have more cash to pull every possible lever of influence. Since 2004, the combined net worth of the Forbes 400 has more than doubled. The Koch brothers alone saw their joint fortune grow tenfold during this period, from $8 billion to over $80 billion. George Soros's net worth more than tripled, and Michael Bloomberg's grew sevenfold, soaring to over $35 billion. The upper class is much larger, too, which means more people have the means to get into the influence game. A 2015 study found that 69,560 individuals living in the United States have assets of $30 million or more—a huge jump from a decade ago.

What's also new is that donors are getting more strategic about blending various forms of influence spending. Many now grasp that there's a wide spectrum of choices for converting wealth into power—from traditional campaigns gifts at one end to cause-focused philanthropy at the other. In between are 501(c)(4)s that can drive messages and mobilize voters, as well as hard-hitting 501(c)(3)s that are skilled at pushing policy agendas. The wealthiest, and savviest donors, can and do take advantage of all these choices.[4]

According to *Forbes* magazine, which keeps track of such things, there are more billionaires in the USA than any other country. In 2016, the 540 billionaires who lived in America exceeded all of those in all the European countries combined.[5] Given that the rich can contribute to political causes through 501(c) organizations, super PACs and other ways to hide their identity, it is hard to determine how many of them are using their fortunes to elect politicians and influence policies that they support. Many of them are probably content to count their money, cars, houses, yachts and wives. But some of them, like the Kochs, are very active in attempts to influence elections and government decisions.

The *New York Times* identified just 158 families that contributed $176 million to the early stage of the 2016 presidential campaign, which amounted to nearly half of the total collected by the candidates.[6] Never before had so much been given so early by a group of people that would not be big enough to fill a movie theater. And much of that giving was mainly made possible by the Citizens United decision.

Besides being rich, the vast majority of politically active billionaires were white, male and older. They also lean overwhelmingly to the right politically and frequently made their money in just two areas—finance and energy.[7]

Below is a short list of billionaires who used their fortunes to amplify their voices in the debate over the Iran nuclear deal or who spent heavily supporting politicians who took a strong stand in favor or against it. There were super-rich individuals on both sides of the debate, but those in opposition were more numerous and spent far more than those who were in favor of the deal. Their net worth estimates are taken from *Forbes* magazine.

BILLIONAIRES PUBLICLY AGAINST THE DEAL

1. Sheldon Adelson—$32.9 billion, casino owner and pro-Israel extremist who once suggested the USA should detonate a nuclear device in the desert in Iran just to show them America means business.[8] He spent hundreds of millions of dollars attempting to get Newt Gingrich and other Republican candidates elected.[9] He spent so lavishly that a trip to Las Vegas to solicit his backing became a virtual requirement for anyone seeking the Republican presidential nomination. Adelson was also one of the main funders of a number of anti-deal organizations including the Republican Jewish Coalition, Foundation for Defense of Democracies, Zionist Organization of America, Christians United for Israel, Endowment for Middle East Truth, Israeli American Council and the World Values Network. To enhance his influence in Israel, Adelson owns a newspaper in Israel, which is distributed for free. He has also invested in other ways to affect politics in Israel. According to an article in the Jewish newspaper *The Forward*:

> Adelson has devoted large sums to supporting a cadre of hawkish pro-Israel scholars who provide intellectual

backing for Netanyahu's policies. Key to this effort is his support for the Jerusalem Center for Public Affairs, a conservative think tank headed by Dore Gold, adviser to Netanyahu and former Israeli ambassador [to] the United Nations. Adelson's $1 million gift last year represented nearly two-thirds of the think tank's budget. In 2007, Adelson gave $4.5 million to establish an institute for strategic affairs carrying his name at the Shalem Center, another Israeli research center known for its hawkish positions and its closeness to Netanyahu. Adelson also recently announced a $25 million contribution to Ariel University, the only Israeli higher education institution in the occupied West Bank.[10]

The same article noted that in 2012 Adelson contributed $32 million to Birthright, which was 40 percent of its budget. Birthright is a program that gives free trips to Israel to young Jewish Americans. The e-mail list from that program was used to encourage past Birthright trip recipients to oppose the Iran deal. In 2012, Adelson also gave $53 million to two super PACs.

In a 2012 article in Forbes, Adelson explained why he was giving so much money to influence the presidential election that year: "I'm against very wealthy people attempting to or influencing elections. But as long as it's doable I'm going to do it. Because I know that guys like Soros have been doing it for years, if not decades."[11]

2. Haim Saban—$2.9 billion, an avid supporter of Hillary Clinton, he nonetheless harshly criticized Obama for negotiating with Iran and called the agreement a bad deal. According to an article in the *Forward*, Saban and Adelson tried to "out-hawk" each other at a joint

appearance at the inaugural conference of the Israeli American Council. At the event, Saban suggested the way to deal with Iran was to "bomb the sons of bitches."[12] Once the deal was concluded, Saban tried to walk back from that position apparently wanting to avoid putting Clinton into a difficult position or harming their relationship. Saying the agreement was a fait accompli, he asserted it was necessary to focus on making sure Iran did not acquire nuclear weapons.[13]

3. Rupert Murdoch—$12 billion, he did not take a public position on the deal, but he controls the content of the media outlets that he owns like Fox News and the *Wall Street Journal* and others that railed against it.[14]
4. Bernard Marcus—$4.3 billion, the owner of Home Depot, he has given over $10 million to the Foundation of Defense of Democracies, a major anti-deal organization.[15]
5. Paul Singer: $2.6 billion, a hedge fund manager who contributed $250,000 to Senator Cotton's campaign.[16] He also donated a million dollars to The Israel Project, another anti-deal group, which may be a supporter of an Islamophobic hate group. A board member of the Republican Jewish Coalition, he also gave $3.6 million to the Foundation for the Defense of Democracies (FDD).[17, 18]
6. Seth Klarman—$1.6 billion, another hedge fund manager who is on the board of, and a huge contributor to, The Israel Project (nearly $4 million between 2008 and 2011). He also contributes to the Foundation for the Defense of Democracies, the Middle East Media Research Institute, the Middle East Forum, another Islamophobic group, and the David Project. Klarman, believing the coverage of Israel in Israeli newspapers

was biased, started his own called the *Times of Israel*.[19] In 2014, he donated $100,000 to Arkansas Horizon, the super PAC supporting Tom Cotton.[20]

7. Ronald Lauder—$3.4 billion, heir to the Estee Lauder cosmetics business, ambassador to Austria under Reagan and president of the World Jewish Conference. He issued a statement in February 2017 that accused Iran of repeated subversion of the nuclear agreement and welcomed the US Treasury Department's decision to announce new sanctions against the Islamic Republic following its recent ballistic missile test.[21]
8. Richard Perry—$1.2 billion, the owner of Barneys clothing stores and a hedge fund manager who supported Hillary Clinton and contributed to Obama but also gave a million dollars to The Israel Project.[22]
9. Daniel Loeb—$2.9 billion, a hedge fund manager and supposedly a Democrat, Loeb supported Romney because he was angered by Obama's effort to regulate financial markets. A key financial backer of the Emergency Fund for Israel, which pushes for the bombing of Iran.[23]
10. Norman Braman—$1.7 billion, owner of an automobile dealership, he was the biggest underwriter of Marco Rubio's campaign. He also contributed to a nonprofit that funds Israeli settlements in the West Bank.[24]
11. Stewart and Lynda Resnick—$4.2 billion, agri-business owners who fear normalizing relations with Iran would create competition for their pistachios and other products.[25]
12. Mortimer Zuckerman—$2.7 billion, chairman and editor in chief of US News who considers the deal an unforgivable betrayal of Israel.[26]

13. Nina Rosenwald—an heiress to the Sears Roebuck fortune, her net worth is unclear. But she has donated millions of her own money and that of the family foundation to fund numerous Islamophobic organizations. A 2012 article in *The Nation* about her titled "The Sugar Mama of Anti-Muslim Hate," asserted she was responsible for fueling "a rapidly emerging alliance between the pro-Israel mainstream and the Islamophobic fringe."[27] She also founded and is president of the Gatestone Institute. Listed as chairman of that 501(c)(3) think tank is former ambassador to the UN, John Bolton, another advocate of a military attack on Iran.[28]

Billionaires Publicly For the Deal

1. George Soros—$25.2 billion, he is one of the richest people in the world thanks to investments and his hedge fund. He is also the billionaire the right loves to hate since he is a generous supporter of liberal causes and the Democratic Party. The readers of one right-wing website voted him "the single most destructive leftist demagogue in the country" because he "gives billions to left-wing causes."[29] Even though Soros is Jewish, he has been attacked by right-wing Israelis for funding Palestinian groups.[30] Conspiracy theorist Alex Jones labeled him the head of a "Jewish mafia."[31] Some of the criticism of him has more than a whim of anti-Semitism involved like the effort of the increasingly authoritarian government of Hungary to shut down a university in that country because Soros helps fund it.[32]
2. Eli Broad—$7.7 billion, one of "98 prominent Hollywood Jews" who wrote an open letter[33] in favor of

the agreement, Broad made his billions in tract housing and insurance.[34]
3. Steven Spielberg—$3.7 billion, moviemaker and supporter of Obama, he gave the president an award for his work.[35]
4. Ted Turner—$2.3 billion, media mogul and founder of CNN and the United Nations Foundation, Turner tweeted support for the agreement.[36]
5. S. Daniel Abraham—$2.1 billion, he made his wealth from SlimFast diet drinks. A Jewish philanthropist, he e-mailed Democratic senators urging that they support the deal.[37]
6. Bill Oberndorf—a hedge fund manager and the largest donor to Ploughshares, which was the most important pro-deal organization.[38]

The Somewhat Ambiguous Billionaires

(Those who did not take a clear position but made statements about the deal or supported politicians that had a very clear position on it.)

1. Warren Buffett—$74.1 billion, the third richest American, he stated that sanctions should be lifted only if there is complete assurance that Iran doesn't get a nuclear weapon.[39] Buffett is the rare billionaire who thinks it unfair that his secretary pays a higher income tax rate than he does.
2. Michael Bloomberg—$49.8 billion, he criticized the Obama administration for politicizing the debate over the deal and said he had deep reservations about the agreement but was still assessing it.[40]
3. Harold Hamm—$11.6 billion, an oil and gas entrepreneur who wrote about the deal but only in terms of the need to allow more US oil exports.[41]

4. Brian Chesky—$3.8 billion, only in his mid-thirties, he accumulated his wealth creating Airbnb. He has taken no position on the agreement but has said he wants to expand Airbnb into Iran in the future.[42] He and his two cofounders of the alternative lodging site have pledged, along with Bill Gates and Warren Buffet, to give the majority of their fortunes away.[43]
5. Tom Streyer—$1.6 billion, did not take a public position, but through his super PAC, NextGen, he made significant contributions to the Truman National Security Project, which advocates for the Iran deal.[44]
6. Robert Mercer—net worth unknown, he contributed $11 million to Ted Cruz's Super PAC, Keep the Promise.[45] Attempts to determine how rich he is by *Bloomberg* failed, but he does own a $90 million yacht.[46] He also funded the Breitbart website and was deeply involved with Donald Trump's rise to power. Jane Mayer's profile of him in the *New Yorker* describes him as reclusive, libertarian and anti-establishment.
7. Donald Sussman—a hedge fund manager who is married to a Democratic congresswoman, he is long-time supporter of the Clintons and Democrats. He gave millions to the Party in soft money before Citizens United and since then has donated millions to House Majority PAC, which works to elect Democrats to the House of Representatives.[47]
8. Maurice Hank Greenberg—a huge donor to Republican Party who contributed $10 million to Jeb Bush's campaign. He was a former chairman of AIG, an international insurance company that had to be bailed out by the Federal Reserve during the 2008 financial crisis to the tune of nearly $185 billion.[48]

9. Elizabeth and Richard Uihlein—Billionaire Republican mega-donors to far-right PACs and Republican candidates. Their family-owned business, Uline, sells shipping and packing materials and other industrial goods.[49]
10. James Simons—$18 billion, a hedge fund manager, he is one of the most reliable donors to the Democratic Party.[50]
11. Ferris and Dan Wilks—donated $15 million to the Keep the Promise super PAC that advocated for Ted Cruz. They made their money during the fracking boom in west Texas.[51]
12. Steven Cohen—another hedge fund manager whose fund was shut down in one of the biggest insider trading scandals in history.[52] He nonetheless swiftly started another one and is now worth around $13 billion. A major supporter of Chris Christie.
13. Charles Koch—$47.4 billion, he and his brother David are among the ten richest Americans. They support a number of libertarian causes and think tanks like the Mercatus Center at George Mason University. He is a big donor to the CATO Institute,[53] which called the agreement a clear success.[54] At the same time, he gave to a number of Republican candidates who opposed it. The two brothers pledged to spend nearly $900 million during the 2016 elections.[55]
14. Robert McNair—$3.5 billion, he donated half a million dollars to each of the super PACs backing Graham, Walker, Cruz and Bush.[56]
15. Lawrence Ellison—$55.6 billion, the CEO of Oracle Corporation and one of the four big donors to Marco Rubio's super PAC.[57]
16. Diane Hendricks—$4.8 billion, a fortune that came from a roofing supply business. She is a major contrib-

utor to Wisconsin governor Scott Walker with whom she shares a desire to destroy the power of labor unions.[58] According to Forbes, she is America's richest self-made woman.[59]
17. Leonard Blavatnik—$16.7 billion, a Ukrainian-born American investor in real estate and entertainment companies, he made major contributions to Scott Walker's super PAC.[60]
18. Ben Klein—another huge supporter of Ted Cruz, he hosted a fund raiser with Israel NorPAC, an organization that opposed the Iran nuclear deal. He donated directly to the Cruz campaign as well as giving $250,000 to the Cruz super PAC, Stand for Truth.[61] He is the CEO of a health care company that was charged with stealing over $1 million from Social Security, Medicare and Medicaid payments to its patients. The suit was settled without public disclosure of the terms.

This list and other lists of wealthy contributors to political campaigns demonstrate how their donations are almost always exclusively to one party or the other. OpenSecrets.org looked at the top 99 funders whose donations to PACs and Super PACs had been made public. It found that 92 of them gave only to conservatives or liberals. And of the seven that did split their donations, six of them gave over 90 percent to one of the two political ideologies.[62]

With such wealth, one might think they might hedge their bets more. One reason they might not, is that hedge fund managers like to fund Republicans to avoid real tax reform. The most successful of the managers can make over a billion dollars a year as they take a percentage of profits as well as charging the people whose money they handle a fixed fee.

Despite the fact that this income comes from managing other people's money, it is taxed at the lower rate for long-term capital gains instead of the rate for ordinary income. If that loophole were eliminated, the top tax rate for them would increase from 23.8 percent to 39.6 percent.[63]

During the 2016 election campaign, Donald Trump repeatedly said that he would eliminate this feature of the tax code, called the carried interest loophole, because "the hedge fund guys are getting away with murder." However, his early tax plans showed no evidence that he was going to follow through on that particular campaign promise.[64]

The carried interest loophole is the main reason Warren Buffet's secretary pays a higher tax rate than he does. While Buffet thinks that is unfair, most of his fellow billionaires disagree. They work to elect politicians whose ideas on tax reform always lower taxes on the super-rich.[65] Their investment in politics has paid off handsomely. When Bill Clinton was president, the 400 taxpayers who earned the most paid 27 percent of their income to the government. By 2012, it had fallen below 17 percent, about the same percentage paid by a family making $100,000 a year.[66]

In addition to investing in politicians who lowered their taxes, a few of the billionaires spent heavily to undermine the Iran agreement. Four large Republican donors—Sheldon Adelson, Bernard Marcus, Paul Singer and Seth Klarman—bankrolled a number of the opposition groups.[67] All are Jewish and they all poured millions into organizations that opposed the agreement including the Foundation for Defense of Democracy, the Washington Institute for Near East Policy, the American Enterprise Institute, the Republican Jewish Coalition, United Against a Nuclear Iran and the Israel American Council.[68] On the other side of the Iran debate, there were also billionaires putting their money behind groups that supported the deal. George Soros, also Jewish, was the most prominent and made major contributions to the Ploughshares Fund and J Street.

There is an old saying that the only things in life are death and taxes. The super-rich don't let death prevent their efforts to lower their taxes or influence other government policies. They do that not just by advocating the abolition of the inheritance tax. They also do it by setting up foundations to continue their work long after they are gone.

One example of a foundation with influence is the Lynde and Harry Bradley Foundation. They were two brothers and cofounders of the Allen Bradley Company, which manufactured automation equipment. Lynde died in 1942 and Harry in 1965, but the Foundation lives on as one of the most significant source of funds for ultraconservative causes.

The Foundation describes itself as dedicated to strengthening "the American democratic-capitalist system," which when "properly understood accords men and women the dignity they deserve as human beings."[69] The Center for Media and Democracy, which describes itself as "a national watchdog group that conducts in-depth investigations into corruption and the undue influence of corporations on media and democracy," had a different spin on the Foundation's activities.[70]

CMD details how the Foundation, using its status as a 501(c)(3) charitable organization, is building a "conservative infrastructure" throughout the country. It is doing that by funding receptive politicians, right-wing think tanks, symbiotic "grassroots" groups, friendly media, litigation centers, and opposition research that are all working toward conservative goals including dismantling labor unions. To achieve those objectives, CMD describes this "infrastructure" as designed to benefit the Republican Party while at the same time attempting to crush supporters of the Democratic Party.[71]

One media outlet that is friendly to Republicans is a news website called the Daily Signal, which is run by the Heritage Foundation, a far-right think tank. Both benefit from Bradley Foundation support.[72] A search of the Daily Signal website using the phrase "Iran nuclear" yielded 157 stories, none of which reported the agreement in a positive light.

Another contribution of the Bradley Foundation to the opposition to the nuclear agreement was funding anti-Muslim hate groups. Research by the Center for American Progress, which analyzed the Form 990 the Bradley Foundation is required to submit to the IRS, showed that between 2001 and 2012 it had given $6,540,000 to three organizations that belong to what the center called the Islamophobia network— the David Horowitz Freedom Center ($5,090,000), the Center for Security Policy of Frank Gaffney ($1,020,000), and the Middle East Forum of Daniel Pipes ($430,000).[73]

Gaffney, a former acting assistant secretary of defense in the Reagan administration, is such an anti-Islam extremist that even the Bradley Foundation stopped supporting him and some conservative groups shunned. He once claimed that the logo for the Missile Defense Agency appeared to morph the logo of the Obama campaign with the Islamic crescent star, arguing it was part of a "worrying pattern of official U.S. submission to Islam."[74]

The Bradley Foundation gave Gaffney's center $1.4 million over the years.[75] In 2012, Gaffney handed the foundation his center's Sacred Honor Award in recognition of its "philanthropy in the service of national security."[76] Despite the award, the foundation stopped funding for Gaffney's center in 2013 after their connection received some media attention. While the head of the foundation refused to explain that decision, he "dismissed any suggestion that his group is helping to spread anti-Islamic views."[77]

Another right-wing foundation, the Sarah Scaife Foundation, gave Gaffney's organization $175,000 in 2013. Gaffney's support came not just from right-wing foundations. Other contributors included Texas oil man T. Boone Pickens, ($50,000) and major defense contractors like General Electric—($5000), Raytheon ($20,000), Lockheed Martin ($150,000), Northrup Grumman ($5000) and General Dynamics ($15,000). He also received a $100,000 contribution from the Middle East Forum.

About two dozen other foundations, funds and individuals[78] provided much of the rest of Gaffney's $3.5 million funds in that year. Although the center's revenue declined by $1.5 million the following year, Gaffney still paid himself over $300,000 in both years.[79]

An anonymous donor or donors with the address of 1901 Pennsylvania Avenue NW in Washington gave Gaffney's three gifts totaling nearly $600,000.[80] There is a large office building at that address with a number of tenants, but one of them is The Israel Project. The Project's CEO is Josh Block, who was paid $425,000 in 2014 out of TIP's $6.6 million budget. He worked for nearly a decade as the spokesman for the American Israel Public Affairs Committee, which as will be discussed shortly. AIPAC is the organization that worked the hardest and spent the most to prevent the nuclear agreement.[81]

Aside from billionaires and their foundations, there were a large number of religious organizations that took sides in the debate over the Iran nuclear agreement. Ironically, those organizations were often at odds with the sentiment of the groups they claim to represent. Many Jewish organizations opposed the deal even though a poll, commissioned by the pro-deal group J Street, showed there was greater support for it among American Jews than the general public.[82]

Peter Beinart, who writes for *The Atlantic* magazine and the liberal Israeli newspaper *Haaretz*, noted the fact that nearly all the major Jewish organizations opposed the Iran nuclear deal despite the surveys that showed the overwhelming majority of American Jews supported it. In an article in *Haaretz*, he offered an explanation of why this was the case: "Because the American Jewish establishment is not a democracy. It's a plutocracy."[83] In other words, the major Jewish organizations were more interested in reflecting the views of their big donors than they were worried about the opinion of the majority of their members.

Jewish groups were not the only ones taking sides in the debate or the only ones whose leaders did not represent their rank and file. Evangelicals, Catholics and other Christians also came out for or against the deal with some of their leaders falsely claiming they spoke for their members. A group of pastors and other religious leaders, who claimed to be the voice of tens of millions of "pro-Israel Christians," sent a petition to the White House opposing any agreement that did not "completely dismantle" Iran's ability to build a bomb. An organization of Hispanic evangelicals, claiming to be comprised of 40,000 churches across the USA, urged that the deal be rejected outright.[84] At the same time, some on the "Evangelical Left" were said to favor it.[85]

As religious leaders petitioned government, asserting they represented the views of their congregations, a survey from the University of Maryland attempted to measure public opinion on the agreement. It found "a deal based on limited enrichment was favored not only by 61 percent overall, but also 61 percent of Republicans, 54 percent of Evangelicals, and a plurality (46 to 41 percent) of strong Tea Party sympathizers. Even 55 percent of the viewers of Fox News favored the agreement, but only if they tuned in just two or three times a week. Frequent viewers of Christian broadcasting networks were the exception to the pro-deal majorities in other groups. They favored more sanctions by 58 percent."[86]

Pope Francis and other Catholic leaders endorsed the agreement and the Pope even met with Iran's president, Hassan Rouhani, in January 2016. It was the first such meeting since 1999 between the head of the Catholic Church and the leader of Iran.[87] The Pope did not speak for every member of his faith however. All of the six Catholics (Jeb Bush, Marco Rubio, Rick Santorum, Chris Christie, Bobby Jindal and George Pataki) running to be the Republican presidential candidate put party and politics ahead of the Pope and opposed the agreement.

The Quakers, through their organization, the Friends Committee on National Legislation, were particularly active in supporting the deal. For instance, the Friends Committee arranged for a letter, signed by over 50 religious leaders from a wide number of groups, to be delivered to Congress urging the legislators to "remember the wisdom of Jesus" and approve the agreement.[88]

While the religious argued over whose side God was on, a whole host of other organizations pitched in with their opinions, expertise and pressure. As the debate attracted public opinion and aroused serious passions, the number of actors involved grew rapidly. As Cameron Harris's fabricated news story about ballot stuffing in Ohio demonstrated, today all one needs to try and make some money is an idea and a website. And the idea is optional. Once the website is set up, which anyone can do for a few dollars, the rest is marketing.

It helps to have a cause in addition to the website. The proponents of any cause will assert it is just and that they are the right people doing the right thing in the right way to produce the right results. In reality, it can be any cause, promoted by anyone, using any means with any results. They are usually nonprofit organizations, which makes their fund-raising efforts easier since contributions to them are tax deductible. Too frequently, they spend more on themselves and raising money than they do on the people they are supposedly in business to help.

One example of the disparity between a group's stated intentions and its expenditures is the Wounded Warrior Project. It was created to raise money to help military veterans who were injured while in service. After dozens of employees of the Project became whistle blowers, the Senate Judiciary Committee investigated the organization. The Committee issued a 500-page report in May 2017, documenting numerous abuses including misleading advertising and excessive spending on travel, fund-raising and parties for the Project's staff members.[89]

The sheer number of nonprofits and the potential for them being inefficient, if not corrupt, has given rise to websites like GuideStar and Charity Navigator. They evaluate and rank nonprofits on certain indicators including what percentage of their money they spend on themselves for administrative purposes. Charity Navigator lists 184 charities working on international issues including peace, security, human rights and foreign policy research and advocacy.[90] GuideStar lists nearly 14,000 nonprofit groups of all types in the District of Columbia alone.

Among the nonprofits are a large number of think tanks. They are often thought of as places where wonky experts and former government officials produce impartial research and policy papers. A series of articles in 2013 in the *Boston Globe*, however, described how think tanks have become just one more weapon in the partisan policy battle in Washington. As the *Globe* described it:

> Not long ago, Washington's think tanks constituted a rarefied world of policy-minded scholars supported by healthy endowments and quietly sought solutions to some of the nation's

biggest challenges. But now Congress and the executive branch are served a limitless feast of supposedly independent research from hundreds of nonprofit institutions that are pursuing fiercely partisan agendas and are funded by undisclosed corporations, wealthy individuals, or both. The shift is upending the role of think tanks, prompting some researchers to worry it is eroding trust in these institutions. Indeed, it now is difficult to tell the difference between truly objective advice and high-priced advocacy for political or private profit, according to a Globe review of public and internal documents and interviews with dozens of current and former think tank scholars, management staff, and donors.[91]

Just as there are nonprofits like GuideStar and Charity Navigator that track and evaluate thousands of other nonprofits, there are also now many think tanks that there is at least one doing the same evaluation and ranking process for other think tanks. It is the Think Tanks and Civil Societies Program at the University of Pennsylvania, which issues an annual report that ranks 6846 think tanks throughout the world.[92]

Like religious organizations, think tanks took sides in the debate over the Iran nuclear agreement. One of the more prominent opponents was the right-wing Heritage Foundation, which was founded to support conservative causes and policy prescriptions. Among the companies that contribute to Heritage are many defense contractors. Leaked e-mails revealed why. They described multiple meetings between Heritage officials and Lockheed Martin following a Pentagon decision to cut funding for the F-22 program.[93] The F-22, a state of the art fighter plane, was plagued by missed deadlines and cost overruns as the price per aircraft soared to over $400 million.[94] As Heritage experts diligently wrote and advocated in favor of building more F-22s, Heritage officials urged Lockheed to increase its contributions to the organization.

With regard to the Iran nuclear agreement, in October 2015, Heritage published a seven-point program that it urged Obama's successor to adopt. Not surprisingly, the plan emphasized additional spending on the military.[95] The steps suggested were:

1. Expand sanctions on Iran.
2. Strengthen U.S. military forces.
3. Strengthen U.S. alliances, especially with Israel, by boosting arms sales to Israel, Saudi Arabia, and other Persian Gulf countries and transferring to Israel bunker-busting bombs, which it could use to attack hardened nuclear facilities in Iran.
4. Put a high priority on missile defense.
5. Deter nuclear proliferation.
6. Expand domestic oil and gas production and lift the ban on US oil exports to put downward pressure on world prices.
7. Negotiate a better deal with Iran.

As if its line between policy analysis and advocacy were not blurred enough, Heritage created a new organization called Heritage Action to engage in hardball politics. Heritage used it not just to attack Democrats but went after any Republican deemed insufficiently conservative. That was too much even for the right-wing *Washington Examiner*, a conservative website and magazine. It editorialized:

> A think tank should arrive at its politics through serious thought and study. It should not arrive at its thoughts by reference to its political agenda. Back in 2010, Heritage "grew fangs" with the launch of Heritage Action, a 501(c)4 lobbying

arm. That addition has become the tail that wags the dog. Loved by some but loathed by most, Heritage Action throws grenades and burns bridges on Capitol Hill. It assembled a grassroots army numbering in the tens of thousands, and created an odd creature—a powerful lobby for limited government. Too often Heritage seemed to be attacking differences in tactics as abandonment of principles.[96]

Heritage is but one of many think tanks in and around Washington and elsewhere in the USA. A list of some of the more prominent ones can be found in Appendix C sorted out by their ideological tendencies. Below is a breakdown of the average number of employees, annual revenue and number of think tanks in each ideological category.

Libertarianism used to be seen as a far-right fringe philosophy that even the vast majority of conservatives did not fully embrace. That may be changing thanks to the bankrolls of billionaires like the Koch brothers who are using their wealth to push the philosophy which boils down to eliminating most of government and taxes on the rich. Libertarians have run in every presidential election since 1972.[97] In 2016, the party's candidate, Gary Johnson, got just three percent of the vote. But that was, in percentage terms, three time greater than the party had ever received in the past.

The fact that there are 14 such think tanks working toward mainstreaming libertarian principles is another demonstration of how billionaires and their foundations use their wealth for political purposes. Johnson's showing may have reflected a widespread dislike of both major party candidates, but it may also mean the investment by billionaires in libertarian think tanks is having at least a modest return (Table 3.1).

While the open wallets of billionaires help to explain why there are so many think tanks representing different political ideologies, philosophy offers another reason when applied to

Table 3.1 Number, average staff and revenue of think tanks

Category	Number	Staff	Revenue $ million
Liberal	9	61	12.44
Centrist	18	246	47.43
Conservative	11	74	19.70
Libertarian	14	60	8.46

the environment within the beltway. The nineteenth-century German philosopher Georg Wilhelm Friedrich Hagel is remembered for the dialectic method where a proposition goes through three stages of development. First, there is a thesis. It gives rise to a reaction, or antithesis, which contradicts or negates the thesis. Finally, the tension between the two is resolved by means of a synthesis.

In Washington things evolve differently. Those who have a thesis to promote create a nonprofit association to defend it. Those who oppose the thesis create their own group to counter the arguments of the first. And there is never a synthesis because that would involve compromise and, more importantly, it would put both the first two groups out of business.

There are so many nonprofit associations because some people profit from their existence. The people they employ do and they often compensate themselves very well for their efforts. The salary of the president of the USA is $400,000 a year. In one organization alone that opposed to the Iran nuclear agreement, at least 11 people received higher salaries than that.

The remainder of this chapter describes ten of the organizations involved in the Iran deal debate. They are grouped in pairs not necessarily because they went head-to-head against each other but because they provide competing points of view and a further explanation of the way partisan politics, technology, globalization, the elusiveness of truth and money have affected the way foreign policy is made.

AIPAC Versus J Street

How Partisan Politics Divides

The American Israel Public Affairs Committee: AIPAC is widely believed to be one of the most powerful organizations in Washington. In terms of political muscle, it ranks in the same league as the National Rifle Association and the American Association of Retired Persons. AARP does not have a foreign policy agenda, however. The NRA does, as it often works to prevent restrictions on guns abroad, but it devotes most of its efforts to fighting even the most common-sense restrictions on firearms at home.

Because AIPAC devotes itself to issues related to Israel, it is inherently the one organization of the three that is most involved in foreign policy. Of all the groups working against the nuclear agreement the Obama administration reached with Iran, AIPAC worked the hardest and spent the most to demolish it.

AIPAC says its mission is "to strengthen, protect and promote the U.S.-Israel relationship in ways that enhance the security of the United States and Israel."[98] When translated into policy, that mission becomes an effort to influence policy, reward congressmen who cooperate with AIPAC and target those who refuse to play along.

In Washington, power is money and money is power. AIPAC commands lots of both. In 2015, its budget was $89 million and at least 11 of its highest-paid officials had salaries exceeding the $400,000 the president of the USA is paid annually. According to M. J. Rosenberg, who worked for 6 years at AIPAC and 15 years on Capitol Hill and is a writer for *The Nation* magazine:

> AIPAC is not an aberration. Basically, every decision Congress makes is made with an eye on who has the money and how can

a legislator either get some of it or avoid it being deployed against them. No, not every decision is based on money. Issues like abortion, for instance, which is a religious kind of issue, are not based on money. But everything else is, most notably issues relating to banks, guns, Wall Street, labor, regulations to protect the consumer, health care, the environment, etc. And especially combatting any effort to prevent or reduce the effects of climate change, like when the Koch Brothers fight and lobby and use their money to prevent the development of alternative energy sources. Yes, Middle East policy is determined by the highest bidder, which is AIPAC. But pretty much every policy discussed on Capitol Hill is determined by those with the money.[99]

In addition to contributions from pro-Israel billionaires, AIPAC's wealth comes from its more than 100,000 members and its annual policy conference. Held in Washington each spring, the meeting draws a crowd of more than 18,000 activists who pay a minimum of $500 to attend. It also attracts hundreds of senators, congressmen and other politicians who always seem to be in a contest to see who can express the most support for Israel.

In July 2015, AIPAC created a group called Citizens for a Nuclear Free Iran for the sole purpose of opposing the Iran accord and to pressure members of Congress to reject it.[100] CNFI's goal was to target Democrats in the House and Senate who were seen to be hawkish or in districts with significant Jewish populations.[101]

CNFI was registered as a 501(c)(4) organization, which is granted to "social welfare" groups that supposedly devote the majority of their efforts to "promoting in some way the common good and general welfare of the people of the community."[102] That designation allowed CNFI to engage in lobbying and other political activity aimed at defeating the nuclear agreement, which is not allowed for AIPAC itself to do given its 501(c)(3) status.

AIPAC's 2015 form 990 shows a transfer of $19 million to CNFI.[103] The AIPAC funding allowed CNFI to run a series of dishonest and misleading television advertisements against the agreement.[104] The ad campaign was estimated to have cost some $20 million.[105] AIPAC may have spent twice that amount altogether. Whether it was the failure of that campaign or not, no mention of CNFI was to be found on AIPAC's website when checked in May 2017. CNFI still has a Facebook page, but it had not been updated since September 2015 and CNFI's website address simply redirects to AIPAC's homepage.

Like Prime Minister Netanyahu, AIPAC claims to support a two-state solution for the Israeli-Palestinian problem. Like Netanyahu, that support is insincere and comes with conditions that no Palestinian leader would be able to accept. According to Peter Beinart, writing in *The Atlantic*, AIPAC saying it supports a two-state solution is mainly an effort to keep Jewish Democrats as members.[106] Netanyahu knows he has to pay occasional lip service to the creation of a Palestinian state as well, but the reason for his duplicity is equally as political as AIPAC's. He knows that if he ever moved seriously in that direction, his government would immediately fall since most of the political parties in his coalition are hard-liners who oppose dismantling any settlements or returning any territory.

An example of AIPAC's duplicity is described in a September 2014 article in the *New Yorker* by Connie Bruck in which she describes the organization's reaction to Oslo Accords that were signed by Israeli Prime Minister Yitzhak Rabin and Yasser Arafat, the leader of the Palestine Liberation Organization, in 1993. The aim of the accords was to build a formal peace process between the PLO and Israel. Bruck quotes Keith Weissman, a former AIPAC analyst as saying, "AIPAC couldn't act like they were rejecting what the government of Israel did, but the outcry in the organization about Oslo was so great that they found ways to sabotage it."[107]

Also like Netanyahu, AIPAC has a clear preference for Republicans over Democrats to the point where it often appears to be as much an extension of the GOP as Fox News. In an article in *Haaretz*, Beinart noted that AIPAC's staff is "militantly bipartisan," but he pointed that is because "they must maintain their influence no matter who runs Washington."[108] AIPAC and Netanyahu have one other thing in common. Ironically, the political power of both would be at grave risk if Israel were ever to make peace with the Palestinians.

AIPAC's rightward tilt applies to Israeli as well as American politics. Its relations with Rabin's Labor Party government contrasted sharply with its lockstep agreement with Netanyahu and his Likud Party. Daniel Kurtzer, who was Deputy Assistant Secretary of State for Near Eastern Affairs at the time, and later served as ambassador to Israel, told Bruck that "Rabin was furious with AIPAC. He felt they were allied with Likud and would undermine him in what he was trying to do."[109]

AIPAC's political preferences pose a problem since two-thirds to three-quarters of Jewish voters consistently vote for the Democratic presidential candidate two-thirds to three-quarters of the time. But as mentioned earlier, Beinart pointed out that major Jewish organizations are plutocracies and not democracies. AIPAC's political orientation, therefore, demonstrates another truism about Washington. Whatever an organization's stated purpose, its own preservation is its top priority and the key to survival is power and money.

In the case of AIPAC, one of the things it decided to do to increase its power was to reach out to Evangelical

Christians. This reflects the fact that Jews are declining as a percentage of the US population but is more a pure political calculation. This would seem an unlikely pair of allies given that many evangelicals look forward to events like the Second Coming of Christ and end times when all the Jews wind up either dead or converted to Christianity. But it is just an example of another old saying—politics makes for strange bedfellows.

Evangelicals are the bedrock of the Republican Party base voters and three-quarters of evangelical voters cast their ballots for the Republican candidate in the last five presidential elections.[110] The support of white evangelicals for Israel is even stronger than that of Jews or Catholics. While some 82 percent of them believe God gave Israel to the Jewish people, less than half of those in the other two religions share the same sentiments. Another poll even showed that 60 percent of evangelicals thought the USA should support Israel even if its interests diverge with those of the USA.[111]

One evangelical group, which claims to have 900,000 members, is Christians United for Israel. It was founded specifically "to provide a national association through which every pro-Israel church, parachurch organization, ministry or individual in America can speak and act with one voice in support of Israel in matters related to Biblical issues."[112] The group asserts it is relying on the Bible for information and other moral matters in the support for Israel.[113]

CUFI was founded by John Hagee, a best-selling author and pastor from San Antonio.[114] Among Hagee's pronouncements was "the day we validate this Iran nuclear deal as signed, sealed and delivered, will be the day we stick our finger in the eye of God."[115] He has also claimed that the spread of Ebola was punishment from God because President Obama sought to divide Jerusalem.[116]

Hagee is a regular speaker at AIPAC's annual conference. As Peter Beinart noted in a *Haaretz* column: "AIPAC has repeatedly hosted speeches by Pastor John Hagee, who called Hurricane Katrina 'the judgment of God against the city of New Orleans' because 'there was to be a homosexual parade there on the Monday that the Katrina came.' To AIPAC, it doesn't matter. Hagee leads Christians United for Israel, which lobbies the United States government to support anything Benjamin Netanyahu does."[117]

Outreach to Christian evangelicals as a way to influence American policy in the Middle East is not new. In a 2002 article in *Mother Jones* by Michael Scherer and Ken Silverstein described how it began:

> The active alliance between evangelical Christians, American Jewish organizations, and conservative Israeli leaders dates to the tenure of Prime Minister Menachem Begin, who took office in 1977. Begin and his Likud Party used religious arguments to justify confiscation of Arab land and shared in common with American evangelicals—though not most American Jews—highly conservative views on social questions like abortion and welfare. Begin cultivated ties to emerging evangelical leaders like the Reverend Jerry Falwell, honoring him with a dinner in New York in 1980 and presenting him with a Learjet for his efforts on behalf of Israel. Since then, all subsequent Likud prime ministers have carefully strengthened ties to American evangelicals. In 1996, Benjamin Netanyahu created the Israel Christian Advocacy Council and flew 17 Christian leaders to Israel, where they signed a pledge that "America never, never desert Israel."[118]

AIPAC copied the outreach to Christian evangelicals of Begin and Netanyahu. It continues to forge those links today as well as having programs to reach out to African American and Hispanic religious leaders. Engaging African Americans has been credited by one writer on Tikkun Daily, a progressive interfaith website, as having successfully prevented use of the word "occupation" in relation to Israel's control of the West Bank when the 2016 Democratic Party platform was drafted.[119] The Republican Party, not to be outdone, dropped all mention of a two-state solution from its 2016 platform.

In addition to reaching out to a wide range of constituencies, AIPAC is able to operate successfully in another arena of Washington politics—the use of leaked information for political purposes. In 2004, Lawrence Franklin, who worked as the Iran desk office at the Pentagon, was being investigated by the FBI for leaking classified information.[120] Franklin plead guilty and was eventually sentenced to 12 years in prison. During the investigation, he cooperated with prosecutors and wore a recording device when he met with two AIPAC officials, Steven Rosen, director of foreign policy issues, and Keith Weissman, the AIPAC senior analyst who Brock quoted in her *New Yorker* article.[121] As a result of those meetings, Rosen was charged with "two counts related to unlawful disclosure of national defense information" and Weissman was charged with one count of "conspiracy to illegally communicate classified information." The two AIPAC representatives had immediately passed the information received from Franklin to other AIPAC staff members and Israeli embassy officials.[122] As the investigation progressed, the FBI raided AIPAC offices twice to gather evidence.[123]

At first AIPAC paid Rosen and Weissman's legal fees, but after about nine months fired both of them even though they continued to deny any wrongdoing.[124] AIPAC donors stepped in to support them, however, and Rosen collected at least $670,000 including $100,000 from Haim Saban.[125] Rosen then sued AIPAC over his dismissal and the case became very contentious as both sides traded salacious charges.¹²⁶ So salacious that one writer who read the court documents said he felt like taking a shower afterwards.

The charges against Rosen and Weissman were finally dropped in 2009. The judge in the case required prosecutors to show the defendants were aware they had classified information and they acted in "bad faith" knowing it could damage the country's security. At that point, the government dropped the case.¹²⁷ The sentence given to Franklin was later reduced to 10 months of house arrest and probation.¹²⁸

Franklin was apparently motivated by the belief that Secretary of State Powell was resisting Pentagon attempts for a more hawkish approach toward Iran. He thought he could use AIPAC to lobby President Bush for a more aggressive policy, ignoring the fact that the USA at that point was already deeply involved in two wars in the Middle East.¹²⁹

Some Washington observers thought Rosen and Weissman had solicited the information from Franklin in order to pass it to the Israelis. One former congressman characterized the whole affair as business as usual, saying, "The number one game in Washington is making the people talking to you feel like you're an insider, that you've got information no else has."¹³⁰ Whatever game the AIPAC officials were playing, the organization's hardline policies gave rise to its opposite number, which was one of the most active groups that supported the Iran nuclear deal.

J Street

J Street is the antithesis of AIPAC's thesis. It was created in 2008 as a reaction to AIPAC's adherence to far-right politics both in the United States and Israel. For all its political muscle and estimated 100,000 members, AIPAC does not represent where most American Jews stand with regard to Israel and the Iran deal because it values its biggest donors more.

While J Street has some significant donors, it cannot count on nearly as many as AIPAC does. George Soros gave it about $250,000 from 2007 to 2010.[131] The Nathan Cummings Foundation was another major contributor and the Skoll Global Threats Fund, a Jewish organization, donated at least $200,000 over the same three-year period. The Soros affiliated Democracy Alliance also listed J Street in their spring 2014 portfolio under the section "Progressive Infrastructure Map."[132] In 2015, AIPAC's revenue was 27 times the $3.3 million that J Street received. In 2014, J Street's president Jeremy Ben-Ami made $234,000, while AIPAC's CEO made over six times that amount.

J Street is pro-Israel but seeks a peaceful end to the conflict with the Palestinians that includes a two-state solution.[133] It has not been reluctant to take on those who take a hard-line. On one occasion Ben-Ami said: "We cannot proceed as if we believe in the third incarnation of Netanyahu and believe he wants a two-state solution, or believe that he is not a racist, and we must react to this new reality."[134]

J Street supported the Iran nuclear agreement, calling it "historic" and asserting that it avoids "disastrous war."[135] Those views provoked some harsh criticism from the right. An opinion article in *The Hill* accused J Street of just caring about being progressive and helping to provide funds to politicians who let money to flow to Hamas, the group that controls Gaza and is considered a terrorist organization by Israelis and the American government. That article was written by Paul Miller who was only described as a contributor to the Franklin Center for Government and Public Integrity.[136] The Franklin Center has been characterized as "a purveyor of political propaganda dressed up as journalism."[137] The Center is largely funded by the Koch brothers, the Bradley Foundation and Donors Trust.

Another critic of J Street was David Friedman, who said that Ben Ami and those who share his politics were "worse than *kapos*" and not really Jews.[138] *Kapos* were the Jews who worked for the Nazis in the concentration camps. Friedman, who was President Trump's bankruptcy lawyer, was named by him as ambassador to Israel. Friedman, an opponent of a two-state solution, was the second Trump ambassadorial nominee confirmed by the Senate but received the votes of only two Democratic senators.[139] Never before had a person nominated for this ambassadorship received so little support.

The political divide between AIPAC and J Street has increasingly taken on partisan overtones. That divide has been made deeper by the contributions by a few fervently pro-Israel billionaires to Republicans as well as AIPAC.[140] And they were not the only recipients of money given to opponents of the nuclear agreement.

The Foundation for Defense of Democracies Versus Ploughshares

The Impact of Money

The lobbying muscle of AIPAC was an important part of the efforts to oppose the Iran nuclear agreement as it worked to increase public pressure on Congress to block the deal. AIPAC had no experts in nuclear weapons to draw on however. Experts were essential in order to be talking heads for television news shows and to give testimony at congressional hearings. Republican legislators used their majority status to arrange hearings that were mainly a platform for critics of the agreement. It was another opportunity for Washington's political theater as it provided video clips and quotes for media outlets that opposed the deal.

For example, the Senate Banking Committee held a hearing on August 5, 2015, with two panels to discuss "The Implications of Sanctions Relief Under the Iran Agreement." The first panel had two Obama administration officials and the second had four experts, three of them opposed to the agreement. The day before, the Senate Foreign Relations Committee held a hearing on the "JCPOA: Non-Proliferation, Inspections, and Nuclear Constraints" with three witnesses. Two were opposed to the agreement, while the third gave it a limited endorsement.[141] That person was Gary Samore who at the time of the hearing was the president of an organization called United Against a Nuclear Iran, which will be discussed later in this chapter. Less than a week after the hearing, UANI announced that Samore was no longer the president of the organization.[142]

Another hearing, ostensibly about ISIS, was designed to showcase opponents of Iran. It was held on April 29, 2015, by the Subcommittee on Terrorism, Non-Proliferation and Trade of the House Foreign Affairs Committee.[143] One of the witnesses at that session was a case study in how to get things done in Washington. She was Maryam Rajavi, the President of the National Council of Resistance of Iran. The NCRI is a political front for a cult called the Mujahedeen-e-Khalq. The MEK had for years been considered a terrorist organization by the State Department but was taken off the terrorism list in 2012 after a classic image makeover. The MEK hired a lobbyist, made contributions to key congressmen and paid a host of former Democratic and Republican officials $10,000–$50,000 to attend lavish dinners and give short speeches.[144]

At the hearing, Rajavi essentially made a pitch that the best way to fight ISIS, a Sunni terrorist group, is removing the Shiite regime in Tehran.[145] Rajavi likes to portray the MEK as a democratic alternative to the Iranian regime, but the group is widely despised in Iran because it fought on the Iraqi side with Saddam Hussein in the war between the two countries.

Press reports in 2008 asserted that the MEK was receiving cash and other assistance from the Bush administration to conduct covert operations in Iran, which was four years before the MEK was removed from the State Department's terrorism list.[146] Bush administration officials denied the reports, but if they were true they should have added the USA to the State Department's list of state sponsors of terrorism.

Just where the MEK got its cash to spread around Washington was unclear, but they spent heavily. Those who have addressed the group for tens of thousands of dollars include former Democratic senators Evan Bayh, Bill Bradley and Robert Torricelli (who is also the group's lawyer); former congressmen Patrick Kennedy and Lee Hamilton; former generals Wesley Clark, James T. Conway, James Jones, Michael Hayden, Peter Pace, Richard Myers, Anthony Zinni and Hugh Shelton; former governors Ed Rendell, Bill Richardson and Howard Dean; former officials in the Bush 43 administration including Andrew Card, Anita McBride, Michael Mukasey, Dana Perino, Tom Ridge, Frances Townsend and John Bolton; former State Department officials Paula Dobriansky, Philip Zelikow, Mitchell Reiss and Dell Dailey and former FBI Director Louis Freeh.[147] Elaine Chao, Trump's Secretary of Transportation and the wife of Senator Mitch McConnell, received $50,000 for a five minute speech in 2015.[148] Former New York City Mayor Rudy Giuliani has given speeches at multiple MEK events over the years and has been one of its biggest advocates.[149]

Ten days before President Trump's inauguration, 22 individuals including Giuliani, Torricelli and former senator Joe Lieberman sent the president-elect a letter urging him to adopt a policy of regime change in Iran, asserting that "the

MEK and all those supporting the organization have now been comprehensively cleared and vindicated by judicial investigations."[150] At least, half of the signers have, according to press reports, accepted speaking fees from the MEK.

The MEK was not the only group financing critics of Iran. Opponents of the deal counted on their own experts who benefitted from the generous financial support of several of the aforementioned billionaires.

The Foundation for the Defense of Democracies
FDD was founded just after the 9/11 attacks and describes itself as "a non-profit, non-partisan 501(c)3 policy institute." Its website says it focuses "on foreign policy and national security that combines policy research, democracy and counterterrorism education, strategic communications and investigative journalism in support of its mission to promote pluralism, defend democratic values and fight the ideologies that drive terrorism."

While FDD does have some representation from Democrats, it has a decidedly Republican tilt and its president, Clifford May, is a former communications director of the Republican National Committee. John Hannah, a Senior Counselor at FDD, was Dick Cheney's national security advisor.[151] FDD's vice president, Toby Dershowitz, was the spokesperson for AIPAC for 14 years.[152] It is a small organization, but has some wealthy backers. Five big Republican donors, including Bernard Marcus, who is also a director of FDD, Paul Singer and Sheldon Adelson, contributed $19 million to it between 2008 and 2011.[153]

That investment bought considerable exposure as FDD was very active on Capitol Hill and in the media. In 2014 and until August 2015, FDD's experts testified against the Iran agreement 17 times before congressional committees. During the same period, the staff from two much larger right-wing think tanks, the American Enterprise Institute and the Heritage Foundation, appeared only once.[154]

One article described FDD's impact and attributed its influence to its focus on the Iran nuclear deal and the ability of the analysts who work there:

> Over the last 10 years, the organization has bulked up considerably, adding a former CIA specialist on Iran and two other Farsi speakers as well as a onetime Treasury official with expertise in illicit finance and an investigative reporter from the *Wall Street Journal* with a deep knowledge of sanctions and financial markets. Their work has caught the attention of influential policymakers, especially sanctions hawks who have used the research to argue that the White House is being conned by a country that for decades has dubbed America "the great Satan" and has threatened to wipe Israel off the face of the map.[155]

Like other groups opposing the agreement, particularly United Against a Nuclear Iran, FDD has worked to prevent private companies from trading with Iran. That effort has led to some curious partnerships. A series of leaked e-mails showed close coordination between FDD officials and the ambassador of the United Arab Emirates in Washington.[156] The foundation provided the ambassador with a long list of non-US companies that were doing business or considering investing in Iran and that also had operations in the UAE or Saudi Arabia. The UAE, which does not recognize Israel diplomatically, seems to be willing to work with an organization funded by extremely pro-Israel billionaires in an effort to economically undermine their common enemy Iran.

According to an article in *The Middle East Observer*, the e-mails revealed another target of the joint efforts as they "appear to show clear collaboration between the FDD and the

UAE on a campaign to downgrade the image and importance of Qatar as a regional and global power." This effort was said to have included collusion with journalists who published articles accusing Qatar and Kuwait of supporting terrorism.[157] The accuracy of that report is hard to determine, but the strained relations between Qatar and other Persian Gulf states is not. In June 2017, the UAE, Saudi Arabia and several other countries in the region broke diplomatic relations with Qatar. That country is a key American ally as it houses the forward headquarters of the United States Central Command, which oversees all American military operations in Afghanistan and the Middle East, as well as an air base used by US forces.[158]

One of those in close touch with the UAE ambassador was Mark Dubowitz, a former venture capitalist who switched careers to become FDD's CEO. He argued in a March 2017 opinion piece in the *Wall Street Journal* that it was delusional to rigorously enforce the nuclear agreement. By doing so, he reasoned, Iran could develop capabilities that were not restricted under the agreement and then, once it expired, would be able to produce a bomb in a matter of weeks.[159]

Dubowitz's suggested policy alternative was a two-step strategy. The first phase was to develop a comprehensive assault on Iran that uses both covert and overt economic, financial, political, diplomatic, cyber and military power to subvert and roll back the Iranian threat. The second step was for the USA should reinvigorate the sanctions regime, intimidate any companies thinking of doing business with Iran, threaten military action and signal to the other P5+1 countries the USA is ready to negotiate a new agreement. In other words, he thinks it is necessary to kill the nuclear deal in order to save it. Not discussed in his article is any consideration of how Iran or the other P5+1 countries might react to all his suggested steps.

The Ploughshares Fund

The Fund is the most important organization in the pro-deal camp and sought to build and energize a group of like-minded organizations to support it. According to its website, PF seeks to "identify and fund astute strategies for creating a more secure world" and to "amplify funding with our own issue expertise, lobbying, relationship building and media savvy."[160] Joe Cirincione, a nuclear expert who served as a staff member on the House Armed Services Committee and the Committee on Government Operations, is president of the fund.[161] He also worked at the Carnegie Endowment for International Peace as director for Non-Proliferation and co-wrote a book called Deadly Arsenals: Nuclear, Biological, and Chemical Threats.[162] Other notable figures associated with the group include former Secretary of State George Shultz and former Secretary of Defense William Cohen.[163]

FDD and PF once again demonstrate that the opponents of the Iran nuclear deal are paid better than the advocates. In 2013, at FDD, Clifford May pulled down $432,000, while Dubowitz earned $330,000.[164] At Ploughshares that same year, Cirincione's compensation was listed as $255,000 and its Executive Director at $210,000.

Another difference is the transparency of Ploughshares. Unlike FDD, which offers hardly any information on where its money comes from and where it goes, Ploughshares provides an annual report with considerable detail on both on its website. The report for 2016 records gifts of greater than $100,000 from the Rockefeller Brothers Fund, Carnegie Corporation of New York, and William and Flora Hewlett Foundation, and the Schooner Foundation. Everyone who gave more than $1000 is listed.[165] In the past, George Soros's Open Society Foundation has been a significant donor.[166]

On the expenditure side, the Ploughshares report lists over 90 grants that were awarded totaling $4.5 million. About half the grants and 60 percent of the funds went to a variety of groups that supported the Iran nuclear deal including the Atlantic Council, the Center for New American Security, Friends Committee on National Legislation, MoveOn.org, J Street and the National Iranian American Council. Ploughshares also paid Alan Dershowitz, an emeritus law professor at Harvard and harsh critic of the nuclear deal, $25,000 to participate in a discussion of it.

Dershowitz, writing in *Newsweek*, once urged Congress to not only pass a law authorizing the president to use military action against Iran, but compelling him "to destroy—without warning or negotiation—any attempt by Tehran to build an atomic bomb."[167] Since Iran would not test a nuclear device, or ever give any other incontrovertible proof of possessing such a weapon, any assertion that it was attempting to build a bomb would have to be based on an intelligence assessment.

As the Bush administration demonstrated in the invasion of Iraq, intelligence reports can be cherry picked, based on unreliable sources or even completely fabricated to justify a decision that has already been taken. Whether such a law would act as a deterrent to the Iranians if they were determined to cheat is unclear, but it would certainly allow the president to go to war at any time and for any reason. If that were the case, it would not even require bringing Colin Powell out of retirement to give another address to the UN General Assembly as he did on February 5, 2003, to justify the invasion of Iraq based on intelligence that proved to be false.

Besides Dershowitz, there were other Ploughshares grant recipients who were controversial. It has given National Public Radio $100,000 to "support national security reporting with an emphasis on themes and stories related to nuclear security topics." In a 2016 article in the *New York Times*, one of President Obama's closest advisors was quoted as saying groups like Ploughshares helped spread the administration's message on the nuclear agreement.[168] While that is no surprise to anyone who has read the organization's annual report, it was taken by critics of the deal to mean that Ploughshares had bought favorable air time through its contribution to NPR.[169]

The NPR ombudsman denied that there would ever be any such connection since NPR's rules strictly forbid such a pay to play arrangement. To prove the point, NPR analyzed the 254 stories on the agreement it aired in 2015 and the first half of 2016. It found 118 to be neutral and, in the other 136, there were 160 people who spoke in favor of the deal and 102 against it.

Critics of the deal undoubtedly remained unconvinced that NPR was not influenced. That is because when it comes to an issue as divisive, partisan and controversial as the Iran nuclear agreement, truth is in the eye of the beholder.

UANI Versus the Arms Control Association

What's Truth Got to Do with It

The debate over the Iran nuclear deal was so intense in part because it took on the aspects of a morality play. Opponents of the deal saw Iran as an evil regime bent on acquiring nuclear weapons at all costs. Supporters of the deal saw it as a way to avoid another war.

The assessment of the U.S. government's intelligence community remains much more nuanced predicting neither war nor any Iranian attempt to cheat. The first annual report under the Trump administration titled "Worldwide Threat Assessment of the US Intelligence Community" was presented to the Senate Select Committee on Intelligence on May 11, 2017, by Director of National Intelligence, and former senator, Daniel Coats. The conclusion of the intelligence community was that Iran wants to abide by the agreement, but at the same time keeps some options open:

> Tehran's public statements suggest that it wants to preserve the Joint Comprehensive Plan of Action (JCPOA)—because it views the JCPOA as a means to remove sanctions while preserving some nuclear capabilities, it expects the P5+1 members to adhere to their obligations, although Iran clearly recognizes the new US Administration is concerned with the deal. Iran's implementation of the JCPOA has extended the amount of time Iran would need to produce enough fissile material for a nuclear weapon from a few months to about a year. The JCPOA has also enhanced the transparency of Iran's nuclear activities, mainly through improved access by the international Atomic Energy Agency (IAEA) and its investigative authorities under the Additional Protocol to its Comprehensive Safeguards Agreement.
>
> Iran is pursuing capabilities to meet its nuclear energy and technology goals and to give it the capability to build missile-deliverable nuclear weapons if it chooses to do so. Its pursuit of these goals will influence its level of adherence to the JCPOA. We do not know whether Iran will eventually decide to build nuclear weapons.[170]

Elsewhere in the report, the intelligence community concludes that "Despite Supreme Leader Khamenei's conditional support for the JCPOA nuclear deal implemented in January 2016, he is highly distrustful of US intentions."[171] If the Supreme Leader is distrustful as the report claims, it may have something to do with the number of Islamophobic and other organizations in Washington promoting the idea that Iran cannot be trusted, the popularity of a hawkish foreign policy in Republican circles and the erratic behavior of the Trump administration in its first year in office.

Supporters of the deal hold a different opinion than that of the pessimists. They believe the best hope to prevent the spread of nuclear weapons and avoid American involvement in another war against a Muslim country is to uphold the agreement and insist that all the parties implement it. Both sides are convinced they are right and that their course of action is the best. Each side began from a different starting point and arrived at a different conclusion because they are sure their version of the truth is the correct one.

United Against Nuclear Iran

UANI describes itself as a nonpartisan, nonprofit advocacy organization that seeks to prevent Iran from fulfilling "its desire and intent to possess nuclear weapons."[172] The organization is at the forefront of efforts to pressure companies to stop doing business with Iran. According to its mission statement, "UANI's private sanctions campaign and state and Federal legislative initiatives focus ending the economic and financial support of the Iranian regime by corporations, firms entities and individuals at a time when the international community is attempting to compel Iran to abandon its illegal nuclear weapons program, support for terrorism and gross human rights violations."[173]

One UANI project is a maritime monitoring system using satellite technology to track ship movements in order to detect and call out violators of the sanctions imposed on Iran.[174] As will be discussed in the next chapter, UANI's tactics in exposing companies doing business with Iran prompted Victor Restis, a billionaire Greek businessman who was named as a violator, to sue UANI for defamation. The suit was dismissed after the Obama Justice Department intervened and asserted that national security information would be revealed if it were allowed to proceed.[175]

In June 2015, UANI launched a multimillion-dollar TV, print, radio and digital campaign with the message that America cannot trust Iran and that too many concessions had been granted in negotiating the agreement. Nearly one-third UANI's, budget came from Sheldon Adelson, who routed his $500,000 donations to UANI through family foundation.

The CEO of UANI is Mark Wallace, who served as US ambassador to the United Nations under George W. Bush. He is also CEO of the Counter Extremism Project, which states its mission is to maintain a "database of extremist groups and their supporters, mapping the social and financial networks, tools and methodologies on which these groups rely." The President of UANI, David Ibsen, is the Executive Director for the Counter Extremism Project. UANI works closely with the Institute for Strategic Dialogue (ISD) in London in a transatlantic partnership dedicated to combatting the threat of a nuclear-armed Iran.

As mentioned earlier, in August 2015, Dr. Gary Samore, a nuclear weapons expert, stepped down as president of UANI after he had decided that the nuclear agreement was a success.[176] In an interview with the *New York Times*, Samore said he was worried that "the American capacity to have a reasoned debate about national security issues has really been damaged by the polarization in Washington. There are still experts, but their voices are really muted by the politics." Samore was immediately replaced as president of UANI by former senator Joseph Lieberman who labelled the agreement "a bad deal."

Arms Control Association
ACA is a nonpartisan membership organization that operates as a think tank specializing in arms control and other defense

issues.[177] It works to provide "policy-makers, the press and the interested public with authoritative information, analysis and commentary on arms control proposals, negotiations and agreements, and related national security issues."[178] The group was a strong advocate of the Iran deal and publicized the fact that "a group of 30 leading nuclear nonproliferation specialists" labeled it a "vitally important step forward" for the security and stability of the world.[179]

One of the individuals associated with the group is Greg Thielmann who worked on the Senate Select Committee on Intelligence and in the Bureau of Intelligence and Research in the Department of State.[180] He was a critic of the invasion of Iraq and resigned from the department because of the false intelligence used to justify the war.[181] In an article written for *The Hill*, he argued that the transparency measures in the deal were sufficient for keeping track of Iran's nuclear activities.[182]

On its website, ACA notes it gets support from the Colombe Foundation, the Ploughshares Fund[183] ($36,500 in 2011)[184] and the William and Flora Hewlett Foundation[185] ($275,000 in 2010). UANI and ACA have different opinions of the chances for the deal to succeed and the intentions of Iran. One works to lessen the benefit of the deal to Iran by encouraging companies not to do business there. The other supports the deal by providing expert opinion on its merits. Both are convinced they are right and will continue their efforts.

NIAC VERSUS THE CENTER FOR SECURITY POLICY

The Power of Globalization

Another feature of the Iran debate was the number of Islamophobic organizations that often seemed be making thinly veiled appeals to fear, xenophobia and racism in their arguments against the agreement. They invoked the threat of terrorism and used images like mushroom clouds in the same way the Bush administration did in justifying the invasion of Iraq. On the other side of the debate, there have been groups trying to promote tolerance, an understanding of Persian culture and acceptance of the estimated one million Iranian-Americans.[186]

Two of the major actors in that struggle are the Center for Security Policy and the National Iranian American Council. These two organizations represent different sides of the debate but also reflect the impact of globalization. Many of the Iranian-Americans immigrated to the USA after the overthrow of the Shah. Like the millions of refugees from the Middle East heading toward Europe in recent years, they were trying to escape political unrest in their country. Migration for political and economic reasons has become easier and more common today with the number of those who are refugees, internally displaced or seeking asylum having risen to over 65 million people according to UN estimates.[187] That is the highest level ever exceeding the number reached in the aftermath of World War II and amounting to 1 out of every 113 people on the planet.

Among those who are migrating are a very small number bent on committing acts of terrorism. The propagation of ideologies of hate, bomb-making technology and the social networking of potential terrorists is part of the downside of globalization that makes it easier to commit acts of terrorism. Never mind that as a potential cause of death to Americans, terrorism ranks along aside getting struck by lightning on a clear day, the threat of it is still an opportunity for fund-raising for some organizations and as another reason to oppose the nuclear agreement. And one of those cashing in on that fear was a former Reagan administration official.

Center for Security Policy

CSP was founded by Frank Gaffney who was nominated in April 1987 to be Assistant Secretary of Defense for International Security Policy in the Reagan administration.[188] He was never confirmed and served in the position in an acting capacity for only seven months. When Frank Carlucci replaced Casper Weinberger as Secretary of Defense, Gaffney was fired within a matter of hours.[189] Once outside government, Gaffney set up CSP and used it as a platform to criticize the arms control agreements that were negotiated by the Reagan administration.

In the absence of new arms agreements to criticize, Gaffney has taken up the banner of Islamophobia and raised it to a level that is more like Islamo-paranoia. For instance, he has spread the idea that Sharia law is becoming more commonly used in the USA, that the Muslim Brotherhood has placed its agents in the federal government and that the Brotherhood controls all the mosques in the USA. Major funders of CSP, not mentioned earlier, include the William Rosenwald Family, Newton and Rochelle Becker Family Foundation, Irving Moskowitz Foundation, and Paul Singer Family Foundation.[190]

According to the Southern Poverty Law Center, which tracks hate groups including anti-Muslim organizations, Gaffney's center has evolved from "a hawkish think tank on foreign affairs to a promoter of baseless conspiracy theories and groundless accusations."[191]

CSP and the Middle East Forum of Daniel Pipes are not the only anti-Muslim hate groups. While those two organizations have been around for years, Islamophobia became a cottage industry in the wake of the terrorist attacks of 9/11. Two organizations, the Council on American Islamic Relations and the Southern Poverty Law Center, track such groups and have counted a total of 65 of them. Half of them came into being after 9/11. They are listed in Appendix F.

Among Gaffney's admirers is Steven Bannon, Trump's political strategist who described him as "one of the senior thought leaders and men of action in this whole war against Islamic radical jihad."[192] Trump and officials of his administration, including former National Security Advisor Michael Flynn, have done much to make anti-Islamic sentiments mainstream and Gaffney has benefited from that trend. During the election campaign in speeches and press releases, Trump mentioned CSP on dozens of occasions.[193] While Gaffney had long been considered a pariah, even among conservatives, he has found friends in the White House and, as a result, has gained new prominence and acceptability.

National Iranian American Council
NIAC describes itself as the largest grassroots Iranian-American organization, with over 65,000 supporters and over 8000 donors. Those individual donors, with a median donation of $50, are the core of NIAC's support, providing the overwhelming majority of NIAC's funding every year. NIAC also receives support from the Ploughshares and Rockefeller Brothers Fund. Another organization that provides grants to the NIAC is the PARSA Community Foundation that contributed a total of $591,500 between 2006 and 2015.[194] Based in the USA, the PARSA Community Foundation advocates on behalf of Persians and is a philanthropic organization that is "promoting social entrepreneurship around the globe."[195] NIAC has links to 12 years of its tax returns on its website.[196]

An article in *Business Insider* in 2015 noted the organization has been at the forefront of encouraging engagement with Iran, but because of that it has attracted controversy.[197] NIAC sued a blogger for defamation after he claimed the organization lobbied for the Iranian government.[198] The US District Court ruled against the NIAC but not because what the blogger said was proven true. The judge found that many of NIAC's positions could be construed as siding with what the Iranian government advocated and therefore the accusation did not meet the definition of defamation.[199]

Trita Parsi, who is the president of the NIAC, wrote an article in *The Atlantic* explaining that the outcome of the nuclear negotiations benefits the USA because "hardliners in Iran have figured out how to present a nuclear deal as a win for themselves."[200] The article points out that such statements are necessary for Iranian leaders to sell the deal to people in their country. In other words, a successful negotiation requires giving the other side something it can take home and defend.

Both CSP and NIAC derive their core missions from the effects of globalization. The former gets to sell the idea that Iranians and other Muslims are a threat. The latter organization has the challenge of getting people to accept and understand Iranian culture and the loyalty of Iranian-Americans.

ReThink Versus Secure America Now

Using Technology to Influence Policy

Since much of the battle over the Iran nuclear agreement was fought to win over public opinion, both sides relied on organizations that specialized in the media, communications and advertising. The proponents of the deal had the help of ReThink Media, while the opponents had a group called Secure America Now (SAN). Both groups used technology to spread the arguments of their side and to assist other organizations to do the same.

ReThink Media
ReThink was founded in 2008, with the support of Ploughshares Fund, the Ford Foundation, the Rockefeller Brothers Fund and the Colombe Foundation. It aims to build

the media and communications capacity of think tanks, advocacy organizations and experts working toward "a more constructive US foreign policy." Since its founding, its work with the peace and security community has grown and it is now supported by the Connect U.S. Fund, the Carnegie Corporation of New York and the Hewlett Foundation.[201] It describes itself as a unique organization with the mission "to provide our member groups and the campaigns we serve with affordable access to state-of-the-art media technologies, communications training, professional media outreach support, reporter intel, strategic messaging advice, and both public opinion and media analysis—and ultimately, to help them win."[202] Some of the methods used by ReThink will be described further in the next chapter.

Secure America Now

SAN was founded by polling specialists Pat Caddell, a Democrat, and John McLaughlin, a Republican. The group does not reveal its donors but claims to have 4.3 million members in its grassroots network.[203] According to the Sunlight Foundation, SAN is "run by a longtime political aide of conservative billionaire Ronald Lauder, a cosmetics heir who has become a patron of Jewish causes and Republican candidates."[204]

SAN poured $1 million into a media blitz that targeted three Democratic senators, while they were still undecided on how to vote on the Iran nuclear agreement. The organization is linked to right-wing pro-Israel factions in the USA and abroad. The Rightweb website's profile of SAN includes the following observations:

> Secure America Now produces a steady stream of advertisements and web videos, most of which appear to circulate primarily on rightwing websites. Though the ads cover a range of subjects, the most common recurring theme is Iran's nuclear

enrichment program, which Secure America Now's publications continually insist—against the assessments of the U.S. intelligence community—is geared toward producing nuclear weapons.

"Push polls," which spread politically driven talking points under the guise of gauging public opinion, have been a hallmark of SAN's work. A particularly egregious example was a poll McLaughlin and Caddell released in July 2011 purporting to demonstrate that Jewish Americans were abandoning the Democratic Party. According to the Washington Post, the poll was "laughably bogus" because of its flawed sampling techniques and misleading questions. In contrast to the poll's key finding that "only two in five Jewish voters (43%) say they would vote to re-elect President Obama," Obama ultimately won nearly 70 percent of the Jewish vote in 2012, handily defeating Republican rival Mitt Romney.

SAN, connected to two Republican billionaires, seeks to convince Americans that an aggressively militant foreign policy is vital to securing American national security interests in Israel, Iran and the greater Middle East.

The ten organizations profiled are among the most important ones that were involved in the debate on the Iran nuclear deal, but they just scratch the surface when it comes to describing all the groups that participated. They do illustrate, however, some of the ways that partisan politics, money, globalization, the elusiveness of truth and technology have affected such debates.

The use of technology has enabled ReThink and SAN to spread their respective messages and expand their audiences. The techniques of both are not only useful in the debate over controversial foreign and domestic policy issues, but they have also become essential. Those techniques will be described further in the next chapter.

Notes

1. CNN. 2013. "Document: IG's Report on IRS Targeting Tea Party." http://www.cnn.com/interactive/2013/05/politics/irs-timeline/ Accessed on (6/11/2017).
2. The Center for Media and Democracy. "The U.S. Tax Code and Non-Profits." http://www.sourcewatch.org/index.php/The_U.S._tax_code_and_non_profits Accessed on (6/11/2017).
3. Strupp, Joe. 2013. "Franklin Center Top Donor Is Right-Wing's "Dark Money ATM." Media Matters for America. https://www.mediamatters.org/blog/2013/02/22/franklin-center-top-donor-is-right-wings-dark-m/192770 Accessed on (6/11/2017).
4. Callahan, David. 2016. "The Super-Rich Have Found a New Way to Wield Political Power: Philanthropy." *The Nation*. https://www.thenation.com/article/the-super-rich-have-found-a-new-way-to-wield-political-power-philanthropy/ Accessed on (6/11/2017).
5. Peterson-Withorn, Chase. 2016. "The Full List of Every American Billionaire 2016." *Forbes*. https://www.forbes.com/sites/chasewithorn/2016/03/01/the-full-list-of-every-american-billionaire-2016/#74de93f37acb Accessed on (6/11/2017).
6. Confessore, Nicholas, Sarah Cohen and Karen Yourish. 2015. "Here Are 120 Million Monopoly Pieces, Roughly One for Every Household in the United States." *The New York Times*. https://www.nytimes.com/interactive/2015/10/11/us/politics/2016-presidential-election-super-pac-donors.html Accessed on (6/11/2017).
7. Ibid.
8. Ho, Catherine. 2015. "Mega-Donors Opposing Iran Deal Have Upper Hand in Fierce Lobbying Battle." *The Washington Post*. https://www.washingtonpost.com/news/powerpost/wp/2015/08/13/mega-donors-opposing-iran-deal-have-upper-hand-in-fierce-lobbying-battle/ Accessed on (6/11/2017).

9. Ball, Molly. 2012. "Who Is Sheldon Adelson, the Gingrich Super PAC's Billionaire Backer?" *The Atlantic*. https://www.theatlantic.com/politics/archive/2012/01/who-is-sheldon-adelson-the-gingrich-super-pacs-billionaire-backer/252003/ Accessed on (6/11/2017).
10. Guttman, Nathan. 2014. "Sheldon Adelson Is a Philanthropist Like No Other." *Forward*. http://forward.com/news/israel/208220/sheldon-adelson-is-a-philanthropist-like-no-other/ Accessed on (6/11/2017).
11. Bertoni, Steven. 2012, February 21. "Billionaire Sheldon Adelson Says He Might Give $100 M to Newt Gingrich or Other Republican." *Forbes*. https://www.forbes.com/sites/stevenbertoni/2012/02/21/billionaire-sheldon-adelson-says-he-might-give-100m-to-newt-gingrich-or-other-republican/#7bbb6f644003 Accessed on (6/20/17).
12. Guttman, Nathan. 2014. "Adelson and Saban Try to Out-Hawk Each Other." *Forward*. http://forward.com/opinion/208924/adelson-and-saban-try-to-out-hawk-each-other/ Accessed on (6/11/2017).
13. Davis, Julie Hirschfeld. 2015. "Top Hillary Clinton Donor Clarifies Stance on Iran Nuclear Deal." *The New York Times*. https://www.nytimes.com/politics/first-draft/2015/08/13/top-hillary-clinton-donor-clarifies-stance-on-iran-nuclear-deal/ Accessed on (6/11/2017).
14. Greenslade, Roy. 2015. "Iran Nuclear Deal: What Britain's National Newspapers Think." *The Guardian*. https://www.theguardian.com/media/greenslade/2015/jul/15/iran-nuclear-deal-what-britains-national-newspapers-think Accessed on (6/11/2017).
15. Medea, Benjamin. 2015. "US Lobby Groups Try to Squash Iran Deal Despite Public Support." Telesur. http://www.telesurtv.net/english/opinion/US-Lobby-Groups-Try-to-Squash-Iran-Deal-Despite-Public-Support-20150706-0014.html Accessed on (6/11/2017) and Clifton, Eli. 2013. "Home Depot Founder's Quiet $10 Million Right-Wing Investment." *Salon*. https://www.salon.com/2013/

08/05/home_depot_founder's_quiet_10_million_right_wing_investment/ Accessed on (6/11/2017).
16. Lipton, Eric. 2015. "G.O.P.'s Israel Support Deepens as Political Contributions Shift." *The New York Times.* https://www.nytimes.com/2015/04/05/us/politics/gops-israel-support-deepens-as-political-contributions-shift.html?_r=0 Accessed on (6/11/2017).
17. Clifton, Eli. 2015. "Who Are the Billionaires Attacking Obama's Iran Diplomacy?" *The Nation.* https://www.thenation.com/article/who-are-billionaires-attacking-obamas-iran-diplomacy/ Accessed on (6/11/2017).
18. Ho, Catherine. 2015. "Mega-Donors Opposing Iran Deal Have Upper Hand in Fierce Lobbying Battle." *The Washington Post.* https://www.washingtonpost.com/news/powerpost/wp/2015/08/13/mega-donors-opposing-iran-deal-have-upper-hand-in-fierce-lobbying-battle/ Accessed on (6/11/2017).
19. Right Web. 2015. "Klarman, Seth." http://rightweb.irc-online.org/profile/klarman_seth/ Accessed on (6/11/2017).
20. Blau, Uri. 2016. "Times of Israel Cofounder Gave $1.5 Million to Right-Wing Media Watchdog That Routinely Goes After News Outlets." *Haaretz.* http://www.haaretz.com/israel-news/1.740340 Accessed on (6/11/2017).
21. World Jewish Congress. 2017. "WJC President Ronald Lauder Welcomes 'Firm and Appropriate' US Response to Renewed Iran Aggression." https://www.worldjewishcongress.org/en/news/wjc-president-ronald-s-lauder-welcomes-firm-and-appropriate-us-response-to-renewed-iran-aggression-2-1-2017?printable=true Accessed on (6/11/2017).
22. Clifton, Eli. 2015. "Who Are the Billionaires Attacking Obama's Iran Diplomacy?" *The Nation.* https://www.thenation.com/article/who-are-billionaires-attacking-obamas-iran-diplomacy/ Accessed on (6/11/2017).

23. Right Web. 2013. "Loeb, Daniel." http://rightweb.irc-online.org/profile/loeb_daniel/ Accessed on (6/11/2017).
24. Clifton, Eli. 2015. "Meet Marco Rubio's Far-Right Neocon Donors." *The Nation.* https://www.thenation.com/article/meet-marco-rubios-far-right-neocon-donors/ Accessed on (6/11/2017).
25. Levine, Lasha. 2013. "Oligarch Valley: How Beverly Hills Billionaire Farmers Lynda and Stewart Resnick Profit from the Iran Sanctions They Lobbied for." *Mondoweiss.* http://mondoweiss.net/2013/07/oligarch-valley-how-beverly-hills-billionaire-farmers-lynda-and-stewart-resnick-profit-from-the-iran-sanctions-they-lobbied-for/ Accessed on (6/11/2017).
26. Zuckerman, Mortimer B. 2015. "Obama's Unforgivable Betrayal." US News. http://www.usnews.com/opinion/articles/2015/04/17/obamas-iran-nuclear-deal-is-an-unforgivable-betrayal-of-israel Accessed on (6/11/2017).
27. Blumenthal, Max. 2012. "The Sugar Mama of Anti-Muslim Hate." *The Nation.* https://www.thenation.com/article/sugar-mama-anti-muslim-hate/ Accessed on (6/11/2017).
28. Gatestone. "About Gatestone Institute." https://www.gatestoneinstitute.org/about/ Accessed on (6/11/2017).
29. Human Events. 2011. "Top 10 Reasons George Soros Is Dangerous."http://humanevents.com/2011/04/02/top-10-reasons-george-soros-is-dangerous/ Accessed on (6/11/2017).
30. NGO Monitor. 2016. "Soros Documents Highlight Irresponsible and Unaccountable Funding to Political NGOs."http://www.ngo-monitor.org/press-releases/soros-documents-highlight-irresponsible-and-unaccountable-funding-to-political-ngos/ Accessed on (6/11/2017).
31. Media Matters Staff. 2017. "Trump Ally Alex Jones: "The Head of the Jewish Mafia Is George Soros." https://www.mediamatters.org/video/2017/03/29/trump-ally-alex-jones-head-jewish-mafia-george-soros/215864 Accessed on (6/11/2017).

32. JTA. 2017. "EU Official: Hungarian PM's Crusade Against George Soros Is Anti-Semitic." *Forward*. http://forward.com/fast-forward/371121/eu-official-hungarian-prime-minister-s-crusade-against-george-soros-is-anti/ Accessed on (6/11/2017).
33. Abramovitch, Seth. 2015. "98 Prominent Hollywood Jews Back Iran Nuclear Deal in Open Letter (Exclusive)." *The Hollywood Reporter*. http://www.hollywoodreporter.com/news/98-prominent-hollywood-jews-back-814855 Accessed on (6/11/2017).
34. Bruck, Connie. 2010. "The Art of the Billionaire." *The New Yorker* Magazine. http://www.newyorker.com/magazine/2010/12/06/the-art-of-the-billionaire Accessed on (6/11/2017).
35. Hod, Itay. 2015. "Hollywood Jewish Moguls Torn on Iran Nuke Deal, Impact on Hillary Clinton." *The Wrap*. http://www.thewrap.com/hollywood-jewish-moguls-torn-on-iran-nuke-deal-impact-on-hillary-clinton/ Accessed on (6/11/2017).
36. Turner, Ted. 2015. "I Just Expressed My Support for the Iran Deal. You Can, Too, by Joining @ThunderclapIt. // @NTI_WMD." Tweet. https://twitter.com/tedturneriii/status/629306362036662272 Accessed on (6/11/2017).
37. Weisman, Jonathan and Nicholas Confessore. 2015. "Donors Descend on Schumer and Others in Debate on Iran." *The New York Times*. https://www.nytimes.com/2015/08/13/us/politics/in-efforts-to-sway-iran-debate-big-money-donors-are-heard.html?_r=0 Accessed on (6/11/2017).
38. Ho, Catherine. 2015. "Mega-Donors Opposing Iran Deal Have Upper Hand in Fierce Lobbying Battle." *The Washington Post*. https://www.washingtonpost.com/news/powerpost/wp/2015/08/13/mega-donors-opposing-iran-deal-have-upper-hand-in-fierce-lobbying-battle/ Accessed on (6/11/2017).

39. Melin, Mark. 2015. "Warren Buffett Warns About a Nuclear Iran." *Value Walk*. http://www.valuewalk.com/2015/03/warren-buffett-warns-about-a-nuclear-iran/ Accessed on (6/11/2017).
40. Bloomberg, Michael R. 2015. "White House Should Leave Politics Out of Iran Deal." *Bloomberg*. https://www.bloomberg.com/view/articles/2015-08-10/white-house-should-leave-politics-out-of-iran-deal Accessed on (6/11/2017).
41. Hamn, Harold. 2015. "America's Self-Punishing Oil Export Ban." *The Wall Street Journal*. https://www.wsj.com/articles/americas-self-punishing-oil-export-ban-1434922352 Accessed on (6/11/2017).
42. Edward, Baig C. 2015. "Airbnb CEO Wants to Expand into Iran—Seriously." *USA Today*. https://www.usatoday.com/story/tech/columnist/baig/2015/05/27/brian-chesky-at-code-conference/27672975/ Accessed on (6/11/2017).
43. Gallagher, Leigh. 2016. "Airbnb Cofounders Join Buffett and Gates' 'Giving Pledge'." *Fortune*. http://fortune.com/2016/06/01/airbnb-cofounders-join-buffett-and-gates-giving-pledge/ Accessed on (6/11/2017).
44. Guillén, Alex. 2014. "Steyer Puts Another $15 Million into Super PAC—Total CEO Dies in Moscow Plane Accident—Pebble Mine Developers Sue EPA for Communications with Greens—New Infrastructure Non-Profit." *Politico*. http://www.politico.com/tipsheets/morning-energy/2014/10/steyer-puts-another-15-million-into-super-pac-total-ceo-dies-in-moscow-plane-accident-pebble-mine-developers-sue-epa-for-communications-with-greens-new-infrastructure-non-profit-212543 Accessed on (6/11/2017).
45. Zezima, Katie. 2015. "Cruz Super PAC Launches Seven-Figure, Nationwide Ad Campaign." *The Washington Post*. https://www.washingtonpost.com/news/post-politics/wp/2015/08/04/cruz-super-pac-launches-seven-figure-nationwide-ad-campaign/ Accessed on (6/11/2017).

46. Roux, Pamela. 2017. "Is Trump Backer Robert Mercer a Billionaire? I Tried to Find Out." *Bloomberg*. https://www.bloomberg.com/news/articles/2017-04-25/is-trump-backer-robert-mercer-a-billionaire-i-tried-to-find-out Accessed on (6/11/2017).
47. Biersack, Bob, Viveca Novak, and Will Tucker. 2015. "A Few New Faces – but Not Many – Among Mega Donors to Presidential Super PACs." *The Guardian*. https://www.theguardian.com/us-news/2015/aug/01/donors-presidential-super-pacs Accessed on (6/11/2017).
48. Mccaskill, Nolan D. 2016. "Former AIG Chairman Hank Greenberg Invests $10 Million in Jeb Bush." *Politico*. http://www.politico.com/story/2016/01/hank-greenberg-jeb-bush-217439 Accessed on (6/11/2017).
49. Savchuk, Katia. 2014. "The Little Known CEO Spending Millions to Elect Far-Right Republicans." *Forbes*. https://www.forbes.com/sites/katiasavchuk/2014/11/04/the-little-known-ceo-spending-millions-to-elect-far-right-republicans/#1dc6a0dd5cad Accessed on (6/11/2017).
50. Vogel, Kenneth P. 2015. "Blue Billionaires on Top." *Politico*. http://www.politico.com/story/2015/01/blue-billionaires-on-top-114151 Accessed on (6/11/2017).
51. Schleifer, Theodore. 2015. "First on CNN: Billionaire Brothers Give Cruz Super PAC $15 Million." CNN. http://www.cnn.com/2015/07/25/politics/ted-cruz-wilks-brothers/ Accessed on (6/11/2017).
52. Laub, Gillian. 2016. "Inside Billionaire Steve Cohen's Comeback." *Fortune*. http://fortune.com/steve-cohen-billionaire-point72-hedge-fund/ Accessed on (6/11/2017).
53. Source Watch. 2017. "Cato Institute." http://www.sourcewatch.org/index.php/Cato_Institute#Finances_and_Funding
54. Glaser, John and Justin Logan. 2015. "Iran Nuclear Deal a Clear Success." Cato Institute. https://www.cato.org/publications/commentary/iran-nuclear-deal-clear-success Accessed on (6/11/2017).

55. Goodman, Leah Mcgrath. 2016. "A Top Clinton Donor Says It's Time to Stand Up to Trump." *Newsweek*. http://www.newsweek.com/clinton-donor-jb-pritzker-stop-donald-trump-434171 Accessed on (6/11/2017).
56. Biersack, Bob, Viveca Novak, and Will Tucker. 2015. "A Few New Faces—but not Many—Among Mega Donors to Presidential Super PACs." Open Secrets. https://www.opensecrets.org/news/2015/08/a-few-new-faces-but-not-many-among-megadonors-to-presidential-super-pacs/ Accessed on (6/11/2017).
57. Hook, Janet and Rebecca Ballhaus. 2015. "Larry Ellison Among 4 Big Donors to Marco Rubio Super PAC." *The Wall Street Journal*. https://blogs.wsj.com/washwire/2015/07/31/pac-backing-marco-rubio-gets-16-million-mostly-from-4-donors/ Accessed on (6/11/2017).
58. McCormick, John and Julie Bykowicz. 2015. "Meet the Billionaire Roofer Behind Scott Walker." *Bloomberg*. https://www.bloomberg.com/politics/features/2015-03-12/meet-the-billionaire-roofer-behind-scott-walker Accessed on (6/11/2017).
59. O'Connor, Clare. 2016. "Trump Adds Richest Self-Made Woman Diane Hendricks to Economic Advisory Team." *Forbes*. https://www.forbes.com/sites/clareoconnor/2016/08/11/trump-adds-richest-self-made-woman-diane-hendricks-to-economic-advisory-team/#451fe0b26c85 Accessed on (6/11/2017).
60. Confessore, Nicholas, Sarah Cohen and Karen Yourishaug. 2015. "Small Pool of Rich Donors Dominates Election Giving." *The New York Times*. https://www.nytimes.com/2015/08/02/us/small-pool-of-rich-donors-dominates-election-giving.html Accessed on (6/11/2017).
61. Posner, Sarah. 2016. "Mysterious Ted Cruz Super PAC Donors Tied to Company Accused of Stealing Seniors' Social Security." *Huffington Post*. http://www.huffingtonpost.com/entry/ted-cruz-super-pac-social-security_us_56e83bbfe4b0b25c918361cd Accessed on (6/11/2017).

62. Open Secrets. 2014. "2014 Top Donors to Outside Spending Groups." https://www.opensecrets.org/outside-spending/summ.php?cycle=2014&disp=D&type=V Accessed on (6/11/2017).
63. Roberston, Lori. 2015. "Hedge Fund Managers' Tax Rates." Fact Check. http://www.factcheck.org/2015/09/hedge-fund-managers-tax-rates/ Accessed on (6/11/2017).
64. Goldstein, Matthew and Ben Protess. 2017. "Trump Tax Plan Silent on Carried Interest, a Boon for the Very Rich." *The New York Times*. https://www.nytimes.com/2017/04/27/business/dealbook/trump-tax-plan-silent-on-carried-interest-a-boon-for-the-very-rich.html Accessed on (6/11/2017).
65. Isidore, Chris. 2013. "Buffett Says He's Still Paying Lower Tax Rate Than His Secretary." CNN. http://money.cnn.com/2013/03/04/news/economy/buffett-secretary-taxes/ Accessed on (6/11/2017).
66. Scheiber, Noam and Patricia Cohen. 2015. "For the Wealthiest, a Private Tax System That Saves Them Billions." *The New York Times*. https://www.nytimes.com/2015/12/30/business/economy/for-the-wealthiest-private-tax-system-saves-them-billions.html Accessed on (6/11/2017).
67. Tossi, Sina. 2015. "The Bomb Iran Lobby Gears Up For 2016." Moyers & Company. http://billmoyers.com/2015/06/08/bomb-iran-lobby-gears-2016/ Accessed on (6/11/2017).
68. Ho, Catherine. 2015. "Mega-donors Opposing Iran Deal Have Upper Hand in Fierce Lobbying Battle." *The Washington Post*. https://www.washingtonpost.com/news/powerpost/wp/2015/08/13/mega-donors-opposing-iran-deal-have-upper-hand-in-fierce-lobbying-battle/?utm_term=.f9e10a6f156c Accessed on (6/11/2017).
69. The Lynde and Harry Bradley Foundation. http://www.bradleyfdn.org Accessed on (6/11/2017).
70. Exposed by CMD. "About CMD." http://www.exposedbycmd.org/about-cmd/ Accessed on (6/11/2017).

71. Bottari, Mary. 2017. "Weaponized Philanthropy: Document Trove Details Bradley Foundation's Efforts to Build Right-Wing 'Infrastructure' Nationwide." Exposed by CMD. http://www.exposedbycmd.org/2017/05/05/documents-detail-bradley-foundation-efforts-build-right-wing-infrastructure-nationwide/ Accessed on (6/11/2017).
72. Media Bias/Fact Check. "Right Bias." https://mediabiasfactcheck.com/daily-signal/ Accessed on (6/11/2017).
73. Fear Inc. "Lynde and Harry Bradley Foundation." https://islamophobianetwork.com/funder/lynde-and-harry-bradley-foundation Accessed on (6/11/2017).
74. Clifton, Eli. 2014. "Far-Right Birther's Secret Funders: Look Who's Backing Islamophobe Frank Gaffney." *Salon*. https://www.salon.com/2014/10/01/far_right_birthers_secret_funders_look_whos_backing_islamophobe_frank_gaffney/ Accessed on (6/11/2017).
75. Bice, Daniel. 2015. "Bradley Foundation, Ron Johnson Distance Themselves from Anti-Islam Group." *Journal Sentinel*. http://archive.jsonline.com/watchdog/noquarter/bradley-foundation-ron-johnson-distance-themselves-from-anti-islam-group-b99632721z1-361746331.html Accessed on (6/11/2017).
76. The Lynde and Harry Bradley Foundation. 2017. "Center for Security Policy Gives Sacred Honor Award to Bradley Foundation." http://www.bradleyfdn.org/On-Lion-Letter/ID/1231/Center-for-Security-Policy-gives-Sacred-Honor-Award-to-Bradley-Foundation Accessed on (6/11/2017).
77. Bice, op. cit.
78. Anschutz Foundation 50,000, Summer Foundation, 5000, Ed Snider Foundation 5000, Henderson Foundation 5000, Gerrardine Laffey Connolly Foundation 15,000, Charles Evans Foundation 10,000, F. M. Kirby Foundation 15,000, Sunmark Foundation 13,000, Schwab Charitable Fund 100,000, MZ Foundation 85,000, Diana Davis Spencer Foundation 15,000, William H. Donner Foundation 25,000, Helen Diller Family 25,000, GB Anderson Fund

7500, Clinton Family Fund 5000, Templeton Giving Fund 450,000, Eugene & Emily Grant Family Foundation 275,000, Lynda and Harry Bradley Foundation 50,000, Sarah Scaife Foundation 175,000.
79. ProPublica. 2015. "Center for Security Policy Inc." https://projects.propublica.org/nonprofits/organizations/521601976 Accessed on (6/11/2017).
80. Scribd. "Center for Security Policy Inc. Form 990." https://www.scribd.com/doc/240859080/Center-for-Security-Policy-2013-Schedule-B Accessed on (6/11/2017).
81. JTA Staff. 2012. "The Times of Israel: Josh Block to Head The Israel Project, Lobbyist to Take Over PR Project from Founding CEO." The Israel Project. http://www.theisraelproject.org/the-times-of-israel-josh-block-to-head-the-israel-project-lobbyist-to-take-over-pr-project-from-founding-ceo Accessed on (6/11/2017).
82. Lobe, Jim. 2015. "Support for Iran Deal Stronger among US Jews Than General Public." LobeLog. http://lobelog.com/support-for-iran-deal-stronger-among-us-jews-than-general-public/ Accessed on (6/11/2017).
83. Beinart, Peter. 2015. "Why Don't American Jewish Groups Represent American Jews on Iran," Haaretz. http://www.haaretz.com/opinion/.premium-1.668571 Accessed on (6/11/2017).
84. Goodenough, Patrick. 2015. "Pro-Israel Christians 'Representing Tens of Millions' Petition WH, Congress Against Iran Deal." CNS News. https://www.cnsnews.com/news/article/patrick-goodenough/pro-israel-christians-representing-tens-millions-petition-wh Accessed on (6/11/2017).
85. Nothstine, Ray. 2015. "Evangelical Left Slammed for Supporting Iran Nuclear Deal: 'Serious Christians Can't Just Cry Peace, Peace,' IRD President Tooley Says." The Christian Post. http://www.christianpost.com/news/evangelical-left-slammed-for-supporting-iran-nuclear-deal-serious-christians-cant-just-cry-peace-peace-ird-president-tooley-says-141714/ Accessed on (6/11/2017).

86. Kull, Steven and Shibley Telhami. 2015. "What Americans Really Think about an Iran Deal." *The Washington Post*. https://www.washingtonpost.com/news/monkey-cage/wp/2015/03/03/what-americans-really-think-about-an-iran-deal/?utm_term=.1d5415f05706 Accessed on (6/11/2017).
87. Scammell, Rosie. 2016. "Pope Francis Meets Iran's President to Boost Nuke Deal, Mideast Peace." *The Washington Post*. https://www.washingtonpost.com/national/religion/pope-francis-meets-irans-president-to-boost-nuke-deal-mideast-peace/2016/01/26/a6e4559a-c456-11e5-b933-31c93021392a_story.html?utm_term=.e51568497741 Accessed on (6/11/2017).
88. Toosi, Nahal. 2015. "Group of Christian Leaders Backs Iran Deal." *Politico*. http://www.politico.com/story/2015/08/christian-leaders-back-iran-group-121689 Accessed on (6/11/2017).
89. Reid, Chip and Jennifer Janisch. 2017. "Sen. Grassley Releases Report on Wounded Warrior Project Spending." CBS. http://www.cbsnews.com/news/wounded-warrior-project-investigation-grassley-senate-report/ Accessed on (6/11/2017).
90. Charity Navigator. "International." https://www.charitynavigator.org/index.cfm?bay=search.categories&categoryid=7 Accessed on (6/11/2017).
91. Bender, Bryan. 2013. "Many D.C. Think Tanks Now Players in Partisan Wars." *Boston Globe*. http://www.bostonglobe.com/news/nation/2013/08/10/brain-trust-for-sale-the-growing-footprint-washington-think-tank-industrial-complex/7ZifHfrLPlbz0bSeVOZHdI/story.html Accessed on (6/11/2017).
92. McGann, James G. 2017. "2016 Global Go to Think Tank Index Report." University of Pennsylvania. http://repository.upenn.edu/cgi/viewcontent.cgi?article=1011&context=think_tanks Accessed on (6/11/2017).

93. Fang, Lee. 2015. "Emails Show Close Ties Between Heritage Foundation and Lockheed Martin." *The Intercept.* https://theintercept.com/2015/09/15/heritage-foundation/ Accessed on (6/11/2017).
94. Patterson, Thom. 2016. "Congress Looks at Re-Starting the F-22 Raptor Program." CNN. http://www.cnn.com/2016/04/21/politics/f22-raptor-congress/ Accessed on (6/11/2017).
95. Phillips, James. 2015. "The Iran Nuclear Deal: What the Next President Should Do." The Heritage Foundation. http://www.heritage.org/middle-east/report/the-iran-nuclear-deal-what-the-next-president-should-do Accessed on (6/11/2017).
96. Washington Examiner. 2017. "Heritage Must Look to Its Heritage If It Wants a Future." http://www.washingtonexaminer.com/heritage-must-look-to-its-heritage-if-it-wants-a-future/article/2622362 Accessed on (6/11/2017).
97. Wikipedia. 2017. "Electoral History of the Libertarian Party (United States)." https://en.wikipedia.org/wiki/Electoral_history_of_the_Libertarian_Party_(United States) Accessed on (6/11/2017).
98. AIPAC. 2013. "Our Mission." http://www.aipac.org/about/mission Accessed on (6/11/2017).
99. Rosenberg, M. J. "Does Unconditional Support for Israel Endanger Israeli Voices?" The Israeli Lobby. http://israellobbyus.org/transcripts/5.1MJ_Rosenberg.htm Accessed on (6/11/2017).
100. Tau, Byron. 2015. "AIPAC Funds Ads Opposing Iran Nuclear Deal." *The Wall Street Journal.* http://blogs.wsj.com/washwire/2015/07/17/aipac-funds-ads-opposing-iran-nuclear-deal/ Accessed on (6/11/2017).
101. Ho, Catherine. 2015. "Anti-Iran Deal Groups Firing on All Cylinders in Massive Lobbying Push." *The Washington Post.* http://www.washingtonpost.com/news/powerpost/wp/2015/07/21/anti-iran-deal-groups-firing-on-all-cylinders-in-massive-lobbying-push/ Accessed on (6/11/2017).

102. Open Secrets. "Outside Spending: Frequently Asked Questions About 501(c)(4) Groups." https://www.opensecrets.org/outsidespending/faq.php Accessed on (6/11/2017).
103. Available via the ProPublica website.
104. Biscobing, Dave. 2015. "FACT CHECK: Expert Says Iran Nuclear Deal TV Advertisement Is 'Misleading'." ABC 15. http://www.abc15.com/news/national/fact-check-expert-says-iran-nuclear-deal-tv-advertisement-is-misleading Accessed on (6/11/2017).
105. Right Web. 2015. "Citizens for a Nuclear Free Iran." http://rightweb.irc-online.org/profile/citizens_for_a_nuclear_free_iran/ Accessed on (6/11/2017).
106. Beinart, Peter. 2015. "When Bibi Won, AIPAC Lost." *The Atlantic*. http://www.theatlantic.com/international/archive/2015/03/when-bibi-won-aipac-lost/388203/ Accessed on (6/11/2017).
107. Bruck, Connie. 2014. "Friends of Israel." *The New Yorker* Magazine. http://www.newyorker.com/magazine/2014/09/01/friends-israel Accessed on (6/11/2017).
108. Ibid.
109. Ibid.
110. Smith, Gregory A. and Jessica Martínez. 2016. "How the Faithful Voted: A Preliminary 2016 Analysis." Pew Research Center. http://www.pewresearch.org/fact-tank/2016/11/09/how-the-faithful-voted-a-preliminary-2016-analysis/ Accessed on (6/11/2017).
111. Connelly, Christopher. 2016. "Why American Evangelicals Are a Huge Base of Support for Israel." Public Radio International. https://www.pri.org/stories/2016-10-24/why-american-evangelicals-are-huge-base-support-israel Accessed on (6/11/2017).
112. Christians United for Israel. "About Us." http://www.cufi.org/site/PageServer?pagename=about_AboutCUFI Accessed on (6/11/2017).
113. Ibid.

114. Fetcher, Joshua and John Hagee. 2014. "Ebola Is God's Punishment for Obama Dividing Jerusalem." *My San Antonio.* http://www.mysanantonio.com/news/local/article/John-Hagee-Ebola-is-God-s-punishment-for-Obama-5827110.php Accessed on (6/11/2017).
115. Stakelbeck, Erick. 2015. "Hagee on Iran Deal: Final Blood Moon a Divine Warning." CBN News. http://www1.cbn.com/cbnnews/world/2015/September/Hagee-on-Iran-Deal-Blood-Moon-a-Divine-Warning Accessed on (6/11/2017).
116. Ibid.
117. Beinart, Peter. 2016. "Trump at AIPAC: A Jewish Betrayal of the United States." *Haaretz.* http://www.haaretz.com/opinion/.premium-1.710489 Accessed on (6/11/2017).
118. Scherer, Michael and Ken Silverstein. "Born-Again Zionists." *Mother Jones.* http://www.motherjones.com/politics/2002/09/born-again-zionists/ Accessed on (6/11/2017).
119. Harris-Gershon, David. 2016. "How AIPAC Used Black Leaders to Erase Palestinian Suffering from the Democratic Party Platform." *Kkun Daily.* http://www.tikkun.org/tikkundaily/2016/07/09/exclusive-how-aipac-is-using-black-leaders-to-erase-palestinian-suffering-from-the-democratic-party-platform/ Accessed on (6/11/2017).
120. Johnston, David and Eric Schmitt. 2004. "F.B.I. Is Said to Brief Pentagon Bosses on Spy Case; Charges Are Possible." *The New York Times.* http://www.nytimes.com/2004/08/31/politics/campaign/31inquire.html Accessed on (6/11/2017).
121. Eggen, Dan and Jamie Stockwell. 2005. "U.S. Indicts 2 in Case of Divulged Secrets." *The Washington Post.* http://www.washingtonpost.com/wp-dyn/content/article/2005/08/04/AR2005080401129.html Accessed on (6/11/2017).
122. Guttman, Nathan. 2014. "AIPAC Gets Down and Dirty in Pushback vs. Defamation Suit." *Forward.* http://forward.

123. Shannon, Elaine. 2004. "A Second Search of AIPAC." *Time Magazine.* http://content.time.com/time/nation/article/0,8599,845,221,00.html Accessed on (6/11/2017).
124. Eggen, Dan and Jerry Markon. 2005. "2 Senior AIPAC Employees Ousted." *The Washington Post.* http://www.washingtonpost.com/wp-dyn/articles/A6059-2005Apr20.html Accessed on (6/11/2017).
125. The Daily Dish. 2010. "AIPAC's Civil War." *The Atlantic.* https://www.theatlantic.com/daily-dish/archive/2010/11/aipacs-civil-war/179593/ Accessed on (6/11/2017).
126. Guttman, Nathan. 2014. "AIPAC Gets Down and Dirty in Pushback vs. Defamation Suit." *Forward.* http://forward.com/news/133172/aipac-gets-down-and-dirty-in-pushback-vs-defamatio/ Accessed on (6/11/2017).
127. Ibid.
128. Markon, Jerry. 2009. "Nation Digest: Sentence Reduced in Pentagon-AIPAC Case." *The Washington Post.* http://www.washingtonpost.com/wp-dyn/content/article/2009/06/11/AR2009061104280.html Accessed on (6/11/2017).
129. Goldberg, Jeffrey. 2005. "Real Insiders." *The New Yorker.* http://www.newyorker.com/magazine/2005/07/04/real-insiders Accessed on (6/11/2017).
130. Ibid.
131. Good, Chris. 2010. "Raising More Money, J Street Discloses Big Donors." *The Atlantic.* http://www.theatlantic.com/politics/archive/2010/09/raising-more-money-j-street-discloses-big-donors/63520/ Accessed on (6/11/2017).
132. Scribd. "Spring 2014 Democracy Alliance Portfolio Snapshot." http://www.scribd.com/doc/224397893/Spring-2014-Democracy-Alliance-Portfolio-Snapshot Accessed on (6/11/2017).
133. J Street. "About J Street." http://jstreet.org/about Accessed on (6/11/2017).

134. Guttman, Nathan. 2015. "J Street, Newly Combative, Takes on the Jewish Establishment." *Forward*. http://forward.com/news/israel/217456/j-street-newly-combative-takes-on-the-jewish-estab/ Accessed on (6/11/2017).
135. Winer, Stuart. 2015. "J Street Applauds Obama for Iran Nuke Deal." *The Times of Israel*. http://www.timesofisrael.com/j-street-applauds-obama-for-iran-nuke-deal/ Accessed on (6/11/2017).
136. Miller, Paul. 2014. "J Street: Pro-Progressive, Not Pro-Israel." *The Hill*. http://thehill.com/blogs/congress-blog/politics/222366-j-street-pro-progressive-not-pro-israel Accessed on (6/11/2017).
137. Source Watch. 2017. "Franklin Center for Government and Public Integrity." http://www.sourcewatch.org/index.php/Franklin_Center_for_Government_and_Public_Integrity Accessed on (6/11/2017).
138. Ben-Ami, Jeremy. 2016. "Trump's Nominee for Ambassador to Israel Is Unfit to Serve." *The Washington Post*. https://www.washingtonpost.com/opinions/trumps-nominee-for-ambassador-to-israel-is-unfit-to-serve/2016/12/19/5b6ffa08-c543-11e6-bf4b-2c064d32a4bf_story.html?utm_term=.e09e67c778ea Accessed on (6/11/2017).
139. Wilner, Michael. 2017. "Senate Approves David Friedman as Israel Ambassador." *The Jerusalem Post*. http://www.jpost.com/Diaspora/Report-Trumps-pick-for-Israel-envoy-confirmed-by-US-Senate-485050 Accessed on (6/11/2017).
140. Lipton, Eric. 2015. "G.O.P.'s Israel Support Deepens as Political Contributions Shift." *The New York Times*. https://www.nytimes.com/2015/04/05/us/politics/gops-israel-support-deepens-as-political-contributions-shift.html Accessed on (6/11/2017).
141. Samore, Gary. 2015. "Belfer Center for Science and International Affairs." SFRC Testimony. https://www.foreign.senate.gov/imo/media/doc/080415_Samore_Testimony.pdf Accessed on (6/11/2017).

142. United Against Nuclear Iran. 2015. "Senator Joseph I. Lieberman to Lead United Against Nuclear Iran as Chairman." http://www.unitedagainstnucleariran.com/press-releases/senator-joseph-i-lieberman-lead-united-against-nuclear-iran-chairman Accessed on (6/11/2017).
143. Foreign Affairs Committee. 2015. "ISIS: Defining the Enemy." https://foreignaffairs.house.gov/hearing/subcommittee-hearing-isis-defining-the-enemy/ Accessed on (6/11/2017).
144. McGreal, Chris. 2012. "MEK Decision: Multimillion-Dollar Campaign Led to Removal from Terror List." *The Guardian*. https://www.theguardian.com/world/2012/sep/21/iran-mek-group-removed-us-terrorism-list Accessed on (6/11/2017).
145. Gharib, Ali. 2015. "Cult Leader Will Tell Congress: Fight ISIS by Regime Change in Iran." *The Nation*. https://www.thenation.com/article/cult-leader-will-tell-congress-fight-isis-regime-change-iran/ Accessed on (6/11/2017).
146. Warrick, Joby. 2008. "U.S. Is Said to Expand Covert Operations in Iran." *The Washington Post*. http://www.washingtonpost.com/wp-dyn/content/article/2008/06/29/AR2008062901881_pf.html Accessed on (6/11/2017).
147. Wilkie, Christina. 2011. "Mujahideen-e Khalq: Former U.S. Officials Make Millions Advocating for Terrorist Organization." *Huffington Post*. http://www.huffingtonpost.com/2011/08/08/mek-lobbying_n_913233.html Accessed on (6/11/2017).
148. CBS News. 2017. "AP: Trump Appointee Spoke at Event for "Cult-Like" Iran Exile Group." http://www.cbsnews.com/news/elaine-chao-trump-transportation-secretary-paid-iran-exile-group-mek-ap/ Accessed on (6/11/2017).
149. Rogin, Josh. 2016. "Giuliani Was Paid Advocate for Shady Iranian Dissident Group." *The Washington Post*. https://www.washingtonpost.com/news/josh-rogin/wp/2016/11/15/giuliani-was-paid-advocate-for-shady-

iranian-dissident-group/?utm_term=.b4d13775d788 Accessed on (6/11/2017).
150. Scribd. 2017. "Letter to the President-Elect." https://www.scribd.com/document/336646842/Letter-PEOTUS-Final-20170109-w-Attachments Accessed on (6/11/2017).
151. Foundation for Defense of Democracies. "Our Team: John Hannah." http://www.defenddemocracy.org/about-fdd/team-overview/john-hannah/ Accessed on (6/11/2017).
152. Right Web. 2011. "Dershowitz, Toby." http://rightweb.irc-online.org/profile/dershowitz_toby/ Accessed on (6/11/2017).
153. Clifton, Eli. 2013. "Home Depot Founder's Quiet $10 Million Right-Wing Investment." *Salon*. http://www.salon.com/2013/08/05/home_depot_founder's_quiet_10_million_right_wing_investment/ Accessed on (6/11/2017).
154. Judis, John B. 2015. "The Little Think Tank That Could." *Slate*. http://www.slate.com/articles/news_and_politics/foreigners/2015/08/foundation_for_the_defense_of_democracies_inside_the_small_pro_israel_think.html Accessed on (6/11/2017).
155. Cadei, Emily. 2014. "Mark Dubowitz: Waging Financial War on Iran." *Ozy* Magazine. http://www.ozy.com/provocateurs/the-wonks-waging-financial-war-on-iran/4912 Accessed on (6/11/2017).
156. Jilani, Zaid and Ryan Grim. 2017. "Hacked Emails Show Top UAE Diplomat Coordinating with Pro-Israel Think Tank Against Iran." *The Intercept*. https://theintercept.com/2017/06/03/hacked-emails-show-top-uae-diplomat-coordinating-with-pro-israel-neocon-think-tank-against-iran/?link_id=1&can_id=832d57df8f4da8021d00b7725b908f65&source=email-the-most-well-connected-man-in-washington-just-had-his-inbox-hacked-hoo-boy&email_referrer=the-most-well-connected-man-in-washington-just-had-his-inbox-hacked-hoo-boy&email_subject=the-most-well-connected-man-in-washington-just-had-his-inbox-hacked-hoo-boy Accessed on (6/11/2017).

157. Middle East Observer Staff. 2017. "Hackers Release Emails of UAE Ambassador to US." https://www.middleeastobserver.org/2017/06/04/36941/ Accessed on (6/11/2017).
158. Barnard, Anne and David D. Kirkpatrick. 2017. "5 Arab Nations Move to Isolate Qatar, Putting the U.S. in a Bind." *The New York Times.* https://www.nytimes.com/2017/06/05/world/middleeast/qatar-saudi-arabia-egypt-bahrain-united-arab-emirates.html?hp.&action=click&pgtype=Homepage&clickSource=story-heading&module=first-column-region&region=top-news&WT.nav=top-news Accessed on (6/11/2017).
159. Dubowitz, Mark. 2017. "The Delusion of the Iran Nuclear Deal." Foundation for Defense of Democracies. http://www.defenddemocracy.org/media-hit/dubowitz-mark-the-delusion-of-the-iran-nuclear-deal/ Accessed on (6/11/2017).
160. Ploughshares Fund. "About Us." http://www.ploughshares.org/about-us Accessed on (6/11/2017).
161. Ploughshares Fund. 2012. "Who We Are." http://pf.pyramidwest.net/who-we-are/staff/joseph-cirincione Accessed on (6/11/2017).
162. Cirincione, Joseph, Jon Wolfsthal, and Miriam Rajkumar. 2005. "Deadly Arsenals: Nuclear, Biological, and Chemical Threats, Second Edition, Revised and Expanded." Carnegie Endowment for International Peace. http://carnegieendowment.org/2005/07/10/deadly-arsenals-nuclear-biological-and-chemical-threats-second-edition-revised-and-expanded/916 Accessed on (6/11/2017).
163. Ploughshares Fund. 2015. "Board and Advisors." http://www.ploughshares.org/about-us/board-advisors Accessed on (6/11/2017).
164. Form 990 can be found on the ProPublica website.
165. Ploughshares Fund. 2016. "2016 Annual Report." http://www.ploughshares.org/sites/default/files/Ploughshares_AR2016.pdf Accessed on (6/11/2017).
166. Ibid.

167. Dershowitz, Alan. 2015. "Dershowitz: The Case Against the Iran Deal." *News Week.* http://www.newsweek.com/dershowitz-case-against-iran-deal-360911 Accessed on (6/11/2017).
168. Samuels, David. 2016. "The Aspiring Novelist Who Became Obama's Foreign Policy Guru." https://www.nytimes.com/2016/05/08/magazine/the-aspiring-novelist-who-became-obamas-foreign-policy-guru.html Accessed on (6/20/2017). Accessed on (6/28/2017).
169. Cortellessa, Eric. 2016. "Where Did Ploughshares Get Its Money to Sell the Iran Deal?" *Times of Israel.* http://www.timesofisrael.com/where-did-ploughshares-get-its-money-to-sell-the-iran-deal/ Accessed on (6/11/2017).
170. Coats, Daniel R. 2017. "Statement for the Record Worldwide Threat Assessment of the US Intelligence Community." Senate Select Committee on Intelligence, p. 7. https://www.intelligence.senate.gov/sites/default/files/documents/os-coats-051117.pdf Accessed on (6/11/2017).
171. Ibid., p. 22.
172. United Against Nuclear Iran. "About Us." http://www2.unitedagainstnucleariran.com/about Accessed on (6/11/2017).
173. From UANI's website. http://www.unitedagainstnucleariran.com/about/mission Accessed on (6/20/17).
174. Gladstone, Rick. 2013. "Group Keeps Long-Distance Watch on Iran and Possible Sanction Violations." *The New York Times.* http://www.nytimes.com/2013/06/21/world/middleeast/group-keeps-watch-on-iran-and-possible-sanction-violations.html?ref.=world&_r=1& Accessed on (6/11/2017).
175. Apuzo, Matt. 2014. "Billionaire Named in Suit Against Anti-Iran Group." *The New York Times.* http://www.nytimes.com/2014/08/19/us/billionaire-named-in-suit-against-anti-iran-group.html Accessed on (6/11/2017).

176. Gordon, Michael R. 2015. "Head of Group Opposing Iran Accord Quits Post, Saying He Backs Deal." *The New York Times.* https://www.nytimes.com/2015/08/12/world/middleeast/head-of-group-opposing-iran-accord-quits-post-saying-he-backs-deal.html?_r=0 Accessed on (6/11/2017).
177. Arms Control Association. "About the Arms Control Association." http://www.armscontrol.org/about Accessed on (6/11, 2017).
178. Ibid.
179. Arms Control Association. 2015. "The P5+1 Nuclear Agreement with Iran: A Net-Plus for Nonproliferation." https://www.armscontrol.org/pressroom/press-release/The-P5%2B1-Nuclear-Agreement-With-Iran-A-Net-Plus-for-Nonproliferation Accessed on (6/11/2017).
180. Arms Control Association. "Greg Thielmann." http://www.armscontrol.org/about/thielmann Accessed on (6/11/2017).
181. Leung, Rebecca. 2003. "The Man Who Knew." CBS News. http://www.cbsnews.com/news/the-man-who-knew-14-10-2003/ Accessed on (6/11/2017).
182. Thielmann, Greg. 2014. "Can U.S. Intelligence Effectively Monitor Compliance with an Iran Nuclear Deal?" *The Hill.* http://thehill.com/blogs/congress-blog/foreign-policy/223885-can-us-intelligence-effectively-monitor-compliance-with-an Accessed on (6/11/2017).
183. Arms Control Association. "About the Arms Control Association." https://www.armscontrol.org/about Accessed on (6/11/2017).
184. Lake, Eli. "Ploughshares Fund Uses Its Millions to Sway Arms Control Debate." *The Daily Beast.* http://www.thedailybeast.com/articles/2011/12/13/ploughshares-fund-uses-its-millions-to-sway-arms-control-debate.html Accessed on (6/11/2017).
185. Arms Control Association. "About the Arms Control Association." https://www.armscontrol.org/about Accessed on (6/11/2017).

186. Ansari, Azadeh. 2009. "Iranian-Americans Cast Ballots on Iran's Future." CNN. http://www.cnn.com/2009/US/06/12/iran.elections.voting/ Accessed on (6/11/2017).
187. BBC. 2016. "Refugees at Highest Ever Level, Reaching 65 m, Says UN." http://www.bbc.com/news/world-36573082 Accessed on (6/11/2017).
188. Right Web. 2014. "Center for Security Policy." http://www.rightweb.irc-online.org/profile/Center_for_Security_Policy Accessed on (6/11/2017).
189. Blumenthal, Sidney. 1987. "Richard Perle, Disarmed but Undeterred." *The Washington Post*. https://www.washingtonpost.com/archive/lifestyle/1987/11/23/richard-perle-disarmed-but-undeterred/b83a9f49-8d43-41bd-8e6f-1316efd52075/?utm_term=.2eddb1f85058 Accessed on (6/11/2017).
190. Right Web. 2011. "Center for Security Policy 501(c)3 Financing." http://www.rightweb.irc-online.org/images/uploads/Right_Web_-_Dec_2011_-_CSP_Financing.pdf Accessed on (6/11/2017).
191. Southern Poverty Law Center. 2016. "SPLC Publishes Media Guide to Countering prominent Anti-Muslim Extremists." https://www.splcenter.org/news/2016/10/26/splc-publishes-media-guide-countering-prominent-anti-muslim-extremists Accessed on (6/11/2017).
192. Beinart, Peter. 2017. "The Denationalization of American Muslims." *The Atlantic*. https://www.theatlantic.com/politics/archive/2017/03/frank-gaffney-donald-trump-and-the-denationalization-of-american-muslims/519954/ Accessed on (6/11/2017).
193. Ibid.
194. Weiss, Michael. 2015. "Clinton Foundation Donor Violated Iran Sanctions, Tried to Sell 747 s to Tehran." *The Daily Beast*. http://www.thedailybeast.com/articles/2015/07/10/iranian-moneyman-gave-to-clinton-foundation.html Accessed on (6/11/2017).
195. Ibid.

196. National Iranian American Council. "Transparency in Government & Finance." https://www.niacouncil.org/about-niac/transparency-in-governance-finance/ Accessed on (6/11/2017).
197. Rosen, Armin. 2015. "America's Most Prominent Group Advocating Engagement with Iran Was Hit with a Rough Court Decision." *Business Insider.* http://www.businessinsider.com/americas-most-prominent-group-advocating-engagement-with-iran-was-hit-with-a-rough-court-decision-2015-3 Accessed on (6/11/2017).
198. Ibid.
199. Ibid.
200. Parsi, Trita. 2015. "Why Iran's Supreme Leader Wants a Nuclear Deal." *The Atlantic.* http://www.theatlantic.com/international/archive/2015/03/why-irans-supreme-leader-wants-a-nuclear-deal/388664/#disqus_thread Accessed on (6/11/2017).
201. Rethink Media. "Our Partners & the Collaboratives We Serve." https://rethinkmedia.org/partners Accessed on (6/11/2017).
202. Rethink Media. "Our Story." https://rethinkmedia.org/about Accessed on (6/11/2017).
203. Secure America Now. "Home Page." http://www.secureamericanow.org Accessed on (5/30/2017).
204. Fenton, Jacob. 2013. "Among Hagel Attackers: Shadowy Group Run by Aide to Ron Lauder." https://sunlightfoundation.com/2013/01/31/group-tied-lauder-aide-attack-against-hagel/ Accessed on (6/11/2017).

CHAPTER 4

The Tactics Used

There are many ways to influence policymaking in a democracy and the proponents and opponents of the Iran nuclear deal used them all as they fought to have an impact on the outcome. This chapter will discuss the traditional methods and the new avenues that technology and social media have opened up.

Before doing that, it is important to consider the three types of groups that can try to influence government policy. They are professional lobbyists, members of an association and the general public or a subset of it.

Professional lobbyists in Washington number in the tens of thousands and are engaged in a multibillion-dollar industry. Measuring how many there are and how much money they make is difficult to determine since the definition of lobbyist is flexible. Lobbyists often call themselves that, but many of them prefer to describe what they do as strategic advice, public relations, legal services or under other euphemisms. Lobbyists for foreign governments are required by the Foreign Agents Registration Act to register with the Department of

Justice, but that law is rarely enforced. There are no barriers to entry to the lobbying profession and anyone can attempt it.

What professional lobbyists have in common, regardless of what they call themselves and their services, is that they will work to protect the interests of those with the ability to pay their fee. As will be discussed later in the chapter, in the same way there has never been a criminal who could afford a lawyer who could not find one, there has never been anyone so vile that they could not hire a lobbyist if they had the money.

The lobbyists trade on their contacts and expertise in conducting their business. The most popular profession for congressmen and their staff members when they decide to leave government is lobbying. The obvious conflicts of interest inherent in that revolving door prompted Congress to pass a law designed to bring about reform. But it was reform Washington style where the effect fails to match the stated purpose. As a 2016 article in *Politico* explained: "Of the 352 people who left Congress alive since the law took effect in January 2008, Politico found that almost half (47 percent) have joined the influence industry: 84 as registered lobbyists and 80 others as policy advisers, strategic consultants, trade association chiefs, corporate government relations executives, affiliates of agenda-driven research institutes and leaders of political action committees or pressure groups."[1]

The reform only made things worse as in the six-year period prior to enactment of the law only 43 percent of those who left found their way into the influence industry. The reason influence pedaling is such a popular second career is obvious. Congressmen can usually double or triple their $174,000 annual salary and, at times, increase it by a factor of ten or more. One study cited in a 2012 article in *The Nation* looked at the earnings of 12 congressmen turned lobbyists and found they had increased by 1452 percent.[2]

The former members of Congress are so well compensated because they can work the relationships built up during their years on Capitol Hill to gain access to lawmakers to argue on behalf of their clients. They use the knowledge acquired in government on the subject in question and the process of legislating to formulate arguments and to know to whom those arguments should be made. One study found that the income of former staff members who had become lobbyists saw their income decline significantly once the important congressmen they had worked for also left Congress. So, having or developing personal relationships with those in government is essential, but those relationships may not last and have to be constantly nurtured.

The members of associations join together to hire a professional staff to lobby on their behalf. For instance, the manufacturers of small electrical appliances have an association staffed by people who track whatever the government is doing that might affect its members. A proposed new safety regulation for blenders or microwave ovens will draw the association's attention and action. And as will be discussed, there is no limit to who can form an association, which is why there are so many of them in Washington.

Finally, there is the general public, or any subset of it. These are ordinary citizens who do not usually engage in efforts to influence government policy. For a group to do that successfully, it needs three and a half things—focus, intensity, resources and sometimes proximity.

A good example are Cuban Americans, especially those who came to the USA when Castro took power in 1959. Many of them were middle- and upper-class individuals who lost everything after the revolution. Their hatred of Castro was therefore understandable and something Ronald Reagan recognized and shared. While running for president, he went to Miami and gave speeches denouncing Communism and Castro. As a result, what had been a group with a slight majority registered as Democrats became one of the most reliable Republican voting blocks.

They were focused on Cuba policy and they were intensely interested in it. They were single-issue voters when Cuba policy was in play, and after they became successful economically in the States, they were willing to put their money where their passion was. They therefore delivered the two things that get anyone running for office is interested in—money and votes—in that order.

Because they were concentrated in Miami, they had another asset that is not essential to effectiveness but can help—proximity. Proximity enabled Cuban Americans to have major impact on the elections in the congressional districts where they were located most heavily. Any politicians elected from those districts had to make Cuba policy one of their most important issues.

Because of the focus, intensity, resources and proximity of Cuban Americans, the embargo against Cuba has remained in place for over half a century even though there has been little to show for it. And it is also why in even-numbered years, also known as election years, Republican presidents will often promise to tighten the embargo further.

Trump did not even wait that long. In June 2017, he announced the rollback of some of the steps taken by Obama to loosen the restrictions on travel and trade with Cuba. Predictably Trump called Obama's policy a "bad deal," but his new initiative did little more than reinstate more stringent limitations on travel to Cuba. Thus, Cuba remains the only country in the world to which Americans cannot freely travel due to their government's policy. One thing that Trump did not change was Obama's elimination of the preferred status which allowed any Cuban refugee who reached the USA to stay.³ Apparently, sticking with his anti-immigrant stance was more important than taking one more step to please Cuban Americans.

The key to being an effective lobby is therefore to hire a good lobbyist, form an association or to mobilize public opinion. The challenge of having an effect on public opinion is that most people do not have much knowledge about foreign affairs and generally feel unaffected by them.

For that reason, the common viewpoint for many years among those who studied the impact of public opinion on foreign policy was that it was uninformed and volatile and generally ignored by policymakers. One book on the subject concluded that public opinion constrained but did not set foreign policy.⁴ That book focused on four very prominent foreign issues, however—the Vietnam War, the Nicaraguan Contra funding controversy, the Persian Gulf War, and the Bosnia crisis.

The general public is only vaguely aware of less high-profile foreign policy issues. For instance, if the average person in the USA is asked about North Atlantic Treaty Organization, there is a generally positive response. A recent poll by the Pew Research Center showed six out of ten Americans had a favorable opinion of the security alliance.⁵ Even on NATO, however, there was a partisan divide—81 percent of liberals were supportive of the organization, while only 48 percent of conservatives were.

The poll also found that the positive liberal opinion had gone up 23 percentage points since 2016, while the conservative view was unchanged. The liberal uptick was no doubt in reaction to Trump's declarations that NATO was obsolete. Despite that increase in support, it does not seem likely that many Americans would be motivated to use their time, energy, money or votes solely because of their opinion on NATO.

One way to have an impact on policy is, therefore, to raise public awareness and also to energize individuals to become concerned enough to take action. That was the effort of many of the groups described in the previous chapter. Those opposed to the Iran nuclear agreement sought to mobilize evangelical Christians, Jews and others. Supporters of the deal sought to mobilize other Jews and Christians and pro-peace groups like the Quakers.

Successfully mobilizing that effort can influence the opinions of the policy makers. But, policy is made at different levels and those involved can be elected politicians, appointed officials or career bureaucrats. The importance and public profile of an issue can determine where on this spectrum the policy decision lands. The more the public, or particular constituencies, are aware of an issue, the more they can be effectively encouraged to work to move the decision making to a level where public pressure can be brought to bear.

If the issue can be linked to national security or other major foreign policy goals, the higher the level of attention it will receive and the more weight public opinion will have. The fight to get people to care enough about an issue to give their time and money to support efforts to affect the policy, truth is often the first casualty.

A good example is the Convention on the Rights of Persons with Disabilities. Created in 2006, it is a treaty that is modeled on US law to the extent that it would make current American standards for treatment of the disabled the international norm for all nations to follow.[6]

Like virtually every treaty, it is not self-enforcing. There are no world government agencies, black helicopters that don't show up on radar or an international police force that stands ready to compel compliance or impose penalties on those countries that do not adhere to it. This agreement can be characterized as a naming and shaming exercise that would identify those countries who fail to meet the accepted international standards and are not doing enough to correct that situation.

A total of 172 countries and the European Union have signed on to the treaty on the rights of the disabled. So, who would oppose a treaty that holds up American law for the treatment of the disabled as a standard to which other nations should aspire? Those who can be convinced that if the US Senate ratifies the treaty, the rights of parents and states will be infringed and it will be somehow used to promote abortion. The fact that all those arguments are nonsense did not deter the opponents of the agreement in the slightest.

There are in the District of Columbia almost as many associations as there are lawyers. In other words, there are a lot of them. Once established, those who work for the association have to justify their salaries by demonstrating that they are effective at protecting the interests of its members. In many cases, that means inventing threats to those interests where they don't exist and then claiming victory over those threats.

To ward off the nonexistent threat posed by Disabilities Convention, an association of those who educate their children themselves leapt into action. The president of the Homeschool Legal Defense Association sent out an action alert to 170,000 home-schooling parents to warn of the fictitious danger posed by the treaty and urged them to contact their senators to prevent the convention's ratification.[7] Politicians like former Republican senator Rick Santorum and organizations like the right-wing Heritage Foundation repeated and amplified the false narrative about the treaty's impact.

Among the many proponents of the convention were former Republican senator Bob Dole, who is disabled from wounds suffered in World War II, and over 700 groups representing business, veterans and disabled associations. That widely based endorsement of the treaty was not enough, however. When it came to the floor of the Senate for ratification in 2012, a number of Republican senators greeted Dole warmly as he sat in his wheelchair and encouraged their support for it. Enough of them then voted against its ratification so that it failed to secure the two-thirds of the Senate required.[8]

The opposition of the home schoolers, even though based on falsehoods, was intense enough to ensure the defeat of a treaty to which all but a handful of nations like North Korea and Libya adhere. That is because elected politicians, with the exception of a second-term president, care about nothing more than being reelected. They will, therefore, be most responsive on issues that improve their chances to do that by affecting money and votes.

When the number of voters is relatively small, the intensity of their opinion, if focused on a specific issue, can make up for being few in number. When it comes to arousing intensity, appeals to fear can be very effective. And it doesn't matter whether it is based on xenophobia, racism, a general distrust of government or a fear of international organizations.

Fearmongering is a big business in Washington. The prime example of this is the city's most powerful lobby—the National Rifle Association. Studies show there are somewhere between 88 and 112 guns for every 100 Americans. The country is the most heavily armed nation in history and has twice as many weapons per capita as that island of stability, Yemen, which comes in second. One might think that the individual right to bear arms, which the conservative majority on the Supreme Court discovered for the first time in the 2008 Heller decision, would be considered safe.

The problem is that guns don't wear out quickly. In order to keep gun manufacturers happy, the NRA has to constantly expand the opportunities for their use. That has meant opposing any limitations on assault rifles, guns in classrooms, courthouses and mental hospitals or even things like silencers and high-penetration ammunition. The latter item is mainly used for killing deer and police officers wearing bullet proof vests, but that has not stopped the NRA from arguing for its expanded use.[9]

One member of the NRA wrote an opinion article in the *Washington Post* bemoaning the organization's extreme positions that was titled "The NRA Is Pushing Policies That Gun Owners Like Me Don't Want."[10] He backed up his argument with citations from public opinion polls showing that the policies had very little popular support including among NRA members. He also pointed out that of the 76 directors of the NRA, only one is elected by its annual-dues paying members. The organization claims there are five million of those, but that is impossible to verify.

What the writer of the piece in the *Post* didn't understand is that the NRA is not interested in representing its rank-and-file members. It is interested in representing the big contributors to the organization, which means gun manufacturers and not gun owners. In other words, the NRA is like the major Jewish organizations that Peter Beinart described. Those who contribute the most money have the most influence.

And money matters since advocating for the ever-expanding presence of guns may not represent what most Americans want, but it does pay well. Wayne LaPierre, the CEO of the NRA made over $5 million in 2015.[11] While he may ignore the views of the vast majority, LaPierre is exploiting the fears of a small minority who are intensely opposed to any restriction on their right to bear arms.

The use of that fear, no matter how irrational, helps inflate the salaries of people like LaPierre and keeps politicians cowed. The fear factor has less impact on appointed officials as they worry about keeping the president happy and are less directly affected by or responsive to public opinion. Career bureaucrats are most concerned about their careers and their calculation of the national interest and even further removed from the political fray. The ways to influence them are therefore not identical to those used for who have to submit themselves to elections.

The key policymaker is the president and, if he is already committed to a course of action, the struggle will be a fight to win over those in Congress who are undecided and uncommitted. In the case of the Iran deal, reaching an agreement was one of President Obama's highest foreign policy priorities. Even before he became president, he maintained that the USA should be prepared to negotiate with adversaries like Iran. It was a position that his opponent in the contest to be the Democratic presidential candidate in 2008, Hillary Clinton, called naïve and unrealistic. But once he became president, he put that belief into practice. But, just being president is not enough to win a policy battle and Obama needed to ensure he had enough congressional support for the agreement to survive. That required using all his powers of persuasion and communication skills that he could muster.

In a long article in the *New York Times* in 2016, journalist David Samuels did a profile of Ben Rhodes, whose official title was deputy national security adviser for Strategic Communications. Samuels described Rhodes as more than just Obama's speechwriter and characterized him as one of the president's closest aides and his foreign policy guru.[12]

The article also asserted that Rhodes rewrote the rules of diplomacy for the digital age. He was said to have done that by successfully running the messaging campaign to protect the Iran deal from being overturned by Congress. Samuels described how Rhodes and, his assistant, Ned Price, would draw on their relationships with people outside government to accomplish that in the following passage:

> Price turns to his computer and begins tapping away at the administration's well-cultivated network of officials, talking heads, columnists and newspaper reporters, web jockeys and outside advocates who can tweet at critics and tweak their stories backed up by quotations from "senior White House officials" and "spokespeople." I watch the message bounce from Rhodes's brain to Price's keyboard to the three big briefing podiums—the White House, the State Department and the Pentagon—and across the Twitterverse, where it springs to life in dozens of insta-stories, which over the next five hours don formal dress for mainstream outlets. It's a tutorial in the making of a digital news microclimate—a storm that is easy to mistake these days for a fact of nature, but whose author is sitting next to me right now.

The article also describes how the White House created a "war room" where staffers from the White House, State Department, Treasury, the US Mission at the UN and the Pentagon were on hand to respond rapidly to any attacks on the deal, to put out the administration's arguments in favor of the agreement and support others who were doing the same.

When Samuels asked about "the onslaught of freshly minted experts cheerleading for the deal," Rhodes is said to have replied: "We created an echo chamber. They were saying things that validated what we had given them to say."[13] The article also points out Rhodes's contempt for many journalists by quoting him as saying: "All these newspapers used to have foreign bureaus. Now they don't. They call us to explain to them what's happening in Moscow and Cairo. Most of the outlets are reporting on world events from Washington. The average reporter we talk to is 27 years old, and their only reporting experience consists of being around political campaigns. That's a sea change. They literally know nothing."[14]

The profile was panned for the way it was written and how Samuels characterized his interaction with Rhodes.[15] It also left other reporters wondering how Rhodes could have been so candid and careless around a reporter like Samuels who opposed the nuclear agreement and had written an article making a case for Israel to bomb Iran.[16]

Aside from making Rhodes look both foolish and arrogant, the article also set off a firestorm in the right-wing echo chamber as critics of the deal pointed to it as proof of the administration's duplicity and dishonesty. They loudly asserted that a false and misleading narrative had been used to sell it.[17]

Predictably the white supremacists at Breitbart News put the worse possible spin on the Samuels article. One story, by Breitbart's Jerusalem bureau chief, said it demonstrated an "Orwellian public relations strategy" that "utilized so-called arms-control experts." He also claimed Samuels's article contained interviews "with scores of top Obama administration officials" even though Samuels said he talked to "two dozen former and current White House insiders."[18]

As far as untruths go, converting 24 former and current insiders into 40 or 60 or 80 who are now top officials is small potatoes. But it is consistent with the way Breitbart and other so-called news sites approach their work. They never let the facts get in the way of how they want to spin a story. Another example of that is the Washington Free Beacon. It is a collection of Internet trolls with a website who practice what one of them called "combat journalism." That can best be described as a total disregard for journalistic ethics combined with an attitude that is as aggressive and obnoxious as it is dishonest. While Beacon writers like to see themselves combatting the supposed leftist influence of publications like the *New York Times* and the *Washington Post*, they only add to the cacophony of disinformation that some people draw upon to support what they want to believe like the Comet Ping Pong shooter.[19]

The Beacon website was initially set up as the propaganda arm of the Center for American Progress, an organization funded by the billionaire Koch brothers and a host of far-right foundations.[20] One of the center's founders, when confronted with a Free Beacon story that was patently false, attempted to pass it off as an attempt at humor by saying: "We're true believers, but we're also troublemakers, and if you look at the work we do, a lot of it has a sense of humor. We get up every day and say, how do we cause trouble?"[21]

The Free Beacon predictably devotes much of its energy to climate change denial and fake terrorism stories with headlines like "300 Scientists Tell Trump to Leave the UN Climate Agreement"[22] and "Iran Military Sending Elite Fighters into U.S., Europe."[23] Another Beacon story claimed that Ben Rhodes was somehow responsible for the firing of Michael Flynn, Trump's first national security advisor, who lasted all of 24 days in that position before his lying about his connections to Russia caught up with him. Citing anonymous sources, the article claimed Rhodes was part of a plot to "handicap the Trump administration's efforts to disclose secret details of the nuclear deal with Iran that had been long hidden by the Obama administration."[24] The story quickly got repeated by other right-wing outlets, but there were never any "secret details" revealed by the Trump administration.

The Beacon is a good illustration how billionaires can bankroll a fake news site to affect the political process by relentless pushing whatever narrative they want. When stories appear in something like the Free Beacon, they are picked up and replayed by Fox News as they bounce around the right-wing echo chamber even though what the Beacon does bears so little semblance to journalism.

One story that appeared in the Beacon did have an element of truth, however, even though the details were wrong. It was about the efforts by Rhodes to work with pro-deal groups like the Ploughshares Fund to drum up support for the agreement.[25] In essence, the article described the setting up of the kind of echo chamber that Rhodes had bragged about in the Samuels article.

The outrage of the right and the indignation of the Breitbart writer focused on Rhodes and the pro-deal camp. A great deal of coordination and information sharing took place did take place. Information and arguments were shared as well as news about the progress of the negotiations. Discussions of messaging and which congressmen to lobby were also frequent.

This was not done in secret and it was not unique to one side. The reality is that both camps had their echo chambers to aid in organizing and energizing their supporters as they fought to protect or to scuttle the accord. And they both used many of the same tactics as well. Those can be direct or indirect. And they can be traditional or a more modern version enabled by technology.

Efforts to communicate with and influence policymakers directly take many forms and depend on the level of the policymaker. If it is an elected politician, one can write a president, senator or congressman. The expectation that a congressman will be responsive to his or her constituents is a feature of American democracy that is not common in other countries. In parliamentary democracies, the electoral prospects of a politician are dictated by the officials of his/her political party. An aspiring parliamentarian will have his/her success dictated by how high that person is on the party's list of candidates and that is determined by the leadership of the party.

One anecdote will demonstrate that point. In late 1996, Jorge Santistevan de Noriega became the first person to hold a recently created position in the Peruvian government. Called the *Defensor del Pueblo,* or defender of the people, the purpose of job, in essence, was to serve as a national ombudsman. Any Peruvian could come to his office seeking with a problem with the government including violations of human rights.

When Santistevan's office opened for business a long line of people quickly formed. They spilled out on to the sidewalk and down the block as they waited to see members of his staff. When asked by a visiting American diplomat whether all of them were there to report some abuse of human rights, Santistevan said no, many of them were there because they failed to receive their social security check or government pension.

The diplomat observed that citizens in the USA who wanted help with such difficulties would write their congressmen. Santistevan smiled and replied, "write your congressman does not translate into Spanish."

He was right. Peru, like many countries, has a system of proportional representation, where the members of Congress are elected off a list put together by their party. If their party gets half the votes, the top half of the party's list gets a seat. The first allegiance of those elected is therefore to their party. The idea of representing the region they are from or of constituent service is completely foreign. And they are not provided the funds to employ the staff necessary to provide such services.[26]

The system in the USA is quite different, with senators directly elected by voters in their state and congressmen by those in their district. They all have a budget to cover the cost of staff members and offices in their states and districts that are devoted to constituent service.

Because Americans expect a response from their congressmen, they frequently send them letters, petitions, e-mails and faxes and call their offices by phone. Both sides in the Iran fight did their best to encourage those who agreed with their view to contact the White House and Congress directly.

One organization claimed to have amassed the signatures of 400,000 progressives who were urging Democrats in Congress to support the agreement.[27] The petition was organized by CREDO Action, which describes itself as a social change network funded in part by CREDO Mobile, a mobile phone company.[28] CREDO Mobile charges a bit more than most other carriers for its phone service, but its selling point is that a substantial part of its revenue is given to organizations that are popular among progressives like Planned Parenthood and the American Civil Liberties Union.

CREDO was not the only one using telephones to rally support for the Iran deal. President Obama himself did so as well. In July 2015, he held a conference call with the Center for American Progress and dozens of other organizations. In the call, he exhorted them to encourage as many people as possible to contact Congress to express their support for the nuclear agreement.[29] Obama noted that AIPAC and other groups had spent $20 million on TV ads opposing the agreement and he added that some members of Congress that he had met with recently were "getting squishy because they're feeling the political heat."

One other way senators and congressmen can feel the heat is in their interactions with their constituents in town hall type meetings. Some groups opposed to the deal sent out the schedule for the town halls for 70 key members of Congress as a way to encourage people to attend them and forcefully make their views known to those legislators.

The Republican Jewish Coalition, for instance, put out an action alert to the 40,000 people on its e-mail list urging them to use that means to express their opposition to the Iran pact.[30] The online magazine *Politico* characterized this as copying the tactic used by Tea Party groups to intensify opposition to Obamacare in 2009. Ironically, as will be discussed in the last chapter, the same tactic was being used in 2017 by those who support Obamacare to pressure Congress not to repeal it.

Another way to make elected officials feel the heat is for organizations to reach out to anyone on their e-mail lists urging them to vote for or against a particular politician and to give or withhold campaign contributions. E-mail lists are valuable assets in such an effort and the success of advocacy organizations and political campaigns can depend on how effectively such lists are used.

E-mails lists are also an asset that can be sold as Cameroon Harris may have done with those that signed up to receive messages from his fake news site. If he did, he would not be alone in using a news site to profit in that way. Tucker Carlson, a Fox News personality, created a news website named the Daily Caller and also a tax-exempt entity called The Daily Caller News Foundation, which is a 501(c)(3) organization.

The foundation had revenue of just over $3 million in 2015.[31] It employed most of the 50 journalists that provide content to the for-profit Daily Caller website, an arrangement tax experts consulted by the *Washington Post* considered a violation of tax laws. The experts also felt there was no way the IRS would investigate given its experience with the controversy over its profiling Tea Party groups.[32] When asked about the questionable arrangement by a *Post* reporter, the response of Carlson's business partner was, "I'm not doing anything anyone else can't do."[33]

Carlson's operation profited from its e-mail list by taking the addresses of those that signed up on the Daily Caller website and selling it to others interested in a list of conservatives. One of those that bought the list and paid an estimated $150,000 for it was the Trump for president campaign.[34]

E-mail lists can be used to selectively target individuals more likely to contribute to a particular cause. Another way to raise funds is to pay special attention to people who are known to be big donors. They receive individual appeals and are referred to as grass tops instead of grassroots. The theory being that convincing one ten-thousand-dollar donor is easier than influencing a thousand ten-dollar donors. As any congressman knows, one call to a big donor is much more efficient than contacting many small ones. Another difference is the bigger the donation, the more the donor respects in return as Betsy DeVos pointed out.

While money and votes matter most, there are other ways to help elected officials. Groups on both side of the Iran debate provided talking points, message guidance, information and arguments for or against the agreement. This assistance is most effective when personal and directed. Like lobbyists for corporate interests, those who work in Washington advocating for foreign policy issues develop close relationships with congressional staffers as well as the members of Congress. Those personal connections help ensure that the material developed will be received and used.

In addition, the relationships help define who is worth lobbying. The vast majority of congressmen and senators had their minds made up well before the ink was dry on the Iran deal. Every Republican, to a man and woman, opposed the deal. It may have reflected a different view of Iran and the possibilities of diplomacy, but there can be little doubt that it was also a reflection of overall Republican strategy. Throughout the Obama administration, Republicans opposed virtually everything he attempted to do. According to one writer in *Politico*, the strategy generally worked very well for them even though it meant Washington accomplished very little other than creating gridlock on nearly every issue.[35]

For the most part, Democrats automatically supported the President, but not all of them. The key to the battle over the Iran deal was therefore identifying those Democrats who might potentially desert the president and trying to get them to oppose the deal.

In Congress, there are members who are designated as the assistant leader for their party. Known also as the party whip, it is the job of that member to ensure party discipline is maintained on important issues by whipping up support for the party's stance. They also have to know an exact count of the votes for and against each piece of legislation, especially those party members who might not vote the right way.

People outside of Congress, who engage in the business of influencing it, also do whip counts of how congressmen are going to vote in order to know who to target and who can be ignored. Those who are targeted, like the 70 key congressmen identified by the Republican Jewish Coalition, can expect to be subjected to all the direct and indirect methods that can be brought to bear on them.

Congressmen and their staffs were inundated by more than e-mails, phone calls and faxes regarding the Iran deal. Representatives of both sides of the Iran debate also went in person to their offices to meet with as many of them as they could see to make their case. That often required relying on personal relationships in order to secure an appointment, just as lobbyists for corporate interests often do.

Meeting with congressional staffers has become more difficult in recent years as there are fewer of them. A number of scholars and other observers have noted that around 1980, the number of people working for Congress peaked.[36] Since then it has declined not only in absolute terms, but has been accompanied by a shift from Washington-based staff working on policy to more people doing constituent service in congressional district offices.[37] This trend applies not only to those working directly for congressmen and senators, but those in supporting organizations. The Government Accountability Office and the Congressional Research Service, both vital sources of nonpartisan and unbiased program and policy analysis, have 20 percent fewer people working for them than they did in 1979.[38]

Some have described this as a result of the decline of committee system, which happened when the seniority system for choosing the chairmen was eliminated. Then in 1995, Republicans in Congress implemented their "Contract with America."[39] That plan called for the abolishing of one-third of the committee staff positions, some 600 jobs, and term limits on the time that one could serve as committee and subcommittee chairmen. Those steps resulted in a few party leaders being able to impose discipline on their members, which often ensures that partisan politics comes before the national interest.

The result of the staff reductions and consolidation of power has been to downsize the ability of Congress to do its own policy analysis and to make partisan politics an even bigger factor than before. It is a major cause of the dysfunction of Congress, its low standing in the polls and its inability to forge policies that serve the national interest or that respond to the challenges posed by globalization and other problems.

As the ability of Congress to do its job has diminished, there has been a corresponding rise in the number and power of lobbyists working for special interests. Hiring a lobbyist has long been a favorite way to acquire influence in Washington. Al Kamen, who from 1993 to 2015 wrote a column in the *Washington Post* about politics called "In the Loop," once observed that to hire a lobbyist in Washington all one needed was a half a million bucks and a telephone.[40] That observation indicates why there has never been a dictator so vile and corrupt that no one would represent him as a lobbyist. For the right retainer, there are always many who will.

One example of a corrupt and oppressive political leader that has no trouble buying representation in Washington is President Teodoro Obiang of Equatorial Guinea. Because his country is awash in oil, it has a per capita gross domestic product on a par with Portugal. But the vast majority of his people live in abject poverty because the president and his family and friends steal most of the revenue from oil and squander much of it abroad on luxury items that only billionaires can afford.

The president's son, for instance, had a fleet of sports cars that cost millions of dollars each and mansions in Europe and yachts that were bought for hundreds of millions of dollars apiece.[41] That kind of conspicuous corruption is no bar to public service in Equatorial Guinea. The son served for years as agriculture minister, was named second vice president by his father in 2012 and first vice president and thus, his father's probable successor, in 2016.

Despite a level of criminality that would embarrass a Russian oligarch, the importance of oil and the money it generated bought Obiang entrance to the Obama White House on several occasions. It also attracted the fawning attention of energy company executives like the then Exxon CEO, and now Secretary of State, Rex Tillerson. At his confirmation hearings for his new job, Tillerson professed to have "no direct knowledge" of his company's helping to enable Obiang's corruption and would not even say the name of the country.[42]

Obiang was able to gain access to the president and make the secretary of state suffer from amnesia by using his oil money for more than cars, houses and yachts. Among those whose services he employed was Cassidy and Associates, which is one of the most successful lobbying firms in Washington. To help improve Obiang's image, Cassidy contracted with a public relations company called Qorvis. According to its filing under the Foreign Agents Registration Act,[43] Qorvis was paid to provide Cassidy with the following services to help Washington ignore the Obiang regime's reputation:

Ongoing media engagement and message development, including but not limited, to:

- Program management and coverage analytics
- Draft documents, statements, and media releases as needed
- Proactive media relations engagement strategy
- Message development and refinement
- Translation services as needed
- Daily media tracking and reporting
- Manage and update website content
- Provide a fortnightly status report on activities and undertaken
- Letters and speeches as needed
- Online content generation and management
  - YouTube
  - Facebook
  - Twitter
  - Wiki
  - Blogs

The range of services that lobbyists provide to any corrupt dictator with a checkbook can be used by any group battling for public opinion to support particular foreign policy issues. All the actors, think tanks, nonprofit associations, religious groups, advocacy organizations and others used media engagement and message development in its various forms to influence the debate over the Iran nuclear deal.

In addition to acting like lobbyists, another technique used by both sides of the Iran debate was to engage the media by working closely with journalists. For a subject as technical as the nuclear agreement, most of the journalists were as clueless as Rhodes suggested and briefing them became an important objective for both sides in the debate.

Journalists employed by media outlets friendly to one side or the other became the place to go to suggest stories, provide talking points and aim messaging efforts. Another element of the struggle was to react immediately whenever a story appeared by journalists that took the view of the other side and to rally those who could support a counter-narrative. After the Samuels article appeared, a number of experts pushed back. For instance, one expert at the Brookings Institution wrote that Samuels never really made a case for his central thesis that the Obama administration had put out a false narrative.[44]

Another tactic used by both sides was to put together a list of those who would appear to be able to speak with authority on the agreement. Getting the opinion of these "validators" was important to demonstrate the opinion of experts to the general public. Anyone recognized as having experience even vaguely related to the nuclear agreement were brought into the fight. Retired diplomats and generals, arms control experts, and those with supposed moral authority including rabbis, bishops and Christian leaders weighed in for or against the deal.

The involvement of retired generals and admirals as endorsers of candidates or of validators of highly politicized positions is often controversial. Some argue that to play such roles risks politicizing the military in a dangerous way.[45] That did not stop three dozen, retired senior officers from publishing a letter in favor of the deal. The anti-deal camp felt it had to respond in kind and generated a letter that had the signatures of nearly 200 former generals and admirals opposed to the deal.[46] The argument of the second group was not strengthened by the inclusion of two criminals from the Iran-Contra affair, Vice Admiral John Poindexter and Major General Richard Secord.

Because of the threat that Iran poses to Israel, rabbis were seen as important validators, but like the generals, they came down on both sides of the deal. A letter signed by 340 of them was sent to Congress supporting it.[47] Over 840 rabbis added their names to a petition to Congress opposing the agreement.[48]

A number of arms control experts went on the record praising the accord.[49] When the journal *Foreign Affairs* polled a group of 52 experts as to whether Congress should approve the deal, 37 said yes, 11 said no and 4 described themselves as neutral. Among the no votes was that of Elliot Abrams, another Iran Contra criminal who is now a fellow at the Council on Foreign Relations.[50] Former American and Israeli government, military and intelligence officials were encouraged to take a position and many did. Several prominent figures like Colin Powell and Brent Scowcroft came out endorsing the deal.[51]

The problem with validators is that both sides can often produce those with titles and experience that sound impressive even if it means enlisting the support of some with past felony charges for lying about their government activities on their resumes. Invalidating the validators by coming up with those who endorse the opposite side is therefore another required strategy.

As the armies of pro and anti-deal advocates engaged in the fight over the agreement, there were, as in any war, those who had the potential to become collateral damage. Those who opposed the agreement saw one way to undermine it was to minimize the economic benefit that Iran expected in exchange for the limitations placed on its nuclear program. So they set about trying to name, shame and intimidate any company thinking of doing business in Iran.

Officials of the Obama administration attempted to ensure that Iran did see the benefits provided by the agreement as without them there was little incentive for Iran to comply with it. U.S. officials undertook a roadshow to travel around the world explaining the sanctions that remained and to ensure that companies understood what kind of business they could legally engage in with Iran following the signing of the agreement.[52] The administration officials were also advising foreign companies on legal ways to do things that American companies were prohibited from doing. According to an article in the *Financial Times*:

> Although the Obama administration insists that Iran will continue to be barred from the US financial system, US officials are looking at ways that would allow non-US banks to use dollars at some stage in a transaction with Iran as long as the final deal was not in US dollars or involve American banks. It is also examining ways to provide more assurance to non-American insurance companies about what sort of transactions with Iran are legitimate.[53]

Deal opponents were, not surprisingly, doing their best to work the other side of the argument by discouraging companies from doing business with Iran. The group United Against a Nuclear Iran sent letters to hundreds of firms insisting that they "think twice about investing in Iran."[54]

The letters were reported to be lengthy, biting in tone and specific to the company in question. UANI also took out a full-page ad in the *Financial Times* warning companies that the "severe legal, financial and reputational risks associated with Iran business will remain for the foreseeable future."[55] The ad was signed by dozens of those associated with UANI and reads like a list of people from the George W. Bush administration and right-wing think tanks many of whom were advocates for the 2003 invasion of Iraq.

UANI did not just issue ominous warnings to companies that were considering doing business with Iran. It publicly named them. In one case, the naming and shaming effort provoked a legal response. Victor Restis, a billionaire Greek businessman, sued for defamation after he was called out by UANI. Restis was unable to testify at the trial because he was under criminal investigation for unrelated offenses in Greece and could not leave that country. Those charges were subsequently dropped when the Greek Supreme Court decided the activities of Restis had been standard business practice and were therefore not illegal.[56]

The case was particularly noteworthy because of the actions of Obama's Justice Department. As the *New York Times* described it: "The lawsuit has taken on larger importance as it threatens to reveal government secrets. It also could make public the inner workings of United Against Nuclear Iran, which is run by former United States government officials, has lobbied for tough sanctions against Iran and has helped write legislation on Capitol Hill. The Obama administration has temporarily blocked release of the group's internal documents, including its emails and donor lists, saying the records are likely to contain law enforcement secrets."[57]

A number of groups including the American Civil Liberties Union, the Center for Constitutional Rights and the Electronic Frontier Foundation filed a friend of the court brief, even though those declarations are usually made only once a verdict is reached and the case appealed. The organizations expressed their concern about the case by pointing out: "Never before has the government sought dismissal of a suit between private parties on state secrets grounds without providing the parties and the public any information about the government's interest in the case. It is hard to see why, unlike in every other state secrets case in history, meaningful public disclosure to the parties is not possible in this case."[58]

Despite the concerns of the ACLU and others, the judge in the case accepted the government's argument. The suit brought by Restis against UANI was dismissed and the nature of the state secrets was never revealed. There was speculation that secret intelligence obtained from Israel could have been involved because, Meir Dagan, the former head of Israel's intelligence service Mossad, is on UANI's board.[59] In any event, the decision set a precedent that the government can intervene in a suit between two private parties and get it dismissed without ever having to publicly explain why beyond a vague assertion that national security was somehow involved.

Why Obama's Justice Department would protect a group bent on destroying Obama's most significant foreign policy achievement remains a mystery. One possible explanation is that UANI obtained its information on Restis from another country and the U.S. government did not want to embarrass that ally. If that were the case, it would mean a private group of largely former government officials was working with a supposed friendly nation to undermine American foreign policy.

Another way to undermine foreign policy is to make it incoherent and inconsistent by allowing different levels of government to make their own. Opponents of the deal tried to accomplish that by encouraging state and municipal governments to pass their own sanctions against Iran. Normally, Washington would oppose such efforts, but the Republican majorities in the House and the Senate chose instead to encourage them.[60]

Senate Concurrent Resolution 26,[61] for instance, noted that the Comprehensive Iran Sanctions, Accountability, and Divestment Act of 2010 stated that "It is the sense of Congress that the United States should support the decision of any State or local government that for moral, prudential, or reputational reasons divests from, or prohibits the investment of assets of the State or local government in, a person that engages in investment activities in the energy sector of Iran, as long as Iran is subject to economic sanctions imposed by the United States."

The resolution also noted that the 2010 act prohibited such measures from preemption by the federal government and that 30 states and the District of Columbia had enacted divestment legislation or policies against Iran and that 11 states had enacted prohibitions against awarding state or local government contracts to companies or financial institutions that do business with Iran.

The resolution added the ridiculous assertion that "such laws and regulations in no way interfere with the conduct of United States foreign policy." If such laws and regulations had no effect, what would be the point of encouraging them? And if they do have an effect, how can it not interfere with what the federal government is trying to do? Perhaps, it was all just for theatrical purposes as the bill was referred to the Senate Foreign Relations Committee and got no further.

Another bit of congressional theater are the hearings that are held that bring in a panel of experts to give testimony on a subject. Because the party in the majority can largely control who is on the panel, the purpose of the hearing is often not to shed light on the subject. It is to give the spotlight to a particular point of view. Since the Republicans are in the majority and it is the anti-deal political party, it is no surprise that according to *The Nation*, "People associated with groups taking a hard line on Iran sanctions accounted for twenty-two of the thirty-six testimonies solicited by House and Senate committees."[62]

In addition to hearings mentioned in the last chapter, another example was a hearing held by the House Committee on Oversight and Government Reform, chaired by Representative Jason Chaffetz. It was held less than two weeks after the Samuels article on Ben Rhodes appeared in the *New York Times* and its subject was "White House Narratives on the Iran Nuclear Deal."[63] The witnesses were all from right-wing organizations that opposed the deal—the American Enterprise Institute, the Hudson Institute and the Foundation for the Defense of Democracies.

The representative of the Foundation was John Hannah who was Dick Cheney's foreign policy advisor. He focused his testimony on the assertion by Samuels in the article that a successful agreement "would create the space for America to disentangle itself from its established system of alliances with countries like Saudi Arabia, Egypt, Israel and Turkey" and allow the administration to begin a large-scale disengagement from the Middle East.[64] Hannah was not a fan of any such supposed disengagement, real or imagined. As a key aide to Cheney, he had a prominent role in gathering the faulty intelligence and shaping the narrative that led to the invasion of Iraq.[65]

Beyond intimidating companies, congressional theater and dueling narratives, the two sides of the Iran debate used both the traditional and new forms of media to get their messages. In addition to briefing friendly reporters in order to make the argument in the news section of media outlets, the battle was waged on the editorial pages. Editorial boards were provided material and quotes to assist writing statements of their views on the deal. Many of the validators and other experts placed articles they had written on the opinion pages by working their relationships with those same editors.

While some might think that the opinion pages of a newspaper are a blank space waiting to be filled by brilliant submissions, that is not the case. After the normal columnists and the paper's own editorial writers have had their say, there is little space left for outside voices. And to fill that space, the editors will often decide what they want said and who should say it. They will then commission a piece to be written. Frequently articles are given space for no more reason than there is a personal relationship between the contributor and the editor or a desire to have one with the contributor. A very prominent person can get something printed because the editors will assume that people will read the article just because of that person's reputation. And readership can matter more than objectivity or insightful analysis.

Besides placing an opinion piece in a newspaper, another method of getting a point of view published is a letter to the editor. Those are shorter, but instead of being the viewpoint of one expert, they can appear to be more generally representative of what the paper's readers are thinking. Pro-deal groups encouraged the use of all these methods and tracked the number of editorials, opinion articles and letters to the editor carefully since those statistics were a good measure of how successful they were at making their arguments heard.

Those with a desire to take a stand on the Iran deal and unable to make the case in the 700 to 1000-word format of an opinion article can always write a book. Michael Oren, the former Israeli ambassador in Washington did just that. He said he wrote the book to stop the Iran deal and timed its release for June 2015 just as the negotiations were in their crucial final stage.[66] In the book, Oren faulted Obama for the strains in the US-Israel relationship and said any mistakes Israel had made were "honest." Apparently, Oren thinks that his boss, Prime Minister Netanyahu had no responsibility for the strains.

Oren labeled the sanctions relief offered to Iran a "signing bonus." While Oren failed in his attempt to derail the deal, he did get significant free publicity for his book. In it he admittedly engages in some "armchair psychoanalyzing." He speculates that Obama surrounded himself with powerful women because of being reared by his mother and grandmother and suggests his rejection by two Muslim father figures informed his outreach to Islam.[67]

An anti-deal book that came out after the agreement was concluded was written by Jay Solomon, the chief foreign affairs correspondent for the *Wall Street Journal*. Solomon describes Obama's interest in the Iran deal as "obsessive" and claims the agreement "ranks among the riskiest diplomatic bets made by an American president in modern U.S. history."[68] Solomon then goes on to argue that it is a losing bet. Solomon was abruptly fired by the *Journal* in June 2017 when an Associated Press story revealed his involvement with a shadowy, Iranian-born, businessman who was an arms merchant and had been involved in the Iran-Contra scandal.[69]

Another technique used by both sides of the Iran debate to attract attention to their point of view was to exploit the new methods provided by technology. In other words, they utilized social media and its ever-changing platforms to the fullest extent.

A person's age can determine how that person gets information, which can affect the conclusions they draw from that information. The younger a person is, the more likely he or she is to get information through Facebook and other online sources. Beyond information, a point of view can be spread and amplified via social media and opposite points of view attacked.

E-mails for action alerts, retweeting to reinforce and distribute an argument more widely, placing videos on YouTube, creating websites with background information and setting up social media war rooms to respond instantly on an issue that is being debated at that moment are just a few of the ways that technology was used by both sides in the Iran debate to disseminate information, organize and energize people.

Those means did not exist a few years ago and they will continue to evolve and multiply as technology changes and new platforms appear and old ones disappear. They also create new opportunities for those who can exploit them. For instance as mentioned in the last chapter, ReThink Media was founded in 2008 to help show progressive organizations how to navigate and utilize the new technologies. It describes itself as "a unique, non-profit organization focused on building the communications capacity of nonprofit think tanks, experts, and advocacy groups working toward a more constructive US foreign and national security policy, the protection of human and civil rights, and strengthening our democracy."[70]

Organizations like ReThink can help provide guidance to groups that are trying to have an influence on policy and help them get their message out more effectively. They offer tips on organizing in the digital age like how to test run messaging, the best software to use, how to employ mobile phones to fund-raise, ways to make phone calls to supporters more productive, how asking people to share articles can spread the word, how to drive traffic to a website and thereby increase that site's revenue from advertising, creating e-mail lists to raise funds, staying in contact continuously with those who respond, using postscripts in e-mails to more effectively engage the reader and more.

Another technique is to create surveys to put out via e-mail or to place on websites to encourage people to offer their views on an issue. These are done not so much because of any interest in the opinions expressed as they are to identify supporters for fund-raising and mobilization. It is not unlike, when Cameron Harris put on his fabricated story on his fake news website and offered people the opportunity to sign up for future stories about Clinton's imaginary schemes to steal the election. Or when Tucker Carlson's organization gathered e-mail addresses from the Daily Caller website to enable them to be sold to the Trump campaign. The thousands of names collected provided a valuable asset for anyone wanting to make money on conspiracy theories or sell the lists to candidates.

Opinion polls, where the opinions do matter, were also another tool in the battle over the deal. Both sides in the Iran debate paid for polls that were designed to show the general public, or key parts of it, favored their position. The effort was obviously to show that the weight of public opinion favored their point of view and therefore should be taken into consideration by Congress and other policymakers.

In polling, as with pipers, whoever pays gets to call the tune. The questions can be structured in a way to elicit the desired response—a tactic known as push polling. As described in the last chapter, one anti-deal group, Secure America Now, is well known for using that strategy.[71] Even the name of the organization implies that America is insecure and that all that is necessary to change that is to follow the organization's advice.

One of the key audiences in the Iran debate was American Jews. J Street, the pro-peace and pro-Israel group, had a poll done that showed 84 percent of American Jews strongly or somewhat strongly favored an agreement with Iran. J Street asked whether they would support the easing of economic sanctions in return for an agreement that limited Iran's nuclear program to peaceful purposes and provided for inspection of its nuclear facilities.[72]

Another poll, commissioned by the LA *Jewish Journal*, was conducted in July 2015 just a few days after the deal was announced.[73] It surveyed both Jews and the general population and found that Jewish Americans were far more informed and opinionated when it came to the agreement. Among the Jewish respondents, 49 percent favored the deal, while 31 percent opposed it. For the public as a whole, only 28 percent supported it, 24 percent opposed it and the remaining 48 percent "didn't know enough to say."

ReThink Media did an analysis of 17 polls by 11 polling firms that were conducted between September 2013 and January 2015 and were publicly available. It aggregated the results of those polls and came to six major conclusions[74]:

1. Americans saw Iran as unfriendly and many see it as an enemy.
2. Americans nevertheless consistently favored diplomatic negotiations over military intervention.
3. Americans also consistently supported the interim agreement and showed no less support when it came to the final agreement.
4. Americans did not trust Iran and worried that its leaders are not negotiating in good faith. The verifiability of any final agreement therefore would be crucial for garnering public support.
5. Partisan differences on Iran were most prominent with respect to perceptions of the threat and the "best" approach, and less prominent when it came to support for diplomacy.
6. Few Americans followed the negotiations closely. Pollsters did not emphasize the verification processes

built into the agreement, and often tried to force opinions from an uninformed public—all contributing to a strong partisan effect.

It is not surprising, given the highly technical nature of the talks, that the general public was not following the negotiations closely. It is also no surprise that some of the pollsters tried to shape the responses of those being polled. The challenge for the anti-deal group was to make Iran as big a threat as possible by stressing its support for terrorism, missile development program and lack of trustworthiness. Those on the opposite side of the argument had to push the idea that the agreement was verifiable and the only realistic alternative to another war.

In making those arguments, both sides had to raise funds as well as awareness and they used every method they could to do so. Those methods included the more traditional means of influencing public opinion and also utilized the new ones provided by technology and social media. Appeals to partisan politics and occasional disregard for the truth were all elements in the struggle over the deal. But the fact that the agreement was successfully concluded did not mean that the battle was over. The next and final chapter will discuss where that battle might lead and the implications of the debate more generally for the ability of Washington to fashion a foreign policy that responds to the national interests and the challenges that should be faced in today's world.

NOTES

1. Arnsdorf, Isaac. 2016, July 3. "The Lobbying Reform That Enriched Congress." *Politico.*, http://www.politico.com/story/2016/06/the-lobbying-reform-that-enriched-congress-224849 Accessed on (6/28/2017).

2. Fang, Lee. 2012, March 14. "When a Congressman Becomes a Lobbyist, He Gets a 1,452 Percent Raise (on Average)." *The Nation*.https://www.thenation.com/article/when-congressman-becomes-lobbyist-he-gets-1452-percent-raise-average/ Accessed on (6/28/2017).
3. Somin, Ilya. 2017, June 18. "The Good, Bad and Ugly of Trump's New Cuba Policy." *Washington Post*. https://www.washingtonpost.com/news/volokh-conspiracy/wp/2017/06/18/the-good-bad-and-ugly-of-trumps-new-cuba-policy Accessed on (6/20/2017).
4. Sobel, Richard. 2001. "The Impact of Public Opinion on U.S. Foreign Policy." Oxford University Press. https://global.oup.com/ushe/product/the-impact-of-public-opinion-on-us-foreign-policy-since-vietnam-9780195105285?cc=us&lang=en& Accessed on (6/20/2017).
5. Stokes, Bruce. 2017. "NATO's Image Improves on Both Sides of Atlantic." Pew Research Center. http://www.pewglobal.org/2017/05/23/natos-image-improves-on-both-sides-of-atlantic/ Accessed on (6/20/2017).
6. United Nations. 2017. "Convention on the Rights of Persons with Disabilities." https://www.un.org/development/desa/disabilities/convention-on-the-rights-of-persons-with-disabilities.html Accessed on (6/20/2017).
7. Severns, Maggie. 2014. "Bob Dole Battles Home-Schoolers." *Politico*. http://www.politico.com/story/2014/07/bob-dole-home-school-legal-defense-109201 Accessed on (6/20/2017).
8. Steinhauer, Jennifer. 2012. "Dole Appears, but G.O.P. Rejects a Disabilities Treaty." *New York Times*. http://www.nytimes.com/2012/12/05/us/despite-doles-wish-gop-rejects-disabilities-treaty.html Accessed on (6/20/2017).
9. Editorial. 2015, March 12. "Ban the 'Cop Killer' Bullets." *Lost Angeles Times*. http://www.latimes.com/opinion/editorials/la-ed-ammo-atf-delays-ban-on-armor-piercing-bullets-20150312-story.html Accessed on (6/25/2017).

10. Valentine, Matt. 2017, June 16. "The NRA Is Pushing Policies That Gun Owners Like Me Don't Want." *Washington Post*. https://www.washingtonpost.com/outlook/how-the-nra-conquered-washington-and-abandoned-gun-owners-like-me/2017/06/16/e9374238-51e8-11e7-91eb-9611861a988f_story.html?utm_term=.84ce1974dbee Accessed on (6/25/2017).
11. Zezima, Katie. 2017, February 9. "NRA Chief Executive Received Nearly $4 Million Retirement Payout in 2015." *Washington Post*. https://www.washingtonpost.com/news/post-nation/wp/2017/02/09/nra-chief-executive-received-nearly-4-million-retirement-payout-in-2015/?utm_term=.a94aaabe161d Accessed on (6/24/2017).
12. Samuels, David. 2016. "The Aspiring Novelist Who Became Obama's Foreign Policy Guru." https://www.nytimes.com/2016/05/08/magazine/the-aspiring-novelist-who-became-obamas-foreign-policy-guru.html Accessed on (6/20/2017).
13. Ibid.
14. Ibid.
15. Lozado, Carlos. 2016. "Why the Ben Rhodes Profile in the New York Times Magazine Is Just Gross." *New York Times*. https://www.washingtonpost.com/news/book-party/wp/2016/05/06/why-the-ben-rhodes-profile-in-the-new-york-times-magazine-is-just-gross/?utm_term=.2d7105c2f8e9 Accessed on (6/20/2017).
16. Kaplan, Fred. 2016. "Ben Rhodes Needs Some Fresh Air." *Slate*. http://www.slate.com/articles/news_and_politics/war_stories/2016/05/how_to_read_david_samuels_profile_of_obama_foreign_policy_aide_ben_rhodes.html Accessed on (6/20/2017).
17. Klein, Aaron. 2016. "NY Times: White House Used Often Misleading False Narrative to Sell Iran Deal to Clueless Reporters." Breitbart. http://www.breitbart.com/jerusalem/2016/05/06/ny-times-white-house-used-often-misleading-false-narrative-sell-iran-deal-clueless-reporters/ Accessed on (6/20/2017).

18. Klein, Aaron. 2016. "NY Times: White House Used Often Misleading False Narrative to Sell Iran Deal to Clueless Reporters." Breitbart. http://www.breitbart.com/jerusalem/2016/05/06/ny-times-white-house-used-often-misleading-false-narrative-sell-iran-deal-clueless-reporters/ Accessed on (6/20/2017).
19. Right Web. 2013. "Washington Free Beacon." http://rightweb.irc-online.org/profile/washington_free_beacon/ Accessed on (6/20/2017).
20. Conservative Transparency. 2017. "Center for American Progress." http://conservativetransparency.org/recipient/center-for-american-progress/ Accessed on (6/20/2017).
21. Rutenberg, Jim. 2013. "A Conservative Provocateur, Using a Blowtorch and His Pen." *New York Times*. http://www.nytimes.com/2013/02/24/us/politics/michael-goldfarb-gleeful-provocateur-at-intersection-of-many-worlds.html?pagewanted=all Accessed on (6/20/2017).
22. Dorman, Sam. 2017. "300 Scientists Tell Trump to Leave UN Climate Agreement." The Free Beacon. http://freebeacon.com/issues/300-scientists-tell-trump-to-leave-un-climate-agreement/ Accessed on (6/20/2017).
23. Kredo, Adam. 2016. "Military Leader: Iran Sending Elite Fighters into U.S., Europe." The Free Beacon. http://freebeacon.com/national-security/iranian-military-sending-elite-forces-u-s-europe/ Accessed on (6/20/2017).
24. Holt, Jared. 2017. "Right-Wing Media's Shadow Government Conspiracy Theory: Ben Rhodes Edition." Media Matters. https://www.mediamatters.org/research/2017/02/16/right-wing-media-s-shadow-government-conspiracy-theory-ben-rhodes-edition/215368 Accessed on (6/20/2017).
25. Kredo, Adam. 2015. "White House Officials Plot Ways to Press Lawmakers into Supporting Iran Deal." The Free Beacon. http://freebeacon.com/national-security/white-house-officials-plot-ways-to-pressure-lawmakers-into-supporting-iran-deal/ Accessed on (6/20/2017).
26. Author interview with Santistevan in Lima in 1996.

27. Malitz, Zack. 2015. "400,000 Signatures Against War with Iran." *Daily Kos.* http://www.dailykos.com/story/2015/07/30/1407390/-400-000-signatures-against-war-with-Iran Accessed on (6/20/2017).
28. Credo Action. 2017. https://credoaction.com Accessed on (6/20/2017).
29. Edwards, Julia. 2015. "Obama Urges Supporters to Lobby for Iran Deal." Reuters. http://www.reuters.com/article/us-iran-nuclear-obama-idUSKCN0Q5038201507 31 Accessed on (6/20/ 2017).
30. Toosi, Nahal. 2015. "Iran Deal Opponents Steal Tactic from Obamacare Fight." *Politico.* http://www.politico.com/story/2015/07/iran-deal-opponents-tactic-obamacare-fight-120486 Accessed on (6/20/2017).
31. Foundation Center. 2016. "Form 990: Daily Caller News Foundation." http://990s.foundationcenter.org/990_pdf_archive/452/452922471/452922471_201512_990.pdf Accessed on (6/20/2017).
32. Borchers, Callum. 2017. "Charity Doubles as a Profit Stream at the Daily Caller News Foundation." *Washington Post.* https://www.washingtonpost.com/news/the-fix/wp/2017/06/02/charity-doubles-as-a-profit-stream-at-the-daily-caller-news-foundation/?utm_term=.bcd558c48ee9 Accessed on (6/20/2017).
33. Ibid.
34. Sloan, Calvin. 2017. "Exposed: Tucker Carlson, His "Charity," and the Trump Campaign Cash He Didn't Tell Fox Viewers About." Exposed by CMD. http://www.exposedbycmd.org/tucker-carlson Accessed on (6/20/2017).
35. Grunwald, Michael. 2016. "The Victory of No." *Politico.* http://www.politico.com/magazine/story/2016/12/republican-party-obstructionism-victory-trump-214498 Accessed on (6/20/2017).
36. Drutman, Lee and Steven Teles. 2015. "Why Congress Relies on Lobbyists Instead of Thinking for Itself." *The Atlantic.*

http://www.theatlantic.com/politics/archive/2015/03/when-congress-cant-think-for-itself-it-turns-to-lobbyists/387295/ Accessed on (6/20/2017).
37. LaPira, Tim and Herschel Thomas. 2016. "So What If Congressional Staff Levels Are Declining?" Legislative Branch Capacity Working Group. http://www.legbranch.com/theblog/2016/6/27/so-what-if-congressional-staff-levels-are-declining Accessed on (6/20/2017).
38. Drutman and Teles, op. cit.
39. Wolfensberger, Don. 2014. "The New Congressional Staff: Politics at the Expense of Policy." Brookings. https://www.brookings.edu/blog/fixgov/2014/03/21/the-new-congressional-staff-politics-at-the-expense-of-policy/ Accessed on (6/20/2017).
40. Al Kamen. 2005. "Lobbyist to Put in a Good Word for Sudan." *Washington Post*.
41. Burke, Jason. 2017. "French Trial Reveals Vast Wealth of Equatorial Guinean President's Son." *Guardian*. https://www.theguardian.com/world/2017/jan/02/french-trial-teodorin-obiang-wealth-equatorial-guinea Accessed on (6/20/2017).
42. Alleante, Tutu. 2017. "How Our Incoming Secretary of State Helped to Enrich Africa's Nastiest Dictatorship." *Washington Post*. https://www.washingtonpost.com/news/global-opinions/wp/2017/02/01/how-our-incoming-secretary-of-state-helped-to-enrich-africas-nastiest-dictatorship/?utm_term=.11ce9aed94cb Accessed on (6/20/2017).
43. Foreign Agents Registration Act. "Exhibit B." https://www.fara.gov/docs/5483-Exhibit-AB-20101122-24.pdf Accessed on (6/20/2017).
44. Maloney, Suzanne. 2016. "Deception and the Iran Deal: Did the Obama Administration Mislead America, or Did the Rhodes Profile?" Brookings. https://www.brookings.edu/blog/markaz/2016/05/11/deception-and-the-iran-deal-did-the-obama-administration-mislead-america-or-did-the-rhodes-profile/ Accessed on (6/20/2017).

45. Inskeep, Steve. 2016. "Military Leaders' Endorsements of Political Candidates Questioned." NPR. http://www.npr.org/2016/09/08/493073644/military-leaders-endorsements-of-political-candidates-questioned Accessed on (6/20/2017).
46. Morello, Carol. 2015. "Retired Generals and Admirals Urge Congress to Reject Iran Nuclear Deal." *Washington Post.* https://www.washingtonpost.com/world/national-security/retired-generals-and-admirals-urge-congress-to-reject-iran-deal/2015/08/26/8912d9c6-4bf5-11e5-84df-923b3ef1a64b_story.html?utm_term=.e45ffd39f2f6 Accessed on (6/20/2017).
47. JTA. 2015. "340 Rabbis Back Iran Deal in Letter to Congress." *Forward.* http://forward.com/news/breakingnews/319264/340-rabbis-back-iran-deal-in-letter-to-congress/ Accessed on (6/20/2017).
48. JTA. 2015. "Hundreds of U.S. Rabbis Sign Petition Against Iran Deal." *Haaretz.* http://www.haaretz.com/jewish/news/1.672879 (Accessed June 20, 2017).
49. Crowley, Michael. 2015. "Nuclear Experts Fall n Behind Obama." *Politico.* http://www.politico.com/story/2015/08/nuclear-experts-fall-in-behind-obama-iran-121459 Accessed on (6/20/2017).
50. Foreign Affairs. 2015. "Should Congress Approve the Iran Deal?" https://www.foreignaffairs.com/articles/iran/2015-09-07/should-congress-approve-iran-deal Accessed on (6/20/2017).
51. Meyer, Theodoric. 2015. "Colin Powell Defends Iran Nuclear Deal." *Politico.* http://www.politico.com/story/2015/09/powell-defends-iranian-nuclear-deal-213375 Accessed on (6/20/2017).
52. Kerr, Simeon. 2016. "U.S. Roadshows Aim to Guide Groups Through Iran Sanctions Maze," *Financial Times.*
53. Ibid.
54. Toosi, Nahal. 2016. "Lawmakers, Activists Pounce on Companies Flirting with Iran." *Politico.* http://www.

politico.com/story/2016/07/iran-nuclear-companies-225343 Accessed on (6/20/2017).
55. Financial Times. 2015. "Experts Detail Continuing Business Risks in Iran." http://www.unitedagainstnucleariran.com/sites/default/files/Open-Letter_FT_11092015.pdf Accessed on (6/20/2017).
56. Glass, David. 2016. "Greek Shipowner Victor Resitis Cleared of Embezzlement and Money Laundering Charges." Seatrade Maritime News. http://www.seatrade-maritime.com/news/europe/greek-shipowner-victor-restis-cleared-of-embezzlement-and-money-laundering-charges.html Accessed on (6/20/2017).
57. Apuzzo, Matt. 2014. "Billionaire Named in Suit Against Anti-Iran Group." *The New York Times.* https://www.nytimes.com/2014/08/19/us/billionaire-named-in-suit-against-anti-iran-group.html Accessed on (6/20/2017).
58. Gharib, Ali and Eli Clifton. 2014. "IS the Justice Department Shielding an Anti-Iran Smear Campaign?" *The Nation.* https://www.thenation.com/article/justice-department-shielding-anti-iran-smear-campaign/ Accessed on (6/20/2017).
59. Guttman, Nathan. 2014, September 25. "Why Is Government Seeking to Kill United Against Nuclear Iran Lawsuit?" *Forward.* http://forward.com/news/israel/206379/why-is-government-seeking-to-kill-united-against-n/ Accessed on (6/20/2017).
60. Cullis, Tyler. 2017. "Iran Hawks Try a New Congressional Tactic." Lobe Log. http://lobelog.com/iran-hawks-try-a-new-congressional-tactic/ Accessed on (6/20/2017).
61. Congress. "S. Con. Res. 26." https://www.congress.gov/114/bills/sconres26/BILLS-114sconres26is.pdf Accessed on (6/20/2017).
62. Clifton, Eli. 2014. "Why the Hawks Are Winning the Iran Debate." *The Nation.* https://www.thenation.com/article/anti-diplomacy-groups-dominate-congressional-hearings-iran-policy/ Accessed on (6/20/2017).

63. Oversight. 2016. "White House Narrative on the Iran Nuclear Deal." https://oversight.house.gov/hearing/white-house-narratives-on-the-iran-nuclear-deal/ Accessed on (6/20/2017).
64. Samuels, op. cit.
65. Corn, David. 2016. "GOPers Probing Iran Deal Turn to Cheney Aid Who Was Involved with Bogus Iraq Intel." *Mother Jones.* http://www.motherjones.com/politics/2016/05/chaffetz-john-hannah-ben-rhodes-iraq-war-intelligence Accessed on (6/20/2017).
66. Gass, Nick. 2015. "Michael Oren: I Wrote My Book to Stop Obama's Iran Deal." *Politico.* http://www.politico.com/story/2015/06/michael-oren-new-book-obama-iran-deal-119317 Accessed on (6/20/2017).
67. Oren, Michael. 2015. *Ally.* Random House, p. 98.
68. Solomon, Jay. 2016. *The Iran Wars.* Random House, p. 8.
69. Rosen, Amin. 2017, June 23. "Jay Solomon's Firing Is a Cautionary Tale," Table. http://www.tabletmag.com/scroll/238667/jay-solomons-firing-is-a-cautionary-tale Accessed on (6/29/2017).
70. Rethink Media. 2017. "About." https://rethinkmedia.org/about Accessed on (6/20/2017).
71. Right Web. 2014. "Secure America Now." http://rightweb.irc-online.org/profile/secure_america_now/ Accessed on (6/20/2017).
72. LaFranchi, Howard. 2014. "Going Against Netanyahu, 85 Percent of US Jews Favor the Iran Nuclear Deal." The Christian Science Monitor. http://www.csmonitor.com/layout/set/print/USA/Foreign-Policy/2014/1106/Going-against-Netanyahu-84-percent-of-US-Jews-favor-Iran-nuclear-deal Accessed on (6/20/2017).
73. Cohen, Steven. 2015. "New Poll: U.S. Jews Support Iran Deal, Despite Misgivings." *Jewish Journal.* http://jewishjournal.com/news/nation/176121/ Accessed on (6/20/2017).

74. Rethink Media. 2015. "Synthesized Analysis: Public Opinion Polling on Iran." https://rethinkmedia.org/opinion/analysis/synthesized-analysis-public-opinion-polling-iran-january-2015-update?authkey=af6b620aa60539c37e20a41fb46c13de0079dc03e29230a5a188ce60aaca8dca Accessed on (6/20/2017).

CHAPTER 5

The Results and the Future

George Shultz once said, "Nothing ever gets settled in this town. It's not like running a company or even a university. It's a seething debating society in which the debate never stops, in which people never give up, including me, and that's the atmosphere in which you administer."[1] Schultz made his statement in 1986 and the occasion was when he appeared before was the House Foreign Affairs Committee. He was defending his ignorance about the sale to Iran of 1500 anti-tank missiles and spare parts for anti-aircraft missiles, which was part of the Iran-Contra scandal, despite his position as Secretary of State at the time.[2]

The passage of the Iran nuclear agreement did little to settle the debate between its supporters and opponents. Immediately after it was struck, the anti-deal camp began to look for ways to undermine it and diminish Iran's potential benefits. A year after the deal went into effect, The CEO of the Adelson-funded Foundation for the Defense of Democracies, Mark Dubowitz, and "a constellation of pressure groups, analysts, lobbyists and lawmakers" still had hopes of altering the agreement, according to an article in

Politico.³ Dubowitz and "his crew of some 20 sanctions experts, terrorism analysts, nuclear advisors, human rights researchers and Persian-speaking colleagues" were described as "working feverishly in their 'wonk room,' in a gray office building above a Subway sandwich shop six blocks from the White House."[4]

Dubowitz claims he wants a better deal rather than just the destruction of the existing one. But, like Netanyahu's vision of a peace accord with the Palestinians, it would have to be an agreement that he knows the other side would never accept.[5] And he seems to think all that is necessary is to inform the Chinese, Russians, French, Germans and British that they need to return to the negotiating table with the USA to impose such a deal on the Iranians.

One of the initiatives of the opponents has been to try to prevent economic benefits to Iran even when it meant hurting American companies. In 2016, Airbus signed a multibillion-dollar deal to sell commercial jets to airlines in Iran. Boeing, which is always in a fierce competition with Airbus throughout the world, signed two agreements with Iranian airlines to sell a total of 140 planes to carriers in the Islamic Republic for a list price of $22.6 billion. The sales would help sustain 18,000 US jobs, according to Boeing. As the company awaited the Trump administration's approval of the deals, other US firms held back until business relations with Tehran were made clearer.[6] If the sales are disapproved, Airbus will be more than happy to provide the aircraft.

The negative economic impact of sanctions on the USA has apparently not been a persuasive argument in the past. A 2014 study from the National Iranian American Council estimated the cost to the US economy of the sanctions imposed on Iran between 1995 and 2012 at a minimum of $135 billion and perhaps as much as $175 billion.[7]

The impact on the American economy will likely continue to have an insignificant role in determining the ultimate fate of the Iran nuclear agreement, which at least as of mid-2017 was unclear. Whether all parties fulfill it remains to be seen. A larger known unknown is the unpredictability of the Trump administration, which exacerbates the uncertainty.

Some indications were not positive. In June 2017, the *New York Times* reported that the CIA officer who was responsible for the hunt for Osama bin Laden and the campaign of drone strikes, which killed thousands of Islamist militants and hundreds of civilians, had been put in charge of the CIA's operations dealing with Iran. This was interpreted by the *New York Times* as "the first major sign that the Trump administration is invoking the hard line the president took against Iran during his campaign."[8]

The article proceeded to describe how Trump has stocked the National Security Council with hawks that are "eager to contain Iran and push regime change." Counted among the Iran hawks were the National Security Advisor, H. R. McMaster, the senior director for the Middle East, Derek Harvey, and the senior director for intelligence, Ezra Cohen-Watnick.

Cohen-Watnick, a 31-year-old protégé of disgraced former National Security Advisor Michael Flynn, "has told other administration officials that he wants to use American spies to help oust the Iranian government, according to multiple defense and intelligence officials."[9] In addition, the director of the CIA, Mike Pompeo, was one of the fiercest critics of the Iran deal when he was in Congress.

Opponents of the nuclear deal were not just found in the CIA and the NSC. Republicans in Congress continued to focus on Iran's ballistic missile testing, human rights abuses and aggressive role in Yemen, Iraq and elsewhere in the

Middle East. A bill imposing new sanctions on those involved with the ballistic missile programs and against Iran's Islamic Revolutionary Guard Corps worked its way through Congress with strong bipartisan support.[10] Opponents of the Iran agreement argued that imposing additional sanctions would not violate the deal. Supporters, including former Secretary of State John Kerry, warned that it could jeopardize the agreement and urged other measures be taken.

A June 2017 Congressional Research Service report described the potential impact of new sanctions and the benefits Iran had received from the agreement:

> The reimposition of many or all U.S. sanctions would undoubtedly harm Iran's economy. Iran's economy shrank by 9% in the two years that ended in March 2014, before stabilizing since 2015 as a result of modest sanctions relief under an interim nuclear agreement. Iran achieved about 7% growth in 2016. Sanctions caused Iran's crude oil exports to fall from about 2.5 million barrels per day (mbd) in 2011 to about 1.1 mbd by mid-2013, and sanctions relief has enabled the exports to recover to nearly pre-sanctions levels. Sanctions also made inaccessible more than $120 billion in Iranian reserves held in banks abroad, and sanctions relief has enabled Iran to regain access to those funds and Iran's banks to reintegrate into the international financial system. Foreign energy firms have begun making new investments in Iran's energy sector. Nuclear negotiations and sanctions relief helped Iran's President, Hassan Rouhani politically and he was able to defeat a strong hardliner rival in the May 19, 2017, presidential election.[11]

While the future of the Iran nuclear agreement is unclear, one thing is certain. Those who opposed it will continue to look for ways to undermine it because, as George Shultz said more than 30 years ago, nothing is ever settled in Washington. It is therefore worth considering how the five factors discussed earlier might affect the agreement and, more generally, what they imply for the future of foreign policy formulation.

Globalization Is Here to Stay: At Least the Downside

The impact of globalization, defined as the movement of things, people and ideas across borders, has three aspects that are relevant to the future of policy making and could be labeled the good, the bad and the ugly. The good are benefits from globalization like increased trade (the things) and travel by tourists and for business (the people) and the spread of democracy and efforts to protect human rights (the ideas). The bad is the flip side—all those things, people and ideas that involve terrorism, crime or are harmful. And the ugly is the status of the efforts of the international community to rise to the challenges posed by globalization.

It is difficult to interpret politics today because, at least with President Trump in office, words have lost their meaning. They signify what he wants them to stand for one day and changes them to mean something else the next. His repeated emphasis on an "America first" foreign policy, however, would seem to have more the potential for making efforts to deal with globalization even uglier and less effective.

His criticism of trade agreements and NATO are likely to be counterproductive. His withdrawal from the Trans-Pacific Partnership and his insistence on renegotiating the North American Free Trade Agreement are part of his campaign promises to get better trade deals for America. While the economic effects of trade agreements are positive overall, the net gains don't matter much to those workers in industries decimated by foreign competition. It will remain to be seen, however, whether better deals can be reached. As in any negotiation, both sides have to leave the table feeling the resulting agreement will be beneficial. If a "better deal" cannot be struck, then the result will be less trade and less overall economic benefit.

Since the essence of globalization is crossing borders more easily and thereby weakening the governments within those borders, international cooperation is essential to addressing globalization's negative effects. Even the world's only super power cannot prevail against terrorists, the proliferation of weapons of mass destruction and ideologies of hate on its own. Not to mention global health risks and climate change.

The way the world seems to be interpreting "America first," however, is "America alone." The withdrawal of the USA from the Paris climate change agreement reinforced that perception. German Chancellor Angela Merkel summed up this sentiment in a single sentence in May 2017 when she said "The times when we could completely rely on others are, to an extent, over."[12] Although she did not mention Trump specifically, she did not have to say his name for the meaning to be clear. The headline on CNN story put it succinctly: "How a single sentence from Angela Merkel showed what Trump means to the world."

The lack of confidence in Trump is not just a CNN headline but is a worldwide sentiment, according to a survey done by the Pew Research Center. It surveyed attitudes in 37 countries and found a median of just 22 percent of the people in those countries have confidence in Trump to do the right thing when it comes to international affairs. That compared with 64 percent when it came to Obama at the end of his presidency. The only two countries where the confidence level for Trump was greater than that of Obama was Israel where it was 7 percentage points higher at 56 and Russia where Trump was 42 percentage points higher at 53.[13]

The Council on Foreign Relations is one of the oldest and most established think tanks that specializes in international relations. It created a Council of Councils that brought together similar institutions from the wealthiest 25 countries around the world in an attempt "to find common ground on shared threats, build support for innovative ideas, and introduce remedies into the public debate and policymaking processes of member countries."[14]

The Council of Councils produces an annual report card on international cooperation, grading the world's performance at addressing challenges stemming from globalization among other issues. The 2016 report noted: "the world witnessed some of the most significant shocks to multilateralism in twenty-five years, and the future of the rules-based global order was called into question."[15] Among the shocks it cited were the British decision to leave the European Union and the election of Donald Trump. It also downgraded international cooperation efforts from a B in 2015 to a barely passing C– for 2016. And since that was before the Trump administration took office, next year's grade should be even lower.

The prospects for international cooperation have clear implications for the future of the Iran nuclear deal. The most likely scenario for it to fall apart would be a claim from the American government that Iran had violated it. That claim would have to be based on intelligence assessments since Iran is not going to provide proof of its violations by doing something like testing a nuclear device. If the claim is accompanied by a call to action from the USA, what would the reaction of the P-5+1 partners and the rest of the world be? Would they accept American leadership when America seems so interested in shedding its traditional responsibilities in so many other areas? The reaction will in no small measure depend on the degree to which the rest of the world thinks it can believe what the US government is saying.

The Prospects for Truth

Dishonesty is hardly new in Washington, and politicians have always made appeals based on emotions like hope, fear and hate with the facts being, at best, a secondary consideration. President Trump has used this tactic so often and in so many unprecedented ways, however, that it has left the much maligned "main stream media" struggling for ways to report his remarks. Reluctant to simply call the president a liar, "unproven allegations" and other euphemisms have become a standard part of daily reporting. When confronted with such "inconsistencies" reported by journalists, the president and his surrogates just double down and keep repeating them. They simply invent whatever evidence needed to support their allegations. This practice even has a name thanks to the perhaps inadvertent comment by one of his closest advisors who called it "alternative facts."[16]

While running for the presidency, Trump's distortions of the truth repeatedly earned the highest category of the *Washington Post*'s ranking for untruth—four Pinocchios—a level that would win an Olympic gold medal level if lying were a sport. As the *Post* stated:

> There's never been a presidential candidate like Donald Trump—someone so cavalier about the facts and so unwilling to ever admit error, even in the face of overwhelming evidence. As of Nov. 3, 2016, about 64 percent (59 of 92) of our rulings of his statements turned out to be Four Pinocchios, our worst rating. By contrast, most politicians tend to earn Four Pinocchios 10 to 20 percent of the time. (Moreover, most of the remaining ratings for Trump are Three Pinocchios.)[17]

The volume of fake news and disinformation has added to a general distrust of the Washington establishment. Politicians like Bernie Sanders and Donald Trump were able to tap into that cynicism and make it an important part of their campaigns. Distrust of Washington has become such a powerful force it has turned experience there from an asset into a liability.

Trump was the only presidential candidate of either of the two major parties in all of American history who had spent no time in either government or the military. All previous candidates had been former senators, congressmen, governors or generals. Even Wendell Wilke, a progressive Republican businessman who ran against Franklin Roosevelt in 1940, had at least served as an army officer during World War I. While in the past government or military experience has always mattered in the voting process, it was clearly unimportant to many voters in 2016.

Predicting the foreign policy of a president with no experience beyond real estate deals and no track record on policy other than constantly changing pronouncements is difficult. Another question is whether the way a person gets information and his management style, affects his policies. Donald Trump reportedly has little time to read and struggles to name a book that influenced him. His preferred method is to base his decisions on "common sense" rather than lengthy reports or thick briefing books.

President Obama, on the other hand, was described as a voracious reader and very deliberate decision maker, requiring several meetings to consider options. That style prompted former Vice President Cheney to deride such an approach as "dithering."[18] A *Washington Post* reporter had one description of what might be called the process Trump uses to formulate foreign policy: "The process, according to two advisers I spoke with, is this: Trump's foreign policy aides wait for him to say something in public about an international issue and then craft a policy around whatever he said. The details of how Trump utterances fit into his overall international vision are worked out after the fact."[19]

In his first months in office, Trump the president, was indistinguishable from Trump the campaigner. The grandiose promises, a lack of any detail or even apparent interest in policy and the cascade of untruth all continued. Fact checkers at the *Washington Post* catalogued 492 false or misleading statements made by him in his first 100 days in office.[20]

The *New York Times* reported that Trump had begun running campaign-style advertisements that magnified his accomplishments as president even though there were few if any achievements besides naming a conservative to the Supreme Court and signing minor executive orders. To the *Times*, it was an "extraordinarily early return to campaigning when most presidents would be spending their time pushing through their highest legislative priorities."[21]

Trump's use of untruth doesn't only arise from sloppy word choices or even a callous disregard for the facts. It has been the essence of his political strategy. The constant stream of inaccuracies and downright falsehoods by him and his surrogates delights and stimulates his supporters and confounds his opponents.

Despite being its largest beneficiary, Trump is just part of the untruth industry. Paul Horner, who the *Washington Post* described as a 38-year-old impresario of a Facebook fake-news empire, described his success in the following terms:

> Honestly, people are definitely dumber. They just keep passing stuff around. Nobody fact-checks anything anymore—I mean, that's how Trump got elected. He just said whatever he wanted, and people believed everything, and when the things he said turned out not to be true, people didn't care because they'd already accepted it. My sites were picked up by Trump

supporters all the time. It's real scary. I've never seen anything like it. I think Trump is in the White House because of me.[22]

As with conspiracy theories, the tendency to believe untruth is not even distributed along the political spectrum. There is a pronounced tendency on the right to even treat fact checkers with contempt. A study done by the Reporters Lab project at Duke University found that:

- Liberal websites were far more likely to cite fact-checks to make their points than conservative sites were.
- Conservative sites were much more likely to criticize fact-checks and to allege partisan bias.
- Liberal sites made most of the positive references, while the negative references came primarily from the right.
- Conservative sites made the most critical comments about fact-checking, occasionally using quotation marks ("fact-checking") to imply it wasn't legitimate.[23]

It could be possible that Trump is unique and once his term ends, politicians will return to a more traditional level of dishonesty. But the likelihood of that is questionable since untruth has become a business for someone like Horner and an effective political weapon for Trump and other politicians on the right. And it has been made even more possible by the third change—technology.

Technology and Politics

Technology and social media have certainly made the dissemination of untruth easier. According to one company, it also made possible identifying the views of voters and manipulating them without them being aware of it. Cambridge Analytica has asserted it could predict the personality and hidden political leanings of every American adult through what it calls "psychographic" profiles.[24] While the company did not use the profiles in the 2016 presidential election, it received at least $6 million from the Trump campaign for other services.

Some political experts dismissed the supposed power to manipulate voters that Analytica claimed to have, while others saw it as key to Trump's surprise election victory.[25] Aggravating the concern of progressives was the fact that company is largely owned by Robert Mercer, the reclusive billionaire who funded Breitbart News and helped Stephen Bannon become Trump's political advisor.

The potential for creating an individualized blizzard of high-tech, Facebook-optimized propaganda has implications for commerce and foreign policy as well as politics.[26] According to an article in the online magazine *Scout*, Cambridge Analytica's weaponized artificial intelligence is a propaganda machine that "has become the new prerequisite for political success in a world of polarization, isolation, trolls, and dark posts. In the past, political messaging and propaganda battles were arms races to weaponize narrative through new mediums -- waged in print, on the radio, and on TV. This new wave has brought the world something exponentially more insidious -- personalized, adaptive, and ultimately addictive propaganda. Silicon Valley spent the last ten years building platforms whose natural end state is digital addiction. In 2016, Trump and his allies hijacked them."[27]

As with Russian interference in the 2016 election, the magnitude of what technology did to help Trump win is impossible to determine. However, it is unambiguous that his victory caused considerable anguish among liberals and provoked a reaction that was spread through the use of technology and social media.

Included in this reaction was a small group of young progressives who decided to take a page out of the playbook of some conservative groups. They examined the mechanisms that were used to thwart President Obama's agenda, seeking a way to apply the same tactics to obstructing President Trump. In so doing, they have provided an interesting case study in techniques to influence policy that will likely be adopted in the future for both domestic and foreign policy issues.

The group called itself "Indivisible" and originally consisted of about three dozen people, mostly young and many former staff members for Democratic congressmen. They drafted a document and published it online, laying out a strategy for what they hope to achieve.[28] The document went viral and within a few days had millions of views.

Their strategy was to emulate the tactics of their ideological opposites, the Tea Party groups, which had done so much to block many of Obama's initiatives.[29] While they abhorred the more aggressive and racist aspects of Tea Party activism, they admired its effectiveness.[30]

They determined that the Tea Party was successful because it made two strategic choices. First, it was locally focused and thrived on small local groups of dedicated conservatives. The groups were relatively few in number and only one in five self-identified as members of the Tea Party contributed money or attended events. In other words, they discovered a relatively small number of people could have a significant impact on the national debate if they had focus and intensity.

The second strategic choice of the Tea Party groups was not to develop policy, but instead to concentrate on obstruction. They did not offer an alternative or even consider compromise. They viewed concessions to Democrats as betrayal and any Republican members of Congress offering any were targeted for reprisals at the polls. They confronted the congressmen in their home districts and demanded they reject whatever the president proposed. Few Republicans criticized these tactics for fear of retaliation.

The Tea Party activists had an extraordinary clarity of purpose and were united in their opposition to the Obama administration. They went to town hall meetings and took over. They appeared at their congressmen's offices to ask for meetings. And they coordinated blanket calling of those offices at key moments.

The document offered four steps for how progressives could adopt the Tea Party recipe to influence policy in Washington.

- Work on a local level to prevent implementation of Trump's agenda.
- Exploit their congressman's fear of losing an election and looking weak or unlikeable.
- Find, or create, a local group, mobilize others and organize to take action.
- Confront their congressman in town halls, other public events, district office visits and through phone calls, faxes and e-mails. Record the encounters on video, coordinating with the local group and feeding into local media.

The purpose of the activism is to show congressmen and senators the political costs of supporting policies that the activists oppose.

Whether its algorithms and artificial intelligence or activists using social media to coordinate their efforts, the paths to influence policy will expand given the impact of technology. But one method will not change—the ability of the rich to use their wealth to buy access to and influence on politicians.

Money and Partisan Politics

While politicians on the right tried to portray the withdrawal from the Paris climate change agreement as being due to a concern for jobs or American workers, it was prompted by partisan politics and money. Environmental concerns did not cause the decrease in coal mining jobs and withdrawal from the accord will not reverse the decline. Paul Krugman, the *New York Times* columnist and winner of the Nobel Prize for economics, estimated that mechanization was the force behind the loss of two-thirds of the coal mining jobs between 1948 and 1970.[31] With the boom in natural gas brought on by fracking technology, those jobs are not coming back.

A 4600 words article in the *New York Times* in June 2017 described the real cause for the Republican Party leadership going from seeing the need to take action on climate change to denouncing it as fake science.[32] According to the article:

> The Republican Party's fast journey from debating how to combat human-caused climate change to arguing that it does not exist is a story of big political money, Democratic hubris in the Obama years and a partisan chasm that grew over nine years like a crack in the Antarctic shelf, favoring extreme positions and uncompromising rhetoric over cooperation and conciliation.
>
> "Most Republicans still do not regard climate change as a hoax," said Whit Ayres, a Republican strategist. But the entire climate change debate has now been caught up in the broader polarization of American politics. In some ways, it's become yet another of the long list of litmus test issues that determine whether or not you're a good Republican.

This evolution happened quickly. In 2008, when Senator John McCain was running for president, one of his campaign ads touted the fact that he had "stood up to President George

W. Bush and sounded the alarm on global warming."[33] Two things changed. First, the Koch brothers, who own a chain of refineries and 4000 miles of pipelines, and other fossil fuel billionaires got out their checkbooks. And second, denial became good politics because a key constituency of the Republican Party did not want to believe in the science supporting climate change.

The Koch brothers funded a new nonprofit called Americans for Prosperity that claims to represent 3.2 million members. Since that is exactly 1 percent of the population of the USA, perhaps the Kochs just made the wealthiest 1 percent of Americans honorary members. The 1 percent own between 33 percent of 42 percent of the nation's wealth depending on the study cited.[34]

Americans for Prosperity describes itself as being dedicated to lower taxes, less government and economic prosperity for all. On its webpage soliciting donations, AFP adds another goal without any trace of irony—to put a stop to cronyism and corporate welfare.[35]

There are actually two organizations. The Americans for Prosperity Foundation, which is a 501(c)(3) and Americans for Prosperity, which is a 501(c)(4). The former had revenue of $23 million in 2014 while the latter, which can engage more directly in politics and election campaigns, raised $83 million. The revenue of both organizations surged in even numbered years. In the presidential election year of 2012, the (c)(4) organization received $115 million.[36] The organization's members, whether the number 3.2 million or not, are regarded as a standing ground force of activists who can be mobilized quickly for any legislative battle the Koch brothers deem important.[37]

In addition to spending tens of millions of dollars on elections and grassroots mobilization, AFP insisted that candidates sign a no tax pledge that also required them to "oppose any legislation relating to climate change that includes a net increase in government revenue." By Election Day in 2010, 165 candidates had signed the pledge and most of them won including 83 of the 92 new members of Congress.[38] The Kochs and other oil industry executives funded friendly academics and a think tank, the Competitive Enterprise Institute, to generate studies and talking points dismissing the idea that climate change is human driven.[39] The institute had $7 million in revenue in 2014 and compensated each of its two top executives around $200,000 a year.[40]

The no tax pledge effectively doomed any cap and trade legislation or other initiatives to respond to climate change. And the Republicans who prevented any such action did not seem to be suffering despite that a recent poll showed 53 percent of Americans think human activity caused global warming and 69 percent support limiting carbon dioxide emissions from coal-fired power plants.

The *New York Times* article explained why Republicans nonetheless resist taking action: "Most public opinion polls find that voters rank the environment last or nearly last among the issues that they vote on. And views are divided based on party affiliation. In 2001, 46 percent of Democrats said they worried 'a great deal' about climate change, compared with 29 percent of Republicans, according to a Gallup tracking poll on the issue. This year, concern among Democrats has reached 66 percent. Among Republicans, it has fallen, to 18 percent. Until people vote on the issue, Republicans will find it politically safer to question climate science and policy than to alienate moneyed groups like Americans for Prosperity."[41]

One of the reasons Republicans are comfortable with climate change denial is that the bedrock group among the party's base are white evangelical Christians. They tend to have a biblical worldview that includes a distrust •any information that the believe conflicts with their religion.⁴² That outlook often includes unquestioning support for the Israeli government and by association a distrust of Iran and opposition to the nuclear agreement.

That resistance to the deal ensures Republican legislators will continue to oppose it. Over three quarters of white evangelicals identify as, or lean toward, Republican. They make up a third of the party, accounting for about a fifth of the electorate.⁴³ Thus, the political party that controls the White House, Congress and the Supreme Court is dominated by voters who distrust science.

In addition to Republican opposition to the nuclear agreement, another trend that can be safely predicted is the politically active billionaires will continue to use their wealth to influence foreign as well as domestic policy. And the ones who have opposed the nuclear deal have been willing to spend far more than the ones who support it.

While the corrupting influence of money on politics is not going to change, it would help if there were requirements for transparency so that every group that attempts to influence policy has to identify their significant donors. The Center for Responsive Politics has found that campaign ads paid for by dark money drop significantly if there is a requirement for the donors paying for them to be revealed.⁴⁴

Even a modest reform like that will remain out of reach without significant public pressure from grassroots organizations. President Eisenhower warned out the military-industrial complex that arouse during the Cold War and constantly pushed for an ever-larger defense budget. Elections have become a multibillion-dollar industry and those who benefit from it, besides the politicians, will fight to prevent any real reform. The Citizens United decision opened the floodgates and it remains to be seen if they can ever be even partially closed.

In addition to money and religiously motivated worldviews, foreign policy formulation and the future of the Iran nuclear agreement will be subjected to the influence of fragility of truth and the other effects of technology. One would hope that in an increasingly complex world, policymakers could rise above partisan politics on occasion to better serve the national interest instead of serving the rich or certain demographic groups. But someone hoping to see reason triumph in Washington may have a long wait. Meanwhile, globalization will ensure that the Iranian nuclear issue is one that the USA can neither ignore nor deal with on its own.

Winston Churchill reportedly once said, "Democracy is the worst form of government, except for all those other forms that have been tried from time to time." It appears he did actually say those words in a House of Commons debate in 1947 although he did not coin the phrase as he was quoting an unidentified predecessor.[45] So while reform may be unlikely, at least the debate will hopefully continue and the outcome won't be the worst.

Notes

1. Apple, R. W. 1986. "A Lesson from Shultz." *The New York Times*. http://www.nytimes.com/1986/12/09/world/a-lesson-from-shultz.html Accessed on (6/11/2017).
2. *The New York Times*. 1981. "An Iran-Contra Guide: What Happened and When." http://www.nytimes.com/1988/03/17/world/an-iran-contra-guide-what-happened-and-when.html Accessed on (6/11/2017).
3. Lakshmanan, Indira A. R. 2016. "Inside the Plan to Undo the Iran Nuclear Deal." *Politico*. http://www.politico.com/magazine/story/2016/07/iran-nuclear-deal-foreign-policy-barack-obama-hassan-rouhani-javad-zarif-israel-john-kerry-214052#ixzz4EU89xXN2 Accessed on (6/11/2017).

4. Ibid.
5. Dubowitz, Mark. 2017. "The Delusion of the Iran Nuclear Deal." Foundation for Defense of Democracies. http://www.defenddemocracy.org/media-hit/dubowitz-mark-the-delusion-of-the-iran-nuclear-deal/ Accessed on (6/11/2017).
6. Wall, Robert. 2017. "Boeing's Sale of Up to 60 Commercial Jets to Iran Takes Next Step." *Wall Street Journal*.
7. National Iranian American Council. 2014. "Report: Iran Sanctions Cost US Economy up to $175 Billion." https://www.niacouncil.org/report-iran-sanctions-cost-us-economy-175-billion/?gclid=CjwKEAjwvYPKBRCYr5GLgNCJ_jsS-JABqwfw7B0tcLh-pBj7FB0hQy4iWRFuo8PMBiqjBTGnGQMWfVhoCAnjw_wcB Accessed on (6/11/2017).
8. Rosenberg, Matthew and Adam Goldman. 2017. "C.I.A. Names the 'Dark Prince' to Run Iran Operations, Signaling a Tougher Stance." *The New York Times*. https://www.nytimes.com/2017/06/02/world/middleeast/cia-iran-dark-prince-michael-dandrea.html?_r=0 Accessed on (6/11/2017).
9. Stein, Jeff. 2017. "Ezra Cohen-Watnick: Inside the Rise of Trump's Invisible Man in the White House." *News Week*. http://www.newsweek.com/ezra-cohen-watnick-donald-trump-devin-nunes-russia-barack-obama-wiretap-susan-583904 Accessed on (6/11/2017).
10. Kasperowicz, Pete. 2017. "Iran Sanctions Bill Advances in Senate with 18–3 Committee Vote." *The Washington Examiner*. http://www.washingtonexaminer.com/iran-sanctions-bill-advances-in-senate-with-18-3-committee-vote/article/2624127 Accessed on (6/11/2017).
11. Katzman, Kenneth. 2017. "Iran Sanctions." Congressional Research Service. https://fas.org/sgp/crs/mideast/RS20871.pdf Accessed on (6/11/2017).
12. Cillizza, Chris. 2017. "How a Single Sentence from Angela Merkel Showed What Trump Means to the World." CNN. http://www.cnn.com/2017/05/29/politics/merkel-trump-europe/index.html Accessed on (6/11/2017).

13. Wike, Richard. 2017, June 16. "U.S. Image Suffers as Publics Around World Question Trump's Leadership," Pew Research Center. http://www.pewglobal.org/2017/06/26/u-s-image-suffers-as-publics-around-world-question-trumps-leadership/ Accessed on (6/29/2017).
14. Council of Councils. 2017. "About the Council of Councils Report Card on International Cooperation 2016–2017." https://www.cfr.org/councilofcouncils/reportcard2017/#!/about Accessed on (6/11/2017).
15. Council of Councils. 2017. "2016 Overall Grade on International Cooperation." https://www.cfr.org/councilofcouncils/reportcard2017/#!/overall/2016 Accessed on (6/11/2017).
16. Bradner, Eric. 2017. "Conway: Trump White House Offered 'Alternative Facts' on Crowd Size." CNN. http://www.cnn.com/2017/01/22/politics/kellyanne-conway-alternative-facts/ Accessed on (6/11/2017).
17. Kessler, Glenn. 2016. "All of Donald Trump's Four-Pinocchio Ratings, in One Place." *The Washington Post.* https://www.washingtonpost.com/news/fact-checker/wp/2016/03/22/all-of-donald-trumps-four-pinocchio-ratings-in-one-place/?utm_term=.71ce73a419b5 Accessed on (6/11/2017).
18. Fisher, Mark. 2016. "Donald Trump Doesn't Read Much. Being President Probably Wouldn't Change That." *The Washington Post.* https://www.washingtonpost.com/politics/donald-trump-doesnt-read-much-being-president-probably-wouldnt-change-that/2016/07/17/d2ddf2bc-4932-11e6-90a8-fb84201e0645_story.html?wpisrc=nl_rainbow&wpmm=1 Accessed on (6/11/2017) and Mayer, Jane. 2016. "Donald Trump's Ghostwriter Tells All." *The New Yorker.* http://www.newyorker.com/magazine/2016/07/25/donald-trumps-ghostwriter-tells-all?mbid=nl_160718_Daily&CNDID=26200182&spMailingID=9217394&spUserID=MTI5NTY0ODQ3NjUyS0&spJobID=961427027&spReportId=OTYxNDI3MDI3S0 Accessed on (6/11/2017).

19. Rogin, Josh. 2016. "At Their Convention, Republicans Will Overlook Trump's Foreign Policy Incompetence." *The Washington Post.* https://www.washingtonpost.com/opinions/global-opinions/at-their-convention-republicans-will-overlook-trumps-foreign-policy-incompetence/2016/07/17/2f89d9e4-4aa6-11e6-bdb9-701687974517_story.html?postshare=3114688901180088&tid=ss_mail Accessed on (6/11/2017).
20. Kessler, Glenn and Michelle Ye Hee Lee. 2017. "President Trump's First 100 Days: The Fact Check Tally." *The Washington Post.* https://www.washingtonpost.com/news/fact-checker/wp/2017/05/01/president-trumps-first-100-days-the-fact-check-tally/?utm_term=.7a39af86788d Accessed on (6/11/2017).
21. Thrush, Glenn and Julie Hirschfeld Davis. 2017. "Trump Abruptly Ends CBS Interview After Wiretap Question." *The New York Times.* https://www.nytimes.com/2017/05/01/us/politics/trump-cbs-interview.html?hp&action=click&pgtype=Homepage&clickSource=story-heading&module=first-column-region&region=top-news&WT.nav=top-news Accessed on (6/11/2017).
22. Dewey, Caitlin. 2016. "Facebook Fake-News Writer: 'I Think Donald Trump Is in the White House Because of Me'." *The Washington Post.* https://www.washingtonpost.com/news/the-intersect/wp/2016/11/17/facebook-fake-news-writer-i-think-donald-trump-is-in-the-white-house-because-of-me/?tid=sm_tw&utm_term=.7ec941326908 Accessed on (6/11/2017).
23. Iannucci, Rebecca and Bill Adair. 2017, June. "Heroes or Hacks: The Partisan Divide over Fact-Checking." Duke Reporters' Lab. https://drive.google.com/file/d/0BxoyrEbZxrAMNm9HV2tvcXFma1U/view Accessed on (6/25/2017).
24. Confessore, Nicholas and Danny Hakim. 2017. "Data Firm Says 'Secret Sauce' Aided Trump; Many Scoff." *The New York Times.* https://www.nytimes.com/2017/03/06/us/

politics/cambridge-analytica.html?emc=eta1 Accessed on (6/11/2017).
25. Wood, Paul. 2016. "The British Data-Crunchers Who Say They Helped Donald Trump to Win." *The Spectator*. https://www.spectator.co.uk/2016/12/the-british-data-crunchers-who-say-they-helped-donald-trump-to-win/ Accessed on (6/11/2017).
26. Anderson, Berit and Brett Horvath. 2017. "The Rise of the Weaponized AI Propaganda Machine." Scout. https://scout.ai/story/the-rise-of-the-weaponized-ai-propaganda-machine Accessed on (6/11/2017).
27. Ibid.
28. Bethea, Charles. 2016. "The Crowdsourced Guide to Fighting Trump's Agenda." *The New Yorker*. http://www.newyorker.com/news/news-desk/the-crowd-sourced-guide-to-fighting-trumps-agenda?intcid=popular Accessed on (6/11/2017).
29. Levin, Ezra, Leah Greenberg and Angel Padilla. 2017. "To Stop Trump, Democrats Can Learn from the Tea Party." *The New York Times*. https://www.nytimes.com/2017/01/02/opinion/to-stop-trump-democrats-can-learn-from-the-tea-party.html Accessed on (6/11/2017).
30. Which can be found here: https://www.indivisibleguide.com Accessed on (6/11/2017).
31. Krugman, Paul. 2017. "Trump's Energy, Low and Dirty." *The New York Times*. https://www.nytimes.com/2017/05/29/opinion/trump-g-7-summit-energy.html Accessed on (6/11/2017).
32. Davenport, Coral and Eric Lipton. 2017. "How G.O.P. Leaders Came to View Climate Change as Fake Science." *The New York Times*. https://www.nytimes.com/2017/06/03/us/politics/republican-leaders-climate-change.html Accessed on (6/11/2017).
33. Ibid.
34. Lam, Bourree. 2016, March 12. "How Much Wealth and Income Does America's 1 Percent Really Have?" *Atlantic*

Magazine. https://www.theatlantic.com/business/archive/2016/03/brookings-1-percent/473478/ Accessed on (6/29/2017).
35. Americans for Prosperity. "You Can Help Restore Economic Freedom." https://secure.americansforprosperity.org/donate Accessed on (6/11/2017).
36. All data from the form 990s on the ProPublica website.
37. Americans for Prosperity. "We Fight for Freedom." https://americansforprosperity.org Accessed on (6/11/2017).
38. Davenport, op. cit.
39. Gillis, Justin and John Schwartz. 2015. "Deeper Ties to Corporate Cash for Doubtful Climate Researcher." https://www.nytimes.com/2015/02/22/us/ties-to-corporate-cash-for-climate-change-researcher-Wei-Hock-Soon.html Accessed on (6/11/2017).
40. From the institute's form 990 on the ProPublica website.
41. Davenport, op. cit.
42. Bailey, Sarah Pulliam. 2017. "Why So Many White Evangelicals in Trump's Base Are Deeply Skeptical of Climate Change." *The Washington Post*. https://www.washingtonpost.com/news/acts-of-faith/wp/2017/06/02/why-so-many-white-evangelicals-in-trumps-base-are-deeply-skeptical-of-climate-change/?tid=ss_mail&utm_term=.2d298c926c1e Accessed on (6/11/017).
43. Bailey, Sarah Pulliam. 2016. "White Evangelicals Voted Overwhelmingly for Donald Trump, Exit Polls Show." *The Washington Post*. https://www.washingtonpost.com/news/acts-of-faith/wp/2016/11/09/exit-polls-show-white-evangelicals-voted-overwhelmingly-for-donald-trump/?utm_term=.c0bc681b2af9 Accessed on (6/11/2017).
44. Balcerzak, Ashley. 2016. "Dark Money Ads Plunged When Reporting Requirement Kicked in." Open Secrets. https://www.opensecrets.org/news/2016/10/dark-money-ads-plunged-when-reporting-requirement-kicked-in/ Accessed on (6/11/2017).

45. Langworth, Richard M. 2009. "Democracy Is the Worst Form of Government…" https://richardlangworth.com/worst-form-of-government Accessed on (6/11/2017).

Acknowledgments

I would like to thank a number of people without whose support this book could not have been possible. At the School of International Affairs at Penn State my thanks must go to SIA's Director, Dr. Scott Gartner, and the Interim of SIA and the Penn State Law School, Admiral James Houck.

I have also had the invaluable assistance of a number of exceptionally talented research assistance—Marwane Zouaidi, Blair Cooper, Daniela Milan and Briana Casey. Two other RA's were incredibly helpful with editing and other tasks in the final weeks of preparing the manuscript for this book and I am very grateful to them both—Mohammad Sarhan, Parminder Singh.

My former colleague from the University of Florida, Dr. Richard Scher, was kind enough to read the entire draft of the book and made extremely useful suggestions about its content. Dr. Dan Caldwell and Ambassador Adrian Basora also were of great help early in the process.

I have had the good fortune to work with a number of excellent people at Palgrave Macmillan in the course of this book including Michelle Chen, John Stegner, Chris Robinson, Elaine Fan and Brian O'Connor.

Last, and most important, is my debt of gratitude to my wife Lynda Schuster, my best editor and reality check as well as an incredibly gifted writer in her own right. And also to my daughter Noa, who complained only a little about the time the writing of this book took away from the moments we could spend together.

As always, despite all this help any mistakes are mine.

Appendices

Appendix A: Text of the Joint Comprehensive Plan of Action: The Iran Nuclear Deal

Joint Comprehensive Plan of Action

Vienna, 14 July 2015

Preface

The E3/EU+3 (China, France, Germany, the Russian Federation, the United Kingdom and the United States, with the High Representative of the European Union for Foreign Affairs and Security Policy) and the Islamic Republic of Iran welcome this historic Joint Comprehensive Plan of Action (JCPOA), which will ensure that Iran's nuclear program will be exclusively peaceful, and mark a fundamental shift in their approach to this issue. They anticipate that full implementation of this JCPOA will positively contribute to regional and international peace and security. Iran reaffirms that under no circumstances will Iran ever seek, develop or acquire any nuclear weapons.

Iran envisions that this JCPOA will allow it to move forward with an exclusively peaceful, indigenous nuclear program, in line with scientific and economic considerations, in accordance with the JCPOA, and with a view to building confidence and encouraging international cooperation. In this context, the initial mutually determined limitations described in this JCPOA will be followed by a gradual evolution, at a reasonable pace, of Iran's peaceful nuclear program, including its enrichment activities, to a commercial program for exclusively peaceful purposes, consistent with international non-proliferation norms.

The E3/EU+3 envision that the implementation of this JCPOA will progressively allow them to gain confidence in the exclusively peaceful nature of Iran's program. The JCPOA reflects mutually determined parameters, consistent with practical needs, with agreed limits on the scope of Iran's nuclear program, including enrichment activities and R&D. The JCPOA addresses the E3/EU+3's concerns, including through comprehensive measures providing for transparency and verification.

The JCPOA will produce the comprehensive lifting of all UN Security Council sanctions as well as multilateral and national sanctions related to Iran's nuclear program, including steps on access in areas of trade, technology, finance, and energy.

Preamble and General Provisions

i. The Islamic Republic of Iran and the E3/EU+3 (China, France, Germany, the Russian Federation, the United Kingdom and the United States, with the High Representative of the European Union for Foreign Affairs and Security Policy) have decided upon this long-term Joint Comprehensive Plan of Action (JCPOA).

This JCPOA, reflecting a step-by-step approach, includes the reciprocal commitments as laid down in this document and the annexes hereto and is to be endorsed by the United Nations (UN) Security Council.
ii. The full implementation of this JCPOA will ensure the exclusively peaceful nature of Iran's nuclear program.
iii. Iran reaffirms that under no circumstances will Iran ever seek, develop or acquire any nuclear weapons.
iv. Successful implementation of this JCPOA will enable Iran to fully enjoy its right to nuclear energy for peaceful purposes under the relevant articles of the nuclear Non-Proliferation Treaty (NPT) in line with its obligations therein, and the Iranian nuclear program will be treated in the same manner as that of any other non-nuclear-weapon state party to the NPT.
v. This JCPOA will produce the comprehensive lifting of all UN Security Council sanctions as well as multilateral and national sanctions related to Iran's nuclear program, including steps on access in areas of trade, technology, finance and energy.
vi. The E3/EU+3 and Iran reaffirm their commitment to the purposes and principles of the United Nations as set out in the UN Charter.
vii. The E3/EU+3 and Iran acknowledge that the NPT remains the cornerstone of the nuclear non-proliferation regime and the essential foundation for the pursuit of nuclear disarmament and for the peaceful uses of nuclear energy.
viii. The E3/EU+3 and Iran commit to implement this JCPOA in good faith and in a constructive atmosphere, based on mutual respect, and to refrain from any action inconsistent with the letter, spirit and intent of this JCPOA that would undermine its successful implementation. The E3/EU+3 will refrain from imposing

discriminatory regulatory and procedural requirements in lieu of the sanctions and restrictive measures covered by this JCPOA. This JCPOA builds on the implementation of the Joint Plan of Action (JPOA) agreed in Geneva on 24 November 2013.

ix. A Joint Commission consisting of the E3/EU+3 and Iran will be established to monitor the implementation of this JCPOA and will carry out the functions provided for in this JCPOA. This Joint Commission will address issues arising from the implementation of this JCPOA and will operate in accordance with the provisions as detailed in the relevant annex.

x. The International Atomic Energy Agency (IAEA) will be requested to monitor and verify the voluntary nuclear-related measures as detailed in this JCPOA. The IAEA will be requested to provide regular updates to the Board of Governors, and as provided for in this JCPOA, to the UN Security Council. All relevant rules and regulations of the IAEA with regard to the protection of information will be fully observed by all parties involved.

xi. All provisions and measures contained in this JCPOA are only for the purpose of its implementation between E3/EU+3 and Iran and should not be considered as setting precedents for any other state or for fundamental principles of international law and the rights and obligations under the NPT and other relevant instruments, as well as for internationally recognized principles and practices.

xii. Technical details of the implementation of this JCPOA are dealt with in the annexes to this document.

xiii. The EU and E3+3 countries and Iran, in the framework of the JCPOA, will cooperate, as appropriate, in the field of peaceful uses of nuclear energy and engage in mutually determined civil nuclear cooperation projects as detailed in Annex III, including through IAEA involvement.

xiv. The E3+3 will submit a draft resolution to the UN Security Council endorsing this JCPOA affirming that conclusion of this JCPOA marks a fundamental shift in its consideration of this issue and expressing its desire to build a new relationship with Iran. This UN Security Council resolution will also provide for the termination on Implementation Day of provisions imposed under previous resolutions; establishment of specific restrictions; and conclusion of consideration of the Iran nuclear issue by the UN Security Council 10 years after the Adoption Day.

xv. The provisions stipulated in this JCPOA will be implemented for their respective durations as set forth below and detailed in the annexes.

xvi. The E3/EU+3 and Iran will meet at the ministerial level every 2 years, or earlier if needed, in order to review and assess progress and to adopt appropriate decisions by consensus.

Iran and E3/EU+3 will take the following voluntary measures within the timeframe as detailed in this JCPOA and its Annexes

Nuclear

A. Enrichment, Enrichment R&D, Stockpiles

1. Iran's long term plan includes certain agreed limitations on all uranium enrichment and uranium enrichment-related activities including certain limitations on

specific research and development (R&D) activities for the first 8 years, to be followed by gradual evolution, at a reasonable pace, to the next stage of its enrichment activities for exclusively peaceful purposes, as described in Annex I. Iran will abide by its voluntary commitments, as expressed in its own long-term enrichment and enrichment R&D plan to be submitted as part of the initial declaration for the Additional Protocol to Iran's Safeguards Agreement.

2. Iran will begin phasing out its IR-1 centrifuges in 10 years. During this period, Iran will keep its enrichment capacity at Natanz at up to a total installed uranium enrichment capacity of 5060 IR-1 centrifuges. Excess centrifuges and enrichment-related infrastructure at Natanz will be stored under IAEA continuous monitoring, as specified in Annex I.

3. Iran will continue to conduct enrichment R&D in a manner that does not accumulate enriched uranium. Iran's enrichment R&D with uranium for 10 years will only include IR-4, IR-5, IR-6 and IR-8 centrifuges as laid out in Annex I, and Iran will not engage in other isotope separation technologies for enrichment of uranium as specified in Annex I. Iran will continue testing IR-6 and IR-8 centrifuges, and will commence testing of up to 30 IR-6 and IR-8 centrifuges after eight and a half years, as detailed in Annex I.

4. As Iran will be phasing out its IR-1 centrifuges, it will not manufacture or assemble other centrifuges, except as provided for in Annex I, and will replace failed centrifuges with centrifuges of the same type. Iran will manufacture advanced centrifuge machines only for the purposes specified in this JCPOA. From the end of the eighth year, and as described in Annex I, Iran will start

to manufacture agreed numbers of IR-6 and IR-8 centrifuge machines without rotors and will store all of the manufactured machines at Natanz, under IAEA continuous monitoring until they are needed under Iran's long-term enrichment and enrichment R&D plan.

5. Based on its own long-term plan, for 15 years, Iran will carry out its uranium enrichment-related activities, including safeguarded R&D exclusively in the Natanz Enrichment facility, keep its level of uranium enrichment at up to 3.67%, and, at Fordow, refrain from any uranium enrichment and uranium enrichment R&D and from keeping any nuclear material.

6. Iran will convert the Fordow facility into a nuclear, physics and technology center. International collaboration including in the form of scientific joint partnerships will be established in agreed areas of research. 1044 IR-1 centrifuges in six cascades will remain in one wing at Fordow. Two of these cascades will spin without uranium and will be transitioned, including through appropriate infrastructure modification, for stable isotope production. The other four cascades with all associated infrastructure will remain idle. All other centrifuges and enrichment-related infrastructure will be removed and stored under IAEA continuous monitoring as specified in Annex I.

7. During the 15 year period, and as Iran gradually moves to meet international qualification standards for nuclear fuel produced in Iran, it will keep its uranium stockpile under 300 kg of up to 3.67% enriched uranium hexafluoride (UF6) or the equivalent in other chemical forms. The excess quantities are to be sold based on international prices and delivered to the international buyer in return for natural uranium delivered to Iran,

or are to be down-blended to natural uranium level. Enriched uranium in fabricated fuel assemblies from Russia or other sources for use in Iran's nuclear reactors will not be counted against the above stated 300 kg UF6 stockpile, if the criteria set out in Annex I are met with regard to other sources. The Joint Commission will support assistance to Iran, including through IAEA technical cooperation as appropriate, in meeting international qualification standards for nuclear fuel produced in Iran. All remaining uranium oxide enriched to between 5% and 20% will be fabricated into fuel for the Tehran Research Reactor (TRR). Any additional fuel needed for the TRR will be made available to Iran at international market prices.

B. **Arak, Heavy Water, Reprocessing**

8. Iran will redesign and rebuild a modernized heavy water research reactor in Arak, based on an agreed conceptual design, using fuel enriched up to 3.67 %, in a form of an international partnership which will certify the final design. The reactor will support peaceful nuclear research and radioisotope production for medical and industrial purposes. The redesigned and rebuilt Arak reactor will not produce weapons grade plutonium. Except for the first core load, all of the activities for redesigning and manufacturing of the fuel assemblies for the redesigned reactor will be carried out in Iran. All spent fuel from Arak will be shipped out of Iran for the lifetime of the reactor. This international partnership will include participating E3/EU+3 parties, Iran and such other countries as may be mutually determined. Iran will take the leadership role as the owner and as the project manager and the E3/EU+3

and Iran will, before Implementation Day, conclude an official document which would define the responsibilities assumed by the E3/EU+3 participants.
9. Iran plans to keep pace with the trend of international technological advancement in relying on light water for its future power and research reactors with enhanced international cooperation, including assurance of supply of necessary fuel.
10. There will be no additional heavy water reactors or accumulation of heavy water in Iran for 15 years. All excess heavy water will be made available for export to the international market.
11. Iran intends to ship out all spent fuel for all future and present power and research nuclear reactors, for further treatment or disposition as provided for in relevant contracts to be duly concluded with the recipient party.
12. For 15 years Iran will not, and does not intend to thereafter, engage in any spent fuel reprocessing or construction of a facility capable of spent fuel reprocessing, or reprocessing R&D activities leading to a spent fuel reprocessing capability, with the sole exception of separation activities aimed exclusively at the production of medical and industrial radio-isotopes from irradiated enriched uranium targets.

C. **Transparency and Confidence Building Measures**

13. Consistent with the respective roles of the President and Majlis (Parliament), Iran will provisionally apply the Additional Protocol to its Comprehensive Safeguards Agreement in accordance with Article 17(b) of the Additional Protocol, proceed with its ratification within the timeframe as detailed in Annex V and fully

implement the modified Code 3.1 of the Subsidiary Arrangements to its Safeguards Agreement.

14. Iran will fully implement the "Roadmap for Clarification of Past and Present Outstanding Issues" agreed with the IAEA, containing arrangements to address past and present issues of concern relating to its nuclear program as raised in the annex to the IAEA report of 8 November 2011 (GOV/2011/65). Full implementation of activities undertaken under the Roadmap by Iran will be completed by 15 October 2015, and subsequently the Director General will provide by 15 December 2015 the final assessment on the resolution of all past and present outstanding issues to the Board of Governors, and the E3+3, in their capacity as members of the Board of Governors, will submit a resolution to the Board of Governors for taking necessary action, with a view to closing the issue, without prejudice to the competence of the Board of Governors.

15. Iran will allow the IAEA to monitor the implementation of the voluntary measures for their respective durations, as well as to implement transparency measures, as set out in this JCPOA and its Annexes. These measures include: a long-term IAEA presence in Iran; IAEA monitoring of uranium ore concentrate produced by Iran from all uranium ore concentrate plants for 25 years; containment and surveillance of centrifuge rotors and bellows for 20 years; use of IAEA approved and certified modern technologies including on-line enrichment measurement and electronic seals; and a reliable mechanism to ensure speedy resolution of IAEA access concerns for 15 years, as defined in Annex I.

16. Iran will not engage in activities, including at the R&D level, that could contribute to the development of a

nuclear explosive device, including uranium or plutonium metallurgy activities, as specified in Annex I.
17. Iran will cooperate and act in accordance with the procurement channel in this JCPOA, as detailed in Annex IV, endorsed by the UN Security Council resolution.
18. The UN Security Council resolution endorsing this JCPOA will terminate all provisions of previous UN Security Council resolutions on the Iranian nuclear issue— 1696 (2006), 1737 (2006), 1747 (2007), 1803 (2008), 1835 (2008), 1929 (2010) and 2224 (2015)—simultaneously with the IAEA-verified implementation of agreed nuclear-related measures by Iran and will establish specific restrictions, as specified in Annex V.[1]
19. The EU will terminate all provisions of the EU Regulation, as subsequently amended, implementing all nuclear-related economic and financial sanctions, including related designations, simultaneously with the IAEA-verified implementation of agreed nuclear-related measures by Iran as specified in Annex V, which cover all sanctions and restrictive measures in the following areas, as described in Annex II:

   i. Transfers of funds between EU persons and entities, including financial institutions, and Iranian persons and entities, including financial institutions;
   ii. Banking activities, including the establishment of new correspondent banking relationships and the opening of new branches and subsidiaries of Iranian banks in the territories of EU Member States;
   iii. Provision of insurance and reinsurance;
   iv. Supply of specialized financial messaging services, including SWIFT, for persons and entities set out in Attachment 1 to Annex II, including the Central Bank of Iran and Iranian financial institutions;

v. Financial support for trade with Iran (export credit, guarantees or insurance);
vi. Commitments for grants, financial assistance and concessional loans to the Government of Iran;
vii. Transactions in public or public-guaranteed bonds;
viii. Import and transport of Iranian oil, petroleum products, gas and petrochemical products;
ix. Export of key equipment or technology for the oil, gas and petrochemical sectors;
x. Investment in the oil, gas and petrochemical sectors;
xi. Export of key naval equipment and technology;
xii. Design and construction of cargo vessels and oil tankers;
xiii. Provision of flagging and classification services;
xiv. Access to EU airports of Iranian cargo flights;
xv. Export of gold, precious metals and diamonds;
xvi. Delivery of Iranian banknotes and coinage;
xvii. Export of graphite, raw or semi-finished metals such as aluminum and steel, and export or software for integrating industrial processes;
xviii. Designation of persons, entities and bodies (asset freeze and visa ban) set out in Attachment 1 to Annex II; and
xix. Associated services for each of the categories above.

20. The EU will terminate all provisions of the EU Regulation implementing all EU proliferation-related sanctions, including related designations, 8 years after Adoption Day or when the IAEA has reached the Broader Conclusion that all nuclear material in Iran remains in peaceful activities, whichever is earlier.

21. The United States will cease the application, and will continue to do so, in accordance with this JCPOA of the sanctions specified in Annex II to take effect simultaneously with the IAEA-verified implementation of the agreed nuclear-related measures by Iran as specified in Annex V. Such sanctions cover the following areas as described in Annex II:

    i. Financial and banking transactions with Iranian banks and financial institutions as specified in Annex II, including the Central Bank of Iran and specified individuals and entities identified as Government of Iran by the Office of Foreign Assets Control on the Specially Designated Nationals and Blocked Persons List (SDN List), as set out in Attachment 3 to Annex II (including the opening and maintenance of correspondent and payable through-accounts at non-U.S. financial institutions, investments, foreign exchange transactions and letters of credit);

    ii. Transactions in Iranian Rial;

    iii. Provision of U.S. banknotes to the Government of Iran;

    iv. Bilateral trade limitations on Iranian revenues abroad, including limitations on their transfer;

    v. Purchase, subscription to, or facilitation of the issuance of Iranian sovereign debt, including governmental bonds;

    vi. Financial messaging services to the Central Bank of Iran and Iranian financial institutions set out in Attachment 3 to Annex II;

    vii. Underwriting services, insurance, or reinsurance;

    viii. Efforts to reduce Iran's crude oil sales;

ix. Investment, including participation in joint ventures, goods, services, information, technology and technical expertise and support for Iran's oil, gas and petrochemical sectors;
x. Purchase, acquisition, sale, transportation or marketing of petroleum, petrochemical products and natural gas from Iran;
xi. Export, sale or provision of refined petroleum products and petrochemical products to Iran;
xii. Transactions with Iran's energy sector;
xiii. Transactions with Iran's shipping and shipbuilding sectors and port operators;
xiv. Trade in gold and other precious metals;
xv. Trade with Iran in graphite, raw or semi-finished metals such as aluminum and steel, coal, and software for integrating industrial processes;
xvi. Sale, supply or transfer of goods and services used in connection with Iran's automotive sector;
xvii. Sanctions on associated services for each of the categories above;
xviii. Remove individuals and entities set out in Attachment 3 to Annex II from the SDN List, the Foreign Sanctions Evaders List, and/or the Non-SDN Iran Sanctions Act List; and
xix. Terminate Executive Orders 13574, 13590, 13622, and 13645, and Sects. 5–7 and 15 of Executive Order 13628.

22. The United States will, as specified in Annex II and in accordance with Annex V, allow for the sale of commercial passenger aircraft and related parts and services to Iran; license non-U.S. persons that are owned or controlled by a U.S. person to engage in activities with Iran consistent with this JCPOA; and license the importation into the United States of Iranian-origin carpets and foodstuffs.

23. Eight years after Adoption Day or when the IAEA has reached the Broader Conclusion that all nuclear material in Iran remains in peaceful activities, whichever is earlier, the United States will seek such legislative action as may be appropriate to terminate, or modify to effectuate the termination of, the sanctions specified in Annex II on the acquisition of nuclear-related commodities and services for nuclear activities contemplated in this JCPOA, to be consistent with the U.S. approach to other non-nuclear-weapon states under the NPT.
24. The E3/EU and the United States specify in Annex II a full and complete list of all nuclear-related sanctions or restrictive measures and will lift them in accordance with Annex V. Annex II also specifies the effects of the lifting of sanctions beginning on "Implementation Day". If at any time following the Implementation Day, Iran believes that any other nuclear-related sanction or restrictive measure of the E3/EU+3 is preventing the full implementation of the sanctions lifting as specified in this JCPOA, the JCPOA participant in question will consult with Iran with a view to resolving the issue and, if they concur that lifting of this sanction or restrictive measure is appropriate, the JCPOA participant in question will take appropriate action. If they are not able to resolve the issue, Iran or any member of the E3/EU+3 may refer the issue to the Joint Commission.
25. If a law at the state or local level in the United States is preventing the implementation of the sanctions lifting as specified in this JCPOA, the United States will take appropriate steps, taking into account all available authorities, with a view to achieving such implementation. The United States will actively encourage officials at the state or local level to take into account the changes in the U.S. policy reflected in the lifting of sanctions under this JCPOA and to refrain from actions inconsistent with this change in policy.

26. The EU will refrain from re-introducing or re-imposing the sanctions that it has terminated implementing under this JCPOA, without prejudice to the dispute resolution process provided for under this JCPOA. There will be no new nuclear-related UN Security Council sanctions and no new EU nuclear-related sanctions or restrictive measures. The United States will make best efforts in good faith to sustain this JCPOA and to prevent interference with the realization of the full benefit by Iran of the sanctions lifting specified in Annex II. The U.S. Administration, acting consistent with the respective roles of the President and the Congress, will refrain from re-introducing or re-imposing the sanctions specified in Annex II that it has ceased applying under this JCPOA, without prejudice to the dispute resolution process provided for under this JCPOA. The U.S. Administration, acting consistent with the respective roles of the President and the Congress, will refrain from imposing new nuclear-related sanctions. Iran has stated that it will treat such a re-introduction or re-imposition of the sanctions specified in Annex II, or such an imposition of new nuclear-related sanctions, as grounds to cease performing its commitments under this JCPOA in whole or in part.
27. The E3/EU+3 will take adequate administrative and regulatory measures to ensure clarity and effectiveness with respect to the lifting of sanctions under this JCPOA. The EU and its Member States as well as the United States will issue relevant guidelines and make publicly accessible statements on the details of sanctions or restrictive measures which have been lifted under this JCPOA. The EU and its Member States and the United States commit to consult with Iran regarding the

content of such guidelines and statements, on a regular basis and whenever appropriate.
28. The E3/EU+3 and Iran commit to implement this JCPOA in good faith and in a constructive atmosphere, based on mutual respect, and to refrain from any action inconsistent with the letter, spirit and intent of this JCPOA that would undermine its successful implementation. Senior Government officials of the E3/EU+3 and Iran will make every effort to support the successful implementation of this JCPOA including in their public statements.[2] The E3/EU+3 will take all measures required to lift sanctions and will refrain from imposing exceptional or discriminatory regulatory and procedural requirements in lieu of the sanctions and restrictive measures covered by the JCPOA.
29. The EU and its Member States and the United States, consistent with their respective laws, will refrain from any policy specifically intended to directly and adversely affect the normalization of trade and economic relations with Iran inconsistent with their commitments not to undermine the successful implementation of this JCPOA.
30. The E3/EU+3 will not apply sanctions or restrictive measures to persons or entities for engaging in activities covered by the lifting of sanctions provided for in this JCPOA, provided that such activities are otherwise consistent with E3/EU+3 laws and regulations in effect. Following the lifting of sanctions under this JCPOA as specified in Annex II, ongoing investigations on possible infringements of such sanctions may be reviewed in accordance with applicable national laws.
31. Consistent with the timing specified in Annex V, the EU and its Member States will terminate the implementation

of the measures applicable to designated entities and individuals, including the Central Bank of Iran and other Iranian banks and financial institutions, as detailed in Annex II and the attachments thereto. Consistent with the timing specified in Annex V, the United States will remove designation of certain entities and individuals on the Specially Designated Nationals and Blocked Persons List, and entities and individuals listed on the Foreign Sanctions Evaders List, as detailed in Annex II and the attachments thereto.

32. EU and E3+3 countries and international participants will engage in joint projects with Iran, including through IAEA technical cooperation projects, in the field of peaceful nuclear technology, including nuclear power plants, research reactors, fuel fabrication, agreed joint advanced R&D such as fusion, establishment of a state-of-the-art regional nuclear medical center, personnel training, nuclear safety and security, and environmental protection, as detailed in Annex III. They will take necessary measures, as appropriate, for the implementation of these projects.

33. The E3/EU+3 and Iran will agree on steps to ensure Iran's access in areas of trade, technology, finance and energy. The EU will further explore possible areas for cooperation between the EU, its Member States and Iran, and in this context consider the use of available instruments such as export credits to facilitate trade, project financing and investment in Iran.

Implementation Plan

34. Iran and the E3/EU+3 will implement their JCPOA commitments according to the sequence specified in

Annex V. The milestones for implementation are as follows:

i. Finalization Day is the date on which negotiations of this JCPOA are concluded among the E3/EU+3 and Iran, to be followed promptly by submission of the resolution endorsing this JCPOA to the UN Security Council for adoption without delay.
ii. Adoption Day is the date 90 days after the endorsement of this JCPOA by the UN Security Council, or such earlier date as may be determined by mutual consent of the JCPOA participants, at which time this JCPOA and the commitments in this JCPOA come into effect. Beginning on that date, JCPOA participants will make necessary arrangements and preparations for the implementation of their JCPOA commitments.
iii. Implementation Day is the date on which, simultaneously with the IAEA report verifying implementation by Iran of the nuclear-related measures described in Sects. 15.1–15.11 of Annex V, the EU and the United States take the actions described in Sects. 16 and 17 of Annex V respectively and in accordance with the UN Security Council resolution, the actions described in Sect. 18 of Annex V occur at the UN level.
iv. Transition Day is the date 8 years after Adoption Day or the date on which the Director General of the IAEA submits a report stating that the IAEA has reached the Broader Conclusion that all nuclear material in Iran remains in peaceful activities, whichever is earlier. On that date, the EU and the United States will take the actions described in Sects. 20

and 21 of Annex V respectively and Iran will seek, consistent with the Constitutional roles of the President and Parliament, ratification of the Additional Protocol.

v. UN Security Council resolution Termination Day is the date on which the UN Security Council resolution endorsing this JCPOA terminates according to its terms, which is to be 10 years from Adoption Day, provided that the provisions of previous resolutions have not been reinstated. On that date, the EU will take the actions described in Sect. 25 of Annex V.

35. The sequence and milestones set forth above and in Annex V are without prejudice to the duration of JCPOA commitments stated in this JCPOA.

Dispute Resolution Mechanism

36. If Iran believed that any or all of the E3/EU+3 were not meeting their commitments under this JCPOA, Iran could refer the issue to the Joint Commission for resolution; similarly, if any of the E3/EU+3 believed that Iran was not meeting its commitments under this JCPOA, any of the E3/EU+3 could do the same. The Joint Commission would have 15 days to resolve the issue, unless the time period was extended by consensus. After Joint Commission consideration, any participant could refer the issue to Ministers of Foreign Affairs, if it believed the compliance issue had not been resolved. Ministers would have 15 days to resolve the issue, unless the time period was extended by consensus. After Joint Commission consideration—in parallel with (or in lieu of) review at the Ministerial level—either the complaining participant

or the participant whose performance is in question could request that the issue be considered by an Advisory Board, which would consist of three members (one each appointed by the participants in the dispute and a third independent member). The Advisory Board should provide a non-binding opinion on the compliance issue within 15 days. If, after this 30-day process the issue is not resolved, the Joint Commission would consider the opinion of the Advisory Board for no more than 5 days in order to resolve the issue. If the issue still has not been resolved to the satisfaction of the complaining participant, and if the complaining participant deems the issue to constitute significant non-performance, then that participant could treat the unresolved issue as grounds to cease performing its commitments under this JCPOA in whole or in part and/or notify the UN Security Council that it believes the issue constitutes significant non-performance.

37. Upon receipt of the notification from the complaining participant, as described above, including a description of the good-faith efforts the participant made to exhaust the dispute resolution process specified in this JCPOA, the UN Security Council, in accordance with its procedures, shall vote on a resolution to continue the sanctions lifting. If the resolution described above has not been adopted within 30 days of the notification, then the provisions of the old UN Security Council resolutions would be re-imposed, unless the UN Security Council decides otherwise. In such event, these provisions would not apply with retroactive effect to contracts signed between any party and Iran or Iranian individuals and entities prior to the date of application, provided that the activities contemplated under and

execution of such contracts are consistent with this JCPOA and the previous and current UN Security Council resolutions. The UN Security Council, expressing its intention to prevent the reapplication of the provisions if the issue giving rise to the notification is resolved within this period, intends to take into account the views of the States involved in the issue and any opinion on the issue of the Advisory Board. Iran has stated that if sanctions are reinstated in whole or in part, Iran will treat that as grounds to cease performing its commitments under this JCPOA in whole or in part.

Annex I: Nuclear-Related Measures

A. General

1. The sequence of implementation of the commitments detailed in this Annex is specified in Annex V to the Joint Comprehensive Plan of Action (JCPOA). Unless otherwise specified, the durations of the commitments in this Annex are from Implementation Day.

B. Arak Heavy Water Research Reactor

2. Iran will modernize the Arak heavy water research reactor to support peaceful nuclear research and radioisotopes production for medical and industrial purposes. Iran will redesign and rebuild the reactor, based on the agreed conceptual design (as attached to this Annex) to support its peaceful nuclear research and production needs and purposes, including testing of fuel pins and assembly prototypes and structural materials. The design will be such as to minimize the production of plutonium and not to produce weapon-grade plutonium in normal operation. The power of the redesigned

reactor will not exceed 20 MWth. The E3/EU+3 and Iran share the understanding that the parameters in the conceptual design are subject to possible and necessary adjustments in developing the final design while fully preserving the above-mentioned purposes and principles of modernization.
3. Iran will not pursue construction at the existing unfinished reactor based on its original design and will remove the existing calandria and retain it in Iran. The calandria will be made inoperable by filling any openings in the calandria with concrete such that the IAEA can verify that it will not be usable for a future nuclear application. In redesigning and reconstructing of the modernized Arak heavy water research reactor, Iran will maximize the use of existing infrastructure already installed at the current Arak research reactor.
4. Iran will take the leadership role as the owner and as the project manager, and have responsibility for overall implementation of the Arak modernization project, with E3/EU+3 participants assuming responsibilities regarding the modernization of the Arak reactor as described in this Annex. A Working Group composed of E3/EU+3 participants will be established to facilitate the redesigning and rebuilding of the reactor. An international partnership composed of Iran and the Working Group would implement the Arak modernization project. The Working Group could be enlarged to include other countries by consensus of the participants of the Working Group and Iran. E3/EU+3 participants and Iran will conclude an official document expressing their strong commitments to the Arak modernization project in advance of Implementation Day which would provide an assured path forward to modernize the reactor and would define the responsibilities assumed by the E3/EU+3 participants, and subsequently contracts

would be concluded. The participants of the Working Group will provide assistance needed by Iran for redesigning and rebuilding the reactor, consistent with their respective national laws, in such a manner as to enable the safe and timely construction and commissioning of the modernized reactor.

5. Iran and the Working Group will cooperate to develop the final design of the modernized reactor and the design of the subsidiary laboratories to be carried out by Iran, and review conformity with international safety standards, such that the reactor can be licensed by the relevant Iranian regulatory authority for commissioning and operation. The final design of the modernized reactor and the design of the subsidiary laboratories will be submitted to the Joint Commission. The Joint Commission will aim to complete its review and endorsement within three months after the submission of the final design. If the Joint Commission does not complete its review and endorsement within three months, Iran could raise the issue through the dispute resolution mechanism envisaged by this JCPOA.

6. The IAEA will monitor the construction and report to the Working Group for confirmation that the construction of the modernized reactor is consistent with the approved final design.

7. As the project manager, Iran will take responsibility for the construction efforts. E3/EU+3 parties will, consistent with their national laws, take appropriate administrative, legal, technical, and regulatory measures to support co-operation.

   E3/EU+3 parties will support the purchase by Iran, the transfer and supply of necessary materials, equipment, instrumentation and control systems and technologies required for the construction of the redesigned

reactor, through the mechanism established by this JCPOA, as well as through exploration of relevant funding contributions.
8. E3/EU+3 parties will also support and facilitate the timely and safe construction of the modernized Arak reactor and its subsidiary laboratories, upon request by Iran, through IAEA technical cooperation if appropriate, including but not limited to technical and financial assistance, supply of required materials and equipment, state-of-the-art instrumentation and control systems and equipment and support for licensing and authorization.
9. The redesigned reactor will use up to 3.67 percent enriched uranium in the form of UO_2 with a mass of approximately 350 kg of UO_2 in a full core load, with a fuel design to be reviewed and approved by the Joint Commission. The international partnership with the participation of Iran will fabricate the initial fuel core load for the reactor outside Iran. The international partnership will cooperate with Iran, including through technical assistance, to fabricate, test and license fuel fabrication capabilities in Iran for subsequent fuel core reloads for future use with this reactor. Destructive and non-destructive testing of this fuel including Post-Irradiation-Examination (PIE) will take place in one of the participating countries outside of Iran and that country will work with Iran to license the subsequent fuel fabricated in Iran for the use in the redesigned reactor under IAEA monitoring.
10. Iran will not produce or test natural uranium pellets, fuel pins or fuel assemblies, which are specifically designed for the support of the originally designed Arak reactor, designated by the IAEA as IR-40. Iran will store under IAEA continuous monitoring all existing natural uranium pellets and IR-40 fuel assemblies until

the modernized Arak reactor becomes operational, at which point these natural uranium pellets and IR-40 fuel assemblies will be converted to UNH, or exchanged with an equivalent quantity of natural uranium. Iran will make the necessary technical modifications to the natural uranium fuel production process line that was intended to supply fuel for the IR-40 reactor design, such that it can be used for the fabrication of the fuel reloads for the modernized Arak reactor.

11. All spent fuel from the redesigned Arak reactor, regardless of its origin, for the lifetime of the reactor, will be shipped out of Iran to a mutually determined location in E3/EU+3 countries or third countries, for further treatment or disposition as provided for in relevant contracts to be concluded, consistent with national laws, with the recipient party, within one year from the unloading from the reactor or whenever deemed to be safe for transfer by the recipient country.
12. Iran will submit the DIQ of the redesigned reactor to the IAEA which will include information on the planned radio-isotope production and reactor operation program. The reactor will be operated under IAEA monitoring.
13. Iran will operate the Fuel Manufacturing Plant only to produce fuel assemblies for light water reactors and reloads for the modernized Arak reactor.

C. **Heavy Water Production Plant**

14. All excess heavy water which is beyond Iran's needs for the modernized Arak research reactor, the Zero power heavy water reactor, quantities needed for medical research and production of deuterate solutions and

chemical compounds including, where appropriate, contingency stocks, will be made available for export to the international market based on international prices and delivered to the international buyer for 15 years. Iran's needs, consistent with the parameters above, are estimated to be 130 metric tonnes of nuclear grade heavy water or its equivalent in different enrichments prior to commissioning of the modernized Arak research reactor, and 90 metric tonnes after the commissioning, including the amount contained in the reactor.

15. Iran will inform the IAEA about the inventory and the production of the HWPP and will allow the IAEA to monitor the quantities of the heavy water stocks and the amount of heavy water produced, including through IAEA visits, as requested, to the HWPP.

D. Other Reactors

16. Consistent with its plan, Iran will keep pace with the trend of international technological advancement in relying only on light water for its future nuclear power and research reactors with enhanced international cooperation including assurances of supply of necessary fuel.
17. Iran intends to ship out all spent fuel for all future and present nuclear power and research reactors, for further treatment or disposition as provided for in relevant contracts to be concluded consistent with national laws with the recipient party.

E. Spent Fuel Reprocessing Activities

18. For 15 years Iran will not, and does not intend to thereafter, engage in any spent fuel reprocessing or spent

fuel reprocessing R&D activities. For the purpose of this annex, spent fuel includes all types of irradiated fuel.

19. For 15 years Iran will not, and does not intend to thereafter, reprocess spent fuel except for irradiated enriched uranium targets for production of radio-isotopes for medical and peaceful industrial purposes.

20. For 15 years Iran will not, and does not intend to thereafter, develop, acquire or build facilities capable of separation of plutonium, uranium or neptunium from spent fuel or from fertile targets, other than for production of radio-isotopes for medical and peaceful industrial purposes.

21. For 15 years, Iran will only develop, acquire, build, or operate hot cells (containing a cell or interconnected cells), shielded cells or shielded glove boxes with dimensions less than 6 cubic meters in volume compatible with the specifications set out in Annex I of the Additional Protocol. These will be co-located with the modernized Arak research reactor, the Tehran Research Reactor, and radio-medicine production complexes, and only capable of the separation and processing of industrial or medical isotopes and non-destructive PIE. The needed equipment will be acquired through the procurement mechanism established by this JCPOA. For 15 years, Iran will develop, acquire, build, or operate hot cells (containing a cell or interconnected cells), shielded cells or shielded glove boxes with dimensions beyond 6 cubic meters in volume and specifications set out in Annex I of the Additional Protocol, only after approval by the Joint Commission.

22. The E3/EU+3 are ready to facilitate all of the destructive and non-destructive examinations on fuel elements

and/or fuel assembly prototypes including PIE for all fuel fabricated in or outside Iran and irradiated in Iran, using their existing facilities outside Iran. Except for the Arak research reactor complex, Iran will not develop, build, acquire or operate hot cells capable of performing PIE or seek to acquire equipment to build/develop such a capability, for 15 years.

23. For 15 years, in addition to continuing current fuel testing activities at the TRR, Iran will undertake non-destructive post irradiation examination (PIE) of fuel pins, fuel assembly prototypes and structural materials. These examinations will be exclusively at the Arak research reactor complex. However, the E3/EU+3 will make available their facilities to conduct destructive testing with Iranian specialists, as agreed. The hot cells at the Arak research reactor in which non-destructive PIE are performed will not be physically interconnected to cells that process or handle materials for the production of medical or industrial radioisotopes.

24. For 15 years, Iran will not engage in producing or acquiring plutonium or uranium metals or their alloys, or conducting R&D on plutonium or uranium (or their alloys) metallurgy, or casting, forming, or machining plutonium or uranium metal.

25. Iran will not produce, seek, or acquire separated plutonium, highly enriched uranium (defined as 20% or greater uranium-235), or uranium-233, or neptunium-237 (except for use as laboratory standards or in instruments using neptunium-237) for 15 years.

26. If Iran seeks to initiate R&D on uranium metal based TRR fuel in small agreed quantities after 10 years and before 15 years, Iran will present its plan to, and seek approval by, the Joint Commission.

F. Enrichment Capacity

27. Iran will keep its enrichment capacity at no more than 5060 IR-1 centrifuge machines in no more than 30 cascades in their current configurations in currently operating units at the Natanz Fuel Enrichment Plant (FEP) for 10 years.
28. Iran will keep its level of uranium enrichment at up to 3.67 percent for 15 years.
29. Iran will remove the following excess centrifuges and infrastructure not associated with 5060 IR-1 centrifuges in FEP, which will be stored at Natanz in Hall B of FEP under IAEA continuous monitoring:

29.1. All excess centrifuge machines, including IR-2m centrifuges. Excess IR-1 centrifuges will be used for the replacement of failed or damaged centrifuges of the same type on a one-for-one basis.

29.2. UF6 pipework including sub headers, valves and pressure transducers at cascade level, and frequency inverters, and UF6 withdrawal equipment from one of the withdrawal stations, which is currently not in service, including its vacuum pumps and chemical traps.

30. For the purpose of this Annex, the IAEA will confirm through the established practice the failed or damaged status of centrifuge machines before removal.
31. For 15 years, Iran will install gas centrifuge machines, or enrichment-related infrastructure, whether suitable for uranium enrichment, research and development, or stable isotope enrichment, exclusively at the locations and for the activities specified under this JCPOA.

G. Centrifuges Research and Development

32. Iran will continue to conduct enrichment R&D in a manner that does not accumulate enriched uranium.

For 10 years and consistent with its enrichment R&D plan, Iran's enrichment R&D with uranium will only include IR-4, IR-5, IR-6 and IR-8 centrifuges. Mechanical testing on up to two single centrifuges for each type will be carried out only on the IR-2m, IR-4, IR-5, IR-6, IR-6s, IR-7 and IR-8. Iran will build or test, with or without uranium, only those gas centrifuges specified in this JCPOA.

33. Consistent with its plan, Iran will continue working with the 164-machine IR-2m cascade at PFEP in order to complete the necessary tests until 30 November 2015 or the day of implementation of this JCPOA, whichever comes later, and after that it will take these machines out of the PFEP and store them under IAEA continuous monitoring at Natanz in Hall B of FEP.
34. Consistent with its plan, Iran will continue working with the 164-machine IR-4 cascade at PFEP in order to complete the necessary tests until 30 November 2015 or the day of implementation of this JCPOA, whichever comes later, and after that it will take these machines out of the PFEP and store them under IAEA continuous monitoring at Natanz in Hall B of FEP.
35. Iran will continue the testing of a single IR-4 centrifuge machine and IR-4 centrifuge cascade of up to 10 centrifuge machines for 10 years.
36. Iran will test a single IR-5 centrifuge machine for 10 years.
37. Iran will continue testing of the IR-6 on single centrifuge machines and its intermediate cascades and will commence testing of up to 30 centrifuge machines from one and a half years before the end of year 10. Iran will proceed from single centrifuge machines and small cascades to intermediate cascades in a logical sequence.

38. Iran will commence, upon start of implementation of the JCPOA, testing of the IR-8 on single centrifuge machines and its intermediate cascades and will commence the testing of up to 30 centrifuges machines from one and a half years before the end of year 10. Iran will proceed from single centrifuges to small cascades to intermediate cascades in a logical sequence.
39. For 10 years, Iran, consistent with the established practice, will recombine the enriched and depleted streams from the IR-6 and IR-8 cascades through the use of welded pipework on withdrawal main headers in a manner that precludes the withdrawal of enriched and depleted uranium materials and verified by the IAEA.
40. For 15 years, Iran will conduct all testing of centrifuges with uranium only at the PFEP. Iran will conduct all mechanical testing of centrifuges only at the PFEP and the Tehran Research Centre.
41. For the purpose of adapting PFEP to the R&D activities in the enrichment and enrichment R&D plan, Iran will remove all centrifuges except those needed for testing as described in the relevant paragraphs above, except for the IR-1 cascade (No. 1) as described below. For the full IR-1 cascade (No. 6), Iran will modify associated infrastructure by removing UF6 pipework, including sub-headers, valves and pressure transducers at cascade level, and frequency inverters. The IR-1 cascade (No. 1) centrifuges will be kept but made inoperable, as verified by the IAEA, through the removal of centrifuge rotors and the injection of epoxy resin into the sub headers, feeding, product, and tails pipework, and the removal of controls and electrical systems for vacuum, power and cooling. Excess centrifuges and infrastructure will be stored at Natanz in Hall B of FEP

under IAEA continuous monitoring. The R&D space in line No. 6 will be left empty until Iran needs to use it for its R&D program.

42. Consistent with the activities in the enrichment and enrichment R&D plan, Iran will maintain the cascade infrastructure for testing of single centrifuges and small and intermediate cascades in two R&D lines (No. 2 and No. 3) and will adapt two other lines (No. 4 and No. 5) with infrastructure similar to that for lines No. 2 and No. 3 in order to enable future R&D activities as specified in this JCPoA. Adaptation will include modification of all UF6 pipework (including removal of all sub headers except as agreed as needed for the R&D program) and associated instrumentation to be compatible with single centrifuges and small and intermediate cascade testing instead of full scale testing.

43. Consistent with its plan and internationally established practices, Iran intends to continue R&D on new types of centrifuges through computer modeling and simulations, including at universities. For any such project to proceed to a prototype stage for mechanical testing within 10 years, a full presentation to, and approval by, the Joint Commission is needed.

H. Fordow Fuel Enrichment Plant

44. The Fordow Fuel Enrichment Plant (FFEP) will be converted into a nuclear, physics, and technology center and international collaboration will be encouraged in agreed areas of research. The Joint Commission will be informed in advance of the specific projects that will be undertaken at Fordow.

45. Iran will not conduct any uranium enrichment or any uranium enrichment related R&D and will have no nuclear material at the Fordow Fuel Enrichment Plant (FFEP) for 15 years.

46. For 15 years, Iran will maintain no more than 1044 IR-1 centrifuge machines at one wing of the FFEP of which:

46.1. Two cascades that have not experienced UF6 before will be modified for the production of stable isotopes. The transition to stable isotope production of these cascades at FFEP will be conducted in joint partnership between the Russian Federation and Iran on the basis of arrangements to be mutually agreed upon. To prepare these two cascades for installation of a new cascade architecture appropriate for stable isotope production by the joint partnership, Iran will remove the connection to the UF6 feed main header, and move cascade UF6 pipework (except for the dump line in order to maintain vacuum) to storage in Fordow under IAEA continuous monitoring. The Joint Commission will be informed about the conceptual framework of stable isotope production at FFEP.

46.2. For four cascades with all associated infrastructure remaining except for pipework that enables crossover tandem connections, two will be placed in an idle state, not spinning. The other two cascades will continue to spin until the transition to stable isotope production described in the previous subparagraph has been completed. Upon completion of the transition to stable isotope production described in the previous subparagraph, these two spinning cascades will be placed in an idle state, not spinning.

47. Iran will:

47.1. remove the other 2 cascades of IR-1 centrifuges from this wing, by removing all centrifuges and cascade UF6 pipework, including sub headers, valves and pressure transducers at cascade level, and frequency inverters.
47.2. also subsequently remove cascade electrical cabling, individual cascade control cabinets and vacuum pumps. All these excess centrifuges and infrastructure will be stored at Natanz in Hall B of FEP under IAEA continuous monitoring.
48. Iran will:
48.1. remove all excess centrifuges and uranium enrichment related infrastructure from the other wing of the FFEP. This will include removal of all centrifuges and UF6 pipework, including sub headers, valves and pressure gauges and transducers, and frequency inverters and converters, and UF6 feed and withdrawal stations.
48.2. also subsequently remove cascade electrical cabling, individual cascade control cabinets, vacuum pumps and centrifuge mounting blocks. All these excess centrifuges and infrastructure will be stored at Natanz in Hall B of FEP under IAEA continuous monitoring.
49. Centrifuges from the four idle cascades may be used for the replacement of failed or damaged centrifuges in stable isotope production at Fordow.
50. Iran will limit its stable isotope production activities with gas centrifuges to the FFEP for 15 years and will use no more than 348 IR-1 centrifuges for these activities at the FFEP. The associated R&D activities in Iran will occur at the FFEP and at Iran's declared and monitored centrifuge manufacturing facilities for testing, modification and balancing these IR-1 centrifuges.
51. The IAEA will establish a baseline for the amount of uranium legacy from past enrichment operations that

will remain in Fordow. Iran will permit the IAEA regular access, including daily as requested by the IAEA, access to the FFEP in order to monitor Iran's production of stable isotopes and the absence of undeclared nuclear material and activities at the FFEP for 15 years.

I. Other Aspects of Enrichment

52. Iran will abide by its voluntary commitments as expressed in its own long term enrichment and enrichment R&D plan to be submitted as part of the initial declaration described in Article 2 of the Additional Protocol.[3] The IAEA will confirm on an annual basis, for the duration of the plan that the nature and scope and scale of Iran's enrichment and enrichment R&D activities are in line with this plan.
53. Iran will start to install necessary infrastructure for the IR-8 at Natanz in Hall B of FEP after year 10.
54. An agreed template for describing different centrifuge types (IR-1, IR-2m, IR-4, IR-5, IR-6, IR-6s, IR-7, IR-8) and the associated definitions need to be accomplished by implementation day.
55. An agreed procedure for measuring IR-1, IR-2m and IR-4 centrifuge performance data needs to be accomplished by implementation day.

J. Uranium Stocks and Fuels

56. Iran will maintain a total enriched uranium stockpile of no more than 300 kg of up to 3.67% enriched uranium hexafluoride (or the equivalent in different chemical forms) for 15 years.
57. All enriched uranium hexafluoride in excess of 300 kg of up to 3.67% enriched UF6 (or the equivalent in

different chemical forms) will be down blended to natural uranium level or be sold on the international market and delivered to the international buyer in return for natural uranium delivered to Iran. Iran will enter into a commercial contract with an entity outside Iran for the purchase and transfer of its enriched uranium stockpile in excess of 300 kg UF6 in return for natural uranium delivered to Iran. The E3/EU+3 will facilitate, where applicable, the conclusion and implementation of this contract. Iran may choose to seek to sell excess enriched uranium to the IAEA fuel bank in Kazakhstan when the fuel bank becomes operational.

58. All uranium oxide enriched to between 5% and 20% will be fabricated into fuel plates for the Tehran Research Reactor or transferred, based on a commercial transaction, outside of Iran or diluted to an enrichment level of 3.67% or less. Scrap oxide and other forms not in plates that cannot be fabricated into TRR fuel plates will be transferred, based on a commercial transaction, outside of Iran or diluted to an enrichment level of 3.67% or less. In case of future supply of 19.75% enriched uranium oxide (U3O8) for TRR fuel plates fabrication, all scrap oxide and other forms not in plates that cannot be fabricated into TRR fuel plates, containing uranium enriched to between 5% and 20%, will be transferred, based on a commercial transaction, outside of Iran or diluted to an enrichment level of 3.67% or less within 6 months of its production. Scrap plates will be transferred, based on a commercial transaction, outside Iran. The commercial transactions should be structured to return an equivalent amount of natural uranium to Iran. For 15 years, Iran will not build or operate facilities for converting fuel plates or scrap back to UF6.

59. Russian designed, fabricated and licensed fuel assemblies for use in Russian-supplied reactors in Iran do not count against the 300 kg UF6 stockpile limit. Enriched uranium in fabricated fuel assemblies from other sources outside of Iran for use in Iran's nuclear research and power reactors, including those which will be fabricated outside of Iran for the initial fuel load of the modernized Arak research reactor, which are certified by the fuel supplier and the appropriate Iranian authority to meet international standards, will not count against the 300 kg UF6 stockpile limit. The Joint Commission will establish a Technical Working Group with the goal of enabling fuel to be fabricated in Iran while adhering to the agreed stockpile parameters (300 kg of up to 3.67 % enriched UF6 or the equivalent in different chemical forms). This Technical Working Group will also, within one year, work to develop objective technical criteria for assessing whether fabricated fuel and its intermediate products can be readily converted to UF6. Enriched uranium in fabricated fuel assemblies and its intermediate products manufactured in Iran and certified to meet international standards, including those for the modernized Arak research reactor, will not count against the 300 kg UF6 stockpile limit provided the Technical Working Group of the Joint Commission approves that such fuel assemblies and their intermediate products cannot be readily reconverted into UF6. This could for instance be achieved through impurities (e.g. burnable poisons or otherwise) contained in fuels or through the fuel being in a chemical form such that direct conversion back to UF6 would be technically difficult without dissolution and purification. The objective technical criteria will guide the approval process of the Technical Working Group. The IAEA will monitor the fuel fabrication process for any

fuel produced in Iran to verify that the fuel and intermediate products comport with the fuel fabrication process that was approved by the Technical Working Group. The Joint Commission will also support assistance to Iran including through IAEA technical cooperation as appropriate, in meeting international qualification standards for nuclear fuel produced by Iran.

60. Iran will seek to enter into a commercial contract with entities outside Iran for the purchase of fuel for the TRR and enriched uranium targets. The E3/EU+3 will facilitate, as needed, the conclusion and implementation of this contract. In the case of lack of conclusion of a contract with a fuel supplier, E3/EU+3 will supply a quantity of 19.75% enriched uranium oxide (U_3O_8) and deliver to Iran, exclusively for the purpose of fabrication in Iran of fuel for the TRR and enriched uranium targets for the lifetime of the reactor. This 19.75% enriched uranium oxide (U_3O_8) will be supplied in increments no greater than approximately 5 kg and each new increment will be provided only when the previous increment of this material has been verified by the IAEA to have been mixed with aluminum to make fuel for the TRR or fabricated into enriched uranium targets. Iran will notify the E3/EU+3 within 2 year before the contingency of TRR fuel will be exhausted in order to have the uranium oxide available 6 months before the end of the 2 year period.

K. Centrifuge Manufacturing

61. Consistent with its enrichment and enrichment R&D plan, Iran will only engage in production of centrifuges, including centrifuge rotors suitable for isotope separation or any other centrifuge components, to meet the enrichment and enrichment R&D requirements of this Annex.

62. Consistent with its plan, Iran will use the stock of IR-1 centrifuge machines in storage, which are in excess of the remaining 5060 IR-1 centrifuges in Natanz and the IR-1 centrifuges installed at Fordow, for the replacement of failed or damaged machines. Whenever during the 10 year period from the start of the implementation of the JCPOA, the level of stock of IR-1 machines falls to 500 or below, Iran may maintain this level of stock by resuming production of IR-1 machines at a rate up to the average monthly crash rate without exceeding the stock of 500.
63. Consistent with its plan, at the end of year 8, Iran will commence manufacturing of IR-6 and IR-8 centrifuges without rotors through year 10 at a rate of up to 200 centrifuges per year for each type. After year 10, Iran will produce complete centrifuges with the same rate to meet its enrichment and enrichment R&D needs. Iran will store them at Natanz in an above ground location, under IAEA continuous monitoring, until they are needed for final assembly according to the enrichment and enrichment R&D plan.

L. **Additional Protocol and Modified Code 3.1**

64. Iran will notify the IAEA of provisional application of the Additional Protocol to its Safeguards Agreement in accordance with Article 17(b) of the Additional Protocol pending its entry into force, and subsequently seek ratification and entry into force, consistent with the respective roles of the President and the Majlis (Parliament).
65. Iran will notify the IAEA that it will fully implement the Modified Code 3.1 of the Subsidiary Arrangement

to Iran's Safeguards Agreement as long as the Safeguards Agreement remains in force.

M. Past and Present Issues of Concern

66. Iran will complete all activities as set out in paragraphs 2, 4, 5, and 6 of the "Roadmap for Clarification of Past and Present Outstanding Issues", as verified by the IAEA in its regular updates by the Director General of the IAEA on the implementation of this Roadmap.

N. Modern Technologies and Long Term Presence of IAEA

67. For the purpose of increasing the efficiency of monitoring for this JCPOA, for 15 years or longer, for the specified verification measures:
67.1. Iran will permit the IAEA the use of on-line enrichment measurement and electronic seals which communicate their status within nuclear sites to IAEA inspectors, as well as other IAEA approved and certified modern technologies in line with internationally accepted IAEA practice. Iran will facilitate automated collection of IAEA measurement recordings registered by installed measurement devices and sending to IAEA working space in individual nuclear sites.
67.2. Iran will make the necessary arrangements to allow for a long-term IAEA presence, including issuing long-term visas, as well as providing proper working space at nuclear sites and, with best efforts, at locations near nuclear sites in Iran for the designated IAEA inspectors for working and keeping necessary equipment.

67.3. Iran will increase the number of designated IAEA inspectors to the range of 130–150 within 9 months from the date of the implementation of the JCPOA, and will generally allow the designation of inspectors from nations that have diplomatic relations with Iran, consistent with its laws and regulations.

O. Transparency Related to Uranium Ore Concentrate (UOC)

68. Iran will permit the IAEA to monitor, through agreed measures that will include containment and surveillance measures, for 25 years, that all uranium ore concentrate produced in Iran or obtained from any other source, is transferred to the uranium conversion facility (UCF) in Esfahan or to any other future uranium conversion facility which Iran might decide to build in Iran within this period.
69. Iran will provide the IAEA with all necessary information such that the IAEA will be able to verify the production of the uranium ore concentrate and the inventory of uranium ore concentrate produced in Iran or obtained from any other source for 25 years.

P. Transparency Related to Enrichment

70. For 15 years, Iran will permit the IAEA to implement continuous monitoring, including through containment and surveillance measures, as necessary, to verify that stored centrifuges and infrastructure remain in storage, and are only used to replace failed or damaged centrifuges, as specified in this Annex.
71. Iran will permit the IAEA regular access, including daily access as requested by the IAEA, to relevant

buildings at Natanz, including all parts of the FEP and PFEP, for 15 years.
72. For 15 years, the Natanz enrichment site will be the sole location for all of Iran's uranium enrichment related activities including safeguarded R&D.
73. Iran intends to apply nuclear export policies and practices in line with the internationally established standards for the export of nuclear material, equipment and technology. For 15 years, Iran will only engage, including through export of any enrichment or enrichment related equipment and technology, with any other country, or with any foreign entity in enrichment or enrichment related activities, including related research and development activities, following approval by the Joint Commission.

Q. **Access**

74. Requests for access pursuant to provisions of this JCPOA will be made in good faith, with due observance of the sovereign rights of Iran, and kept to the minimum necessary to effectively implement the verification responsibilities under this JCPOA. In line with normal international safeguards practice, such requests will not be aimed at interfering with Iranian military or other national security activities, but will be exclusively for resolving concerns regarding fulfillment of the JCPOA commitments and Iran's other non-proliferation and safeguards obligations. The following procedures are for the purpose of JCPOA implementation between the E3/EU+3 and Iran and are without prejudice to the safeguards agreement and the Additional Protocol thereto. In implementing this procedure as well as other transparency measures, the IAEA will be requested

to take every precaution to protect commercial, technological and industrial secrets as well as other confidential information coming to its knowledge.

75. In furtherance of implementation of the JCPOA, if the IAEA has concerns regarding undeclared nuclear materials or activities, or activities inconsistent with the JCPOA, at locations that have not been declared under the comprehensive safeguards agreement or Additional Protocol, the IAEA will provide Iran the basis for such concerns and request clarification.

76. If Iran's explanations do not resolve the IAEA's concerns, the Agency may request access to such locations for the sole reason to verify the absence of undeclared nuclear materials and activities or activities inconsistent with the JCPOA at such locations. The IAEA will provide Iran the reasons for access in writing and will make available relevant information.

77. Iran may propose to the IAEA alternative means of resolving the IAEA's concerns that enable the IAEA to verify the absence of undeclared nuclear materials and activities or activities inconsistent with the JCPOA at the location in question, which should be given due and prompt consideration.

78. If the absence of undeclared nuclear materials and activities or activities inconsistent with the JCPOA cannot be verified after the implementation of the alternative arrangements agreed by Iran and the IAEA, or if the two sides are unable to reach satisfactory arrangements to verify the absence of undeclared nuclear materials and activities or activities inconsistent with the JCPOA at the specified locations within 14 days of the IAEA's original request for access, Iran, in consultation with the members of the Joint

Commission, would resolve the IAEA's concerns through necessary means agreed between Iran and the IAEA. In the absence of an agreement, the members of the Joint Commission, by consensus or by a vote of 5 or more of its 8 members, would advise on the necessary means to resolve the IAEA's concerns. The process of consultation with, and any action by, the members of the Joint Commission would not exceed 7 days, and Iran would implement the necessary means within 3 additional days.

R. Centrifuge Component Manufacturing Transparency

79. Iran and the IAEA will take the necessary steps for containment and surveillance on centrifuge rotor tubes and bellows for 20 years.
80. In this context:
80.1. Iran will provide the IAEA with an initial inventory of all existing centrifuge rotor tubes and bellows and subsequent reports on changes in such inventory and will permit the IAEA to verify the inventory by item counting and numbering, and through containment and surveillance, of all rotor tubes and bellows, including in all existing and newly produced centrifuges.
80.2. Iran will declare all locations and equipment, namely, flow-forming machines, filament-winding machines and mandrels that are used for production of centrifuge rotor tubes or bellows, and will permit the IAEA to implement continuous monitoring, including through containment and surveillance on this equipment, to verify that this equipment is being used to manufacture centrifuges only for the activities specified in this JCPOA.

S. Other Uranium Isotope Separation Activities

81. For 10 years, Iran's uranium isotope separation-related research and development or production activities will be exclusively based on gaseous centrifuge technology.[4] Iran will permit IAEA access to verify that uranium isotope separation production and R&D activities are consistent with this Annex.

T. Activities Which Could Contribute to the Design and Development of a Nuclear Explosive Device

82. Iran will not engage in the following activities which could contribute to the development of a nuclear explosive device:
82.1. Designing, developing, acquiring, or using computer models to simulate nuclear explosive devices.
82.2. Designing, developing, fabricating, acquiring, or using multi-point explosive detonation systems suitable for a nuclear explosive device, unless approved by the Joint Commission for non-nuclear purposes and subject to monitoring.
82.3. Designing, developing, fabricating, acquiring, or using explosive diagnostic systems (streak cameras, framing cameras and flash x-ray cameras) suitable for the development of a nuclear explosive device, unless approved by the Joint Commission for non-nuclear purposes and subject to monitoring.
82.4. Designing, developing, fabricating, acquiring, or using explosively driven neutron sources or specialized materials for explosively driven neutron sources.

Attachment: Arak conceptual design
Fundamental Principles:

- Maximize use of the current infrastructure of original design of Arak research reactor, designated by the IAEA as IR-40, according to their respective ratings.
- Modernizing of the original design in order to be a multi-purpose research reactor comprising radio-isotope production, structural materials and fuel (pins and assembly prototypes) testing and able to conduct other neutronic experiments which demand high neutron fluxes (more than 10^{14}).
- Using heavy water as coolant, moderator and reflector. Light water would be utilized as an annular ring around the compact new core for safety reasons if necessary.
- Around 78 fuel assemblies in a tight hexagonal grid spacing with the following preliminary characteristics will be loaded.
- Up to 3.67 percent enriched UO_2, in the improved assembly design, will be used as fuel.
- Power will not exceed to 20 MWth.
- Adding different types of beam tubes to the existing beam tubes which being extended to the edge of the new compact core.
- Having one central channel in the center of the new core with passive cooling system for the purpose of structural materials and fuel pins and assembly
- prototypes testing with neutron flux beyond $2 \bullet 10^{14}$, twelve in-core irradiation channels (IIC) inside the core and twelve lateral irradiation channels (LIC) just next to the outer ring of fuel assemblies.

- The location of the in-core and lateral irradiation channels should be designed and fixed to meet the best anticipated performances.
- Consistent with relevant section of Annex 1, subsidiary laboratories are part of the modernization project of the Arak Research Reactor. In Addition, Annex III reinforce design and construction of subsidiary laboratories.
- The highest tolerable pressure for the first and second loop is 0.33 Mpa (at the entrance of the reactor pit).
- The highest possible flow rate for coolant is 610 kg/s at the pressure of 0.33 MPa in the main piping system and 42 kg/s for Moderator with the same conditions.

Preliminary Characteristics:

Core parameters	Values
Power (MW)	20
Number of fuel assemblies	~ 78
Active length (cm)	~ 110
Lattice configuration	Hexagonal
Fuel pellets Material	UO_2
Fuel enrichment level	Up to 3.67%
Clad material	Zr Alloys
Burnable poison	Yes, if necessary
Lattice pitch (cm)	~ 11
Coolant medium	D_2O
Moderator medium	D_2O
Reflector medium	D_2O
Reflector thickness (cm)	~ 50
Purity of D_2O	~ 99.8%
Mass of D_2O (mtons)	~ 60–70
Yearly makeup	Yes
K_{eff}	< 1.25
Core Excess reactivity (pcm)	< 20,000
Cycle length (days) approximately	~ 250

(*continued*)

(continued)

Core parameters	Values
^{239}Pu at EoC (g)	~ 850
^{239}Pu purity at EoC	~ 78%
^{235}U consumption	~ 60%
Maximum Thermal Flux, E < 0.625ev	~ $3 \bullet 10^{14}$
Maximum Fast Flux, E > 0.625ev	~ $1 \bullet 10^{14}$
Minimum Thermal Flux, E < 0.625ev	~ $1 \bullet 10^{14}$
Minimum Fast Flux, E > 0.625ev	~ $1 \bullet 10^{14}$
Fluid velocity in channels (m/s)	~ 3.8
Channel mass flow rate (kg/s)	~ 2.4
Working pressure (MPa)	0.33
Fluid inlet temperature (°C)	~ 47
Fluid outlet temperature (°C)	~ 78
Core material	Mainly S.S. 304
Core wall Thickness (mm)	~ 30
Fuel Pellet Diameter (cm)	~ 0.65
Inner Clad Diameter (cm)	~ 0.67
Outer Clad Diameter (cm)	~ 0.8
Number of pins per assembly	12
Mass of UO_2 in full core load (kg)	~ 350
Core diameter (cm)	~ 240

ANNEX II: SANCTIONS-RELATED COMMITMENTS

The sequence of implementation of the commitments detailed in this Annex is specified in Annex V (Implementation Plan) to this Joint Comprehensive Plan of Action (JCPOA).

A. European Union[5]

1. The EU and EU Member States commit to terminate all provisions of Council Regulation (EU) No 267/2012 (as subsequently amended) implementing all nuclear-related sanctions or restrictive

measures as specified in Sects. 1.1–1.10 below, to terminate all provisions of Council Decision 2010/413/CFSP (as subsequently amended), as specified in Sects. 1.1–1.10 below, and to terminate or amend national implementing legislation as required, in accordance with Annex V:

1.1. **Financial, banking and insurance measures**[6]

1.1.1. Prohibition and authorisation regimes on financial transfers to and from Iran (Article 10 of Council Decision 2010/413/CFSP; Articles 30, 30a, 30b and 31 of Council Regulation (EU) No 267/2012);

1.1.2. Sanctions on banking activities (Article 11 of Council Decision 2010/413/CFSP; Article 33 of Council Regulation (EU) No 267/2012);

1.1.3. Sanctions on insurance (Article 12 of Council Decision 2010/413/CFSP; Article 35 of Council Regulation (EU) No 267/2012);

1.1.4. Sanctions on financial messaging services (Article 20(12) of Council Decision 2010/413/CFSP; Article 23(4) of Council Regulation (EU) No 267/2012);

1.1.5. Sanctions on financial support for trade with Iran (Article 8 of Council Decision 2010/413/CFSP);

1.1.6. Sanctions on grants, financial assistance and concessional loans (Article 9 of Council Decision 2010/413/CFSP);

1.1.7. Sanctions on Government of Iran public-guaranteed bonds (Article 13 of Council Decision 2010/413/CFSP; Article 34 of Council Regulation (EU) No 267/2012); and

1.1.8. Sanctions on associated services[7] for each of the categories above (see the references above).

1.2. **Oil, gas and petrochemical sectors**
1.2.1. Sanctions on the import of oil and gas from Iran (Articles 3a, 3c and 3e of Council Decision 2010/413/CFSP; Articles 11, 12 and 14a, and Annexes IV and IVA of Council Regulation (EU) No 267/2012);
1.2.2. Sanctions on the import of Iranian petrochemical products (Articles 3b and 3d of Council Decision 2010/413/CFSP; Articles 13 and 14, and Annex V of Council Regulation (EU) No 267/2012);
1.2.3. Sanctions on the export of key equipment for the oil, gas and petrochemical sectors (Articles 4, 4a and 4b of Council Decision 2010/413/CFSP; Articles 8, 9 and 10, and Annexes VI and VIA of Council Regulation (EU) No 267/2012);
1.2.4. Sanctions on investment in the oil, gas and petrochemical sectors (Articles 6, 6a and 7 of Council Decision 2010/413/CFSP; Articles 17(1), 17(2)(b) and (c), 17(3), 17(4), 17(5), 20 and 21 of Council Regulation (EU) No 267/2012); and
1.2.5. Sanctions on associated services for each of the categories above (see the references above).
1.3. **Shipping, shipbuilding and transport sectors**
1.3.1. Sanctions related to shipping and shipbuilding (Articles 4g, 4h, 8a, 18a and 18b of Council Decision 2010/413/CFSP; Articles 10a, 10b, 10c, 37a, and 37b, and Annex VIB of Council Regulation (EU) No 267/2012);
1.3.2. Sanctions related to the transport sector (Articles 15, 16, 17 and 18 of Council Decision 2010/413/CFSP; Articles 36 and 37 of Council Regulation (EU) No 267/2012); and

1.3.3. Sanctions on associated services for each of the categories above (see the references above).
1.4. **Gold, other precious metals, banknotes and coinage**
1.4.1. Sanctions on gold, precious metals and diamonds, banknotes and coinage (Articles 4c and 4d of Council Decision 2010/413/CFSP; Articles 15 and 16, and Annex VII of Council Regulation (EU) No 267/2012); and
1.4.2. Sanctions on associated services for each of the categories above (see the references above).
1.5. **Nuclear proliferation-related measures**
1.5.1. Sanctions related to proliferation-sensitive nuclear activities (goods and technology, investment and specialized training) (Articles 1(1) (a), (b), (d), (e), (2), (3) and (4), 2, 3, 5, 14 and 21 of Council Decision 2010/413/CFSP; Articles 2, 3, 4, 5, 6, 7, 17(1) and (2)(a), 18, 19 and 22, and Annexes I, II and III of Council Regulation (EU) No 267/2012); and
1.5.2. Sanctions on associated services for the category above (see the references above).
1.6. **Metals**
1.6.1. Sanctions on metals (Articles 4e and 4f of Council Decision 2010/413/CFSP; Articles 15a, 15b and 15c, and Annex VIIB of Council Regulation (EU) No 267/2012); and
1.6.2. Sanctions on associated services for the category above (see the references above).
1.7. **Software**
1.7.1. Sanctions on software (Articles 4i and 4j of Council Decision 2010/413/CFSP; Articles 10d, 10e and 10f, and Annex VIIA of Council Regulation (EU) No 267/2012); and

1.7.2. Sanctions on associated services for the category above (see the references above).
1.8. **Arms**
1.8.1. Sanctions on arms (Articles 1(1)(c), (3) and (4), and 3 of Council Decision 2010/413/CFSP; Articles 5(1)(a) and (c), 17(1) and (2)(a), and 19 of Council Regulation (EU) No 267/2012); and
1.8.2. Sanctions on associated services for the category above (see the references above).
1.9. **Listing of persons, entities and bodies (asset freeze and visa ban)**
1.9.1. Asset freeze and visa ban measures applicable to:
1.9.1.1. listed Iranian banks and financial institutions, including the Central Bank of Iran;
1.9.1.2. listed persons, entities and bodies related to the oil, gas and petrochemical sectors;
1.9.1.3. listed persons, entities and bodies related to shipping, shipbuilding and transport;
1.9.1.4. other listed persons, entities and bodies not related to proliferation-sensitive nuclear-, arms- and ballistic missile-related activities;
1.9.1.5. listed persons, entities and bodies related to proliferation-sensitive nuclear-, arms- and ballistic missile-related activities; and
1.9.1.6. entities and individuals listed by the UN Security Council,
1.9.1.7. as set out in Attachment 1, Part I to this Annex for categories 1.9.1.1–1.9.1.4, Attachment 2, Part I to this Annex for category 1.9.1.5, and Parts of Attachments 1 and 2 to this Annex for category 1.9.1.6 (Articles 19 and 20, and Annexes I and II to Council Decision 2010/413/CFSP; Articles 23, 24, 25, 26, 27, 28, 28a, 28b and 29, and Annexes VIII and IX to Council Regulation (EU) No 267/2012).

1.10. **Other provisions**
1.10.1. The commitment in Sect. 1 covers all remaining provisions of Council Decision 2010/413/CFSP and Council Regulation (EU) No 267/2012 not specified above.
1.10.1.1. Definitions (Article 1 of Council Regulation (EU) No 267/2012); and
1.10.1.2. General and final provisions (Articles 22, 23, 24, 25, 26, 26a, 27 and 28 of Council Decision 2010/413/CFSP; Articles 38, 39, 40, 41, 42, 43, 43a, 44, 45, 46, 47, 48, 49, 50 and 51, and Annex X of Council Regulation (EU) No 267/2012).
2. The EU represents that the provisions listed in Sect. 1 above constitute the full and complete list of all EU nuclear-related sanctions or restrictive measures. These sanctions or restrictive measures will be lifted in accordance with Annex V.
3. **Effects of the lifting of EU economic and financial sanctions**
3.1. As a result of the lifting of sanctions specified in Sect. 1 above, the following activities, including associated services, will be allowed, beginning on implementation day, in accordance with this JCPOA and provided that such activities are otherwise consistent with EU and EU Member States' laws and regulations in effect[8]:
3.2. **Financial, banking and insurance measures (see Sects. 1.1.1–1.1.8)**
3.2.1. Transfers of funds between EU persons, entities or bodies, including EU financial and credit institutions, and Iranian persons, entities or bodies, including Iranian financial and credit institutions, without the requirement for authorisation or notification;

3.2.2. Opening of new branches, subsidiaries or representative offices of Iranian banks in the territories of EU Member States; and the establishment of new joint ventures, or the taking of an ownership interest or the establishment of new correspondent banking relationships by Iranian banks with EU banks; and opening by EU persons, including EU financial and credit institutions, of representative offices, subsidiaries, joint ventures or bank accounts in Iran;

3.2.3. Provision of insurance or reinsurance to Iran or the Government of Iran, an Iranian legal person, entity or body, or a natural person or a legal person, entity or body acting on their behalf or at their direction;

3.2.4. Supply of specialized financial messaging services to any Iranian natural or legal persons, entities or bodies, including those listed in Attachment 1 to this Annex;

3.2.5. Entering into commitments by EU Member States to provide financial support for trade with Iran, including the granting of export credits, guarantees or insurance; and into commitments for grants, financial assistance and concessional loans to the Government of Iran; and

3.2.6. Sale or purchase of public or public-guaranteed bonds to and from Iran, the Government of Iran, the Central Bank of Iran, or Iranian banks and financial institutions or persons acting on their behalf.

3.3. **Oil, gas and petrochemical sectors (see Sects. 1.2.1–1.2.5)**

3.3.1. Import, purchase, swap or transport of Iranian crude oil and petroleum products, natural gas or petrochemical products and related financing;

3.3.2. Sale, supply, transfer or export of equipment or technology, technical assistance, including training, used in the sectors of the oil, gas and petrochemical industries in Iran covering exploration, production and refining of oil and natural gas, including liquefaction of natural gas, to any Iranian person, in or outside Iran, or for use in Iran; and

3.3.3. Granting of any financial loan or credit to, the acquisition or extension of a participation in, and the creation of any joint venture with, any Iranian person that is engaged in the oil, gas and petrochemical sectors in Iran or outside Iran.

3.4. **Shipping, shipbuilding and transport sectors (see Sects. 1.3.1–1.3.3)**

3.4.1. Sale, supply, transfer or export of naval equipment and technology for ship building, maintenance or refit, to Iran or to any Iranian persons engaged in this sector; the design, construction or the participation in the design or construction of cargo vessels and oil tankers for Iran or for Iranian persons; the provision of vessels designed or used for the transport or storage of oil and petrochemical products to Iranian persons, entities or bodies; and the provision of flagging and classification services, including those pertaining to technical specification, registration and identification numbers of any kind, to Iranian oil tankers and cargo vessels;

3.4.2. Access to the airports under the jurisdiction of EU Member States of all cargo flights operated by Iranian carriers or originating from Iran;

3.4.3. Cessation of inspection, seizure and disposal by EU Member States of cargoes to and from Iran in their territories with regard to items which are no longer prohibited; and

3.4.4. Provision of bunkering or ship supply services, or any other servicing of vessels, to Iranian-owned or Iranian-contracted vessels not carrying prohibited items; and the provision of fuel, engineering and maintenance services to Iranian cargo aircraft not carrying prohibited items.

3.5. **Gold, other precious metals, banknotes and coinage (see Sects. 1.4.1–1.4.2)**

3.5.1. Sale, supply, purchase, export, transfer or transport of gold and precious metals as well as diamonds, and provision of related brokering, financing and security services, to, from or for the Government of Iran, its public bodies, corporations and agencies, or the Central Bank of Iran; and

3.5.2. Delivery of newly printed or minted or unissued Iranian denominated banknotes and coinage to, or for the benefit of the Central Bank of Iran.

3.6. **Metals (see Sects. 1.6.1–1.6.2)**

3.6.1. Sale, supply, transfer or export of graphite and raw or semi-finished metals, such as aluminum and steel to any Iranian person, entity or body or for use in Iran, in connection with activities consistent with this JCPOA.

3.7. **Software (see Sects. 1.7.1–1.7.2)**

3.7.1. Sale, supply, transfer or export of software for integrating industrial processes, including updates, to any Iranian person, entity or body, or for use in Iran, in connection with activities consistent with this JCPOA,

3.8. **Listing of persons, entities and bodies (asset freeze and visa ban) (see Sect. 1.9.1)**

3.8.1. As a result of delisting as specified in this Annex, releasing of all funds and economic resources which belong to, and making available funds or economic resources to, the persons, entities and bodies, including Iranian banks and financial institutions, the Central Bank of Iran, listed in Attachment 1 to this Annex; and

3.8.2. As a result of delisting as specified in this Annex, entry into, or transit through the territories of EU Member States of individuals listed in Attachment 1 to this Annex.

B. United States[9]

4. The United States commits to cease the application of, and to seek such legislative action as may be appropriate to terminate, or modify to effectuate the termination of, all nuclear-related sanctions[10] as specified in Sects. 4.1–4.9 below, and to terminate Executive Orders 13574, 13590, 13622 and 13645, and Sects. 5–7 and 15 of Executive Order 13628, in accordance with Annex V.[11]

4.1. **Financial and banking measures**

4.1.1. Sanctions on transactions with individuals and entities set out in Attachment 3 to this Annex, including: the Central Bank of Iran (CBI) and other specified Iranian financial institutions; the National Iranian Oil Company (NIOC),[12] Naftiran Intertrade Company (NICO), National Iranian Tanker Company (NITC) and other specified individuals and entities identified as Government of Iran by the Office of Foreign Assets Control; and certain designated individuals and entities on the Specially Designated Nationals and Blocked Persons List (SDN List) (Comprehensive Iran Sanctions, Accountability, and Divestment Act of 2010 (CISADA) Section 104(c)(2)(E)(ii)(I);

National Defense Authorization Act for Fiscal Year 2012 (NDAA) Sections 1245(d)(1) and (3); Iran Freedom and Counter-Proliferation Act of 2012 (IFCA) Sections 1244(c)(1) and (d), 1245(a)(1)(A), (a)(1)(C)(i)(II) and (c), 1246(a) and 1247(a); Sections 1(a)(i) and 5(a) of Executive Order (E.O.) 13622 and Sections 2(a)(i) and 3(a)(i) of E.O. 13645);

4.1.2. Sanctions on the Iranian Rial (NDAA Sections 1245(d)(1) and (3); IFCA Sections 1244(c)(1), 1246(a) and 1247(a); Section 5(a) of E.O. 13622 and Sections 1(a), 2(a)(i) and 3(a)(i) of E.O. 13645);

4.1.3. Sanctions on the provision of U.S. banknotes to the Government of Iran (NDAA Sections 1245(d)(1) and (3); IFCA Sections 1244(c)(1) and (d), 1246(a) and 1247(a); Section 5(a) of E.O. 13622 and Sections 2(a)(i) and 3(a)(i) of E.O. 13645);

4.1.4. Bilateral trade limitations on Iranian revenues held abroad, including limitations on their transfer (NDAA Sections 1245(d)(1) and (3); IFCA Sections 1244(c)(1), (d) and (h)(2), 1246(a) and 1247(a); Sections 1(a)(i)–(ii), 2(a)(i) and 5(a) of E.O. 13622 and Sections 2(a)(i) and 3(a)(i) of E.O. 13645);

4.1.5. Sanctions on the purchase, subscription to, or facilitation of the issuance of Iranian sovereign debt, including governmental bonds (NDAA Sections 1245(d)(1) and (3); Iran Threat Reduction and Syria Human Rights Act of 2012 (TRA) Section 213(a); IFCA Sections 1244(c)(1) and (d), 1246(a) and 1247(a); Sections 1(a)(i) and 5(a) of E.O. 13622 and Sections 2(a)(i) and 3(a)(i) of E.O. 13645);

4.1.6. Sanctions on financial messaging services to the CBI and Iranian financial institutions set out in Attachment 3 to this Annex (NDAA Sections 1245(d)(1) and (3); TRA Section 220; IFCA Sections 1244(c)(1) and (d), 1246(a) and 1247(a); Section 5(a) of E.O. 13622 and Sections 2(a)(i) and 3(a)(i) of E.O. 13645); and

4.1.7. Sanctions on associated services[13] for each of the categories above (see individual citation references above).

4.2. **Insurance measures**

4.2.1. Sanctions on the provision of underwriting services, insurance, or re-insurance in connection with activities consistent with this JCPOA, including activities with individuals and entities set forth in Attachment 3 to this Annex (Iran Sanctions Act of 1996 (ISA) Section 5(a)(7); NDAA Sections 1245(d)(1) and (3); TRA Sections 211(a) and 212(a); IFCA Sections 1244(c)(1) and (d), 1246(a) and 1247(a); Section 5(a) of E.O. 13622 and Sections 2(a)(i) and 3(a)(i) of E.O. 13645).

4.3. **Energy and petrochemical sectors**

4.3.1. Efforts to reduce Iran's crude oil sales, including limitations on the quantities of Iranian crude oil sold and the nations that can purchase Iranian crude oil (ISA Section 5(a)(7); NDAA Sections 1245(d)(1) and (3); TRA Section 212(a); IFCA Sections 1244(c)(1) and (d), 1246(a) and 1247(a); Section 1 of E.O. 13574, Sections 1(a)(i)–(ii), 2(a)(i) and 5(a) of E.O. 13622, Section 5 of E.O. 13628, and Sections 2(a)(i) and 3(a)(i) of E.O. 13645);

4.3.2. Sanctions on investment, including participation in joint ventures, goods, services, information, technology and technical expertise and support for Iran's oil, gas, and petrochemical sectors (ISA Sections 5(a)(1)–(2) and (4)–(8); TRA Section 212(a); IFCA Sections 1244(c)(1), and (h)(2), 1245(a)(1)(B), (a)(1)(C)(i)(I)–(II), (a)(1)(C)(ii)(I)–(II) and (c), 1246(a) and 1247(a); Section 1 of E.O. 13574, Section 1 of E.O. 13590, Sections 1(a)(i)–(ii), 2(a)(i)–(iii) and 5(a) of E.O. 13622, and Sections 2(a)(i) and 3(a)(i) of E.O. 13645);

4.3.3. Sanctions on the purchase, acquisition, sale, transportation, or marketing of petroleum, petrochemical products and natural gas from Iran (NDAA Sections 1245(d)(1) and (3); TRA Section 212(a); IFCA Sections 1244(c)(1), (d) and (h)(2), 1246(a) and 1247(a); Sections 1(a)(i)–(iii), 2(a)(i)–(ii) and 5(a) of E.O. 13622, and Sections 2(a)(i) and 3(a)(i) of E.O. 13645);

4.3.4. Sanctions on the export, sale or provision of refined petroleum products and petrochemical products to Iran (ISA Section 5(a)(3); NDAA Sections 1245(d)(1) and (3); TRA Section 212(a); IFCA Sections 1244(c)(1) and (d), 1246(a) and 1247(a); Section 1 of E.O. 13574, Sections 1(a)(i) and 5(a) of E.O. 13622, Section 5 of E.O. 13628, and Sections 2(a)(i) and 3(a)(i) of E.O. 13645);

4.3.5. Sanctions on transactions with Iran's energy sector including with NIOC, NICO and NITC (NDAA Sections 1245(d)(1) and (3); IFCA Sections 1244(c)(1), (d) and (h)(2), 1246(a) and 1247(a); TRA Section 212(a); Sections 1(a)(i)–(iii), 2(a)(i)–(ii) and 5(a) of E.O. 13622, and Sections 2(a)(i) and 3(a)(i) of E.O. 13645); and

4.3.6. Sanctions on associated services for each of the categories above (see individual citation references above).

4.4. Shipping, shipbuilding and port sectors

4.4.1. Sanctions on transactions with Iran's shipping and shipbuilding sectors and port operators including IRISL, South Shipping Line, and NITC, and the port operator(s) of Bandar Abbas[14] (TRA Sections 211(a) and 212(a); IFCA Sections 1244(c)(1) and (d); 1245(a)(1)(B), (a)(1)(C)(i)(I)–(II), (a)(1)(C)(ii)(I)–(II) and (c), 1246(a) and 1247(a); Section 5(a) of E.O. 13622 and Sections 2(a)(i) and 3(a)(i) of E.O. 13645); and

4.4.2. Sanctions on associated services for each of the categories above (see individual citation references above).

4.5. Gold and other precious metals

4.5.1. Sanctions on Iran's trade in gold and other precious metals (NDAA Sections 1245(d)(1) and (3); IFCA Sections 1244(c)(1), 1245(a)(1)(A) and (c), 1246(a) and 1247(a); Section 5(a) of E.O. 13622 and Sections 2(a)(i) and 3(a)(i) of E.O. 13645); and

4.5.2. Sanctions on associated services for each of the categories above (see individual citation references above).

4.6. Software and metals

4.6.1. Sanctions on trade with Iran in graphite, raw or semi-finished metals such as aluminum and steel, coal, and software for integrating industrial processes, in connection with activities consistent with this JCPOA, including trade with individuals and entities set forth in Attachments 3 and 4 to this Annex (NDAA Sections 1245(d)(1) and (3); IFCA Sections 1244(c)(1), 1245(a)(1)(B)–(C) and (c), 1246(a) and 1247(a); Section 5(a) of E.O. 13622 and Sections 2(a)(i) and 3(a)(i) of E.O. 13645); and

4.6.2. Sanctions on associated services for each of the categories above (see individual citation references above).

4.7. **Automotive sector**

4.7.1. Sanctions on the sale, supply or transfer of goods and services used in connection with Iran's automotive sector (NDAA Sections 1245(d)(1) and (3); IFCA Sections 1244(c)(1), 1245(a)(1)(B), (a)(1)(C)(i)(II), (a)(1)(C)(ii)(II) and (c), 1246(a) and 1247(a); Section 5(a) of E.O. 13622 and Sections 2(a)(i), 3(a)(i)–(ii), 5 and 6 of E.O. 13645); and

4.7.2. Sanctions on associated services for each of the categories above (see individual citation references above).

4.8. **Designations and other sanctions listings**

4.8.1. Removal of individuals and entities set out in Attachments 3 and 4 to this Annex from the Specially Designated Nationals and Blocked Persons List (SDN List), the Foreign Sanctions Evaders List, and/or the Non-SDN Iran Sanctions Act List (Removal of designations and/or sanctions imposed under ISA Section 5(a), IFCA Section 1244(d)(1) and TRA Section 212; and removals pursuant to the International Emergency Economic Powers Act of certain persons listed pursuant to E.O. 13382, E.O. 13608, E.O. 13622, and E.O. 13645).

4.9. **Nuclear proliferation-related measures**

4.9.1. Sanctions under the Iran, North Korea and Syria Nonproliferation Act on the acquisition of nuclear-related commodities and services for nuclear activities contemplated in the JCPOA, to be consistent with the U.S. approach to other non-nuclear-weapon states under the NPT;

4.9.2. Sanctions on joint ventures relating to the mining, production, or transportation of uranium (ISA Section 5(b)(2)); and

4.9.3. Exclusion of Iranian citizens from higher education coursework related to careers in nuclear science, nuclear engineering or the energy sector (TRA Section 501).

5. **Other trade measures**

5.1. The United States commits to[15]:

5.1.1. Allow for the sale of commercial passenger aircraft and related parts and services to Iran by licensing the (i) export, re-export, sale, lease or transfer to Iran of commercial passenger aircraft for exclusively civil aviation end-use, (ii) export, re-export, sale, lease or transfer to Iran of spare parts and components for commercial passenger aircraft, and (iii) provision of associated serviced, including warranty, maintenance, and repair services and safety-related inspections, for all the foregoing, provided that licensed items and services are used exclusively for commercial passenger aviation[16];

5.1.2. License non-U.S. entities that are owned or controlled by a U.S. person[17] to engage in activities with Iran that are consistent with this JCPOA; and

5.1.3. License the importation into the United States of Iranian-origin carpets and foodstuffs, including pistachios and caviar.

6. The United States represents that the provisions listed in Sect. 4 above constitute the full and complete list of all U.S. nuclear-related sanctions. These sanctions will be lifted in accordance with Annex V.

7. **Effects of the lifting of U.S. economic and financial sanctions:**
7.1. As a result of the lifting of sanctions specified in Sect. 4 above, beginning on implementation day such sanctions, including associated services, would not apply to non-U.S. persons who carry out the following or that[18]:
7.2. **Financial and banking measures[19] (see Sects. 4.1.1–4.1.7)**
Engage in activities, including financial and banking transactions, with the Government of Iran, the Central Bank of Iran, Iranian financial institutions and other Iranian persons specified in Attachment 3 to this Annex, including the provision of loans, transfers, accounts (including the opening and maintenance of correspondent and payable through accounts at non-U.S. financial institutions), investments, securities, guarantees, foreign exchange (including Rial related transactions), letters of credit and commodity futures or options, the provision of specialized financial messaging services and facilitation of direct or indirect access thereto, the purchase or acquisition by the Government of Iran of U.S. bank notes, and the purchase, subscription to, or facilitation of the issuance of Iranian sovereign debt.[20]
7.3. **Insurance measures (see Sect. 4.2.1)**
Provide underwriting services, insurance, or re-insurance in connection with activities consistent with this JCPOA, including activities with individuals and entities set forth in Attachment 3 to this Annex, including underwriting services, insurance, or re-insurance in connection with activities in the

energy, shipping, and shipbuilding sectors of Iran, for the National Iranian Oil Company (NIOC) or the National Iranian Tanker Company (NITC), or for vessels that transport crude oil, natural gas, liquefied natural gas, petroleum and petrochemical products to or from Iran.

7.4. **Energy and petrochemical sectors (see Sects. 4.3.1–4.3.6)**

Are part of the energy sector of Iran; purchase, acquire, sell, transport or market petroleum, petroleum products (including refined petroleum products), petrochemical products or natural gas (including liquefied natural gas) to or from Iran; provide to Iran support, investment (including through joint ventures), goods, services (including financial services) and technology that can be used in connection with Iran's energy sector, the development of its petroleum resources, its domestic production of refined petroleum products and petrochemical products; or engage in activities with Iran's energy sector, including NIOC, NITC, and NICO).

7.5. **Shipping, shipbuilding and port sectors (see Sects. 4.4.1–4.4.2)**

Are part of the shipping or shipbuilding sectors of Iran; own, operate, control or insure a vessel used to transport crude oil, petroleum products (including refined petroleum products), petrochemical products or natural gas (including liquefied natural gas) to or from Iran; operate a port in Iran, engage in activities with, or provide financial services and other goods and services used in connection with, the shipping and shipbuilding sectors of Iran or a port operator in Iran (including the port operator(s) of Bandar Abbas[21]), including port services, such as bunkering and inspection, classification, and financing, and the sale, leasing, and provision of vessels to Iran, including to the Islamic Republic of Iran Shipping Lines (IRISL), NITC, and South Shipping Line Iran or their affiliates.

7.6. **Gold and other precious metals (see Sects. 4.5.1–4.5.2)**
Sell, supply, export or transfer, directly or indirectly, to or from Iran, gold and other precious metals, or conduct or facilitate a financial transaction or provide services for the foregoing including security, insurance and transportation.

7.7. **Software and metals (see Sects. 4.6.1–4.6.2)**
Sell, supply, or transfer, directly or indirectly, graphite, raw or semi-finished metals such as aluminum and steel, coal, and software for integrating industrial processes, to or from Iran in connection with activities consistent with this JCPOA, including trade with individuals and entities set forth in Attachment 3 to this Annex, and the sale, supply, or transfer of such materials to the energy, petrochemical, shipping and shipbuilding sectors of Iran, and Iranian ports, or conduct or facilitate a financial transaction or provide services for the foregoing, including insurance and transportation.

7.8. **Automotive sector (see Sects. 4.7.1–4.7.2)**
Conduct or facilitate financial or other transactions for the sale, supply or transfer to Iran of goods and services used in connection with the automotive sector of Iran.

7.9. **Designations and other sanctions listings (see Sect. 4.8.1)**

The removal of designations and/or sanctions as described in Sect. 4.8.1, ceasing the application of secondary sanctions for transactions with individuals and entities set out in Attachment 3 to this Annex; and unblocking of property and interests in property within U.S. jurisdiction for individuals and entities set out in Attachment 3 to this Annex.

Attachment 1: Part I

LIST OF PERSONS, ENTITIES AND BODIES SET OUT IN ANNEX II TO COUNCIL DECISION 2010/413/CFSP AND ANNEX IX TO COUNCIL REGULATION (EU) NO 267/2012

ACENA SHIPPING COMPANY LIMITED
ADVANCE NOVEL
AGHAJARI OIL & GAS PRODUCTION COMPANY
AGHAZADEH, Reza
AHMADIAN, Mohammad
AKHAVAN-FARD, Massoud
ALPHA EFFORT LTD
ALPHA KARA NAVIGATION LIMITED
ALPHA NARI NAVIGATION LIMITED
ARIAN BANK
ARVANDAN OIL & GAS COMPANY
ASHTEAD SHIPPING COMPANY LTD
ASPASIS MARINE CORPORATION
ASSA CORPORATION
ASSA CORPORATION LTD
ATLANTIC INTERMODAL
AVRASYA CONTAINER SHIPPING LINES

AZARAB INDUSTRIES
AZORES SHIPPING COMPANY ALIAS AZORES SHIPPING FZE LLC
BANCO INTERNACIONAL DE DESARROLLO CA
BANK KARGOSHAE
BANK MELLAT
BANK MELLI IRAN INVESTMENT COMPANY
BANK MELLI IRAN ZAO
BANK MELLI PRINTING AND PUBLISHING COMPANY
BANK MELLI,
BANK OF INDUSTRY AND MINE
BANK REFAH KARGARAN
BANK TEJARAT
BATENI, Naser
BEST PRECISE LTD
BETA KARA NAVIGATION LTD
BIIS MARITIME LIMITED
BIS MARITIME LIMITED
BONAB RESEARCH CENTER
BRAIT HOLDING SA
BRIGHT JYOTI SHIPPING
BRIGHT SHIP FZC
BUSHEHR SHIPPING COMPANY LIMITED
BYFLEET SHIPPING COMPANY LTD
CEMENT INVESTMENT AND DEVELOPMENT COMPANY
CENTRAL BANK OF IRAN
CHAPLET SHIPPING LIMITED
COBHAM SHIPPING COMPANY LTD
CONCEPT GIANT LTD
COOPERATIVE DEVELOPMENT BANK
CRYSTAL SHIPPING FZE

DAJMAR, Mohammad Hossein
DAMALIS MARINE CORPORATION
DARYA CAPITAL ADMINISTRATION GMBH
DARYA DELALAN SEFID KHAZAR SHIPPING COMPANY
DELTA KARA NAVIGATION LTD
DELTA NARI NAVIGATION LTD
DIAMOND SHIPPING SERVICES
DORKING SHIPPING COMPANY LTD
EAST OIL & GAS PRODUCTION COMPANY
EDBI EXCHANGE COMPANY
EDBI STOCK BROKERAGE COMPANY
EFFINGHAM SHIPPING COMPANY LTD
EIGHTH OCEAN ADMINISTRATION GMBH
EIGHTH OCEAN GMBH & CO. KG
ELBRUS LTD
ELCHO HOLDING LTD
ELEGANT TARGET DEVELOPMENT LIMITED
ELEVENTH OCEAN ADMINISTRATION GMBH
ELEVENTH OCEAN GMBH & CO. KG
EMKA COMPANY
EPSILON NARI NAVIGATION LTD
E-SAIL A.K.A. E-SAIL SHIPPING COMPANY
ETA NARI NAVIGATION LTD
ETERNAL EXPERT LTD.
EUROPÄISCH-IRANISCHE HANDELSBANK
EXPORT DEVELOPMENT BANK OF IRAN
FAIRWAY SHIPPING
FAQIHIAN, Dr Hoseyn
FARNHAM SHIPPING COMPANY LTD
FASIRUS MARINE CORPORATION
FATSA
FIFTEENTH OCEAN ADMINISTRATION GMBH

FIFTEENTH OCEAN GMBH & CO. KG
FIFTH OCEAN ADMINISTRATION GMBH
FIFTH OCEAN GMBH & CO. KG
FIRST ISLAMIC INVESTMENT BANK
FIRST OCEAN ADMINISTRATION GMBH
FIRST OCEAN GMBH & CO. KG
FIRST PERSIAN EQUITY FUND
FOURTEENTH OCEAN ADMINISTRATION GMBH
FOURTEENTH OCEAN GMBH & CO. KG
FOURTH OCEAN ADMINISTRATION GMBH
FOURTH OCEAN GMBH & CO. KG
FUTURE BANK BSC
GACHSARAN OIL & GAS COMPANY
GALLIOT MARITIME INCORPORATION
GAMMA KARA NAVIGATION LTD
GIANT KING LIMITED
GOLDEN CHARTER DEVELOPMENT LTD.
GOLDEN SUMMIT INVESTMENTS LTD.
GOLDEN WAGON DEVELOPMENT LTD.
GOLPARVAR, Gholam Hossein
GOMSHALL SHIPPING COMPANY LTD
GOOD LUCK SHIPPING COMPANY LLC
GRAND TRINITY LTD.
GREAT EQUITY INVESTMENTS LTD.
GREAT METHOD LTD
GREAT PROSPECT INTERNATIONAL LTD.
HAFIZ DARYA SHIPPING LINES
HANSEATIC TRADE TRUST & SHIPPING GMBH
HARVEST SUPREME LTD.
HARZARU SHIPPING
HELIOTROPE SHIPPING LIMITED
HELIX SHIPPING LIMITED
HK INTERTRADE COMPANY LTD

HONG TU LOGISTICS PRIVATE LIMITED
HORSHAM SHIPPING COMPANY LTD
IFOLD SHIPPING COMPANY LIMITED
INDUS MARITIME INCORPORATION
INDUSTRIAL DEVELOPMENT & RENOVATION ORGANIZATION
INSIGHT WORLD LTD
INTERNATIONAL SAFE OIL
IOTA NARI NAVIGATION LIMITED
IRAN ALUMINIUM COMPANY
IRAN FUEL CONSERVATION ORGANIZATION
IRAN INSURANCE COMPANY
IRAN LIQUEFIED NATURAL GAS CO.
IRANIAN OFFSHORE ENGINEERING & CONSTRUCTION CO
IRANIAN OIL COMPANY LIMITED
IRANIAN OIL PIPELINES AND TELECOMMUNICATIONS COMPANY (IOPTC)
IRANIAN OIL TERMINALS COMPANY
IRANO MISR SHIPPING COMPANY
IRINVESTSHIP LTD
IRISL (MALTA) LTD
IRISL EUROPE GMBH
IRISL MARINE SERVICES AND ENGINEERING COMPANY
IRISL MARITIME TRAINING INSTITUTE
IRITAL SHIPPING SRL
ISI MARITIME LIMITED
ISIM AMIN LIMITED
ISIM ATR LIMITED
ISIM OLIVE LIMITED
ISIM SAT LIMITED
ISIM SEA CHARIOT LTD

ISIM SEA CRESCENT LTD
ISIM SININ LIMITED
ISIM TAJ MAHAL LTD
ISIM TOUR COMPANY LIMITED
ISLAMIC REPUBLIC OF IRAN SHIPPING LINES
JACKMAN SHIPPING COMPANY
KALA NAFT
KALAN KISH SHIPPING COMPANY LTD
KAPPA NARI NAVIGATION LTD
KARA SHIPPING AND CHARTERING GMBH
KAROON OIL & GAS PRODUCTION COMPANY
KAVERI MARITIME INCORPORATION
KAVERI SHIPPING LLC
KEY CHARTER DEVELOPMENT LTD.
KHALILIPOUR, Said Esmail
KHANCHI, Ali Reza
KHAZAR EXPL & PROD CO
KHAZAR SHIPPING LINES
KHEIBAR COMPANY
KING PROSPER INVESTMENTS LTD.
KINGDOM NEW LTD
KINGSWOOD SHIPPING COMPANY LIMITED
KISH SHIPPING LINE MANNING COMPANY
LAMBDA NARI NAVIGATION LIMITED
LANCING SHIPPING COMPANY LIMITED
LOGISTIC SMART LTD
LOWESWATER LTD
MACHINE SAZI ARAK
MAGNA CARTA LIMITED
MALSHIP SHIPPING AGENCY
MARBLE SHIPPING LIMITED
MAROUN OIL & GAS COMPANY
MASJED-SOLEYMAN OIL & GAS COMPANY

MASTER SUPREME INTERNATIONAL LTD.
MAZANDARAN CEMENT COMPANY
MEHR CAYMAN LTD.
MELLAT BANK SB CJSC
MELLI AGROCHEMICAL COMPANY PJS
MELLI BANK PLC
MELLI INVESTMENT HOLDING INTERNATIONAL
MELODIOUS MARITIME INCORPORATION
METRO SUPREME INTERNATIONAL LTD.
MIDHURST SHIPPING COMPANY LIMITED (MALTA)
MILL DENE LTD
MINISTRY OF ENERGY
MINISTRY OF PETROLEUM
MODALITY LTD
MODERN ELEGANT DEVELOPMENT LTD.
MOUNT EVEREST MARITIME INCORPORATION
NAFTIRAN INTERTRADE COMPANY
NAFTIRAN INTERTRADE COMPANY SRL
NAMJOO, Majid
NARI SHIPPING AND CHARTERING GMBH & CO. KG
NARMADA SHIPPING
NATIONAL IRANIAN DRILLING COMPANY
NATIONAL IRANIAN GAS COMPANY
NATIONAL IRANIAN OIL COMPANY
NATIONAL IRANIAN OIL COMPANY NEDERLAND (A.K.A.: NIOC NETHERLANDS REPRESENTATION OFFICE)
NATIONAL IRANIAN OIL COMPANY PTE LTD
NATIONAL IRANIAN OIL COMPANY, INTERNATIONAL AFFAIRS LIMITED NATIONAL IRANIAN OIL ENGINEERING AND CONSTRUCTION

COMPANY (NIOEC) NATIONAL IRANIAN OIL PRODUCTS DISTRIBUTION COMPANY (NIOPDC) NATIONAL IRANIAN OIL REFINING AND DISTRIBUTION COMPANY NATIONAL IRANIAN TANKER COMPANY NEUMAN LTD
NEW DESIRE LTD
NEW SYNERGY
NEWHAVEN SHIPPING COMPANY LIMITED
NINTH OCEAN ADMINISTRATION GMBH
NINTH OCEAN GMBH & CO. KG
NOOR AFZA GOSTAR
NORTH DRILLING COMPANY
NUCLEAR FUEL PRODUCTION AND PROCUREMENT COMPANY OCEAN CAPITAL ADMINISTRATION GMBH OCEAN EXPRESS AGENCIES PRIVATE LIMITED
ONERBANK ZAO
OXTED SHIPPING COMPANY LIMITED
PACIFIC SHIPPING
PARS SPECIAL ECONOMIC ENERGY ZONE
PARTNER CENTURY LTD
PEARL ENERGY COMPANY LTD
PEARL ENERGY SERVICES, SA
PERSIA INTERNATIONAL BANK PLC
PETRO SUISSE
PETROIRAN DEVELOPMENT COMPANY LTD PETROLEUM ENGINEERING & DEVELOPMENT COMPANY PETROPARS INTERNATIONAL FZE
PETROPARS IRAN COMPANY
PETROPARS LTD.
PETROPARS OILFIELD SERVICES COMPANY
PETROPARS OPERATION & MANAGEMENT COMPANY

PETROPARS RESOURCES ENGINEERING LTD
PETROPARS UK LIMITED
PETWORTH SHIPPING COMPANY LIMITED
POST BANK OF IRAN
POWER PLANTS' EQUIPMENT MANUFACTURING COMPANY (SAAKHTE TAJHIZATE NIROOGAHI)
PROSPER METRO INVESTMENTS LTD.
RASTKHAH, Engineer Naser
REIGATE SHIPPING COMPANY LIMITED
RESEARCH INSTITUTE OF NUCLEAR SCIENCE & TECHNOLOGY REZVANIANZADEH, Mohammad Reza RISHI MARITIME INCORPORATION
SACKVILLE HOLDINGS LTD
SAFIRAN PAYAM DARYA SHIPPING COMPANY
SALEHI, Ali Akbar
SANFORD GROUP
SANTEXLINES
SECOND OCEAN ADMINISTRATION GMBH
SECOND OCEAN GMBH & CO. KG
SEIBOW LOGISTICS LIMITED
SEVENTH OCEAN ADMINISTRATION GMBH
SEVENTH OCEAN GMBH & CO. KG
SHALLON LTD
SHEMAL CEMENT COMPANY
SHINE STAR LIMITED
SHIPPING COMPUTER SERVICES COMPANY
SILVER UNIVERSE INTERNATIONAL LTD.
SINA BANK
SINO ACCESS HOLDINGS
SINOSE MARITIME
SISCO SHIPPING COMPANY LTD
SIXTEENTH OCEAN ADMINISTRATION GMBH
SIXTEENTH OCEAN GMBH & CO. KG

SIXTH OCEAN ADMINISTRATION GMBH
SIXTH OCEAN GMBH & CO. KG
SMART DAY HOLDINGS LTD
SOLTANI, Behzad
SORINET COMMERCIAL TRUST (SCT)
SOROUSH SARAMIN ASATIR
SOUTH WAY SHIPPING AGENCY CO. LTD
SOUTH ZAGROS OIL & GAS PRODUCTION COMPANY
SPARKLE BRILLIANT DEVELOPMENT LIMITED
SPRINGTHORPE LIMITED
STATIRA MARITIME INCORPORATION
SUREH (NUCLEAR REACTORS FUEL COMPANY)
SYSTEM WISE LTD
TAMALARIS CONSOLIDATED LTD
TENTH OCEAN ADMINISTRATION GMBH
TENTH OCEAN GMBH & CO. KG
TEU FEEDER LIMITED
THETA NARI NAVIGATION
THIRD OCEAN ADMINISTRATION GMBH
THIRD OCEAN GMBH & CO. KG
THIRTEENTH OCEAN ADMINISTRATION GMBH
THIRTEENTH OCEAN GMBH & CO. KG
TOP GLACIER COMPANY LIMITED
TOP PRESTIGE TRADING LIMITED
TRADE CAPITAL BANK
TRADE TREASURE
TRUE HONOUR HOLDINGS LTD
TULIP SHIPPING INC
TWELFTH OCEAN ADMINISTRATION GMBH
TWELFTH OCEAN GMBH & CO. KG
UNIVERSAL TRANSPORTATION LIMITATION UTL
VALFAJR 8TH SHIPPING LINE

WEST OIL & GAS PRODUCTION COMPANY
WESTERN SURGE SHIPPING COMPANY LIMITED
WISE LING SHIPPING COMPANY LIMITED
ZANJANI, Babak
ZETA NERI NAVIGATION

Attachment 1: Part II
LIST OF PERSONS, ENTITIES AND BODIES SET OUT IN ANNEX I TO COUNCIL DECISION 2010/413/CFSP AND ANNEX V III TO COUNCIL REGULATION (EU) NO 267/2012

AGHA-JANI, Dawood
ALAI, Amir Moayyed
ASGARPOUR, Behman
ASHIANI, Mohammad Fedai
ASHTIANI, Abbas Rezaee
ATOMIC ENERGY ORGANISATION OF IRAN (AEOI)
BAKHTIAR, Haleh
BEHZAD, Morteza
ESFAHAN NUCLEAR FUEL RESEARCH AND PRODUCTION CENTRE (NFRPC) AND ESFAHAN NUCLEAR TECHNOLOGY CENTRE (ENTC)
FIRST EAST EXPORT BANK, P.L.C.:
HOSSEINI, Seyyed Hussein
IRANO HIND SHIPPING COMPANY
IRISL BENELUX NV
JABBER IBN HAYAN
KARAJ NUCLEAR RESEARCH CENTRE
KAVOSHYAR COMPANY
LEILABADI, Ali Hajinia
MESBAH ENERGY COMPANY
MODERN INDUSTRIES TECHNIQUE COMPANY

MOHAJERANI, Hamid-Reza
MOHAMMADI, Jafar
MONAJEMI, Ehsan
NOBARI, Houshang
NOVIN ENERGY COMPANY
NUCLEAR RESEARCH CENTER FOR AGRICULTURE AND MEDICINE
PARS TRASH COMPANY
PISHGAM (PIONEER) ENERGY INDUSTRIES
QANNADI, Mohammad
RAHIMI, Amir
RAHIQI, Javad
RASHIDI, Abbas
SABET, M. Javad Karimi
SAFDARI, Seyed Jaber
SOLEYMANI, Ghasem
SOUTH SHIPPING LINE IRAN (SSL)
TAMAS COMPANY

Attachment 2: Part I

LIST OF PERSONS, ENTITIES AND BODIES SET OUT IN ANNEX II TO COUNCIL DECISION 2010/413/CFSP AND ANNEX IX TO COUNCIL REGULATION (EU) NO 267/2012

AEROSPACE INDUSTRIES ORGANISATION, AIO
AL YASIN, Javad
ALUMINAT
ANSAR BANK
ARAN MODERN DEVICES
ARAS FARAYANDE
ARFA PAINT COMPANY
ARFEH COMPANY

ARIA NIKAN,
ARMED FORCES GEOGRAPHICAL ORGANISATION
ASHTIAN TABLO
BABAEI, Davoud
BALS ALMAN
BANK SADERAT IRAN
BANK SADERAT PLC
BARGH AZARAKSH
BEHNAM SAHRIYARI TRADING COMPANY
BONYAD TAAVON SEPAH
BORBORUDI, Sayed Shamsuddin
DANESHJOO, Kamran
DARVISH-VAND, IRGC Brigadier-General Javad
ELECTRONIC COMPONENTS INDUSTRIES
ESNICO (EQUIPMENT SUPPLIER FOR NUCLEAR INDUSTRIES CORPORATION)
ETEMAD AMIN INVEST CO MOBIN
EYVAZ TECHNIC
FADAVI, Rear Admiral Ali
FAJR AVIATION COMPOSITE INDUSTRIES
FARAHI, IRGC Brigadier-General Seyyed Mahdi
FARASEPEHR ENGINEERING COMPANY
FATAH, Parviz
GHANI SAZI URANIUM COMPANY
HAERI, Engineer Mojtaba
HIRBOD CO
HOSEYNITASH, IRGC Brigadier-General Ali
HOSSEINI NEJAD TRADING CO.
INSTITUTE OF APPLIED PHYSICS
IRAN AIRCRAFT INDUSTRIES
IRAN AIRCRAFT MANUFACTURING COMPANY
IRAN CENTRIFUGE TECHNOLOGY COMPANY
IRAN COMMUNICATIONS INDUSTRIES

IRAN COMPOSITES INSTITUTE
IRAN ELECTRONICS INDUSTRIES
IRAN MARINE INDUSTRIAL COMPANY
IRAN POOYA
IRAN SAFFRON COMPANY OR IRANSAFFRON CO.
IRANIAN AVIATION INDUSTRIES ORGANIZATION
IRGC AIR FORCE
IRGC QODS FORCE
IRGC-AIR FORCE AL-GHADIR MISSILE COMMAND
ISFAHAN OPTICS
ISLAMIC REVOLUTIONARY GUARD CORPS
JAFARI, Milad
JAVEDAN MEHR TOOS
JELVESAZAN COMPANY
KARANIR
KARIMIAN, Ali
KHALA AFARIN PARS
KHANSARI, Majid
MAAA SYNERGY
MACPAR MAKINA SAN VE TIC
MAHMUDZADEH, Ebrahim
MARINE INDUSTRIES
MAROU SANAT
MATSA (MOHANDESI TOSEH SOKHT ATOMI COMPANY)
MECHANIC INDUSTRIES GROUP
MEHR BANK
MINISTRY OF DEFENSE AND SUPPORT FOR ARMED FORCES LOGISTICS
MOBIN SANJESH
MODERN TECHNOLOGIES FZC
MOHAMMADI, Mohammad
MOHAMMADLU, Brigadier-General Beik

MOVASAGHNIA, Mohammad Reza
MULTIMAT LC VE DIS TICARET PAZARLAMA LIMITED SIRKETI
NACCACHE, Anis
NADERI, Brigadier-General Mohammad
NAJJAR, IRGC Brigadier-General Mostafa Mohammad
NAQDI, BrigGen Mohammad Reza
NASERI, Mohammad Sadegh
NASERIN VAHID
NEDA INDUSTRIAL GROUP
NEKA NOVIN
NOAVARAN POOYAMOJ
NOURI, Ali Ashraf
OIL INDUSTRY PENSION FUND INVESTMENT COMPANY
ORGANISATION OF DEFENSIVE INNOVATION AND RESEARCH
PAKPUR, BrigGen Mohammad
PARCHIN CHEMICAL INDUSTRIES
PARTO SANAT CO
PASSIVE DEFENSE ORGANIZATION
PAYA PARTO
QASEMI, Rostam (a.k.a. Rostam GHASEMI)
RAAD IRAN
RAKA
RESEARCH CENTRE FOR EXPLOSION AND IMPACT
ROSMACHIN
SAIDI, Hojatoleslam Ali
SALAMI, BrigGen Hossein
SAMAN NASB ZAYENDEH ROOD; SAMAN NASBZAINDE ROOD
SAMAN TOSE'E ASIA
SAMEN INDUSTRIES

SCHILLER NOVIN
SEPANIR OIL AND GAS ENERGY ENGINEERING COMPANY
SHAFI'I RUDSARI, Rear Admiral Mohammad
SHAHID AHMAD KAZEMI INDUSTRIAL GROUP
SHAHID BEHESHTI UNIVERSITY
SHAKHESE BEHBUD SANAT
SHAMS, Abolghassem Mozaffari
SHAMSHIRI, IRGC Brigadier-General Ali
SHARIF UNIVERSITY OF TECHNOLOGY
SHETAB G.
SHETAB GAMAN
SHETAB TRADING
SHIRAZ ELECTRONICS INDUSTRIES
SIMATEC DEVELOPMENT COMPANY
SOLAT SANA, Abdollah
SOLTANI, Hamid
STATE PURCHASING ORGANISATION
STEP STANDART TEKNIK PARCA SAN VE TIC A.S.
SUN MIDDLE EAST FZ COMPANY
SURENA (A.K.A. SAKHD VA RAH-AN- DA-ZI)
TABA (IRAN CUTTING TOOLS MANUFACTURING COMPANY—TABA TOWLID ABZAR BORESHI IRAN)
TAGHTIRAN
TAJHIZ SANAT SHAYAN
TECHNOLOGY COOPERATION OFFICE OF THE IRANIAN PRESIDENT'S OFFICE
TEST TAFSIR
TIDEWATER
TOSSE SILOOHA
TURBINE ENGINEERING MANUFACTURING
VAHIDI, IRGC Brigadier-General Ahmad
WEST SUN TRADE GMBH

Y.A.S. CO. LTD
YARSANAT
YASA PART
ZADEH, Amir Ali Haji

Attachment 2: Part II

LIST OF PERSONS, ENTITIES AND BODIES SET OUT IN ANNEX I TO COUNCIL DECISION 2010/413/CFSP AND ANNEXES V I I I TO COUNCIL REGULATION (EU) NO 267/2012

7TH OF TIR.
ABBASI-DAVANI, Fereidoun
ABZAR BORESH KAVEH CO.
AGHAJANI, Azim
AHMADIAN, Ali Akbar
AMIN INDUSTRIAL COMPLEX
AMMUNITION AND METALLURGY INDUSTRIES GROUP ARMAMENT INDUSTRIES GROUP
BAHMANYAR, Bahmanyar Morteza
BANK SEPAH
BANK SEPAH INTERNATIONAL
BARZAGANI TEJARAT TAVANMAD SACCAL COMPANIES BEHINEH TRADING CO.
CRUISE MISSILE INDUSTRY GROUP
DASTJERDI, Ahmad Vahid
DEFENCE INDUSTRIES ORGANISATION (DIO)
DEFENSE TECHNOLOGY AND SCIENCE RESEARCH CENTER DERAKHSHANDEH, Ahmad
DOOSTAN INTERNATIONAL COMPANY
ELECTRO SANAM COMPANY
ESLAMI, Mohammad
ESMAELI, Reza-Gholi

ETTEHAD TECHNICAL GROUP
FAJR INDUSTRIAL GROUP
FAKHRIZADEH-MAHABADI, Mohsen
FARASAKHT INDUSTRIES
FARAYAND TECHNIQUE
FATER (OR FAATER) INSTITUTE
GHARAGAHE SAZANDEGI GHAEM
GHORB KARBALA
GHORB NOOH
HARA COMPANY
HEJAZI, Mohammad
HOJATI, Mohsen
IMENSAZAN CONSULTANT ENGINEERS INSTITUTE
INDUSTRIAL FACTORIES OF PRECISION (IFP) MACHINERY
JOZA INDUSTRIAL CO.
KALA-ELECTRIC
KAVEH CUTTING TOOLS COMPANY
KETABACHI, Mehrdada Akhlaghi
KHATAM AL-ANBIYA CONSTRUCTION HEADQUARTERS KHORASAN METALLURGY INDUSTRIES M. BABAIE INDUSTRIES
MAKIN
MALEK ASHTAR UNIVERSITY
MALEKI, Naser
MINISTRY OF DEFENSE LOGISTICS EXPORT
MIZAN MACHINERY MANUFACTURING A.K.A.: 3MG
NAQDI, Mohammad Reza
NEJAD NOURI, Mohammad Mehdi
NIRU BATTERY MANUFACTURING COMPANY
OMRAN SAHEL
ORIENTAL OIL KISH

PARCHIN CHEMICAL INDUSTRIES
PARS AVIATION SERVICES COMPANY
PEJMAN INDUSTRIAL SERVICES CORPORATION
QODS AERONAUTICS INDUSTRIES
RAH SAHEL
RAHAB ENGINEERING INSTITUTE
REZAIE, Morteza
SABALAN COMPANY
SAD IMPORT EXPORT COMPANY
SAFARI, Morteza
SAFAVI, Yahya Rahim
SAFETY EQUIPMENT PROCUREMENT (SEP)
SAHAND ALUMINUM PARTS INDUSTRIAL COMPANY
SAHEL CONSULTANT ENGINEERS
SALIMI, Hosein
SANAM INDUSTRIAL GROUP
SEPANIR
SEPASAD ENGINEERING COMPANY
SHAHID BAGHERI INDUSTRIAL GROUP (SBIG)
SHAHID HEMMAT INDUSTRIAL GROUP (SHIG)
SHAHID KARRAZI INDUSTRIES
SHAHID SATARRI INDUSTRIES
SHAHID SAYYADE SHIRAZI INDUSTRIES
SHO'A' AVIATION.
SOLEIMANI, Qasem
SPECIAL INDUSTRIES GROUP
TABATABAEI, Ali Akbar
TIZ PARS
YA MAHDI INDUSTRIES GROUP
YAS AIR
YAZD METALLURGY INDUSTRIES
ZAHEDI, Mohammad Reza
ZOLQADR, General

Attachment 3

IRANIAN FINANCIAL INSTITUTIONS AND INDIVIDUAL AND ENTITIES IDENTIFIED AS GOVERNMENT OF IRAN (GOI) ON THE SDN LIST; DESIGNATED ENTITIES AND INDIVIDUALS ON THE SDN LIST AND ENTITIES AND INDIVIDUALS LISTED ON THE FSE LIST; INDIVIDUALS AND ENTITIES SANCTIONED UNDER ISA; BLOCKED PROPERTY OF THE FOREGOING

AA ENERGY FZCO*[22] ABAN AIR
ADVANCE NOVEL LIMITED AFZALI, Ali AGHA-JANI, Dawood
AL AQILI GROUP LLC
AL AQILI, Mohamed Saeed
AL FIDA INTERNATIONAL GENERAL TRADING AL HILAL EXCHANGE
ALPHA EFFORT LIMITED AMERI, Teymour
AMIN INVESTMENT BANK* ANTARES SHIPPING COMPANY NV ARASH SHIPPING ENTERPRISES LIMITED* ARIAN BANK
ARTA SHIPPING ENTERPRISES LIMITED* ASAN SHIPPING ENTERPRISE LIMITED* ASCOTEC HOLDING GMBH*
ASCOTEC JAPAN K.K.*
ASCOTEC MINERAL & MACHINERY GMBH*
ASCOTEC SCIENCE & TECHNOLOGY GMBH*
ASCOTEC STEEL TRADING GMBH* ASHTEAD SHIPPING COMPANY LIMITED ASIA BANK
ASIA ENERGY GENERAL TRADING (LLC)* ASIA MARINE NETWORK PTE. LTD. ASSA CO. LTD.
ASSA CORP.
ATLANTIC INTERMODAL

ATOMIC ENERGY ORGANIZATION OF IRAN
AZORES SHIPPING COMPANY LL FZE BAHADORI, Masoud*
BANCO INTERNACIONAL DE DESARROLLO, C.A. BANDAR IMAM PETROCHEMICAL COMPANY*
BANK KARGOSHAEE
BANK KESHAVARZI IRAN*
BANK MARKAZI JOMHOURI ISLAMI IRAN* BANK MASKAN*
BANK MELLAT*
BANK MELLI IRAN INVESTMENT COMPANY BANK MELLI IRAN*
BANK MELLI PRINTING AND PUBLISHING CO. BANK OF INDUSTRY AND MINE (OF IRAN)*
ANK REFAH KARGARAN*
BANK SEPAH INTERNATIONAL PLC BANK SEPAH*
BANK TEJARAT*
BANK TORGOVOY KAPITAL ZAO*
BANK-E SHAHR*
BATENI, Naser
BAZARGAN, Farzad*
BEHSAZ KASHANE TEHRAN CONSTRUCTION CO.*
BEHZAD, Morteza Ahmadali
BELFAST GENERAL TRADING LLC
BEST PRECISE LIMITED
BIIS MARITIME LIMITED
BIMEH IRAN INSURANCE COMPANY (U.K.) LIMITED*
BLUE TANKER SHIPPING SA*
BMIIC INTERNATIONAL GENERAL TRADING LTD
BOU ALI SINA PETROCHEMICAL COMPANY*
BREYELLER STAHL TECHNOLOGY GMBH & CO. KG*

BUSHEHR SHIPPING COMPANY LIMITED
BYFLEET SHIPPING COMPANY LIMITED
CAMBIS, Dimitris*
CASPIAN MARITIME LIMITED*
CAUCASUS ENERGY
CEMENT INVESTMENT AND DEVELOPMENT COMPANY
CENTRAL INSURANCE OF IRAN
CISCO SHIPPING COMPANY CO. LTD.
COBHAM SHIPPING COMPANY LIMITED
COMMERCIAL PARS OIL CO.*
CONCEPT GIANT LIMITED
CREDIT INSTITUTION FOR DEVELOPMENT*
CRYSTAL SHIPPING FZE
CYLINDER SYSTEM L.T.D.*
DAJMAR, Mohhammad Hossein
DANESH SHIPPING COMPANY LIMITED*
DARYA CAPITAL ADMINISTRATION GMBH
DAVAR SHIPPING CO LTD*
DENA TANKERS FZE*
DERAKHSHANDEH, AHMAD
DETTIN SPA
DEY BANK*
DFS WORLDWIDE
DIVANDARI, Ali
DORKING SHIPPING COMPANY LIMITED
EDBI EXCHANGE COMPANY
EDBI STOCK BROKERAGE COMPANY
EFFINGHAM SHIPPING COMPANY LIMITED
EGHTESAD NOVIN BANK*
EIGHTH OCEAN ADMINISTRATION GMBH
EIGHTH OCEAN GMBH & CO. KG
ELEVENTH OCEAN ADMINISTRATION GMBH

ELEVENTH OCEAN GMBH & CO. KG
ESFAHAN NUCLEAR FUEL RESEARCH AND PRODUCTION CENTER
ESLAMI, Mansour
EUROPAISCH-IRANISCHE HANDELSBANK AG*
EUROPEAN OIL TRADERS
EVEREX
EXECUTION OF IMAM KHOMEINI'S ORDER*
EXPORT DEVELOPMENT BANK OF IRAN*
EZATI, Ali
FAIRWAY SHIPPING LTD
FAL OIL COMPANY LIMITED
FARNHAM SHIPPING COMPANY LIMITED
FARSOUDEH, Houshang
FAYLACA PETROLEUM
FERLAND COMPANY LIMITED
FIFTEENTH OCEAN GMBH & CO. KG
FIFTH OCEAN ADMINISTRATION GMBH
FIFTH OCEAN GMBH & CO. KG
FIRST EAST EXPORT BANK, P.L.C.
FIRST ISLAMIC INVESTMENT BANK LTD.
FIRST OCEAN ADMINISTRATION GMBH
FIRST OCEAN GMBH & CO. KG
FIRST PERSIA EQUITY FUND
FOURTEENTH OCEAN GMBH & CO. KG
FOURTH OCEAN ADMINISTRATION GMBH
FOURTH OCEAN GMBH & CO. KG
FUTURE BANK B.S.C.*
GALLIOT MARITIME INC
GARBIN NAVIGATION LTD*
GEORGIAN BUSINESS DEVELOPMENT
GHADIR INVESTMENT COMPANY*
GHAED BASSIR PETROCHEMICAL PRODUCTS COMPANY*

GHALEBANI, Ahmad*
GHARZOLHASANEH RESALAT BANK*
GHAVAMIN BANK*
GHEZEL AYAGH, Alireza
GOLDEN RESOURCES TRADING COMPANY L.L.C.*
GOLDENTEX FZE
GOLPARVAR, Gholamhossein
GOMSHALL SHIPPING COMPANY LIMITED
GOOD LUCK SHIPPING L.L.C.
GRACE BAY SHIPPING INC*
GREAT BUSINESS DEALS
GREAT METHOD LIMITED
HADI SHIPPING COMPANY LIMITED*
HAFIZ DARYA SHIPPING CO
HARAZ SHIPPING COMPANY LIMITED*
HATEF SHIPPING COMPANY LIMITED*
HEKMAT IRANIAN BANK*
HERCULES INTERNATIONAL SHIP*
HERMIS SHIPPING SA*
HIRMAND SHIPPING COMPANY LIMITED*
HODA SHIPPING COMPANY LIMITED*
HOMA SHIPPING COMPANY LIMITED*
HONAR SHIPPING COMPANY LIMITED*
HONG KONG INTERTRADE COMPANY*
HORMOZ OIL REFINING COMPANY*
HORSHAM SHIPPING COMPANY LIMITED
HOSSEINPOUR, Houshang
HTTS HANSEATIC TRADE TRUST AND SHIPPING, GMBH IDEAL SUCCESS INVESTMENTS LIMITED
IFIC HOLDING AG*
IHAG TRADING GMBH*
IMPIRE SHIPPING COMPANY*
INDUS MARITIME INC

INDUSTRIAL DEVELOPMENT AND RENOVATION ORGANIZATION OF IRAN*
INTERNATIONAL SAFE OIL
INTRA CHEM TRADING GMBH*
IRAN & SHARGH COMPANY*
IRAN & SHARGH LEASING COMPANY*
IRAN AIR
IRAN FOREIGN INVESTMENT COMPANY*
IRAN INSURANCE COMPANY*
IRAN O HIND SHIPPING COMPANY
IRAN O MISR SHIPPING COMPANY
IRAN PETROCHEMICAL COMMERCIAL COMPANY*
IRAN ZAMIN BANK*
IRANAIR TOURS
IRANIAN MINES AND MINING INDUSTRIES DEVELOPMENT AND RENOVATION ORGANIZATION* IRANIAN OIL COMPANY (U.K.) LIMITED*
IRANIAN-VENEZUELAN BI-NATIONAL BANK / JOINT IRAN-VENEZUELA BANK*
IRASCO S.R.L.*
IRINVESTSHIP LTD.
IRISL (MALTA) LIMITED
IRISL (UK) LTD.
IRISL CHINA SHIPPING CO., LTD.
IRISL EUROPE GMBH
IRISL MARINE SERVICES & ENGINEERING COMPANY
IRISL MULTIMODAL TRANSPORT CO.
IRITAL SHIPPING SRL COMPANY
ISI MARITIME LIMITED
ISIM AMIN LIMITED
ISIM ATR LIMITED

ISIM OLIVE LIMITED
ISIM SAT LIMITED
ISIM SEA CHARIOT LIMITED
ISIM SEA CRESCENT LIMITED
ISIM SININ LIMITED
ISIM TAJ MAHAL LIMITED
ISIM TOUR LIMITED
ISLAMIC REGIONAL COOPERATION BANK*
ISLAMIC REPUBLIC OF IRAN SHIPPING LINES
JABBER IBN HAYAN
JAM PETROCHEMICAL COMPANY
JASHNSAZ, Seifollah*
JUPITER SEAWAYS SHIPPING*
KADDOURI, Abdelhak
KAFOLATBANK*
KALA LIMITED*
KALA PENSION TRUST LIMITED*
KARAFARIN BANK*
KASB INTERNATIONAL LLC*
KAVERI MARITIME INC
KAVOSHYAR COMPANY
KERMAN SHIPPING CO LTD
KHALILI, Jamshid
KHAVARMIANEH BANK*
KHAZAR SEA SHIPPING LINES
KISH INTERNATIONAL BANK*
KISH PROTECTION & INDEMNITY
KONING MARINE CORP*
KONT INVESTMENT BANK
KONT KOSMETIK
KSN FOUNDATION
KUO OIL PTE. LTD
LANCELIN SHIPPING COMPANY LIMITED

LEADING MARITIME PTE. LTD.
LEILABADI, Ali Hajinia
LISSOME MARINE SERVICES LLC
LOGISTIC SMART LIMITED
LOWESWATER LIMITED
MACHINE SAZI ARAK CO. LTD.*
MAHAB GHODSS CONSULTING ENGINEERING COMPANY*
MAHDAVI, Ali
MALSHIP SHIPPING AGENCY LTD.
MARANER HOLDINGS LIMITED
MARBLE SHIPPING LIMITED
MARJAN PETROCHEMICAL COMPANY*
MAZANDARAN CEMENT COMPANY
MAZANDARAN TEXTILE COMPANY
MCS ENGINEERING*
MCS INTERNATIONAL GMBH*
MEHR CAYMAN LTD.
MEHR IRAN CREDIT UNION BANK*
MEHRAN SHIPPING COMPANY LIMITED*
MELLAT BANK SB CJSC
MELLAT INSURANCE COMPANY*
MELLI AGROCHEMICAL COMPANY, P.J.S.
MELLI BANK PLC
MELLI INVESTMENT HOLDING INTERNATIONAL
MELODIOUS MARITIME INC
MERSAD SHIPPING COMPANY LIMITED*
MESBAH ENERGY COMPANY
METAL & MINERAL TRADE S.A.R.L.*
MID OIL ASIA PTE LTD
MILL DENE LIMITED
MINAB SHIPPING COMPANY LIMITED*
MINES AND METALS ENGINEERING GMBH*

MIR BUSINESS BANK ZAO
MOALLEM INSURANCE COMPANY
MOBIN PETROCHEMICAL COMPANY*
MODABER*
MODALITY LIMITED
MOGHADDAMI FARD, Mohammad
MOHADDES, Seyed Mahmoud*
MOINIE, Mohammad*
MONSOON SHIPPING LTD*
MOUNT EVEREST MARITIME INC
MSP KALA NAFT CO. TEHRAN*
N.I.T.C. REPRESENTATIVE OFFICE*
NABIPOUR, Ghasem
NAFTIRAN INTERTRADE CO. (NICO) LIMITED*
NAFTIRAN INTERTRADE CO. (NICO) SARL*
NAFTIRAN TRADING SERVICES CO. (NTS) LIMITED*
NARI SHIPPING AND CHARTERING GMBH & CO. KG
NASIRBEIK, Anahita
NATIONAL IRANIAN OIL COMPANY PTE LTD*
NATIONAL IRANIAN OIL COMPANY*
NATIONAL IRANIAN TANKER COMPANY LLC*
NATIONAL IRANIAN TANKER COMPANY*
NATIONAL PETROCHEMICAL COMPANY*
NAYEBI, Pourya
NEFERTITI SHIPPING COMPANY
NEUMAN LIMITED
NEW DESIRE LIMITED
NEW YORK GENERAL TRADING
NEW YORK MONEY EXCHANGE
NICO ENGINEERING LIMITED*
NIKOUSOKHAN, Mahmoud*

NIKSIMA FOOD AND BEVERAGE JLT
NINTH OCEAN ADMINISTRATION GMBH
NINTH OCEAN GMBH & CO. KG
NIOC INTERNATIONAL AFFAIRS (LONDON) LIMITED*
NIZAMI, Anwar Kamal
NOOR AFZAR GOSTAR COMPANY
NOOR ENERGY (MALAYSIA) LTD.*
NOURI PETROCHEMICAL COMPANY*
NOVIN ENERGY COMPANY
NPC INTERNATIONAL LIMITED*
NUCLEAR RESEARCH CENTER FOR AGRICULTURE AND MEDICINE
NUCLEAR SCIENCE AND TECHNOLOGY RESEARCH INSTITUTE
OCEAN CAPITAL ADMINISTRATION GMBH
OIL INDUSTRY INVESTMENT COMPANY*
OMID REY CIVIL & CONSTRUCTION COMPANY*
ONE CLASS PROPERTIES (PTY) LTD.*
ONE VISION INVESTMENTS 5 (PTY) LTD.*
ONERBANK ZAO*
ORCHIDEA GULF TRADING
P.C.C. (SINGAPORE) PRIVATE LIMITED*
PACIFIC SHIPPING DMCEST
PAJAND, Mohammad Hadi
PARDIS INVESTMENT COMPANY*
PARS MCS*
PARS OIL AND GAS COMPANY*
PARS OIL CO.*
PARS PETROCHEMICAL COMPANY*
PARS PETROCHEMICAL SHIPPING COMPANY*
PARS TRASH COMPANY
PARSAEI, Reza*

PARSIAN BANK*
PARTNER CENTURY LIMITED
PARVARESH, Farhad Ali
PASARGAD BANK*
PEARL ENERGY COMPANY LTD.
PEARL ENERGY SERVICES, SA
PERSIA INTERNATIONAL BANK PLC
PERSIA OIL & GAS INDUSTRY DEVELOPMENT CO.*
PETRO ENERGY INTERTRADE COMPANY*
PETRO ROYAL FZE*
PETRO SUISSE INTERTRADE COMPANY SA*
PETROCHEMICAL COMMERCIAL COMPANY (U.K.) LIMITED*
PETROCHEMICAL COMMERCIAL COMPANY FZE*
PETROCHEMICAL COMMERCIAL COMPANY INTERNATIONAL*
PETROIRAN DEVELOPMENT COMPANY (PEDCO) LIMITED*
PETROLEOS DE VENEZUELA S.A. (PDVSA)
PETROPARS INTERNATIONAL FZE*
PETROPARS LTD.*
PETROPARS UK LIMITED*
PIONEER ENERGY INDUSTRIES COMPANY
POLAT, Muzaffer
POLINEX GENERAL TRADING LLC*
POLYNAR COMPANY*
POST BANK OF IRAN*
POURANSARI, Hashem*
PROTON PETROCHEMICALS SHIPPING LIMITED*
PRYVATNE AKTSIONERNE TOVARYSTVO AVIAKOMPANIYA BUKOVYNA
QANNADI, Mohammad

QULANDARY, Azizullah Asadullah
RAHIQI, Javad
RASOOL, Seyed Alaeddin Sadat
REY INVESTMENT COMPANY*
REY NIRU ENGINEERING COMPANY*
REYCO GMBH.*
REZVANIANZADEH, Mohammed Reza
RISHI MARITIME INC
RISHMAK PRODUCTIVE & EXPORTS COMPANY*
ROYAL ARYA CO.*
ROYAL OYSTER GROUP
ROYAL-MED SHIPPING AGENCY LTD
SABET, Javad Karimi
SACKVILLE HOLDINGS LIMITED
SADAF PETROCHEMICAL ASSALUYEH COMPANY*
SAFDARI, Seyed Jaber
SAFIRAN PAYAM DARYA SHIPPING COMPANY
SAMAN BANK*
SAMAN SHIPPING COMPANY LIMITED*
SAMBOUK SHIPPING FZC*
SANDFORD GROUP LIMITED
SANTEX LINES LIMITED
SARKANDI, Ahmad
SARMAYEH BANK*
SARV SHIPPING COMPANY LIMITED*
SECOND OCEAN ADMINISTRATION GMBH
SECOND OCEAN GMBH & CO. KG
SEIBOW LIMITED
SEIBOW LOGISTICS LIMITED
SEIFI, Asadollah
SEPID SHIPPING COMPANY LIMITED*
SEVENTH OCEAN ADMINISTRATION GMBH
SEVENTH OCEAN GMBH & CO. KG

SEYYEDI, Seyed Nasser Mohammad*
SEYYEDI, Seyedeh Hanieh Seyed Nasser Mohammad
SHAHID TONDGOOYAN PETROCHEMICAL COMPANY*
SHALLON LIMITED
SHAZAND PETROCHEMICAL COMPANY*
SHERE SHIPPING COMPANY LIMITED
SHIPPING COMPUTER SERVICES COMPANY
SHOMAL CEMENT COMPANY
SIMA GENERAL TRADING CO FZE*
SIMA SHIPPING COMPANY LIMITED*
SINA BANK*
SINA SHIPPING COMPANY LIMITED*
SINGA TANKERS PTE. LTD.
SINO ACCESS HOLDINGS LIMITED
SINOSE MARITIME PTE. LTD.
SIQIRIYA MARITIME CORP.
SIXTH OCEAN ADMINISTRATION GMBH
SIXTH OCEAN GMBH & CO. KG
SMART DAY HOLDINGS GROUP LIMITED
SOKOLENKO, Vitaly
SORINET COMMERCIAL TRUST (SCT) BANKERS
SOROUSH SARZAMIN ASATIR SHIP MANAGEMENT COMPANY
SOUTH SHIPPING LINE IRAN
SPEEDY SHIP FZC
SPRINGTHORPE LIMITED
STARRY SHINE INTERNATIONAL LIMITED
SWISS MANAGEMENT SERVICES SARL*
SYNERGY GENERAL TRADING FZE*
SYSTEM WISE LIMITED
TABATABAEI, Seyyed Mohammad Ali Khatibi*
TABRIZ PETROCHEMICAL COMPANY*

TADBIR BROKERAGE COMPANY*
TADBIR CONSTRUCTION DEVELOPMENT COMPANY*
TADBIR ECONOMIC DEVELOPMENT GROUP*
TADBIR ENERGY DEVELOPMENT GROUP CO.*
TADBIR INVESTMENT COMPANY*
TAFAZOLI, Ahmad
TALAI, Mohamad
TAMAS COMPANY
TAT BANK*
TC SHIPPING COMPANY LIMITED*
TENTH OCEAN GMBH & CO. KG
THE EXPLORATION AND NUCLEAR RAW MATERIALS PRODUCTION COMPANY THE NUCLEAR REACTORS FUEL COMPANY THIRD OCEAN ADMINISTRATION GMBH
THIRD OCEAN GMBH & CO. KG
THIRTEENTH OCEAN GMBH & CO. KG
TONGHAM SHIPPING CO LTD
TOP GLACIER COMPANY LIMITED
TOP PRESTIGE TRADING LIMITED
TOSEE EQTESAD AYANDEHSAZAN COMPANY*
TOSEE TAAVON BANK*
TOURISM BANK*
TRADE TREASURE LIMITED
TRUE HONOUR HOLDINGS LIMITED
TWELFTH OCEAN ADMINISTRATION GMBH
TWELFTH OCEAN GMBH & CO. KG
UPPERCOURT SHIPPING COMPANY LIMITED
VALFAJR 8TH SHIPPING LINE CO SSK
VOBSTER SHIPPING COMPANY LTD
WEST SUN TRADE GMBH*
WIPPERMANN, Ulrich

WOKING SHIPPING INVESTMENTS LIMITED
YASINI, Seyed Kamal
YAZDI, Bahareh Mirza Hossein
ZADEH, Hassan Jalil
ZANJANI, Babak Morteza
ZARIN RAFSANJAN CEMENT COMPANY*
ZEIDI, Hossein
ZHUHAI ZHENRONG COMPANY
ZIRACCHIAN ZADEH, Mahmoud*

BLOCKED PROPERTY	PROPERTY OF	TYPE	IMO NUMBER
EP-CFD	IRAN AIR	Aircraft	
EP-CFE	IRAN AIR	Aircraft	
EP-CFH	IRAN AIR	Aircraft	
EP-CFI	IRAN AIR	Aircraft	
EP-CFJ	IRAN AIR	Aircraft	
EP-CFK	IRAN AIR	Aircraft	
EP-CFL	IRAN AIR	Aircraft	
EP-CFM	IRAN AIR	Aircraft	
EP-CFO	IRAN AIR	Aircraft	
EP-CFP	IRAN AIR	Aircraft	
EP-CFQ	IRAN AIR	Aircraft	
EP-CFR	IRAN AIR	Aircraft	
EP-IAA	IRAN AIR	Aircraft	
EP-IAB	IRAN AIR	Aircraft	
EP-IAC	IRAN AIR	Aircraft	
EP-IAD	IRAN AIR	Aircraft	
EP-IAG	IRAN AIR	Aircraft	
EP-IAH	IRAN AIR	Aircraft	
EP-IAI	IRAN AIR	Aircraft	
EP-IAM	IRAN AIR	Aircraft	
EP-IBA	IRAN AIR	Aircraft	
EP-IBB	IRAN AIR	Aircraft	
EP-IBC	IRAN AIR	Aircraft	
EP-IBD	IRAN AIR	Aircraft	

(*continued*)

(continued)

BLOCKED PROPERTY	PROPERTY OF	TYPE	IMO NUMBER
EP-IBG	IRAN AIR	Aircraft	
EP-IBH	IRAN AIR	Aircraft	
EP-IBI	IRAN AIR	Aircraft	
EP-IBJ	IRAN AIR	Aircraft	
EP-IBK	IRAN AIR	Aircraft	
EP-IBL	IRAN AIR	Aircraft	
EP-IBM	IRAN AIR	Aircraft	
EP-IBN	IRAN AIR	Aircraft	
EP-IBP	IRAN AIR	Aircraft	
EP-IBQ	IRAN AIR	Aircraft	
EP-IBS	IRAN AIR	Aircraft	
EP-IBT	IRAN AIR	Aircraft	
EP-IBV	IRAN AIR	Aircraft	
EP-IBZ	IRAN AIR	Aircraft	
EP-ICD	IRAN AIR	Aircraft	
EP-ICE	IRAN AIR	Aircraft	
EP-ICF	IRAN AIR	Aircraft	
EP-IDA	IRAN AIR	Aircraft	
EP-IDD	IRAN AIR	Aircraft	
EP-IDF	IRAN AIR	Aircraft	
EP-IDG	IRAN AIR	Aircraft	
EP-IEB	IRAN AIR	Aircraft	
EP-IEC	IRAN AIR	Aircraft	
EP-IED	IRAN AIR	Aircraft	
EP-IEE	IRAN AIR	Aircraft	
EP-IEF	IRAN AIR	Aircraft	
EP-IEG	IRAN AIR	Aircraft	
EP-IRK	IRAN AIR	Aircraft	
EP-IRL	IRAN AIR	Aircraft	
EP-IRM	IRAN AIR	Aircraft	
EP-IRN	IRAN AIR	Aircraft	
EP-IRR	IRAN AIR	Aircraft	
EP-IRS	IRAN AIR	Aircraft	
EP-IRT	IRAN AIR	Aircraft	

(*continued*)

(continued)

BLOCKED PROPERTY	PROPERTY OF	TYPE	IMO NUMBER
EP-MDD	IRAN AIR	Aircraft	
EP-MDE	IRAN AIR	Aircraft	
UR-BXI	IRAN AIR	Aircraft	
UR-BXL	IRAN AIR	Aircraft	
UR-BXM	IRAN AIR	Aircraft	
UR-CGS	IRAN AIR	Aircraft	
UR-CGT	IRAN AIR	Aircraft	
UR-CHW	IRAN AIR	Aircraft	
UR-CHX	IRAN AIR	Aircraft	
UR-CHY	IRAN AIR	Aircraft	
UR-CHZ	IRAN AIR	Aircraft	
UR-CJQ	IRAN AIR	Aircraft	
UR-BHJ	PRYVATNE AKTSIONERNE TOVARYSTVO AVIAKOMPANIYA	Aircraft	
UR-BXN	PRYVATNE AKTSIONERNE TOVARYSTVO AVIAKOMPANIYA	Aircraft	
UR-CIX	PRYVATNE AKTSIONERNE TOVARYSTVO AVIAKOMPANIYA	Aircraft	
UR-CIY	PRYVATNE AKTSIONERNE TOVARYSTVO AVIAKOMPANIYA	Aircraft	
UR-CJA	PRYVATNE AKTSIONERNE TOVARYSTVO AVIAKOMPANIYA	Aircraft	

(*continued*)

(continued)

BLOCKED PROPERTY	PROPERTY OF	TYPE	IMO NUMBER
UR-CJK	PRYVATNE AKTSIONERNE TOVARYSTVO AVIAKOMPANIYA	Aircraft	
RIONA	HAFIZ DARYA SHIPPING CO	Vessel	9349588
MIRZA KOCHEK KHAN	ISLAMIC REPUBLIC OF IRAN SHIPPING LINES	Vessel	7027899
ASSA	ISLAMIC REPUBLIC OF IRAN SHIPPING LINES	Vessel	7632814
AMITEES	ISLAMIC REPUBLIC OF IRAN SHIPPING LINES	Vessel	7632826
HORMUZ 2	ISLAMIC REPUBLIC OF IRAN SHIPPING LINES	Vessel	7904580
PARMIDA	ISLAMIC REPUBLIC OF IRAN SHIPPING LINES	Vessel	8105284
BARSAM	ISLAMIC REPUBLIC OF IRAN SHIPPING LINES	Vessel	8107581
PANTEA	ISLAMIC REPUBLIC OF IRAN SHIPPING LINES	Vessel	8108559
IRAN AKHAVAN	ISLAMIC REPUBLIC OF IRAN SHIPPING LINES	Vessel	8113009
SARINA	ISLAMIC REPUBLIC OF IRAN SHIPPING LINES	Vessel	8203608

(*continued*)

(continued)

BLOCKED PROPERTY	PROPERTY OF	TYPE	IMO NUMBER
SABRINA	ISLAMIC REPUBLIC OF IRAN SHIPPING LINES	Vessel	8215742
ATTRIBUTE	ISLAMIC REPUBLIC OF IRAN SHIPPING LINES	Vessel	8309593
ALIAS	ISLAMIC REPUBLIC OF IRAN SHIPPING LINES	Vessel	8309608
AQUARIAN	ISLAMIC REPUBLIC OF IRAN SHIPPING LINES	Vessel	8309610
ADVENTIST	ISLAMIC REPUBLIC OF IRAN SHIPPING LINES	Vessel	8309622
AGEAN	ISLAMIC REPUBLIC OF IRAN SHIPPING LINES	Vessel	8309634
ANGEL	ISLAMIC REPUBLIC OF IRAN SHIPPING LINES	Vessel	8309646
AGILE	ISLAMIC REPUBLIC OF IRAN SHIPPING LINES	Vessel	8309658
AJAX	ISLAMIC REPUBLIC OF IRAN SHIPPING LINES	Vessel	8309672
ACROBAT	ISLAMIC REPUBLIC OF IRAN SHIPPING LINES	Vessel	8309684
SHADFAR	ISLAMIC REPUBLIC OF IRAN SHIPPING LINES	Vessel	8309696

(continued)

(continued)

BLOCKED PROPERTY	PROPERTY OF	TYPE	IMO NUMBER
AMPLIFY	ISLAMIC REPUBLIC OF IRAN SHIPPING LINES	Vessel	8309701
IRAN HORMUZ 21	ISLAMIC REPUBLIC OF IRAN SHIPPING LINES	Vessel	8314263
IRAN HORMUZ 22	ISLAMIC REPUBLIC OF IRAN SHIPPING LINES	Vessel	8314275
IRAN HORMUZ 23	ISLAMIC REPUBLIC OF IRAN SHIPPING LINES	Vessel	8319782
IRAN SHALAK	ISLAMIC REPUBLIC OF IRAN SHIPPING LINES	Vessel	8319940
IRAN YOUSHAT	ISLAMIC REPUBLIC OF IRAN SHIPPING LINES	Vessel	8319952
AEROLITE	ISLAMIC REPUBLIC OF IRAN SHIPPING LINES	Vessel	8320121
ADRIAN	ISLAMIC REPUBLIC OF IRAN SHIPPING LINES	Vessel	8320133
NAGHMEH	ISLAMIC REPUBLIC OF IRAN SHIPPING LINES	Vessel	8320145
RONAK	ISLAMIC REPUBLIC OF IRAN SHIPPING LINES	Vessel	8320157
ACCURATE	ISLAMIC REPUBLIC OF IRAN SHIPPING LINES	Vessel	8320169

(*continued*)

(continued)

BLOCKED PROPERTY	PROPERTY OF	TYPE	IMO NUMBER
TABANDEH	ISLAMIC REPUBLIC OF IRAN SHIPPING LINES	Vessel	8320171
GULAFSHAN	ISLAMIC REPUBLIC OF IRAN SHIPPING LINES	Vessel	8320183
ALAMEDA	ISLAMIC REPUBLIC OF IRAN SHIPPING LINES	Vessel	8320195
IRAN PARAK	ISLAMIC REPUBLIC OF IRAN SHIPPING LINES	Vessel	8322064
IRAN CHARAK	ISLAMIC REPUBLIC OF IRAN SHIPPING LINES	Vessel	8322076
IRAN HORMUZ 25	ISLAMIC REPUBLIC OF IRAN SHIPPING LINES	Vessel	8422072
IRAN HORMUZ 26	ISLAMIC REPUBLIC OF IRAN SHIPPING LINES	Vessel	8422084
DORITA	ISLAMIC REPUBLIC OF IRAN SHIPPING LINES	Vessel	8605234
IRAN SHALAMCHEH	ISLAMIC REPUBLIC OF IRAN SHIPPING LINES	Vessel	8820925
AAJ	ISLAMIC REPUBLIC OF IRAN SHIPPING LINES	Vessel	8984484
IRAN HORMUZ 12	ISLAMIC REPUBLIC OF IRAN SHIPPING LINES	Vessel	9005596

(continued)

(continued)

BLOCKED PROPERTY	PROPERTY OF	TYPE	IMO NUMBER
IRAN KONG	ISLAMIC REPUBLIC OF IRAN SHIPPING LINES	Vessel	9007582
VISTA	ISLAMIC REPUBLIC OF IRAN SHIPPING LINES	Vessel	9010711
VIANA	ISLAMIC REPUBLIC OF IRAN SHIPPING LINES	Vessel	9010723
IRAN HORMUZ 14	ISLAMIC REPUBLIC OF IRAN SHIPPING LINES	Vessel	9020778
HAMD	ISLAMIC REPUBLIC OF IRAN SHIPPING LINES	Vessel	9036052
SOBHAN	ISLAMIC REPUBLIC OF IRAN SHIPPING LINES	Vessel	9036935
SATTAR	ISLAMIC REPUBLIC OF IRAN SHIPPING LINES	Vessel	9040479
ABBA	ISLAMIC REPUBLIC OF IRAN SHIPPING LINES	Vessel	9051624
BEHDAD	ISLAMIC REPUBLIC OF IRAN SHIPPING LINES	Vessel	9051636
PARSHAN	ISLAMIC REPUBLIC OF IRAN SHIPPING LINES	Vessel	9051648
VALERIAN	ISLAMIC REPUBLIC OF IRAN SHIPPING LINES	Vessel	9051650

(*continued*)

(continued)

BLOCKED PROPERTY	PROPERTY OF	TYPE	IMO NUMBER
NEGEEN	ISLAMIC REPUBLIC OF IRAN SHIPPING LINES	Vessel	9071519
ATTAR	ISLAMIC REPUBLIC OF IRAN SHIPPING LINES	Vessel	9074092
PARIN	ISLAMIC REPUBLIC OF IRAN SHIPPING LINES	Vessel	9076478
TEEN	ISLAMIC REPUBLIC OF IRAN SHIPPING LINES	Vessel	9101649
GOWHAR	ISLAMIC REPUBLIC OF IRAN SHIPPING LINES	Vessel	9103087
IRAN DALEER	ISLAMIC REPUBLIC OF IRAN SHIPPING LINES	Vessel	9118551
PATRIS	ISLAMIC REPUBLIC OF IRAN SHIPPING LINES	Vessel	9137210
NARDIS	ISLAMIC REPUBLIC OF IRAN SHIPPING LINES	Vessel	9137246
KADOS	ISLAMIC REPUBLIC OF IRAN SHIPPING LINES	Vessel	9137258
ZOMOROUD	ISLAMIC REPUBLIC OF IRAN SHIPPING LINES	Vessel	9138044
BRELYAN	ISLAMIC REPUBLIC OF IRAN SHIPPING LINES	Vessel	9138056

(*continued*)

(continued)

BLOCKED PROPERTY	PROPERTY OF	TYPE	IMO NUMBER
NILDA	ISLAMIC REPUBLIC OF IRAN SHIPPING LINES	Vessel	9165786
JOVITA	ISLAMIC REPUBLIC OF IRAN SHIPPING LINES	Vessel	9165798
MANOLA	ISLAMIC REPUBLIC OF IRAN SHIPPING LINES	Vessel	9165803
GLADIOLUS	ISLAMIC REPUBLIC OF IRAN SHIPPING LINES	Vessel	9165815
ELYANA	ISLAMIC REPUBLIC OF IRAN SHIPPING LINES	Vessel	9165827
NEGAR	ISLAMIC REPUBLIC OF IRAN SHIPPING LINES	Vessel	9165839
SAVIZ	ISLAMIC REPUBLIC OF IRAN SHIPPING LINES	Vessel	9167253
GLOXINIA	ISLAMIC REPUBLIC OF IRAN SHIPPING LINES	Vessel	9167265
NESHAT	ISLAMIC REPUBLIC OF IRAN SHIPPING LINES	Vessel	9167277
BEHSHAD	ISLAMIC REPUBLIC OF IRAN SHIPPING LINES	Vessel	9167289
JAIRAN	ISLAMIC REPUBLIC OF IRAN SHIPPING LINES	Vessel	9167291

(*continued*)

(continued)

BLOCKED PROPERTY	PROPERTY OF	TYPE	IMO NUMBER
IRAN SHAHED	ISLAMIC REPUBLIC OF IRAN SHIPPING LINES	Vessel	9184691
GOLSAR	ISLAMIC REPUBLIC OF IRAN SHIPPING LINES	Vessel	9193185
ZARSAN	ISLAMIC REPUBLIC OF IRAN SHIPPING LINES	Vessel	9193197
ARVIN	ISLAMIC REPUBLIC OF IRAN SHIPPING LINES	Vessel	9193202
ARTAVAND	ISLAMIC REPUBLIC OF IRAN SHIPPING LINES	Vessel	9193214
TERESA	ISLAMIC REPUBLIC OF IRAN SHIPPING LINES	Vessel	9209324
GABRIELA	ISLAMIC REPUBLIC OF IRAN SHIPPING LINES	Vessel	9209336
SARITA	ISLAMIC REPUBLIC OF IRAN SHIPPING LINES	Vessel	9209348
SILVER CRAFT	ISLAMIC REPUBLIC OF IRAN SHIPPING LINES	Vessel	9209350
MAHNAM	ISLAMIC REPUBLIC OF IRAN SHIPPING LINES	Vessel	9213387
TERMEH	ISLAMIC REPUBLIC OF IRAN SHIPPING LINES	Vessel	9213399

(continued)

(continued)

BLOCKED PROPERTY	PROPERTY OF	TYPE	IMO NUMBER
MAHSAN	ISLAMIC REPUBLIC OF IRAN SHIPPING LINES	Vessel	9226944
HAMADAN	ISLAMIC REPUBLIC OF IRAN SHIPPING LINES	Vessel	9226956
TARADIS	ISLAMIC REPUBLIC OF IRAN SHIPPING LINES	Vessel	9245304
PARMIS	ISLAMIC REPUBLIC OF IRAN SHIPPING LINES	Vessel	9245316
ZAR	ISLAMIC REPUBLIC OF IRAN SHIPPING LINES	Vessel	9260160
ZIVAR	ISLAMIC REPUBLIC OF IRAN SHIPPING LINES	Vessel	9260172
VALILI	ISLAMIC REPUBLIC OF IRAN SHIPPING LINES	Vessel	9270646
SHAMIM	ISLAMIC REPUBLIC OF IRAN SHIPPING LINES	Vessel	9270658
IRAN SHAHR-E-KORD	ISLAMIC REPUBLIC OF IRAN SHIPPING LINES	Vessel	9270684
IRAN KASHAN	ISLAMIC REPUBLIC OF IRAN SHIPPING LINES	Vessel	9270696
SININ	ISLAMIC REPUBLIC OF IRAN SHIPPING LINES	Vessel	9274941

(*continued*)

(continued)

BLOCKED PROPERTY	PROPERTY OF	TYPE	IMO NUMBER
PARMIS	ISLAMIC REPUBLIC OF IRAN SHIPPING LINES	Vessel	9283007
AZARGOUN	ISLAMIC REPUBLIC OF IRAN SHIPPING LINES	Vessel	9283019
SALIS	ISLAMIC REPUBLIC OF IRAN SHIPPING LINES	Vessel	9283021
GOLBON	ISLAMIC REPUBLIC OF IRAN SHIPPING LINES	Vessel	9283033
PARDIS	ISLAMIC REPUBLIC OF IRAN SHIPPING LINES	Vessel	9284142
TANDIS	ISLAMIC REPUBLIC OF IRAN SHIPPING LINES	Vessel	9284154
SHERE	ISLAMIC REPUBLIC OF IRAN SHIPPING LINES	Vessel	9305192
UPPERCOURT	ISLAMIC REPUBLIC OF IRAN SHIPPING LINES	Vessel	9305207
TONGHAM	ISLAMIC REPUBLIC OF IRAN SHIPPING LINES	Vessel	9305219
VOBSTER	ISLAMIC REPUBLIC OF IRAN SHIPPING LINES	Vessel	9305221
GOLAFRUZ	ISLAMIC REPUBLIC OF IRAN SHIPPING LINES	Vessel	9323833

(continued)

(continued)

BLOCKED PROPERTY	PROPERTY OF	TYPE	IMO NUMBER
ADALIA	ISLAMIC REPUBLIC OF IRAN SHIPPING LINES	Vessel	9328900
SHABGOUN	ISLAMIC REPUBLIC OF IRAN SHIPPING LINES	Vessel	9346524
AGATA	ISLAMIC REPUBLIC OF IRAN SHIPPING LINES	Vessel	9346536
BENITA	ISLAMIC REPUBLIC OF IRAN SHIPPING LINES	Vessel	9346548
MARISOL	ISLAMIC REPUBLIC OF IRAN SHIPPING LINES	Vessel	9349576
ORIANA	ISLAMIC REPUBLIC OF IRAN SHIPPING LINES	Vessel	9349590
MERCEDES	ISLAMIC REPUBLIC OF IRAN SHIPPING LINES	Vessel	9349667
RAMONA	ISLAMIC REPUBLIC OF IRAN SHIPPING LINES	Vessel	9349679
GILDA	ISLAMIC REPUBLIC OF IRAN SHIPPING LINES	Vessel	9367982
SANIA	ISLAMIC REPUBLIC OF IRAN SHIPPING LINES	Vessel	9367994
SARIR	ISLAMIC REPUBLIC OF IRAN SHIPPING LINES	Vessel	9368003

(*continued*)

(continued)

BLOCKED PROPERTY	PROPERTY OF	TYPE	IMO NUMBER
SOMIA	ISLAMIC REPUBLIC OF IRAN SHIPPING LINES	Vessel	9368015
GLORY	ISLAMIC REPUBLIC OF IRAN SHIPPING LINES	Vessel	9369710
ARIES	ISLAMIC REPUBLIC OF IRAN SHIPPING LINES	Vessel	9369722
ABTIN 1	ISLAMIC REPUBLIC OF IRAN SHIPPING LINES	Vessel	9379636
ARSHAM	ISLAMIC REPUBLIC OF IRAN SHIPPING LINES	Vessel	9386500
PARSHAD	ISLAMIC REPUBLIC OF IRAN SHIPPING LINES	Vessel	9387786
HAADI	ISLAMIC REPUBLIC OF IRAN SHIPPING LINES	Vessel	9387798
RAAZI	ISLAMIC REPUBLIC OF IRAN SHIPPING LINES	Vessel	9387803
SAEI	ISLAMIC REPUBLIC OF IRAN SHIPPING LINES	Vessel	9387815
ARTMAN	ISLAMIC REPUBLIC OF IRAN SHIPPING LINES	Vessel	9405930
BASKAR	ISLAMIC REPUBLIC OF IRAN SHIPPING LINES	Vessel	9405942

(continued)

(continued)

BLOCKED PROPERTY	PROPERTY OF	TYPE	IMO NUMBER
BAHJAT	ISLAMIC REPUBLIC OF IRAN SHIPPING LINES	Vessel	9405954
HAAMI	ISLAMIC REPUBLIC OF IRAN SHIPPING LINES	Vessel	9405966
SHAADI	ISLAMIC REPUBLIC OF IRAN SHIPPING LINES	Vessel	9405978
SHAYAN 1	ISLAMIC REPUBLIC OF IRAN SHIPPING LINES	Vessel	9420356
TABAN 1	ISLAMIC REPUBLIC OF IRAN SHIPPING LINES	Vessel	9420368
YARAN	ISLAMIC REPUBLIC OF IRAN SHIPPING LINES	Vessel	9420370
AMIN	ISLAMIC REPUBLIC OF IRAN SHIPPING LINES	Vessel	9422366
AVANG	ISLAMIC REPUBLIC OF IRAN SHIPPING LINES	Vessel	9465746
KIAZAND	ISLAMIC REPUBLIC OF IRAN SHIPPING LINES	Vessel	9465758
BATIS	ISLAMIC REPUBLIC OF IRAN SHIPPING LINES	Vessel	9465760
WARTA	ISLAMIC REPUBLIC OF IRAN SHIPPING LINES	Vessel	9465849

(*continued*)

(continued)

BLOCKED PROPERTY	PROPERTY OF	TYPE	IMO NUMBER
SALIM	ISLAMIC REPUBLIC OF IRAN SHIPPING LINES	Vessel	9465851
ARDAVAN	ISLAMIC REPUBLIC OF IRAN SHIPPING LINES	Vessel	9465863
NAMI	LISSOME MARINE SERVICES LLC	Vessel	8419178
GAS CAMELLIA	LISSOME MARINE SERVICES LLC	Vessel	8803381
TESS	LISSOME MARINE SERVICES LLC	Vessel	8913564
KATERINA 1	LISSOME MARINE SERVICES LLC	Vessel	9031959
MARIA	LISSOME MARINE SERVICES LLC	Vessel	9110626
SUN OCEAN	LISSOME MARINE SERVICES LLC	Vessel	9408358
YOUNES×	NATIONAL IRANIAN TANKER COMPANY	Vessel	8212465
YOUSEF×	NATIONAL IRANIAN TANKER COMPANY	Vessel	8316106
YAGHOUB×	NATIONAL IRANIAN TANKER COMPANY	Vessel	8316168
TOLOU×	NATIONAL IRANIAN TANKER COMPANY	Vessel	8318178
VALFAJR2×	NATIONAL IRANIAN TANKER COMPANY	Vessel	8400103
BADR×	NATIONAL IRANIAN TANKER COMPANY	Vessel	8407345
BANEH×	NATIONAL IRANIAN TANKER COMPANY	Vessel	8508462
SARDASHT×	NATIONAL IRANIAN TANKER COMPANY	Vessel	8517231

(*continued*)

(continued)

BLOCKED PROPERTY	PROPERTY OF	TYPE	IMO NUMBER
MARIVAN˟	NATIONAL IRANIAN TANKER COMPANY	Vessel	8517243
BRIGHT˟	NATIONAL IRANIAN TANKER COMPANY	Vessel	9005235
CARIBO˟	NATIONAL IRANIAN TANKER COMPANY	Vessel	9011246
AURA˟	NATIONAL IRANIAN TANKER COMPANY	Vessel	9013749
BICAS˟	NATIONAL IRANIAN TANKER COMPANY	Vessel	9077850
MAHARLIKA˟	NATIONAL IRANIAN TANKER COMPANY	Vessel	9079066
NAPOLI˟	NATIONAL IRANIAN TANKER COMPANY	Vessel	9079078
NYOS˟	NATIONAL IRANIAN TANKER COMPANY	Vessel	9079080
NAINITAL˟	NATIONAL IRANIAN TANKER COMPANY	Vessel	9079092
NATIVE LAND˟	NATIONAL IRANIAN TANKER COMPANY	Vessel	9079107
ATLANTIC˟	NATIONAL IRANIAN TANKER COMPANY	Vessel	9107655
SPARROW˟	NATIONAL IRANIAN TANKER COMPANY	Vessel	9171450
SWALLOW˟	NATIONAL IRANIAN TANKER COMPANY	Vessel	9171462
SUPERIOR˟	NATIONAL IRANIAN TANKER COMPANY	Vessel	9172038
SPOTLESS˟	NATIONAL IRANIAN TANKER COMPANY	Vessel	9172040
SABRINA˟	NATIONAL IRANIAN TANKER COMPANY	Vessel	9172052
DESTINY˟	NATIONAL IRANIAN TANKER COMPANY	Vessel	9177155

(*continued*)

(continued)

BLOCKED PROPERTY	PROPERTY OF	TYPE	IMO NUMBER
HUMANITY×	NATIONAL IRANIAN TANKER COMPANY	Vessel	9180281
ORIENTAL×	NATIONAL IRANIAN TANKER COMPANY	Vessel	9183934
SHONA×	NATIONAL IRANIAN TANKER COMPANY	Vessel	9187629
ABELIA×	NATIONAL IRANIAN TANKER COMPANY	Vessel	9187631
ALERT×	NATIONAL IRANIAN TANKER COMPANY	Vessel	9187643
SUNDIAL×	NATIONAL IRANIAN TANKER COMPANY	Vessel	9187655
SILVER CLOUD×	NATIONAL IRANIAN TANKER COMPANY	Vessel	9187667
HUWAYZEH×	NATIONAL IRANIAN TANKER COMPANY	Vessel	9212888
HORIZON×	NATIONAL IRANIAN TANKER COMPANY	Vessel	9212890
HAPPINESS×	NATIONAL IRANIAN TANKER COMPANY	Vessel	9212905
MARINA×	NATIONAL IRANIAN TANKER COMPANY	Vessel	9212917
HALISTIC×	NATIONAL IRANIAN TANKER COMPANY	Vessel	9212929
DELVAR×	NATIONAL IRANIAN TANKER COMPANY	Vessel	9218454
DAYLAM×	NATIONAL IRANIAN TANKER COMPANY	Vessel	9218466
DAMAVAND×	NATIONAL IRANIAN TANKER COMPANY	Vessel	9218478
DENA×	NATIONAL IRANIAN TANKER COMPANY	Vessel	9218480
DARAB×	NATIONAL IRANIAN TANKER COMPANY	Vessel	9218492

(continued)

(continued)

BLOCKED PROPERTY	PROPERTY OF	TYPE	IMO NUMBER
IRAN FAZEL[x]	NATIONAL IRANIAN TANKER COMPANY	Vessel	9283746
FIANGA[x]	NATIONAL IRANIAN TANKER COMPANY	Vessel	9283760
IRAN FAHIM[x]	NATIONAL IRANIAN TANKER COMPANY	Vessel	9286140
IRAN FALAGH[x]	NATIONAL IRANIAN TANKER COMPANY	Vessel	9286152
DECESIVE[x]	NATIONAL IRANIAN TANKER COMPANY	Vessel	9356593
SANCHI[x]	NATIONAL IRANIAN TANKER COMPANY	Vessel	9356608
MAJESTIC[x]	NATIONAL IRANIAN TANKER COMPANY	Vessel	9357183
SUCCESS[x]	NATIONAL IRANIAN TANKER COMPANY	Vessel	9357353
SUNEAST[x]	NATIONAL IRANIAN TANKER COMPANY	Vessel	9357365
SPLENDOUR[x]	NATIONAL IRANIAN TANKER COMPANY	Vessel	9357377
COURAGE[x]	NATIONAL IRANIAN TANKER COMPANY	Vessel	9357389
HONESTY[x]	NATIONAL IRANIAN TANKER COMPANY	Vessel	9357391
AMBER[x]	NATIONAL IRANIAN TANKER COMPANY	Vessel	9357406
DAL LAKE[x]	NATIONAL IRANIAN TANKER COMPANY	Vessel	9357717
JUSTICE[x]	NATIONAL IRANIAN TANKER COMPANY	Vessel	9357729
HYDRA[x]	NATIONAL IRANIAN TANKER COMPANY	Vessel	9362059
DOVE[x]	NATIONAL IRANIAN TANKER COMPANY	Vessel	9362061

(*continued*)

(continued)

BLOCKED PROPERTY	PROPERTY OF	TYPE	IMO NUMBER
ZEUS˟	NATIONAL IRANIAN TANKER COMPANY	Vessel	9362073
IMICO NEKA 455˟	NATIONAL IRANIAN TANKER COMPANY	Vessel	9404546
IMICO NEKA 456˟	NATIONAL IRANIAN TANKER COMPANY	Vessel	9404558
IMICO NEKA 457˟	NATIONAL IRANIAN TANKER COMPANY	Vessel	9404560
SUNSHINE˟	NATIONAL IRANIAN TANKER COMPANY	Vessel	9569205
DOJRAN˟	NATIONAL IRANIAN TANKER COMPANY	Vessel	9569619
ATLANTIS˟	NATIONAL IRANIAN TANKER COMPANY	Vessel	9569621
FORTUN˟	NATIONAL IRANIAN TANKER COMPANY	Vessel	9569633
SALALEH˟	NATIONAL IRANIAN TANKER COMPANY	Vessel	9569645
SMOOTH˟	NATIONAL IRANIAN TANKER COMPANY	Vessel	9569657
SKYLINE˟	NATIONAL IRANIAN TANKER COMPANY	Vessel	9569669
INFINITY˟	NATIONAL IRANIAN TANKER COMPANY	Vessel	9569671
DEMOS˟	NATIONAL IRANIAN TANKER COMPANY	Vessel	9569683
YANGZHOU DAYANG DY905˟	NATIONAL IRANIAN TANKER COMPANY	Vessel	9575424
SUNRISE˟	NATIONAL IRANIAN TANKER COMPANY	Vessel	9615092
ANTHEM	SIQIRIYA MARITIME CORP	Vessel	8310669

(*continued*)

(continued)

BLOCKED PROPERTY	PROPERTY OF	TYPE	IMO NUMBER
JAFFNA	SIQIRIYA MARITIME CORP	Vessel	8609515
OLYSA	SIQIRIYA MARITIME CORP	Vessel	9001605

ˣDenotes blocked property of individual and entities identified as GOI by the Office of Foreign Assets Control. U.S. persons and foreign entities owned or controlled by a U.S. person will continue to be prohibited from transactions with these individuals and entities, pursuant to the Iranian Transactions and Sanctions Regulations

Attachment 4

ABBASI-DAVANI, Fereidoun
ADVANCE ELECTRICAL AND INDUSTRIAL TECHNOLOGIES SL
ALUMINAT
ANDISHEH ZOLAL
ARIA NIKAN MARINE INDUSTRY
BUJAR, Farhad
DAYENI, Mahmoud Mohammadi
EYVAZ TECHNIC MANUFACTURING COMPANY
FAKHRIZADEH-MAHABADI, Mohsen
FARATECH
FARAYAND TECHNIQUE
FULMEN GROUP
IMANIRAD, Arman
IMANIRAD, Mohammad Javad
IRAN CENTRIFUGE TECHNOLOGY COMPANY
IRAN POOYA
JAHAN TECH ROOYAN PARS
JAVEDAN MEHR TOOS
KAHVARIN, Iradj Mohammadi

KALAYE ELECTRIC COMPANY
KHAKI, Parviz
MANDEGAR BASPAR KIMIYA COMPANY
MARO SANAT COMPANY
MODERN INDUSTRIES TECHNIQUE COMPANY
NEDA INDUSTRIAL GROUP
NEKA NOVIN
PARTO SANAT CO.
PAYA PARTOV CO.
PENTANE CHEMISTRY INDUSTRIES
PETRO GREEN
PISHRO SYSTEMS RESEARCH COMPANY
POUYA CONTROL
PUNTI, Pere
RAHIMYAR, Amir Hossein
SIMATIC DEVELOPMENT CO.
TAGHTIRAN KASHAN COMPANY
TANIDEH, Hossein
TARH O PALAYESH
THE ORGANIZATION OF DEFENSIVE INNOVATION AND RESEARCH
TOWLID ABZAR BORESHI IRAN
WISSER, Gerhard
YASA PART
ZOLAL IRAN COMPANY

Annex III: Civil Nuclear Cooperation

A. General

1. Iran and E3/EU+3 decided to co-operate, among others, including through IAEA technical cooperation, where appropriate, and without prejudice to the existing bilateral agreements, in different areas of civil nuclear co-operation to be developed within the framework of

this JCPOA, as detailed in this Annex. In this context, the Joint Commission will also support assistance to Iran, including through IAEA technical cooperation projects, as appropriate.
2. All civil nuclear cooperation projects under this JCPOA will be mutually determined by the participating states and will be consistent with the JCPOA and the national laws and regulations of the participating parties.
3. The civil nuclear and scientific cooperation projects envisioned between Iran and the E3/EU+3 as part of this JCPOA may be undertaken in a variety of formats, with a variety of potential participants. A given project undertaken by the E3/EU+3 will not necessarily include participation by all E3/EU+3 parties:
3.1. bilateral or multilateral cooperation arrangements with Iran. Such arrangements would be mutually determined by the participating states.
3.2. projects under the auspices of the IAEA, either through IAEA technical co-operation projects including through Project and Supply Agreements.
3.3. through International Science and Technology Centres. Specifically, E3/EU+3 parties will undertake, to develop nuclear co-operation with Iran, in particular within the following areas:

B. **Reactors, Fuels and Associated Technologies, Facilities and Processes**

4. **Modern light water power and research reactors and associated equipment, technologies and facilities**

E3/EU+3 parties, as appropriate, will facilitate Iran's acquisition of light-water research and power reactors, for research, development and testing, and for the supply of electricity and desalination, with arrangements for the assured supply of nuclear fuel and the removal of spent fuel as provided for in relevant contracts, for each reactor provided. This may include the following areas for co-operation:

4.1. Construction as well as effective and safe operation of new light water power reactors and associated equipment, according to Generation III+ requirements, including small and medium sized nuclear reactors, including joint design and manufacturing, as appropriate.

4.2. Construction of state of the art light water moderated multipurpose research reactors capable of testing fuel pins, assembly prototypes and structural materials with associated related facilities, including joint design and manufacturing, as appropriate.

4.3. Supply of state-of-the-art instrumentation and control systems for the above research and power reactors, including joint design and manufacturing, as appropriate;

4.4. Supply of nuclear simulation and calculation codes and software solutions with regard to the above areas, including joint development, as appropriate;

4.5. Supply of first and second loop main equipment as well as core of the above research and power reactors, including joint design and manufacturing, as appropriate;

4.6. On-the-job training on fuel management scenarios and reshuffling for the above research and power nuclear reactors;

4.7. Joint technical review of Iran's current nuclear reactors, upon the request by Iran, in order to upgrade current equipment and systems, including concerning nuclear safety;

5. **Arak Modernization Project**

5.1. As described in Section B of Annex I, an international partnership composed of E3/EU+3 parties and Iran, which may subsequently be enlarged to include mutually determined third countries will be established, to support and facilitate the redesign and rebuilding of the IR-40 reactor at Arak into a modernized, not exceeding 20MWth, heavy-water moderated and cooled research reactor, based on the agreed conceptual design (as attached to Annex I).

5.2. Iran will take the leadership role as the owner and as the project manager, and have responsibility for overall implementation of the Arak modernization project. A Working Group composed of E3/EU+3 participants will be established to support and facilitate the redesigning and rebuilding of the reactor. An international partnership composed of Iran and the Working Group would implement the Arak modernization project, with E3/EU+3 participants assuming responsibilities as described in Annex I. The Working Group could be enlarged to include other countries by consensus of the participants of the Working Group and Iran.

E3/EU+3 participants and Iran will conclude an official document expressing their strong commitments to the Arak modernization project in advance of Implementation Day which would provide an assured path forward to modernize the reactor and would define the responsibilities assumed by the E3/EU+3 participants, especially in the key areas such as redesign, design review and certification, reactor core manufacturing, fuel design, fabrication and supply, safety and security, spent fuel treatment or disposition, as well as concerning the supply of materials, equipment, instrumentation and control systems, and subsequently contracts would be concluded. The participants of the Working Group will provide assistance needed by Iran for redesigning and rebuilding the reactor, consistent with their respective national laws, in such a manner as to enable the safe and timely construction and commissioning of the modernized reactor.

5.3. Iran and the Working Group will cooperate to develop the final design of the modernized reactor and the design of the subsidiary laboratories to be carried out by Iran, and review conformity with international safety standards, such that the reactor can be licensed by the relevant Iranian regulatory authority for commissioning and operation.

5.4. Iran will continue to assume the primary responsibility for financing the modernization project. Additional funding arrangements for the project, including for IAEA projects supporting the Arak modernization project, will be determined based on the official document and contracts to be subsequently concluded.

6. **Nuclear Fuel**

6.1. E3/EU+3 parties, as appropriate, will support assistance to Iran, including through the IAEA, as appropriate, in meeting international qualification standards for nuclear fuel fabricated by Iran.

6.2. E3/EU+3 parties will seek to cooperate regarding the supply of modern fuels, including, as appropriate, joint design and fabrication, the relevant licenses and fabrication technologies and equipment and related infrastructure, for current and future nuclear research and power reactors, including technical assistance on purification processes, forming and metallurgical activities for different types of nuclear fuel clads and cladding for the modernized Arak heavy water research reactor.

C. Research and Development (R&D) Practices

7. To implement other aspects of this JCPOA and in support of a broader opening of scientific engagements between the E3/EU+3 and Iran, the E3/EU+3 and Iran will seek cooperation and scientific exchange in the field of nuclear science and technology:

7.1. Accelerator-based nuclear physics and nuclear astrophysics research, and stable isotope production in international collaboration at the nuclear, physics, and technology center at the Fordow facility. Iran will request from the E3/EU+3 and other interested parties' specific proposals for cooperative international nuclear, physics, and technology projects and will host an international workshop to review these proposals. The goal is to realize international collaborative projects within a few years. The transitioning to stable isotope production of two cascades will be conducted in a joint partnership between the Russian Federation and Iran on the basis of arrangements to be mutually agreed upon.

7.2. Plasma physics and nuclear fusion;
7.3. Research reactor applications at the TRR, modernized Arak reactor, or at other future research reactors in Iran, such as:
7.3.1. Training
7.3.2. Radio-isotope production and utilization
7.3.3. Nuclear desalination
7.3.4. Neutron transmutation doping
7.3.5. Neutron activation analysis
7.3.6. Neutron capture therapy
7.3.7. Neutron imaging and materials characterization studies using neutron beams
7.3.8. E3/EU+3 parties and Iran could also explore co-operation in the following additional areas:
7.3.9. Design, manufacture and/or assembly of in-core measuring instrumentation and technologies;
7.3.10. Nuclear instrumentation and control, systems and electronics design, manufacture and/or assembly;
7.3.11. Fusion technology and plasma physics and related infrastructure and facilitating contribution of Iran to the International Thermonuclear Experimental Reactor (ITER) Project and/or similar projects, including relevant IAEA technical cooperation projects;
7.3.12. Neutrino astronomy;
7.3.13. Design and manufacturing, and supply, of different types of accelerators and supply of related equipment including through relevant IAEA technical cooperation projects;
7.3.14. Data acquisition and processing software and interface equipment;

D. **Nuclear Safety, Safeguards and Security**

8. **Nuclear safety**

E3/EU+3 parties, and possibly other states, as appropriate, are prepared to cooperate with Iran to establish a Nuclear Safety Centre in Iran, engage in workshops and training events in Iran to support interactions between Iranian nuclear regulatory authorities and those from the E3/EU+3 and elsewhere to, among other things, share lessons learned on establishing and maintaining regulatory independence and effectiveness, and training on implementing nuclear safety culture and best practices; facilitate exchanges and visits to nuclear regulatory authorities and nuclear power plants outside of Iran focusing on best practices for safe operation; and enhance and strengthen domestic emergency preparedness and severe accident management capability.

Provide support and assistance to enable Iran to join relevant conventions on nuclear safety and security, e.g. through workshops or seminars furthering accession to such commitments. Such workshops or seminars could also take place under the auspices of the IAEA.

E3/EU+3 parties, and possibly other states, as appropriate, will co-operate with Iran in the following areas of nuclear safety, as well as in other areas to be mutually agreed:

8.1. Conclusion of bilateral/multilateral agreements with related organizations and research centers;

8.2. Supply of valid codes, instruments and equipment related to nuclear safety;

8.3. Facilitate exchange of knowledge and experience in the area of nuclear safety;
8.4. Enhance and strengthen domestic emergency preparedness and severe accident management capability;
8.5. Arrange on-the-job training and apprenticeship courses for reactor and facility operators, regulatory authority personnel and related supportive organizations in the area of nuclear safety inside and outside of Iran;
8.6. Establish a Nuclear Safety Centre in Iran, which shall be equipped with necessary tools, techniques and equipment, in order to support and facilitate technical and professional training and exchange of lessons-learned for reactor and facility operators, regulatory authority personnel and related supportive organizations;
9. **Nuclear Safeguards**
 E3/EU+3 parties, and possibly other states, as appropriate, are prepared to cooperate with Iran on the effective and efficient implementation of IAEA safeguards and transparency measures in Iran. Co-operation in the following areas can be envisaged:
9.1. Cooperation in the form of on-the-job trainings and workshops to strengthen nuclear material accounting and control process, human resource development, and quality assurance/quality control processes;
9.2. E3/EU+3 parties, and other states, as appropriate, are prepared to cooperate with Iran for the effective and efficient implementation of IAEA safeguards and transparency measures in Iran.

9.3. This cooperation could take the form of training and workshops to strengthen Iran's safeguards regulatory authority, nuclear material accounting and control processes, human resource development, and quality assurance/quality control processes.

10. **Nuclear Security**

    E3/EU+3 parties, and possibly other states, as appropriate, are prepared to cooperate with Iran on the implementation of nuclear security guidelines and best practices. Co-operation in the following areas can be envisaged:

10.1. Co-operation in the form of training courses and workshops to strengthen Iran's ability to prevent, protect and respond to nuclear security threats to nuclear facilities and systems as well as to enable effective and sustainable nuclear security and physical protection systems;

10.2. Co-operation through training and workshops to strengthen Iran's ability to protect against, and respond to nuclear security threats, including sabotage, as well as to enable effective and sustainable nuclear security and physical protection systems.

E. **Nuclear Medicine and Radioisotopes, Associated Technologies, Facilities and Processes**

11. E3/EU+3 parties, as appropriate, are prepared to cooperate with Iran to improve the utilization of nuclear medicine in Iran in order to enhance Iran's expertise in diagnostic imaging and radiotherapy, increase the availability of medical radioisotopes for diagnosis and treatment of Iranian citizens, and facilitate Iran's participation in the broader international

scientific and nuclear medicine community. Such cooperation may include:

11.1. Upgrades to the infrastructure associated with existing cyclotron facilities, including for medical radioisotopes production.

11.2. Facilitating Iranian acquisition of a new cyclotron, and associated radio-pharmacy equipment, for medical radioisotopes production.

11.3. Acquisition of state-of-the-art diagnostic imaging and radiotherapy equipment for existing or new nuclear medicine centers, including co-operation between hospitals for the treatment of individual patients.

11.4. Cooperation on occupational and patient dosimetry procedures.

11.5. Improved target utilization to increase radioisotope production.

11.6. Acquisition of radioisotope sources for brachytherapy, and radiotherapy instrument calibration, and other medical and industrial applications.

11.7. Supply of state-of-the art radio-medicine center and necessary laboratories.

F. Waste Management and Facility Decommissioning

12. E3/EU+3 parties, as appropriate, are prepared to cooperate with Iran in the safe, effective, and efficient management and disposition of nuclear and radiological wastes derived from Iran's nuclear fuel cycle activities and nuclear medicine, radioisotope production and/or consumption activities.

13. E3/EU+3 parties, as appropriate, are prepared to cooperate with Iran in areas of safe, effective, and environmentally friendly best practices for facility

decontamination and decommissioning, including co-operation on long term storage facilities for the repository of low and medium level waste.
14. E3/EU+3 parties, as appropriate, are prepared to facilitate exchanges and visits to relevant sites and locations outside of Iran related to effective waste management and best practices.
15. E3/EU+3 parties, as appropriate, will facilitate the supply of appropriate equipment and systems for waste management and depository facilities in Iran.

G. Other projects

16. Other projects may be implemented between the relevant E3/EU+3 parties and Iran, as mutually determined by the participants in the JCPOA, including in the following areas:
16.1. Construction of nuclear desalination and associated infrastructure in Iran;
16.2. Development of laser technology for medical applications (e.g. for eye surgery);

Annex IV: Joint Commission

1. **Establishment, Composition, and Coordinator**
1.1. The Joint Commission is established to carry out the functions assigned to it in the JCPOA, including its Annexes.
1.2. The Joint Commission is comprised of representatives of Iran and the E3/EU+3 (China, France, Germany, the Russian Federation, the United Kingdom, and the United States, with the High

Representative of the Union for Foreign Affairs and Security Policy), together, the JCPOA participants.

1.3. The Joint Commission may establish Working Groups in particular areas, as appropriate.

1.4. The High Representative of the Union for Foreign Affairs and Security Policy ('High Representative'), or his/her designated representative will serve as the Coordinator of the Joint Commission.

2. **Functions**

2.1. The Joint Commission will perform the following functions:

2.1.1. Review and approve the final design for the modernized heavy water research reactor and the design of the subsidiary laboratories prior to the commencement of construction, and review and approve the fuel design for the modernized heavy water research reactor as provided for in Section B of Annex I;

2.1.2. Review and approve, upon request by Iran, development, acquisition, construction or operation of hot cells (containing a cell or interconnected cells), shielded cells or shielded glove boxes with dimensions beyond 6 cubic meters in volume and specifications set out in Annex I of the Additional Protocol, as provided for in paragraph 21 of Annex I;

2.1.3. Review and approve plans submitted by Iran to initiate R&D on uranium metal based TRR fuel, as provided for in paragraph 26 of Annex I;

2.1.4. Review and approve, upon request by Iran, projects on new types of centrifuges to proceed to a prototype stage for mechanical testing, as provided for in paragraph 43 of Annex I;

2.1.5. Receive information in advance about the specific projects that will be undertaken at Fordow, as provided for in paragraph 44 of Annex I;

2.1.6. Receive information about the conceptual framework of stable isotope production at Fordow, as provided for in paragraph 46.1 of Annex I;

2.1.7. Assess and then approve, upon request by Iran, that fuel assemblies manufactured in Iran and their intermediate products cannot be readily reconverted into UF6, based on the objective technical criteria, with the goal of enabling fuel to be fabricated in Iran, as provided in paragraph 59 of Annex I;

2.1.8. Support assistance to Iran, including through IAEA technical cooperation as appropriate, in meeting international qualification standards for nuclear fuel produced by Iran, as provided for in paragraph 59 of Annex I;

2.1.9. Review and approve in advance, upon request by Iran, engagement by Iran, including through export of any enrichment or enrichment related equipment and technology, with any other country, or with any foreign entity in enrichment and enrichment related activities, including related research and development, as provided for in paragraph 73 in Annex I;

2.1.10. Provide consultation, and advise on the necessary means in the context of access as specified in paragraph 78 of Annex I;

2.1.11. Review and approve in advance, upon request by Iran, the design, development, fabrication, acquisition, or use for non-nuclear purposes of multi-point explosive detonation systems suitable for a nuclear explosive device and explosive diagnostic systems (streak cameras, framing cameras and flash x-ray cameras) suitable for the development of a nuclear explosive device, as provided for in paragraphs 82.2 and 82.3 of Annex I;

2.1.12. Review and consult to address issues arising from the implementation of sanctions lifting as specified in this JCPOA and its Annex II;

2.1.13. Review and decide on proposals for nuclear-related transfers to or activities with, Iran, in accordance with Sect. 6 of this Annex and the United Nations Security Council resolution endorsing this JCPOA;

2.1.14. Review, with a view to resolving, any issue that a JCPOA participant believes constitutes nonperformance by another JCPOA participant of its commitments under the JCPOA, according to the process outlined in the JCPOA;

2.1.15. Adopt or modify, as necessary, procedures to govern its activities;

2.1.16. Consult and provide guidance on other implementation matters that may arise under the JCPOA.

3. **Procedures**

3.1. The Joint Commission will meet on a quarterly basis and at any time upon request of a JCPOA participant to the Coordinator. The Coordinator will convene a meeting of the Joint Commission to be held no later than one week following receipt of such a request, except for consultations in accordance with Section Q of Annex I and any other matter that the Coordinator and/or a JCPOA participant deem urgent, in which case the meeting will be convened as soon as possible and not later than three calendar days from receipt of the request.

3.2. Meetings of the Joint Commission will be held in New York, Vienna, or Geneva as appropriate. The host country should facilitate entry formalities for those attending such meetings.

3.3. The Joint Commission may decide by consensus to invite observers to attend its meetings.

3.4. Except as provided in Sect. 6 of this Annex which will be subject to the confidentiality procedure of the UN, the work of the Joint Commission is confidential and may be shared only among JCPOA participants and observers as appropriate, unless the Joint Commission decides otherwise.

4. **Decisions**

4.1. Except as stated otherwise in this Annex, decisions by the Joint Commission are to be made by consensus.

4.2. Each JCPOA participant will have one vote. Decisions of the Joint Commission are to be taken by the Representative or the Deputy Representative or other such alternate as the JCPOA participant may designate.

4.3. The vote of each JCPOA participant will be made known to all other JCPOA participants if any JCPOA participant requests a recorded vote.

4.4. Matters before the Joint Commission pursuant to Section Q of Annex I are to be decided by consensus or by affirmative vote of five JCPOA participants. There is no quorum requirement.

4.5. The Coordinator will not take part in decision-making on nuclear-related transfers and activities as set out in Sect. 6 of this Annex.

5. **Other**
5.1. Each JCPOA participant will be responsible for its own costs of participating in the Joint Commission, unless the Joint Commission decides otherwise.
5.2. JCPOA participants may request that the Coordinator circulates a notification to the other JCPOA participants at any time. Upon such a request, the Coordinator will circulate such notification without delay to all JCPOA participants.
6. **Procurement Working Group**
6.1. With the purpose of establishing a procurement channel, the Joint Commission will, except as otherwise provided by the United Nations Security Council resolution endorsing this JCPOA, review and decide on proposals by states seeking to engage in:
6.1.1. the supply, sale or transfer directly or indirectly from their territories, or by their nationals or using their flag vessels or aircraft to, or for the use in or benefit of, Iran, and whether or not originating in their territories, of all items, materials, equipment, goods and technology set out in INFCIRC/254/Rev.12/Part 1, and, if the end-use will be for Iran's nuclear program set out in this JCPOA or other non-nuclear civilian end-use, all items, materials, equipment, goods and technology set out in INFCIRC/254/Rev.9/Part 2 (or the most recent version of these documents as updated by the Security Council), as well as any further items if the relevant State determines that they could contribute to activities inconsistent with the JCPOA; and,

6.1.2. the provision to Iran of any technical assistance or training, financial assistance, investment, brokering or other services related to the supply, sale, transfer, manufacture, or use of the items, materials, equipment, goods and technology described in subparagraph (a) above;

6.1.3. acquisition by Iran of an interest in a commercial activity in another State involving uranium mining, production or use of nuclear materials and technologies as listed in INFCIRC/254/Rev.12/Part 1, and such investments in territories under their jurisdiction by Iran, its nationals, and entities incorporated in Iran or subject to its jurisdiction, or by individuals or entities acting on their behalf or direction, or by entities owned or controlled by them.

6.2. The Joint Commission will discharge its responsibility for reviewing and making recommendations on proposals for nuclear-related transfers to or activities with Iran through a Procurement Working Group.

6.3. Each E3+3 State and Iran will participate in the Procurement Working Group. The High Representative will serve as the Coordinator of the Procurement Working Group.

6.4. Except as otherwise provided by the Joint Commission or the United Nations Security Council resolution endorsing this JCPOA, the Procurement Working Group will consider proposals according to the following process:

6.4.1. Upon receipt of a proposal, including all necessary supporting information, by a State seeking to engage in transfers and activities referenced in Sect. 6.1, the Coordinator will forward the proposal, through appropriate means, without delay to the Procurement

Working Group and, when the proposal relates to items, material, equipment, goods and technology intended to be used in nuclear activities authorized by the JCPOA, to the IAEA. The Procurement Working Group will have up to 30 working days to consider and decide on the proposal.

6.4.2. "Necessary supporting information" for purposes of Sect. 6.4.1 means: (a) a description of the item; (b) the name, address, telephone number, and email address of the exporting entity; (c) the name, address, telephone number, and email address of the importing entity; (d) a statement of the proposed end-use and end use location, along with an end-use certification signed by the AEOI or the appropriate authority of Iran attesting the stated end-use; (e) export license number if available; contract date, if available; and (g) details on transportation, if available; provided that if any of the export license number, contract date, or details on transportation are not available as of the time of submittal of the proposal, such information will be provided as soon as possible and in any event as condition of approval prior to shipment of the item.

6.4.3. Each participant in the Procurement Working Group will have to communicate to the Coordinator, within 20 working days, whether it approves or rejects the proposal. The timeline for consideration may be extended for an additional period of 10 working days at the request of a participant of the Procurement Working Group.

6.4.4. The proposal will be recommended for approval as soon as the Coordinator receives formal approvals from all the Procurement Working Group Participants or if, at the end of the 30 working day period, the Coordinator has received no disapprovals from any of the Procurement Working Group Participants. If at the end of the 30 working day period, the proposal has not been recommended for approval, the proposal may, at the request of at least two Working Group Participants within 5 working days, be referred to the Joint Commission, which would decide on approval of the proposal by consensus within 10 working days. Otherwise the proposal will be recommended for disapproval. The disapproving JCPOA participant(s) should provide relevant information regarding the disapproval to the Joint Commission as appropriate, taking into account the need to protect confidential information.

6.4.5. The Coordinator will communicate the recommendation of the Joint Commission to the United Nations Security Council no later than 35 working days, or in case of referral to the Joint Commission no later than 45 working days from the date the Coordinator transmitted the proposal and all necessary supporting information to the Procurement Working Group.

6.4.6. Except as decided otherwise by consensus, the Procurement Working Group will meet every three weeks for reviewing the proposals. When some of the proposals to be reviewed relate to items, material, equipment, goods and technology intended to be used in nuclear activities authorized by the JCPOA, the IAEA may be invited to attend the meeting as an observer.

6.5. All JCPOA participants will act in accordance with the procurement channel and will only engage in transfers and activities referenced in Sect. 6.1 following approval by the Joint Commission and the United Nations Security Council. Iran will not use, acquire, or seek to procure the items, materials, equipment, goods, and technology referred to in Sect. 6.1 of this Annex for nuclear activities which are inconsistent with this JCPOA.

6.6. Any JCPOA participant may refer a procurement-related activity to the Joint Commission under the dispute settlement mechanism if it is concerned that such activity is inconsistent with this JCPOA.

6.7. Iran will provide to the IAEA access to the locations of intended use of all items, materials, equipment, goods and technology set out in INFCIRC/254/Rev.12/Part 1 (or the most recent version of these documents as updated by the Security Council) imported following the procedure under Sect. 6 of this Annex.

6.8. Iran will permit the exporting state to verify the end-use of all items, materials, equipment, goods and technology set out in INFCIRC/254/Rev.9/Part 2 (or the most recent version of these documents as updated by the Security Council) imported following the procedure under Sect. 6 of this Annex. Upon request of the exporting state, or if the Joint Commission deems necessary when approving a proposal for transfer, the Joint Commission will provide expertise to the exporting state, including experts, as needed, to participate in the end-use verification.

6.9. The Procurement Working Group will respond to requests for guidance on procurement activities from third parties, as communicated by the Coordinator. The Procurement Working Group will endeavor to respond to such requests for guidance within 9 working days from the date the Coordinator submits it to the Procurement Working Group.

6.10. The Joint Commission will report to the United Nations Security Council at least every 6 months on the status of the Procurement Working Group's decisions and on any implementation issues.

7. **Working Group on Implementation of Sanctions Lifting**

7.1. The Joint Commission will discharge its responsibilities for reviewing and consulting on issues related to the implementation of sanctions lifting as specified in this JCPOA assisted by a working group on the implementation of sanctions lifting.

7.2. The Joint Commission participants will participate in this working group. The High Representative will serve as coordinator of this working group.

7.3. If at any time following the implementation day Iran believes that any other nuclear-related sanction or restrictive measure including related designations of the E3/EU+3 is preventing the full implementation of the sanctions lifting as specified in this JCPOA, the JCPOA participant in question will consult with Iran with a view to resolving the issue. If they are not able to resolve the issue, Iran or any member of the E3/EU+3 may refer the issue to the working group.

7.4. The participants of the working group will review and consult, with a view to resolving the issue within 30 working days.

7.5. If after involvement of the working group, the issue remains unresolved, any participant of the JCPOA may refer it to the Joint Commission.

ANNEX V: IMPLEMENTATION PLAN[23]

1. This Annex describes the sequence of the actions specified in Annexes I and II to this JCPOA.

A. Finalization Day

2. Upon conclusion of the negotiations of this JCPOA, the E3/EU+3 (China, France, Germany, the Russian Federation, the United Kingdom and the United States, with the High Representative of the European Union for Foreign Affairs and Security Policy) and Iran will endorse this JCPOA.
3. Promptly after the conclusion of the negotiations of this JCPOA, the proposed UN Security Council resolution referred to in Sect. 18 of this Annex will be submitted to the UN Security Council for adoption without delay.
4. The EU will promptly endorse the UN Security Council resolution referred to above through Council Conclusions.
5. Iran and the IAEA will start developing necessary arrangements to implement all transparency measures provided for in this JCPOA so that such arrangements are completed, in place, and ready for implementation on Implementation Day.

B. Adoption Day

6. Adoption Day will occur 90 days after the endorsement of this JCPOA by the UN Security Council through the resolution referred to above, or at an earlier date by mutual consent of all JCPOA participants, at which point this JCPOA comes into effect.

7. Beginning on Adoption Day, JCPOA participants will make necessary arrangements and preparations, including legal and administrative preparations, for the implementation of their JCPOA commitments.
8. Iran will officially inform the IAEA that, effective on Implementation Day, Iran will provisionally apply the Additional Protocol, pending its ratification by the Majlis (Parliament), and will fully implement the modified code 3.1.
9. Iran will implement paragraph 66 from Section M on "Past and Present Issues of Concern" of Annex I.
10. The EU and its Member States will adopt an EU Regulation, taking effect as of Implementation Day, terminating all provisions of the EU Regulation implementing all nuclear-related economic and financial EU sanctions as specified in Sect. 16.1 of this Annex, simultaneously with the IAEA-verified implementation by Iran of agreed nuclear-related measures.
11. The United States, acting pursuant to Presidential authorities, will issue waivers, to take effect upon Implementation Day, ceasing the application of the statutory nuclear-related sanctions as specified in Sects. 17.1–17.2 of this Annex. The President will also take action to direct that all appropriate additional measures be taken to implement the cessation of application of sanctions as specified in Sects. 17.1–17.4 of this Annex, including the termination of Executive orders as specified in Sect. 17.4, and the licensing of activities as specified in Sect. 17.5.
12. E3/EU+3 participants and Iran will begin discussions on an official document to be concluded in advance of Implementation Day which will express strong commitments of the E3/EU+3 participants to the Arak Heavy

Water Reactor modernization project and define the responsibilities assumed by the E3/EU+3 participants.

13. The EU, its Member States and the United States will begin consultation as appropriate with Iran regarding relevant guidelines and publicly accessible statements on the details of sanctions or restrictive measures to be lifted under this JCPOA.

C. Implementation Day

14. Implementation Day will occur upon the IAEA-verified implementation by Iran of the nuclear-related measures described in paragraph 15 below, and, simultaneously, the E3/EU+3 taking the actions described in paragraphs 16 and 17 below, and with the actions described in paragraph 18 below taking place at the UN level in accordance with the UN Security Council resolution.
15. **Iran will implement the nuclear-related measures as specified in Annex I**:
15.1. Paragraphs 3 and 10 from Section B on "Arak Heavy Water Research Reactor";
15.2. Paragraphs 14 and 15 from Section C on "Heavy Water Production Plant";
15.3. Paragraphs 27, 28, 29, 29.1 and 29.2 from Section F on "Enrichment Capacity";
15.4. Paragraphs 32, 33, 34, 35, 36, 37, 38, 39, 40, 41 and 42 from Section G on "Centrifuges Research and Development";
15.5. Paragraphs 45, 46, 46.1, 46.2, 47.1, 48.1 from Section H on "Fordow Fuel Enrichment Plant";
15.6. Paragraphs 52, 54 and 55 from Section I on "Other Aspects of Enrichment";

15.7. Paragraphs 57 and 58 from Section J on "Uranium Stocks and Fuels";

15.8. Paragraph 62 from Section K on "Centrifuge Manufacturing";

15.9. Complete the modalities and facilities-specific arrangements to allow the IAEA to implement all transparency measures provided for in Annex I;

15.10. Paragraphs 64 and 65 from Section L on "Additional Protocol and Modified Code 3.1";

15.11. Paragraphs 80.1 and 80.2 from Section R on "Centrifuge Component Manufacturing Transparency"; and

15.12. Within one year from Implementation Day, Iran will have completed the measures specified in paragraphs 47.2 and 48.2 of Section H on "Fordow Fuel Enrichment Plant".

16. **The European Union will:**

16.1. Terminate the provisions of Council Regulation (EU) No 267/2012 and suspend the corresponding provisions of Council Decision 2010/413/CFSP specified in Sects. 1.1.1–1.1.3; 1.1.5–1.1.8; 1.2.1–1.2.5; 1.3.1, 1.3.2 (in so far as it concerns Articles 16 and 17 of Council Decision 2010/413/CFSP) and 1.3.3; 1.4.1 and 1.4.2; 1.10.1.2 (in so far as it concerns Articles 39, 43, 43a of Council Regulation (EU) No 267/2012) of Annex II. EU Member States will terminate or amend national implementing legislation as required.

16.2. Amend the provisions of Council Regulation (EU) No 267/2012 and the corresponding provisions of Council Decision 2010/413/CFSP specified in Sects. 1.6.1–1.7.2 of Annex II, in connection with activities consistent with this JCPOA.

16.3. Remove individuals and entities set forth in Attachment 1 to Annex II of this JCPOA from Annexes VIII and IX to Council Regulation (EU) 267/2012. Suspend the provisions of Council Decision 2010/413/CFSP specified in Sect. 1.9.1 of Annex II in relation to individuals and entities set forth in Attachment 1 to Annex II.

16.4. Amend the provisions of Council Regulation (EU) No 267/2012 and Council Decision 2010/413/CFSP specified in Sects. 1.5.1 and 1.5.2 of Annex II to implement the relevant provisions of the UN Security Council resolution referred to above.

17. **The United States will**[24]:

17.1. Cease the application of the sanctions set forth in Sects. 4.1–4.5 and 4.7 of Annex II, with the exception of Section 211(a) of the Iran Threat Reduction and Syria Human Rights Act of 2012 (TRA);

17.2. Cease the application of the sanctions set forth in Sect. 4.6 of Annex II, in connection with activities consistent with this JCPOA, including trade with individuals and entities set forth in Attachment 3 to Annex II;

17.3. Remove individuals and entities set forth in Attachment 3 to Annex II from the Specially Designated Nationals and Blocked Persons List (SDN List), the Foreign Sanctions Evaders List (FSE List), and/or the Non-SDN Iran Sanctions Act List as set forth in Sect. 4.8.1 of Annex II;

17.4. Terminate Executive Orders 13574, 13590, 13622, 13645 and Sects. 5–7 and 15 of Executive Order 13628 as set forth in Sect. 4 of Annex II; and

17.5. License activities as set forth in Sect. 5 of Annex II.

18. **UN Security Council**
18.1. In accordance with the UN Security Council resolution endorsing this JCPOA, the provisions imposed in UN Security Council resolutions 1696 (2006), 1737 (2006), 1747 (2007), 1803 (2008), 1835 (2008), 1929 (2010) and 2224 (2015) will be terminated subject to re-imposition in the event of significant non-performance by Iran of JCPOA commitments, and specific restrictions, including restrictions regarding the transfer of proliferation sensitive goods will apply.[25]
18.2. The E3/EU+3 will take appropriate measures to implement the new UNSC resolution.

D. Transition Day

19. Transition Day will occur 8 years from Adoption Day or upon a report from the Director General of the IAEA to the IAEA Board of Governors and in parallel to the UN Security Council stating that the IAEA has reached the Broader Conclusion that all nuclear material in Iran remains in peaceful activities, whichever is earlier.
20. **The European Union will**:
20.1. Terminate the provisions of Council Regulation (EU) No 267/2012 and suspend the corresponding provisions of Council Decision 2010/413/CFSP specified in Sects. 1.1.4, 1.3.2 (in so far as it concerns Articles 15 and 18 of Council Decision and Articles 36 and 37 of Council Regulation); 1.5.1 and 1.5.2 (in so far as it concerns Ballistic Missiles restrictions); 1.6.1–1.9.1 of Annex II.
20.2. Remove individuals and entities set forth in Attachment 2 to Annex II from Annexes VIII and IX to Council Regulation (EU) 267/2012.

20.3. Remove individuals and entities set forth in Attachment 1 to Annex II from Annexes I and II to Council Decision 2010/413/CFSP.
20.4. Terminate all provisions in Council Decision 2010/413/CFSP suspended on Implementation Day.
21. **The United States will**:
21.1. Seek such legislative action as may be appropriate to terminate, or modify to effectuate the termination of, the statutory sanctions set forth in Sects. 4.1–4.5, 4.7 and 4.9 of Annex II;
21.2. Seek such legislative action as may be appropriate to terminate, or modify to effectuate the termination of, the statutory sanctions described in Sect. 4.6 of Annex II, in connection with activities consistent with this JCPOA, including trade with individuals and entities set forth in Attachments 3 and 4 to Annex II; and
21.3. Remove individuals and entities set out in Attachment 4 to Annex II from the SDN List and/or the FSE List as set forth in Sect. 4.8.1 of Annex II.
22. **Iran will**:
22.1. Seek, consistent with the Constitutional roles of the President and Parliament, ratification of the Additional Protocol.

E. **UNSCR Termination Day**

23. UNSCR (UN Security Council resolution) Termination Day will occur in accordance with the terms of the UN Security Council resolution endorsing the JCPOA, which is 10 years from Adoption Day, provided that the provisions of previous resolutions have not been reinstated.
24. On UNSCR Termination Day, the provisions and measures imposed in that resolution would terminate

and the UN Security Council would no longer be seized of the Iran nuclear issue.

25. **The European Union will:**
25.1. Terminate all remaining provisions of Council Regulation (EU) No 267/2012 and Council Decision 2010/413/CFSP.

F. **Other**

26. The terminations described in this Annex V are without prejudice to other JCPOA commitments that would continue beyond such termination dates.

Appendix B: Detailed Chronology Courtesy of the Arms Control Association

1960s

November 1967: Iran's first nuclear reactor, the U.S. supplied five-megawatt Tehran Research Reactor (TRR) goes critical. It operates on uranium enriched to about 93 percent (it is converted to run on 20 percent in 1993), which the United States also supplies.

1970s

February 1970: The Iranian parliament ratifies the nuclear Nonproliferation Treaty (NPT).

1974: Shah Reza Pahlavi establishes the Atomic Energy Organization of Iran (AEOI) and announces plans to generate about 23,000 megawatts of energy over 20 years, including the construction of 23 nuclear power plants and the development of a full nuclear fuel cycle.

1979: The Iranian Revolution and the seizure of the U.S. embassy in Tehran result in a severing of U.S.-Iranian ties and damages Iran's relationship with the West. Iranian nuclear projects are halted.

1980s

January 19, 1984: The U.S. Department of State adds Iran to its list of state sponsors of terrorism, effectively imposing sweeping sanctions on Tehran.

1987: Iran acquires technical schematics for building a P-1 centrifuge from the Abdul Qadeer Khan network.

1990s

1992: Congress passes the Iran-Iraq Arms Nonproliferation Act of 1992, which prohibits the transfer of controlled goods or technology that might contribute "knowingly and materially" to Iran's proliferation of advanced conventional weapons.

1993: Conversion of the TRR is completed by Argentina's Applied Research Institute. It now runs on fuel enriched to just less than 20 percent, 115 kilograms of which is provided by Argentina; the contract for the conversion was signed in 1987.

August 5, 1996: The U.S. Congress passes the Iran-Libya Sanctions Act, also known as the Iran Sanctions Act, that penalizes foreign and U.S. investment exceeding $20 million in Iran's energy sector in one year.

2000s

August 2002: The National Council of Resistance on Iran, the political wing of the terrorist organization Mujahideen-e Khalq (MeK), holds a press conference and declares Iran has built nuclear facilities near Natanz and Arak.

September 12, 2003: The International Atomic Energy Agency (IAEA) Board of Governors adopts a resolution calling for Iran to suspend all enrichment—and reprocessing-related activities. The resolution requires Iran to declare all material relevant to its uranium-enrichment program and allow IAEA inspectors to conduct environmental sampling at any location. The resolution requires Iran to meet its conditions by October 31st 2003.

October 21, 2003: Iran agrees to meet IAEA demands by the October 31st deadline. In a deal struck between Iran and European foreign ministers, Iran agrees to suspend its uranium–enrichment activities and ratify an additional protocol requiring Iran to provide an expanded declaration of its nuclear activities and granting the IAEA broader rights of access to sites in the country.

June 18, 2004: The IAEA rebukes Iran for failing to cooperate with IAEA inspectors. Iran responds by refusing to suspend enrichment-related activities as it had previously pledged.

November 14, 2004: Iran notifies the IAEA that it will suspend enrichment-related activities following talks with France, Germany, and the United Kingdom. According to the so-called Paris Agreement, Iran would maintain the suspension for the duration of talks among the four countries. As a result, the IAEA Board of Governors decides not to refer Tehran to the UN Security Council.

February 27, 2005: Russia and Iran conclude a nuclear fuel supply agreement in which Russia would provide fuel for the Bushehr reactor it is constructing and Iran would return the spent nuclear fuel to Russia. The arrangement is aimed at preventing Iran from extracting plutonium for nuclear weapons from the spent nuclear fuel.

August 8, 2005: Iran begins producing uranium hexafluoride at its Isfahan facility. As a result, France, Germany, and the United Kingdom halt negotiations with Tehran.

September 24, 2005: The IAEA adopts a resolution finding Iran in noncompliance with its safeguards agreement by a vote of 22-1 with 12 members abstaining. The resolution says that the nature of Iran's nuclear activities and the lack of assurance in their peaceful nature fall under the purview of the UN Security Council, paving the way for a future referral.

February 4, 2006: A special meeting of the IAEA Board of Governors refers Iran to the UN Security Council. The resolution "deems it necessary for Iran to" suspend its enrichment-related activities, reconsider the construction of the Arak heavy-water reactor, ratify the additional protocol to its safeguards agreement, and fully cooperate with the agency's investigation.

February 6, 2006: Iran tells the IAEA that it will stop voluntarily implementing the additional protocol and other non-legally binding inspection procedures.

April 11, 2006: Iran announces that it has enriched uranium for the first time. The uranium enriched to about 3.5 percent was produced at the Natanz pilot enrichment plant.

June 6, 2006: China, France, Germany, Russia the United Kingdom, and the United Sates (the P5 + 1) propose a framework agreement to Iran offering incentives for Iran to halt its enrichment program for an indefinite period of time.

July 31, 2006: The UN Security Council adopts Resolution 1696, making the IAEA's calls for Iran to suspend enrichment-related and reprocessing activities legally binding for the first time.

August 22, 2006: Iran delivers a response to the P5 + 1 proposal, rejecting the requirement to suspend enrichment but declaring that the package contained "elements which may be useful for a constructive approach."

December 23, 2006: The UN Security Council unanimously adopts Resolution 1737, imposing sanctions on Iran for its failure to suspend its enrichment-related activities. The sanctions prohibit countries from transferring sensitive nuclear- and missile-related technology to Iran and require that all countries freeze the assets of ten Iranian organizations and twelve individuals for their involvement in Iran's nuclear and missile programs.

March 24, 2007: The UN Security Council unanimously adopts Resolution 1747 in response to Iran's continued failure to comply with the council's demand to suspend Uranium enrichment.

August 21, 2007: Following three rounds of talks in July and August, the IAEA and Iran agree on a "work plan" for Iran to answer long-standing questions about its nuclear activities, including work suspected of being related to nuclear weapons development.

December 3, 2007: The United States publicly releases an unclassified summary of a new National Intelligence Estimate report on Iran's nuclear program. The NIE says that the intelligence community judged "with high confidence" that Iran halted its nuclear weapons program in the fall of 2003 and assessed with moderate confidence that the program had not resumed as of mid-2007. The report defines Iran's nuclear weapons program as "design and weaponization work" as well as clandestine uranium conversion and enrichment. The NIE also said that Iran was believed to be technically capable of producing enough highly enriched uranium for a nuclear weapon between 2010 and 2015.

March 3, 2008: The UN Security Council passes Resolution 1803, further broadening sanctions on Iran. It requires increased efforts on the part of member states to prevent Iran from acquiring sensitive nuclear or missile technology and adds 13 persons and seven entities to the UN blacklist.

June 14, 2008: The P5 + 1 present a new comprehensive proposal to Iran updating its 2006 incentives package. The new proposal maintained the same basic framework as the one in 2006, but highlighted an initial "freeze-for-freeze" process wherein Iran would halt any expansion of its enrichment activities while the UN Security Council agreed not to impose additional sanctions.

February 3, 2009: Iran announces that it successfully carried out its first satellite launch, raising international concerns that Iran's ballistic missile potential was growing.

April 8, 2009: Following an Iran policy review by the new Obama administration, the United States announces that it would participate fully in the P5 + 1 talks with Iran, a departure from the previous administration's policy requiring Iran to meet UN demands first.

June 12, 2009: Iran holds presidential elections. Incumbent Mahmoud Ahmadinejad is declared the winner amid many indications that the election was rigged. This sparks weeks of protests within Iran and delays diplomatic efforts to address Iran's nuclear program.

September 25, 2009: United States President Barack Obama, British Prime Minister Gordon Brown, and French President Nicolas Sarkozy announced that Iran has been constructing a secret, second uranium-enrichment facility, Fordow, in the mountains near the holy city of Qom. IAEA spokesman Marc Vidricaire said that Iran informed the agency September 21 about the existence of the facility, but U.S. intelligence officials said Iran offered the confirmation only after learning that it had been discovered by the United States.

October 1, 2009: The P5 + 1 and Iran agree "in principle" to a U.S.-initiated, IAEA-backed, proposal to fuel the TRR. The proposal entails Iran exporting the majority of its 3.5 percent enriched Uranium in return for 20 percent-enriched uranium fuel for the TRR, which has exhausted much of its supply. This agreement was later met with domestic political opposition in Iran, resulting in attempts by Tehran to change the terms of the "fuel swap."

2010

February 9, 2010: Iran begins the process of producing 20 percent enriched uranium, allegedly for the TRR.

May 17, 2010: Brazil, Iran, and Turkey issue a joint declaration attempting to resuscitate the TRR fuel-swap proposal. In the declaration, Iran agrees to ship 1200 kilograms of 3.5 percent enriched uranium to Turkey in return for TRR fuel from France and Russia. France, Russia, and the United States reject the arrangement, citing Iran's larger stockpile of 3.5 percent-enriched uranium and the failure of the declaration to address Iran's enrichment to 20 percent.

June 9, 2010: The UN Security Council adopts Resolution 1929, significantly expanding sanctions against Iran. In addition to tightening proliferation-related sanctions and banning Iran from carrying out nuclear-capable ballistic missile tests, the resolution imposes an arms embargo on the transfer of major weapons systems to Iran.

June 24, 2010: Congress adopts the Comprehensive Iran Sanctions, Accountability, and Divestment Act; tightening U.S. sanctions against firms investing in Iran's energy sector, extending those sanctions until 2016, and imposing new sanctions on companies that sell refined petroleum to Iran.

July 26, 2010: The EU agrees to further sanctions against Iran. A statement issued by EU member state foreign ministers refers to the new sanctions as "a comprehensive and robust package of measures in the areas of trade, financial services, energy, [and] transport, as well as additional designations for [a] visa ban and asset freeze.

September 16, 2010: The Stuxnet computer virus is first identified by a security expert as a directed attack against an Iranian nuclear-related facility, likely to be the Natanz enrichment plant.

2011

January 21–22, 2011: Following a December meeting in Geneva, the P5 + 1 meets with Iran in Istanbul, but the two sides do not arrive at any substantive agreement. Iran's two preconditions for further discussions on a fuel-swap plan and transparency measures, recognition of a right to enrichment and the lifting of sanctions, were rejected by the P5 + 1.

February 16, 2011: U.S. intelligence officials tell a Senate committee that Iran has not yet decided whether it wants to develop nuclear weapons but is keeping that option open through development of its material capabilities.

May 8, 2011: Iran's Bushehr nuclear power plant begins operations and successfully achieves a sustained chain reaction two days later, according to Atomstroyexport, the Russian state-owned company constructing and operating the plant.

June 8, 2011: Iran announces that it intends to triple the rate of 20 percent-enriched uranium production using more-advanced centrifuge designs. It also says it will move production to the Fordow enrichment plant near Qom, which is still under construction.

July 12, 2011: Russian foreign minister Sergey Lavrov unveils a proposal wherein Iran would take steps to increase cooperation with the IAEA and carry out confidence-building measures in return for a gradual easing of sanctions.

October 21, 2011: EU foreign policy chief, Catherine Ashton, sends a letter to Iranian nuclear negotiator Saeed Jalili calling for "meaningful discussions on concrete confidence-building steps" to address international concerns about Iran's nuclear ambitions.

November 8, 2011: The IAEA releases a report detailing a range of activities related to nuclear weapons development in which Iran is suspected to have engaged as part of a structured program prior to 2004. The report raises concerns that some weapons-related activities occurred after 2003. The information in the report is based primarily on information received from other countries, but also includes information from the agency's own investigation. The findings appear consistent with the U.S. 2007 National Intelligence Estimate on Iran.

December 31, 2011: As part of the fiscal year 2012 National Defense Authorization Act, Congress passes legislation that will allow the United States to sanction foreign banks if they continue to process transactions with the Central Bank of Iran.

2012

January 2012: The EU passes a decision that will ban all member countries from importing Iranian oil beginning July 1, 2012. Other provisions of the decision will prevent member countries from providing the necessary protection and indemnity insurance for tankers carrying Iranian oil.

January 29–31, 2012: Following an exchange of letters between Iran and the IAEA, it was agreed that an Agency team would travel to Tehran to begin discussions on the IAEA's investigations into the possible military dimensions of Iran's nuclear program laid out in the November 2011 IAEA report.

February 15, 2012: Jalili responds to Ashton's Oct. 21 letter, while Iran simultaneously announces a number of nuclear advances, including the domestic production of a fuel plate for the TRR.

April 14, 2012: Iran meets with the P5 + 1 in Istanbul for talks both sides call "positive." They agree on a framework of continuing negotiations with a step-by-step process and reciprocal actions.

May 23–24, 2012: Iran and the P5 + 1 meet in Baghdad for a second set of talks.

June 18–19, 2012: Talks between Iran and the P5 + 1 continue in Moscow. Representatives discuss the substance of a P5 + 1 proposal and an Iranian proposal. Ashton and Jalili announce that will determine if political-level talks will continue after a technical-level meeting in July.

July 3, 2012: Experts representing the six parties meet in Istanbul to discuss the technical aspects of the P5 + 1 proposal and the Iranian proposal.

July 24, 2012: Schmid and Bagheri meet in Istanbul to discuss the outcome of the technical level experts meeting and confirm that Ashton and Jalili will talk to determine the future of the negotiations.

August 30, 2012: The IAEA reports that Iran increased the number of centrifuges installed at the Fordow enrichment plant and is continuing to produce uranium enriched to 20 percent in excess of its needs for the Tehran Research Reactor.

September 2012: Ashton and Jalili meet in Istanbul to assess "common points" reached at the low-level expert talks held in early July. The meeting was not considered a formal negotiation.

September 27, 2012: In a speech to the UN General Assembly, Israeli Prime Minister Benjamin Netanyahu draws a red-line for an Israeli attack on Iran. Netanyahu defines his red-line as Iran amassing enough uranium enriched to 20 percent (approximately 250 kilograms), which, when further enriched, will be enough for one bomb.

November 16, 2012: The IAEA reports that since August, Iran completed installation of the approximately 2800 centrifuges that Fordow is designed to hold, although the number enriching remains constant. The number of cascades producing 20 percent enriched uranium remains constant at Fordow. The report also notes that Iran installed more centrifuges at Natanz, and continued producing uranium enriched to 20 percent.

2013

February 26, 2013: Iran and the P5 +1 resume negotiations in Almaty, Kazakhstan over Iran's nuclear program. The P5 + 1 offers Iran an updated proposal based largely on the 2012 package.

April 5–6, 2013: Iran and the P5 + 1 meet again in Almaty for a second round of talks. At the end of the meetings, negotiators announce that no further meetings are scheduled and the sides remain far apart.

June 3, 2013: At the quarterly meeting of the IAEA Board of Governors, Director General Yukiya Amano says that the agency's talks with Iran over clarifying the possible military dimensions of Iran's nuclear program have not made any progress.

June 14, 2013: Hassan Rouhani is elected president of Iran. A former nuclear negotiator, he asserts that Iran will maintain its nuclear program, but offers to be more transparent.

August 6, 2013: Three days after his inauguration, Iran's President Hasan Rouhani calls for the resumption of serious negotiations with the P5 + 1 on Iran's nuclear program.

September 26, 2013: The P5 + 1 foreign ministers meet with Iranian Foreign Minister Javad Zarif on the sidelines on the UN General Assembly meeting in New York. Zarif presents the P5 + 1 with a new proposal that U.S. Secretary of State John Kerry describes as "very different in the vision" of possibilities for the future. Zarif and Kerry meeting for a bilateral exchange after the larger group meeting. Zarif later says he and Kerry move to agree "first, on the parameters of the end game." Zarif says Iran and the P5 + 1 will think about the order of steps that need to be implemented to "address the immediate concerns of [the] two sides" and move toward finalizing a deal within a year. The parties agree to meet again on October 15 in Geneva.

September 27, 2013: President Barack Obama calls Iranian President Hassan Rouhani, marking the highest level contact between the U.S. and Iran since 1979. While President Obama says that there will be significant obstacles to overcome, he believes a comprehensive resolution can be reached.

In Vienna, Iran's new envoy to the IAEA, Reza Najafi, meets with IAEA deputy director Herman Nackaerts to resume negotiations on the structured approach to resolving the agency's concerns about the possible military dimensions of Iran's nuclear program. Both sides describe the meeting as constructive and agree to meet again on October 28.

October 15–16, 2013: Iran and the P5 + 1 meet in Geneva to resume negotiations over Iran's nuclear program. At the end of the talks, the parties release a joint statement describing the meetings as "substantive and forward looking." The statement also says that Iran presented a new proposal that the P5 + 1 carefully considered as an "important contribution" to the talks. The proposal is understood to contain a broad framework for a comprehensive agreement and an interim confidence building measure to be instituted over the next 3–6 months, but no details are given as the parties agreed to keep the negotiations confidential.

Wendy Sherman, Undersecretary of State for Political Affairs, says after the talks that Iran approached the meetings "with a candor" she had not heard in her two years of negotiating with Tehran. The parties agree to meet again November 7–8 in Geneva with an experts level meeting October 30–31.

October 28–29, 2013: Iran meets with the IAEA to continue discussions over the agency's investigations into Iran's past nuclear activities with possible military dimensions. According to a joint statement, Iran presented a new proposal at the talks that contained "practical measures" to "strengthen cooperation and dialogue with a view to future resolution of all outstanding issues." Iran and the IAEA agree to meet again in Tehran on November 11.

November 7–10, 2013: The P5 + 1 and Iran meet in Geneva to continue negotiations over Iran's nuclear program. On November 8, with the expectation that a deal is close, U.S. Secretary of State John Kerry flies to Geneva to join the talks, as do the foreign ministers from the other P5 + 1 countries. The parties fail to reach an agreement on a first-phase deal, but announce that talks will continue on November 20 in Geneva.

Secretary Kerry says in Nov. 10 press conference that the parties "narrowed the differences" and made significant progress toward reaching an agreement during the talks.

November 11, 2013: IAEA Director General Yukiya Amano and Ali Akbar Salehi meet in Tehran to continue talks on an approach for the agency's investigations into Iran's past nuclear activities with possible military dimensions. Amano and Salehi sign a Framework for Cooperation Agreement.

The framework lays out initial practical steps to be taken by Iran within three months, including allowing IAEA access to the Heavy Water Production Plant at Arak and the Gchine uranium mine, and providing the agency with information on new research reactors and nuclear power plants that Iran intends to build. The statement commits the parties to cooperation "aimed at ensuring the exclusively peaceful nature of Iran's nuclear program through the resolution of all outstanding issues that have not already been resolved by the IAEA."

November 20–24, 2013: Iran and the P5 + 1 meet again in Geneva to continue negotiations. On November 23, the foreign ministers from the P5 + 1 join the negotiations. Early on November 24, Iranian Minister Javad Zarif and Catherine Ashton, leader of the P5 + 1 negotiating team, sign an agreement called the Joint Plan of Action. It lays out specific steps for each side in a six-month, first-phase agreement, and the broad framework to guide negotiations for a comprehensive solution.

The first-phase pauses further developments in Iran's nuclear program, rolls back significant elements like the stockpile of 20 percent enriched uranium, and requires more extensive IAEA monitoring and access to nuclear sites. In return, Iran receives limited sanctions relief, repatriation of limited assets frozen abroad, and a commitment that no new nuclear-related sanctions will be imposed on Iran for the duration of the agreement.

The plan will establish a Joint Commission to monitor the agreement and work with the IAEA. The six-month period can be extended by mutual consent of both parties.

December 8, 2013: Under the terms of the Framework for Cooperation Agreement the IAEA visits the Arak Heavy Water Production Plant.

December 9–12, 2013: The P5 + 1 and Iran meet in Geneva at the technical level to begin discussions on the implementation of the Nov. 24 Joint Plan of Action.

December 11, 2013: Iran and the IAEA meet again in Vienna to review progress made on the six actions that Iran agreed to take as part of the Framework for Cooperation Agreement. The parties also begin discussing the next practical steps for Iran to take and initially plan to meet again on Jan. 21 to finalize the measures. The meeting is later postponed at the request of Iran to Feb. 8.

December 30–31, 2013: Technical level discussions between Iran and the P5 + 1 on implementing the Joint Plan of Action continue in Geneva.

2014

January 9–10, 2014: Iran and the P5 + 1 meet for a third time in Geneva to discuss implementation. The parties reach an agreement and return to their respective capitals for approval.

January 12, 2014: Iran and the P5 + 1 announce that implementation of the Joint Plan of Action will begin on Jan. 20.

January 20, 2014: Implementation of the Joint Plan of Action begins. The IAEA issues a report on Iran's compliance with the deal. The report states that Iran is adhering to the terms of the agreement, including, halting enrichment of uranium to 20 percent, beginning to blend down half of the stockpile of 20 percent enriched uranium to 3.5 percent, and halting work on the Arak Heavy Water Reactor. The IAEA also begins more intrusive and frequent inspections.

The United States and the European Union also issue statements saying they have taken the necessary steps to waive the specific sanctions outlined in the Nov. 24 deal and release a schedule of payments for Iran to receive oil money held up in the other countries.

February 9, 2014: Iran and the IAEA meet to discuss further actions for Iran to take under the November 11 framework agreement to resolve the agency's concerns about Iran's nuclear program. They agree on additional actions, including Iran's past work on exploding bridgewire detonators, one of the past activities with possible military dimensions.

February 17–20, 2014: Negotiations between Iran and the P5 + 1 on the comprehensive agreement begin in Vienna. The parties agree on an agenda and framework to guide the talks.

March 17–20, 2014: The P5 + 1 and Iran meet in Vienna to continue negotiations.

April 7–9, 2014: Another round of talks between Iran and the P5 + 1 take place in Vienna.

May 13–16, 2014: The P5 + 1 and Iran begin drafting the comprehensive agreement.

May 21, 2014: Iran and the IAEA announce an additional five actions for Iran to complete before August 25. Two of the activities that Iran agrees to provide information on relate to possible military dimensions.

June 2–6, 2014: At the IAEA board meeting Director General Yukiya Amano says that Iran is complying with the terms of the interim agreement and the agency's investigation into the unresolved concerns about Iran's nuclear program. The agency's quarterly report shows that Iran has neutralized nearly all of its stockpile of 20 percent uranium gas buy dilution or conversion to powder form.

June 16–20, 2014: Iran and the P5 + 1 hold another round of negotiations in Vienna.

July 2–19, 2014: Iran and the P5 + 1 continue talks in Vienna on a comprehensive nuclear agreement. Early on June 19, the parties announce that they will extend the talks through November 24 and keep the measures agreed to in the interim agreement in place. The parties also announce additional actions that Iran will take, namely, converting 25 kg of uranium powder enriched to 20 percent into fuel plates and blending down about 3 tons of uranium enriched to less than 2 percent. The P5 + 1 will also repatriate $2.8 billion in funds. The parties agree to resume talks in August.

August 25, 2014: Iran misses a deadline to complete actions on five areas of concern to the IAEA as part of the agreement that Iran and the agency reached in November 2013.

September 5, 2014: The IAEA's quarterly report on Iran's nuclear program shows that Iran is complying with the interim deal, but did not provide the IAEA with information about past activities with possible military dimensions (PMDs) by the Aug. 25 deadline.

September 18, 2014: Talks between Iran and the P5 + 1 resume in New York City on the sidelines of the UN General Assembly. Both sides say that little progress was made at the end of the talks.

October 14–16: Iran and the P5 + 1 meet in Vienna to continue negotiations. Officials say that they remain focused on reaching an agreement by the Nov. 24 deadline and progress was made during the talks.

November 9–10: Iranian Foreign Minister Zarif and U.S. Secretary of State Kerry meet in Muscat, Oman to continue talks. P5 + 1 lead negotiator Catherine Ashton is also present.

November 18–24: Iran and the P5 + 1 meet in Vienna to continue negotiations on a comprehensive agreement. U.S. Secretary of State John Kerry joins the talks on Nov. 20.

French Foreign Minister Fabiusu, British Foreign Secretary Hammond, and German Foreign Minister Steinmeier all join the talks between Nov. 20 and 22. Russian Foreign Minister Lavrov arrives on Nov. 23 and Chinese Foreign Minister Wang on Nov. 24.

November 24: Iran and the P5 + 1 announce that negotiations will be extended because progress was made on the difficult issues and both sides see a path forward. The parties announce that they now aim to reach a political agreement by March and then complete the technical annexes by June 30. Both sides will continue to implement the conditions of the interim Joint Plan of Action from November 2013. Iran and the P5 + 1 also make additional commitments.

December 15: Talks between the P5 + 1 and Iran continue in Geneva. U.S. State Department officials say the talks are "good and substantive." Parties plan to meet again in January.

December 24: Iran's Foreign Minister Mohammad Javad Zarif says in a letter to his foreign counterparts that Iran's goal remains to reach a comprehensive nuclear deal that assures the world its nuclear program is exclusively peaceful.

2015

January 15–18: The P5 + 1 and Iran meet in Geneva to continue negotiations.

January 21: In testimony before the Senate Foreign Relations Committee on Jan. 21, U.S. Deputy Secretary of State Antony Blinken says: "We assess that we still have a credible chance of reaching a deal that is in the best interest of America's security, as well as the security of our allies."

January 23–24: Undersecretary of State Wendy Sherman and European Union Political Director Helga Schmid meet again with Iranian Deputy Foreign Minister Abbas Araghchi in Zurich, Switzerland.

February 18–20: Talks between the P5 + 1 and Iran resume in Vienna.

February 19: A report by the Director General of the IAEA confirms that Iran is upholding its commitments under the interim deal, including additional provisions from the November 2014 extension. The report notes "Iran has continued to provide the Agency with managed access to centrifuge assembly workshops, centrifuge rotor production workshops and storage facilities."

March 3: Prime Minister Netanyahu delivers a speech to a joint session of Congress. His speech claims that the Iran deal "would all but guarantee that Iran gets [nuclear] weapons, lots of them."

March 9: Senator Tom Cotton and 46 other senators sign an open letter to the Parliament of Iran. The letter warns that any deal reached without legislative approval could be revised by the next president "with the stroke of a pen."

March 17–20: Talks between the P5 + 1 and Iran continue in Lausanne. The head of Iran's Atomic Energy Organization, Ali Akbar Salehi, says to reporters "We have made progress on technical issues. One or two issues remain and need to be discussed."

March 25–April 2: Negotiations continue in Lausanne. By March 29, all of the Foreign Ministers from the seven countries involved and EU foreign policy chief Federica Mogherini are present.

April 2: Iran and the P5 + 1 announce agreement on a general framework that outlines the broad parameters of a nuclear deal. The United States issues a more specific factsheet on the details. Iran and the P5 + 1 agree to continue meeting to finalize a deal before June 30.

April 14: The Senate Foreign Relations Committee unanimously passes legislation authored by Senator Bob Corker (R-Tenn.) that will require the President to submit the deal to Congress for a vote of approval or disapproval. According to the legislation, the President will not be able to waive sanctions during the 30-day Congressional review period.

April 15: Iran and the IAEA meet in Tehran to continue discussing the agency's investigations into the possibly military dimensions of Iran's nuclear program.

April 27: U.S. Secretary of State John Kerry and Iranian Foreign Minister Mohammad Javad Zarif meet in New York on the sidelines of the nuclear Nonproliferation Treaty Review Conference. Technical drafting work on the annexes of the agreement is underway.

May 7: The Senate passes the Corker legislation 98-1 on congressional review of an Iran nuclear deal.

May 12: EU and Iranian negotiators meet in Vienna to continue drafting a comprehensive agreement.

June 26: U.S. Secretary of State John Kerry arrives in Vienna to continue negotiations on a nuclear deal with Iran and the P5 + 1. U.S. Secretary of Energy Ernest Moniz joins Kerry.

July 14: Iran and the P5 + 1 announce a comprehensive deal. Iran and the IAEA announce a roadmap for the agency's investigation into the possible military dimensions of Iran's nuclear program.

July 19: The Obama administration sends the comprehensive deal and supporting documents to Congress, beginning the 60-day review period mandated by the Iran Nuclear Deal Review Act.

July 20: The UN Security Council unanimously passes a resolution endorsing the nuclear deal and the lifting of UN

Security Council nuclear sanctions once key steps are taken in the deal.

August 15: The IAEA confirms that Iran submitted documents and explanations to answer the agency's unresolved concerns about past activities that could be related to nuclear weapons development.

September 2: The 34th Senator announces support for the nuclear deal with Iran, meaning that Congress will not have the support to override a presidential veto on a resolution disapproving of the deal.

September 8: Four additional Senators announce that they will support the nuclear deal with Iran, bringing the total number to 42. This important milestone will prevent the Senate from reaching the 60-vote threshold required for ending debate and moving to vote on a resolution of disapproval.

September 9: The IAEA announces that is submitted follow-up questions to Iran based on the information provided by Iran on Aug. 15. The IAEA is ahead of its Sept. 15 deadline to submit the questions.

September 10: A vote to end debate and move to vote on a resolution of disapproval fails to reach the required 60 votes on the Senate floor. The measure fails 58–42. Four democrats joined the 54 Republicans in favor of moving to vote on the resolution of disapproval. Similar votes fail on Sept. 15 and Sept. 17.

September 11: A vote on a resolution of approval fails in the House of Representatives, 269-162, with 25 Democrats voting joining the Republicans in voting against the measure.

September 17: The congressional review period ends without passage of a resolution of approval or a resolution of disapproval.

September 20: IAEA Director General Yukiya Amano and Deputy Director General Tero Varjoranta visit the Parchin site at Iran. The IAEA has concerns about Iran conducting explosive activities there relevant to a nuclear device. Amano and Varjoranta confirm that environmental sampling was done at the site under IAEA surveillance and the agency is now testing the samples.

October 4: A panel of Iranian lawmakers reviewing the JCPOA release their assessment of the deal. The report issued says that the agreement contains some security threats, such as allowing inspectors access to military sites, but should go ahead.

October 10: Iran tests a medium-range ballistic missile, the Emad. The Emad is a more precise version of the Shahab-3, believed to be capable of carrying a 750 kg payload over 1700 kilometers. The test is a violation of UN Security Council Resolution 1929 (2010), which prohibits Iran from testing nuclear-capable ballistic missiles.

October 10: Iran's parliament approves a preliminary bill supporting the Iran deal.

October 13: Iran's parliament approves a detailed bill supporting the Iran deal.

October 14: Iran's Guardian Council ratifies the bill approved by the parliament, completing Iran's internal review of the agreement.

October 15: The IAEA announces the activities laid out in the July 14 roadmap for the investigation into the past possible military dimensions of Iran's nuclear program has been completed. The IAEA aims to complete its report by Dec. 15.

October 18: Iran and the P5 + 1 formally adopt the nuclear deal. Iran begins taking steps to restrict its nuclear program. The United States issues waivers on nuclear-related sanctions to come into effect on implementation day. The EU announces it passed legislation to lift nuclear-related sanctions on implementation day.

October 18: Iran notifies the IAEA of that it will provisionally implement its additional protocol and modified Code 3.1 to its safeguards agreement as of implementation day.

October 19: The first meeting of the Joint Commission takes place in Vienna. One of the purposes of the meeting is to set up working groups called for under the deal, such as the working group on procurement and the Arak reactor modification.

October 20: The Supreme Leader issues a statement endorsing the nuclear deal and bill passed by the Iranian parliament.

October 21: The United States raises Iran's ballistic missile test as a possible violation of UN Security Council Resolution 1929 at a meeting of the Security Council.

November 21: Iran tests another medium-range ballistic missile in violation of UN Security Council Resolution 1929.

December 2: The IAEA issues its assessment of Iran's past activities related to nuclear weapons development (PMDs). The IAEA assess that Tehran had an organized weapons program prior to 2003 and that some activities continued, although not as an organized effort, through 2009. The report says that the agency has no credible indication that nuclear material was diverted from Iran's declared program or that any activities continued after 2009.

December 15: The IAEA Board of Governors holds a special meeting to consider the Dec. 2 report on Iran's weaponization activities. The board passes a resolution terminating past resolutions on Iran's nuclear program and ending the investigation. The board requests that the IAEA continue reporting on Iran's nuclear activities under the nuclear deal and report immediately on any concerns that arise with Iran's implementation.

December 28: Iran announces that it shipped 8.5 tons of low-enriched uranium, including the 20 percent enriched material in scrap and waste, out of the country to Russia. In return, Iran receives 140 tons of uranium yellowcake.

2016

January 11: Iranian officials announce that the Arak reactor core is being disabled. Iranian and P5 + 1 officials say that implementation day is close.

January 16: The IAEA verifies that Iran met its nuclear related commitments. Based on the IAEA report, Zarif and Mogherini announce implementation day, triggering the lifting of sanctions. UN Security Council Resolution 2231, which the Council passed in July to endorse the deal and trigger the lifting of UN sanctions comes into effect. Prior resolutions on Iran's nuclear program are terminated.

January 17: The U.S. Treasury Department issues an announcement that new sanctions will be imposed on 11 individuals and entities involved with Iran's ballistic missile programs. U.S. President Barack Obama says that with implementation of the nuclear deal Iran will not obtain nuclear weapons and that "the region, the United States, and the world will be more secure." Iranian President Hassan Rouhani gives a speech saying that "Iran's nuclear rights have been accepted by all."

January 26: Behrouz Kamalvandi, spokesman for the Atomic Energy Organization of Iran, says that Iran and China had signed a basic agreement to formalize China's assistance in redesigning the Arak reactor during Chinese President Xi Jinping's visit to Iran the previous week.

February 11: Abbas Qaidaari, director of the Defense and Security Studies Department at the Center for Strategic Studies in the Office of the Iranian President, writes in a piece for the Atlantic Council that "Iran's strategic defense plan currently sees no justification" for missile ranges greater than 2000–2300 kilometers. Qaidaari said that although Tehran is committed to developing its "deterrent conventional defense capabilities," it will limit its ballistic missiles to that range.

February 26: The IAEA issues its first quarterly report on Iran's post-implementation day nuclear activities. The report notes that Iran is meeting its nuclear obligations, although it slightly exceeded a cap set on the stockpile of heavy water allowed under the agreement. The IAEA notes that Iran had 130.9 metric tons of heavy water, slightly above the 130 metric ton limit set by the deal, but shipped out 20 metric tons on February 24 to stay below the limit.

March 9: Iran test launches two different variations of the Qadr medium-range ballistic missile.

March 14: U.S. Ambassador to the UN Samantha Power says she raised Iran's ballistic missile tests at a Security Council meeting, saying that the tests are inconsistent with UN Security Council Resolution 2231.

March 15: Iranian Foreign Minister Mohammad Javad Zarif defends Iran's missile launches saying that the missiles are permissible under UN Security Council Resolution 2231 because the missiles are not designed to be capable of carrying nuclear warheads.

April 22: Officials from Iran and the United States meet in Vienna sign a purchase agreement for Washington to buy 32 metric tons of heavy water for $8.6 million. U.S. Secretary of State John Kerry and Iranian Foreign Minister Mohammad Javad Zarif meet in New York to discuss implementation of the deal. In remarks after the meeting Kerry says that Washington is working to clarify confusion among foreign banks about the sanctions lifted in January.

May 27: The IAEA issues its quarterly report on Iran's implementation of the nuclear deal. The report shows Iran is abiding by restrictions under the agreement and inspectors have been able to access certain Iranian sites using complimentary access visits.

July 18: Iran's research and development plan for advanced centrifuge machines, leaked to the AP, is reported on in the press.

July 29: In a statement, the IAEA notes it sent a letter to Iran denying it was the source of leaked information about Iranian plans for phasing in advanced centrifuges in 2027.

September 8: The IAEA releases its third quarterly report since JCPOA implementation day, confirming Iran's continued compliance with the agreement. The report notes that Iran removed 96 IR-1 centrifuges from the storage area at Natanz to replace damaged centrifuges that were enriching uranium.

September 21: The U.S. Department of the Treasury Office of Foreign Assets Control grants Airbus and Boeing permission to sell planes to Iran. The licenses were made possible by sanctions waived as part of the JCPOA.

September 22: Iran and the P5 + 1 meet in New York to review progress on JCPOA implementation and the pace of sanctions relief. The meeting marks the first ministerial-level meeting since the announcement of the deal's implementation in January. Speaking to the UN General Assembly on the same day, Iranian President Hassan Rouhani expresses concern over the slow pace of sanctions relief and claims the U.S. has been in lack of compliance.

September 26: Sergei Kireienko, head of Rosatom, the state-run Russian nuclear energy company, announces that Moscow purchased 38 tons of heavy-water from Iran. The material was delivered to Russia in mid-September.

November 2: IAEA Director General Yukiya Amano expresses concern to Iranian leaders regarding the size of Iran's heavy water stock. On November 8th, the Agency confirms that Iran's heavy water stock, at 130.1 tons, exceeds the 130 metric ton limit outlined in the deal, marking the second time Iran has exceeded the limit. On November 9th, Iran informs the IAEA of plans to remain in compliance by transferring heavy water out of the country.

November 8: Donald Trump is elected as the 45th President of the United States. During the presidential campaign, Trump referred to the JCPOA as the worst deal ever negotiated and pledged to renegotiate it. The U.S.'s European allies in the P5 + 1 previously signaled they would resist efforts to renegotiate the deal.

November 20: IAEA releases its fourth quarterly report on Iranian nuclear program since JCPOA implementation day. The report notes that Iran had 130.1 metric tons of heavy water, slightly over the 130 metric tons permitted under the deal. The IAEA report says Iran plans to transfer heavy water out of the country.

December 1: Congress passes a 10-year extension of the Iran Sanctions Act (ISA), which becomes law on December 15th. Extension of the ISA is consistent with U.S. obligations under the JCPOA, although many of the ISA's provisions are being waived under Washington's commitments under the agreement.

December 6: IAEA verifies that all 11 metric tons of heavy water shipped out of Iran have reached their destination and are in storage, bringing Iran back within the limit on heavy water of 130 metric tons established by the JCPOA.

December 13: President Rouhani announces Iran will respond to Washington's extension of the Iran Sanctions Act by researching and developing nuclear propulsion for marine vessels.

December 15: U.S. Secretary of State John Kerry reissues sanctions waivers early, on the same day that the ISA renewal comes into effect, to demonstrate the U.S. commitment to the JCPOA.

December 18: IAEA Director General Yukiya Amano visits Iran, meeting with President Rouhani and Ali Akbar Salehi, head of Iran's Atomic Energy Organization. Amano and Salehi discussed issues related to implementation. Further, Amano sought clarification on Iran's announcement regarding naval nuclear reactor research and development.

December 23: The IAEA, at the request of Federica Mogherini, circulates decisions made by the Joint Commission set up to oversee implementation of the nuclear deal. The documents contain additional information on hot cells, recovering waste uranium, describing and calculating efficiency for advanced centrifuges, and utilizing the procurement channel.

2017

January 12: In his confirmation hearing for the position of Secretary of Defense, General Jim Mattis tells Congress that, while he believes the JCPOA is an imperfect agreement, "when America gives her word, we have to live up to it and work with our allies." His remarks echo a previous statement in April, when he noted there is "no going back" on the deal absent a clear violation of the agreement.

Iran receives the first shipment in an order of 100 planes purchased from Airbus. Sanctions waived as part of the nuclear deal allow Iran to purchase new commercial aircraft.

January 15: IAEA verifies that Tehran has taken certain steps to remove infrastructure and excess centrifuges from Fordow within the necessary timeframe required by the JCPOA (one year after Implementation Day). Secretary of Energy Moniz releases a statement noting "Iran successfully met the milestone of removing excess centrifuges and infrastructure from Fordow, demonstrating that the deal continues to limit Iran's nuclear program so as to provide confidence that Iran is not developing a nuclear weapon and maintain at least a one year breakout time."

January 28: Iran test fires a medium-range ballistic missile, in defiance of UN Security Council Resolution 2231. The test prompts former NSA Michael Flynn, on February 1, to declare the United States has placed Iran "on notice."

February 9: EU foreign policy chief Federica Mogherini travels to Washington for meetings with Secretary of State Rex Tillerson, former National Security Advisor Michael Flynn, and members of Congress. Mogherini notes that the JCPOA is key for the security of Europe given its geographic proximity to Iran.

February 24: IAEA releases its first quarterly report on Iranian nuclear activity in 2017, reporting on the size of Iran's stockpile of uranium enriched to 3.67 percent for the first time. The report notes that the stockpile was 101.7 kilograms. The limit established by the deal is 300 kilograms.

March 23: Senator Bob Corker (R-Tenn.) introduces a new Iran sanctions bill, the Countering Iran's Destabilizing Activities Act of 2017, targeting Iran's ballistic missile program and support for terrorism.

March 31: Former Deputy Secretary of State Tony Blinken and six former Obama administration officials release an op-ed in Foreign Policy outlining their opposition to the Countering Iran's Destabilizing Activities Act of 2017.

April 18: Secretary of State Rex Tillerson, in a letter to speaker of the House Paul Ryan, certifies to Congress that Iran is compliant in meeting its obligations under the JCPOA.

April 23: Iran and China resolve a price dispute and complete an agreement to modify Iran's Arak reactor. China will work with Iran to carry out modifications stipulated by the JCPOA to reduce the reactor's output of weapons-grade plutonium.

May 16: Ambassador Wendy Sherman, the lead U.S. negotiator for the JCPOA, states her opposition to the Countering Iran's Destabilizing Activities Act of 2017, noting its potential to undermine the nuclear accord.

May 17: The U.S. renews sanctions waivers as required by its JCPOA obligations, marking the first time the Trump administration has waived sanctions and taken a proactive step to implement the deal.

May 19: Iranian President Hassan Rouhani is re-elected to a second term. EU foreign policy chief Federica Mogherini congratulates Rouhani on Twitter and reaffirms the EU's commitment to full JCPOA implementation.

Appendix C: Short Descriptions of Some of the Organizations for and Against the Deal

Opposition Groups

The Jewish Institute for National Security Affairs: JINSA's mission is "educating congressional, military and civilian national security decision-makers on the American defense and strategic interests, primarily in the Middle East, the cornerstone of which is a robust U.S.-Israeli security cooperation."[26]

William Kristol, a neoconservative writer and founder of the right-wing magazine *The Weekly Standard*, is featured prominently on the JINSA's website. Kristol is known for supporting the invasion of Iraq and for saying the war would last only two months. He nonetheless has consistently pushed for a hawkish response on nearly every issue.[27] He and JINSA CEO Dr. Michael Makovsky called on Congress to scuttle the entire agreement with Iran.[28] In 2012 the organization had a dispute with a staff member, Shoshana Bryen, who worked on security policy, which prompted some on its advisory board including Richard Perle and James Woolsey to quit.[29] The same article reporting the dispute also noted that the organization tends to get lost in the shuffle with other organizations of a similar nature. One of JINSA's programs is to bring senior military officers to Israel for a tour. The contacts that provided by that program allowed it to quickly put together a letter to congress signed by 190 admirals and generals urging the Iran agreement be rejected.[30]

Emergency Committee for Israel: ECI's works to ensure the protection of Israel from "hostile regimes that refuse to accept the Jewish State."[31] It focuses on Iran, in particular, and its pursuit of nuclear material as well as its support for terrorist organizations.[32] William Kristol is the chairman of ECI and Gary Bauer, an evangelical Christian leader, is on its board. Noah Pollak, executive director of the group, issued a statement opposing the Iran agreement.[33] ECI contributed nearly a million dollars to election campaign of Tom Cotton.[34] Evidently, it must have stepped up fund raising as its IRS form 990 from 2010 listed only about $717, 000 in revenue.[35] It characterized the Iran deal as a "litany of concessions" and made a video about it in 2013 entitled "Obama's March to War," which ended with a mushroom cloud.[36]

Republican Jewish Coalition: Founded in 1985, RJC has Sheldon Adelson on its Board of Directors and works to serve as "a unique bridge between the Jewish community and Republican decision-makers."[37] In 2015 the group met in Las Vegas at Adelson's hotel and hosted a number of Republican presidential contenders including Ted Cruz, Rand Paul, and Rick Perry.[38] A main focus of the event was to attack President Obama's foreign policy, especially related to Iran nuclear agreement.[39] RJC organizers claim that attendance has risen at their events in recent years, reflecting more support from Jewish donors.[40] Because it is designated a 501(c)(4) organization, many of its donors are unknown but include wealthy lawyers such as Brad Rose who donated $50,000 and others on the board such as hedge-fund manager Phil Singer and home-builder Larry Mizel.[41]

Center for Strategic and Budgetary Assessments: CSBA is a research institute designed to "promote innovative thinking and debate about national security strategy, defense planning and military investment options for the 21st century."[42] It provides research and analysis for senior leaders in the executive and legislative branches of government.[43] Eric Edelman, a former Undersecretary of Defense for Policy and former Ambassador to Turkey, is a distinguished fellow at CSBA. During his career in the Foreign Service he served as Vice President Cheney's principal deputy assistant for national security affairs. In congressional testimony before a House of Representatives committee, he asserted the deal made too many concessions to Iran.[44] Among its projects, CSBA has provided information on how to proceed if the United States goes to war with Iran. For example, the CSBA believes that the United States military would have to "develop a new operational concept for future Persian Gulf contingencies" and would have to start a "massive blinding campaign."[45] Another article by Edelman points out how presidents can terminate the arms control and other agreements of their predecessors.[46] Little donor information available, but CSBA had nearly 6 million dollars in revenue in 2012 and nearly 5.4 million in expenses from compensation and other salaries.[47]

The Washington Institute: TWI describes itself as being "dedicated to injecting realism, balance, and scholarship" for Middle East peace and security and providing analysis to public policy officials. It is really little more than an AIPAC-linked think tank.[48] The organization has bipartisan appeal as it includes very pro-Israel Democrats such as former Senator Joe Lieberman and former Representative Howard Berman from California.[49] One key official involved in the organization is Dennis Ross, who worked in the George H.W. Bush, Clinton and Obama administrations on Middle East issues. He was particularly involved in negotiations between Israelis and Palestinians, where he was generally regarded as overtly pro-Israel. Ross's opposition to the deal was somewhat nuanced as he stated in one interview "The deal itself buys you 15 years. One of my main concerns is what happens after year 15, when they basically can have as large a program as they want, and the gap between threshold status and weapon status becomes very small."[50]

Patrick Clawson, who has a PhD in economics and is director of research and a senior fellow in the organization, took a much harder line.[51] In fact, in 2012, Clawson suggested Israel should create a "false flag operation," drawing the United State into a war with Iran after Iraq.[52] According to *Foreign Policy Magazine*, Larry and Barbi Weinberg created TWI in 1985 while they were the president and vice president of AIPAC.[53]

Foreign Policy initiative: FPI is another 501(c)(3) group that is a rightwing think tank which "promotes continued U.S. engagement" as well as "robust support for America's democratic allies and opposition to rogue regimes that threaten American interests."[54] FPI was founded in 2009 and its board of directors includes Eric Edelman. In 2014, he and

Dennis Ross wrote a letter on arguing any Iran aid provides in defeating the Islamic State does not warrant a new relationship with Iran.[55] In another example of the positions the organization takes, an article featured on its website by board member William Kristol, argued that the invasion of Iraq was correct.[56] Information on donors is hard to find, but its IRS Form 990 showed that for 2013 the organization had revenue of about $1.45 million dollars while expenses were $974,000, which went mainly to salaries.[57] The other expenses totaling around $557,000 are not specified.[58] Apparently one of FPI's biggest donors was Paul Singer, the hedge fund billionaire. According to an article in the Atlantic, Singer decided to cut his contribution to FPI and as a result its board decided to cease operations in August 2017.[59] According to a Republican operative with ties to FPI, the reason for the closure was because "The initial impetus for the thing was always to sort of beat back the isolationist strain in the party at the beginning of the Obama era." Singer was also said to have decided he was getting to little return on his investment.

American Security Initiative: ASI is a national security 501(c)(4) founded by former Republican Senators Saxby Chambliss and Norm Coleman and Democrat Evan Bayh. In 2014, Coleman became a registered lobbyist for the Saudi regime, providing the Saudis with legal services on issues including policy developments involving Iran. ASI was part of the successful effort to pass the Corker Menendez bill, which forced Obama to submit the agreement to Congress before signing it. In March 2015, even before the deal was made public, ASI launched a $1.4 million ad campaign aimed at Democratic Senator Chuck Schumer and other key senators with the message that the deal is great for Iran and dangerous for the US.[60,61]

Christians United For Israel: CUFI describes its purpose as "to provide a national association through which every pro-Israel church, parachurch organization, ministry or individual in America can speak and act with one voice in support of Israel in matters related to Biblical issues."[62] The group asserts it is relying on the Bible for information and other moral matters in the support for Israel.[63] CUFI was founded by John Hagee, a best-selling author and pastor from San Antonio.[64] Among Hagee's pronouncements was "And the day we validate this Iran nuclear deal as signed, sealed and delivered, will be the day we stick our finger in the eye of God."[65] He also claimed that the spread of Ebola was punishment from God because President Obama sought to divide Jerusalem.[66] Sheldon Adelson is a major contributor to CUFI and received an award from Hagee in 2014.[67] At one point, Glenn Beck also pledged a $100,000 donation to the group.[68]

United With Israel: Founded by businessman Michael Gerbitz, this group has used social media to construct a wide network of activists[69] to "spread the truth about Israel to the entire world" and fight to "win the battle of public opinion for Israel."[70] It claims to have 3 million supporters and counts among them former Governor Mike Huckabee and Prime Minister Netanyahu.[71] Its website features a large number of news stories related to Israel, opinion pieces with titles like "The UN Declares War on Judeo-Christian Civilization" and links for ways to urge senators and congressmen to take steps like cutting funding to the Palestinian Authority and increasing sanctions on Iran.

International Christian Embassy Jerusalem (ICEJ): The ICEJ is a Christian organization created in 1980 when its founders "heard an exhortation from heaven" that called on them to "speak comfort to Jerusalem."[72] It aims to increase support for Israel among Christians and works to encourage Jews to make Aliyah to Israel.[73] It receives financial support from individual born-again Christians.[74] In the 1980s, the organization received backing from Pat Robertson and his Christian Broadcasting Network.[75]

Americans for a Safe Israel: Founded in 1970 in the United States, and similar to Land of Israel group that exists internationally, it asserts that Israel should keep the land gained in the 1967 war for legal, historic, and religious reasons[76] and it rejects any compromise on territory as being necessary for peace.[77] Irving Moskowitz, a Florida-based bingo and gambling magnate, who is associated with numerous pro-Israel and neoconservative organizations, is a major funder of the organization.[78]

National Center for Policy Analysis: A free-market think tank funded by the billionaire Koch brothers, NCPA seeks "to develop and promote private, free-market alternatives to government regulation and control, solving problems by relying on the strength of the competitive, entrepreneurial private sector."[79] In other words, it aims to rid business of taxes and environmental and other government regulations. The Charles G. Koch and David H. Koch brothers' charitable foundation provided over $260,000 in 2009.

Major funders included a number of other rightwing organizations such as the Scaife Family Foundation and Sarah Scaife Foundation, which donated a combined amount of about $2,000,000 around 2009.[80] Exxon Mobil contributed $520,000 presumably with Secretary Tillerson's blessing.

Several articles and videos on the NCPA website feature its executive director Allen West. He is a one-term congressman who was defeated for reelection. He retired from the Army following his conviction on charges of beating and threatening to execute an Iraqi policeman whom he suspected had information regarding attacks on American soldiers.[81]

Endowment for Middle East Truth: Sheldon Adelson has contributed hundreds of thousands of dollars[82] to this organization, which describes itself as a different kind of think tank that is "insightful, passionate, connected and unabashedly pro-American and pro-Israel." EMET (which means truth in Hebrew) charges a minimum of $200 for membership and is a 501(c)3 charitable organization. It focuses on Middle East policy, giving monthly seminars to educate members of congress and their staff by providing them with "research and analysis which challenges misrepresentations and never bows to political correctness."[83]

Another big supporter of EMET is the Leader Family Foundation, run by Lennert J. Leader, a former president of AOL Time Warner Ventures who is also on the board of the Foundation for the Defense of Democracies and the Israel Project.[84]

Zionist Organization of America: ZOA, founded in 1897, is the oldest pro-Israel organization in the United States and is one of the most extreme. It says it is dedicated to "educating the public, elected officials, media and students about the truth of the ongoing and relentless Arab war against Israel."[85] But it has taken an increasingly partisan and uncompromising line. For instance, it condemned Democrats who did not attend Netanyahu's speech to Congress in March 2015 and considered their refusal to endorse his speech similar to Jews in the 1930s that did not speak out against Nazis.[86] Recent ZOA opinion articles assert that the idea Jerusalem is holy to Muslims is a propaganda myth, a Palestinian state is impossible, and not moving the American embassy to Jerusalem rewards terrorists.[87]

ZOA claims to have only 25,000 members nationwide and lost its tax-exempt status in 2012 after failing to file tax returns for three years.[88] It regained that status as its 2015 form 990 was filed showing revenue of $4.8 million and the salary of its president, Morton Klein, at a little $500,000 that year.[89] Its major funders include Sheldon Adelson (between 2009 and 2010 almost $500,000), the Irving Moskowitz Foundation ($200,000) and the Newton Becker Foundation.[90] ZOA, like CUFI and other Adelson-funded groups has pushed hard for Trump to relocate the American embassy from Tel Aviv to Jerusalem,[91] a move many Middle East experts think would be a disaster and that Trump has refused to take, at least in early 2017, despite his campaign promises to do so.[92]

At a ZOA meeting in June 2017, Sebastian Gorka was a speaker. When Gorka mentioned Stephen Bannon some in the audience cheered. Gorka, a national security advisor in the Trump White House has been associated with an anti-Semitic, Hungarian group and Bannon, according to his former wife, has been hostile to Jews.[93]

Stand With Us: Also known as the Israel Emergency Alliance, SWU is a 501(c)(3) organization that says it believes that "education is the road to peace" and is "dedicated to educating people of all ages about Israel and to combating the extremism and anti-Semitism that often distorts the issues."[94] It has aggressively challenged the "pro-Israel" credentials of moderate Jewish-American groups, however, and suggested that receiving money from Arab donors and supporters of Human Rights Watch undermines a group's commitment to Israel and peace. Its major funders include Susan Wexner ($850,000 from 2005 to 2009)[95] whose family founded The Limited and brands such as Bath and Body Works, Victoria's Secret, and The White Barn Candle Company.[96] SWU is also said to be "determined to prove moderate groups like J Street are working to undermine Israeli security."[97]

Simon Wiesenthal Center: This organization is dedicated to protecting global human rights, research on the Holocaust and working against anti-Semitism.[98] It is committed to guaranteeing the safety of Jews around the world and opposed the

Iran accord because of Tehran's views of Israel. Wiesenthal Center officials asserted that "Since 1979, no Iranian leader has changed his mind or actions about Israel, about the U.S. or about human rights. It is the height of folly and naiveté to believe that the Iranian regime will change its stripes in the next decade. No one denies that this agreement will allow Iran in 10 years to produce nuclear weapons in a matter of weeks."[99]

NORPAC (North Jersey PAC): Founded in 1992 By Rabbi Menachem Genack, this New Jersey-based, political action committee funnels money to legislators "who demonstrate a genuine commitment to the strength, security and survival of Israel."[100] In addition to raising funds for those legislators, it distributes talking points and organizes an annual citizen lobby visit-day to their offices in Washington. It claims to be "the largest pro-Israel PAC and was one of the major contributors to congressional opponents of the Iran nuclear agreement."

For instance, it was the largest contributor in 2014 to Representative Ed Royce, a California Republican and the Chairman of the House Foreign Affairs Committee. Royce, however, won reelection that year by 30 percentage points so NORPAC's $48,000 contribution may not have been necessary.[101] NORPAC opposed anyone whose commitment to Israel it deemed insufficient. It fought the nomination of Chuck Hagel to be Secretary of Defense, accusing him of "consistent solicitude toward Iran and the terrorist organizations it funds."[102] That position was so extreme that not even AIPAC agreed with it publicly.

Americans for Peace and Tolerance: This Boston-based organization describes itself as "non-profit organization composed of concerned citizens, academics, and community activists" who are "dedicated to promoting peaceful coexistence in an ethnically diverse America and a climate of tolerance and civil society."[103] Its critics, however, have called it "an outpost of hate and intolerance for its anti-Islamic rhetoric and campaigns against Boston-area mosques and cultural centers. Its website includes news stories of examples of Islamic extremism in the United States including a documentary called "Al Qaeda's Base at MIT."[104] Its founder, Charles Jacobs, has described mosques as "victory markers."[105] It has received financial support from The Middle East Forum, founded by Daniel Pipes, and the Alan and Hope Winters Family Foundation,[106] which has also contributed to other Islamophobic organizations.[107]

One Israel Fund: OIF encourages Israeli settlements on the West Bank by dedicating itself to "supporting the welfare and safety of the men, women and children of Judea, Samaria, the Jordan Valley and the reemerging communities of Gaza evacuees."[108] It describes the settlers in the occupied territories as "430,000 citizens of Israel who are the vanguard of Israel's security and sovereignty as a Jewish State." In 2015, OIF along with four other U.S. based and self-described charitable organizations were sued for allegedly providing funding to "violent Israeli settlers in the occupied West Bank."[109] The plaintiffs, thirteen Palestinians, a mosque and a Greek Orthodox monastery, all claimed to have been the victims of violent attacks by settlers and that the five, tax-exempt organizations violated the Anti-Terrorism Act by providing millions of dollars to the settlers. The suit was dismissed and an appeals court agreed with that decision.[110]

Middle East Forum: Founded by Daniel Pipes, the group says its aim is to protect western values from Middle East threats and to defeat radical Islam.[111] A report by the Center for American Progress, entitled "The Islamophobia Network's Effort to Manufacture Hate in America," described the MEF as "a controversial far-right think thank (sic) that is known for its anti-Islam views and hawkish foreign policy recommendations."[112] For instance, Pipes has suggested that instead of siding with and arming the Syrian rebels against Assad, the United States should work to ensure that the civil war was fought to a stalemate so both sides would inflict lasting damage on each other.[113]

Tax records indicate that donors from other anti-Muslim hate groups donate to MEF.[114] It also received $240,000 from Lynde and Harry Bradley Foundation, $200,000 from Newton and Rochelle Becker Charitable Trust and $2,000,000 from Donors Capital Fund and Rosenwald Family Fund.[115]

American Center for Democracy: ACD says it is dedicated to exposing and monitoring the enemies of freedom and democracy while identifying political, economic, and security threats to the United States from within and without. It also pinpoints "strategies used by radical regimes and movements to subvert America's Judeo-Christian values, Constitutional rights and political and economic systems."[116]

Classified as a 501(c)(3) nonprofit association, its board members include former CIA Director and Ambassador James Woolsey, former Attorney General Michael Mukasey, and former Department of Defense official and hardline hawk Richard Perle.[117] Its board also includes Dmitry Radyshevsky, a journalist who is director of the group Jerusalem Summit,[118] which is another Islamophobic group.[119]

Israeli American Council: The IAC exists to "build an engaged and united Israeli-American community that strengthens our next generations, the American Jewish community and the State of Israel."[120] In 2015, the group announced plans for a $10,000,000 community center for Israeli expatriates living in the San Fernando Valley.[121] Major donors include Sheldon Adelson, who has given it tens of millions of dollars, and another billionaire, Haim Saban.[122]

Religious Zionists of America: RZA seeks to promote a commitment to Religious Zionism and Israel in the American Jewish community.[123] The chairman of the organization argued that Prime Minister Netanyahu was obligated to give his speech to Congress to call attention to the existential threat to Israel from Iran and because "an agreement with Iran would transform it into a nuclear power."[124]

Scholars for Peace in the Middle East: According to its website, SPME seeks "to promote honest, fact-based, and civil discourse, especially in regard to Middle East issues, and opposes ethnic, national, and religious hatreds, including anti-Semitism and anti-Israelism in institutions, disciplines, and communities. We employ academic means to address these issues."[125] SPME also opposes the Boycott, Divestment, and Sanctions movement.[126] Daniel Pipes of the Middle East Forum "has taken credit for funding the projects of several other board members of SPME, including the Brandeis Center and the NGO Monitor."[127]

The World Values Network: While WVN claims to serve "to disseminate universal Jewish values in politics, culture, and media, making the Jewish people a light unto the nations," it is used to promote its founder Shmuley Boteach.[128] He is a reality television star and author of dozens of books, who characterizes himself as America's rabbi. Boteach took out a full-page ad in the *New York Times* in 2015 to denounce National Security Advisor Susan Rice for ignoring the Rwanda genocide in 1994 after she criticized Prime Minister Netanyahu.[129] The ad was widely denounced by other Jewish organizations.[130] In other ads, Boteach has accused Palestinians of embracing child sacrifice.[131] Sheldon Adelson provided

$639,000 to the Network in 2013.¹³² Adelson also backed Boteach when he ran for congress in 2012.¹³³

A long article on Boteach in the Jewish magazine *Tablet* noted that his father was a Jewish immigrant from Iran. It also pointed out that WVN's name on its website appears as "This World: The Values Network," while on tax forms, the name is given as "This World: The Jewish Values Network." The article concludes that this difference exists because "It's as though the very name of the organization reflects Boteach's ambivalence toward the 'Jewish' label, his uncertainty whether he is called to promote Judaism, or to promote himself, to the wider world."¹³⁴ Given Boteach's desire for publicity, it would seem to be the latter.

Friends of Ariel: This group supports Ariel, which was established in 1978 as a settlement in the heart of the West Bank ten miles east of the 1967 borders and only 30 miles from Tel Aviv and Jerusalem. It has grown to a city of 20,000.¹³⁵ Ariel, according to an article in the Israeli newspaper *Haaretz*, has been largely ignored by mainstream Jewish philanthropy, but has received financial support from evangelical Christians.¹³⁶ A story in the Jewish Chronicle, however, says it receives funds from Jewish philanthropists around Los Angeles including real estate developer Larry Field (over a million dollars) and the Milken Family Foundation.¹³⁷

Norman Braman, a billionaire auto dealer, through his foundation, provided over $300,000 to Ariel from 2004 to 2008.¹³⁸ Braman has also largely bankrolled the political career of Florida senator Marco Rubio and was the single biggest funder of his presidential campaign with an estimated $10 million.¹³⁹

American Principles Project: APP is a political action committee (PAC) that contributes to "principled" leaders who advance conservative issues.¹⁴⁰ Articles on its website demonstrate its strong support for Israel and opposition to the Iran nuclear accord.[141] Other writings focused on their outrage over the National Jewish Democratic Council supporting the Iran accord. APP also asserted the opposition to David Friedman, Trump's nominee for ambassador to Israel, was from Muslim groups and "the notorious Jewish pro-Palestinian operatives at J Street."[142] OpenSecrets lists nearly a hundred members of Congress, all Republicans, to whose campaigns APP contributed in 2014.[143] The man listed as treasurer of APP is also president of a company called Electoral Strategies, which received eight payments totaling $4875 from APP during 2016.[144] According to same source, from 2013 to 2014, APP received funding from individuals in the real estate industry, financial services, and other capital and investing companies.[145]

Human Rights Coalition Against Radical Islam: This group claims it seeks to make the world a safer place for everyone by confronting radical political Islam, which it regards as one of the most dangerous ideologies sweeping the world.[146] The group stresses that it is not against Muslims but the political ideology espoused by the radical segment.[147] The chairman of the board of HRCARI justified its creation in an interview by claiming that "The liberal establishment, the Western academy, and the media seem to be controlled by multicultural relativists who have become apologists for Islamic radicalism."[148]

Jewish National Fund: Founded in 1901 to develop land in pre-state Israel, the JNF has invested in parks, reservoirs, dams and land development.[149] While it does not receive funds from the government of Israel, it is tax exempt. After years of refusing to disclose its finances, it revealed in 2015 that is owns property worth $2 billion that comprises 13% of the land in Israel. Its 950 employees worldwide have an average salary of

$80,000.[150] According to its Form 990 for 2014, Ronald Lauder was the chairman of its board, it had revenue of $206 million, expenses of $62 million and its CEO made $463,000 that year.[151]

Jewish Political Education Foundation: This nonprofit organization seeks to eliminate anti-Semitism and advance Zionism by defending Israel and Jewish traditions.[152] In 2011, JPEF participated in an event that celebrated the holiday of Purim at the Iranian UN Mission in New York.[153]

Investigative Project on Terrorism: Founded by Steven Emerson in 1995, the IPT presents itself as a nonprofit research group "recognized as the world's most comprehensive data center on radical Islamic groups."[154] The website also describes Emerson, IPT's executive director and founder, as being "in great demand as one of the most astute, insightful and knowledgeable experts in the world today on the threat and prospects of militant Islamic terrorism."

Emerson displayed his expertise in 2015 on Fox News when he claimed that Birmingham, England was a mostly Muslim city where non-Muslims didn't enter and that in parts of London "there are actually Muslim religious police that actually beat and actually wound anyone who doesn't dress according to Muslim, religious Muslim attire." Those assertions prompted Prime Minister David Cameron to label Emerson a "complete idiot."[155]

According to *The Tennessean* newspaper, IPT also directed money toward a production company called SAE Productions for "management services." SAE Productions lists Emerson himself as its sole officer.[156] In 2008 alone, it received $3.4 million from IPT.[157] ITP's financial backers include Donors Capital Fund ($400,000 from 2007 through 2008),[158] the Becker Foundation ($100,000) and $250,000 from Daniel Pipes's Middle East Forum.[159] According to the Southern

Poverty Law Center, Pipes is anti-Muslim extremist and the Middle East Forum is "a major funder of Muslim-bashers even more radical than himself."[160]

Republican Friends of Israel: A nonprofit organization founded in 2010 in New Jersey that seeks "to generate support for a free and secure Israel among Republican officeholders, candidates and rank and file Republicans."[161] Its website gives little evidence of recent activity however.

The Phyllis Chesler Organization: The website identifies her as "an Emerita Professor of Psychology at City University of New York, best-selling author, a legendary feminist leader, a retired psychotherapist and expert courtroom witness."[162] Her publications focus on the rights of women in the Islamic world, especially in regard to honor killings, as well as supporting banning the burka and head scarfs.[163] She is also a Shillman-Ginsburg Fellow at Daniel Pipes's Middle East Forum.[164] Prior to this, she was also a former director of the Scholars for Peace in the Middle East from 2005 to 2007, an anti-BDS group that had Daniel Pipes on its board.[165]

American Friends of Likud: A not-for-profit American educational organization that claims it has developed "unparalleled relationships" with members of Prime Minister Netanyahu's political party, Likud, based on "a mutual belief in Likud's philosophy."[166] At the same time, AFL's website asserts its name is slightly a misnomer since the organization is not an extension of the Likudparty, but rather directs any money received toward "education programs and events."[167]

AFL hosted a webcast of Prime Minister Benjamin Netanyahu designed to reach the American Jewish community to ask for unity against the nuclear agreement with Iran and to express the agreement's "implications for Israel, the Middle East and the world."[168] According to an article in Buzzfeed, the vast majority of campaign funds of Netanyahu and other Likud politicians are raised in the U.S. with the help of the AFL, which has led several of their trips to Washington, D.C., "where they can fundraise and network with pro-Israel groups."[169]

Pro-Deal Groups

Democracy Alliance: This group is a collection of major donors dedicated to liberal causes. In the 2014 election cycle, 21 DA aligned organizations pledged to spend over $374 million for various liberal groups and causes.[170] George Soros is a major supporter of DA as well as Amber and Steve Mostyn, who are trial lawyers from Houston.[171] More than 120 wealthy Democratic donors, including members of DA, wrote to congress urging the nuclear agreement be approved since rejecting it would "either lead to a nuclear-armed Iran, another costly military campaign, or both."[172]

Center for a New American Security: While CNAS has been described as a "haven for hawkish Democrats," this national defense think tank labels itself as "an independent, bipartisan, nonprofit organization that develops strong, pragmatic, and principled national security and defense policies."[173] It has representation from both political parties among its board members including Richard Armitage, who was Deputy Secretary of State under Colin Powell, Richard Fontaine, a former advisor of Senator John McCain, Madeline Albright, and retired Senator Joe Lieberman (a strong opponent of the deal).[174]

A press release from the organization called the nuclear agreement a "major step forward," stating that its mechanisms would "make it too risky for Iran to pursue a nuclear weapon without being caught and punished."[175]

The organization's website includes a donor list for 2016 with gifts ranging from the hundreds of dollars to half a million, a degree of transparency that few other organizations provide.[176] Defense contractors and other major corporations were significant contributors.

Women's Action for New Directions: WAND seeks to increase women involvement in the goals of eliminating weapons of mass destruction and violence.[177] OpenSecrets.com reports WAND's political donations were made mostly to female Democratic candidates, but only amounted to $11,425 in 2014.[178] WAND has received grants in the neighborhood of $10,000 from the Tides Foundation, which provides grants to accelerate social change "toward a healthy society, one which is founded on principles of social justice, broadly shared economic opportunity, a robust democratic process, and sustainable environmental practices".[179]

National Security Network: NSN was founded in 2006 and ceased operations in March 2016 apparently because of a lack of funding and difficulty carving out a niche in area crowded with similar organizations. It was dedicated toward solutions to national security issues that are based in pragmatism including solving problems with diplomacy alongside allies but also with a military if it's absolutely necessary.[180] It worked with various organizations to try to persuade public officials to seek pragmatic solutions for the United States.[181] Two people involved in the organization were Rand Beers, a longtime national security expert and civil servant who also worked for the Kerry-Edwards campaign in 2004, and former Clinton National Security Adviser Sandy Berger.[182] Beers worked on the National Security Council in the Obama administration and in the Department of Homeland Security as counselor to then Secretary Janet Napolitano.[183] Another NSN official, retired Major General Paul Eaton was featured in an article in *The National Interest* where he said the Iran deal would keep diplomacy in place, while the alternative would be war.[184] He was also quoted in *The Washington Post* as categorizing Senator

Tom Cotton's letter to Iranian leader as "mutinous" act that undermined diplomatic efforts.[185] For 2012, the organization held assets of about $429,000.[186]

Israel Policy Forum: IPS lists its mission to "promote Israel's future as a Jewish and democratic state by advancing a diplomatic resolution to the Arab-Israeli Conflict."[187] It seeks the United States to have a close relationship with Israel, but also be instrumental in a peaceful resolution between the Arabs and Israelis.[188] In 2012 *Haaretz* reported that IPF had "nearly disappeared in influence and presence" but was hoping "to revive itself with some of Jewish life's heavy hitters, people who hint they are frustrated with the seemingly partisan politics of J Street and others" by committing to stay above partisan politics.[189] Alan Solomont, former ambassador to Spain in the Obama administration, was an IPF donor.[190]

Institute for Policy Studies: IPS seeks to encourage those that link "peace, justice, and the environment in the U.S. and globally" through social justice initiatives."[191] It advertises itself as the "first progressive multi-issue think tank" that fights for world security "based on principles of mutual respect, human rights, and international law" and aims to facilitate "true democracy and challenge concentrated wealth, corporate influence, and military power." Other security issues related to Middle East, an IPS fellow, Phyllis Bennis, defended the nuclear agreement in an article in Al Jazeera where she explained how the IAEA inspections worked.[192] IPS lists several years of IRS documents on its website including an IRS Form 990 from 2013 where it reported $1,747,514 in net assets.[193] On its website IPS claims its income is obtained "approximately 75% of our income from private and family donations, about 20% from individual donors, and the remaining 5% from income through events."[194] George Soros's Open

Society Foundation has provided support to IPS.[195] It appears that Soros's foundation donated $260,000 to IPS in 2009[196] and $200,000 the following year.[197]

Appendix D: List of Think Tanks by Political Orientation

Conservative Think Tanks

1. American Enterprise Institute[198]:
   - 225 staff
   - $54.6 million in revenue
   - Donors: Koch Brothers, Richard and Helen DeVos Foundation, Donald and Paula Smith Family Foundation, Searle Freedom Trust, Lynde and Harry Bradley Foundation, and the John M. Olin Foundation
   - Founded 1938
   - Mission: The American Enterprise Institute is a public policy think tank dedicated to defending human dignity, expanding human potential, and building a freer and safer world, committed to making the intellectual, moral, and practical case for expanding freedom, increasing individual opportunity, and strengthening the free enterprise system in America and around the world.

2. Center for Immigration Studies[199]:
   - Staff: 30
   - $2.05 million in revenue (2011)
   - Donors: William H. Donner Foundation, Lynde and Harry Bradley Foundation, Armstrong Foundation, Scaife Family Foundation, Sarah Scaife Foundation, Weiler Foundation, Colcom Foundation, Smith Richardson Foundation, Donors Trust anonymous

donor, Carthage Foundation, John M. Olin Foundation, Jacqueline Hume Foundation, Philip M. McKenna Foundation, Justice Department and Census Bureau.
- Founded 1985
- Mission: providing immigration policymakers, the academic community, news media, and concerned citizens with reliable information about the social, economic, environmental, security, and fiscal consequences of legal and illegal immigration into the United States.

3. Center for Security Policy[200]:
   - Staff: 13
   - Revenue: $4.5 million (2011)
   - Donors: Boeing ($25,000), General Dynamics ($15,000), Lockheed Martin ($15,000), Northrup Grumman ($5000), Raytheon ($20,000), General Electric ($5000), Lynde and Harry Bradley Foundation, Sarah Scaife Foundation
   - Founded 1988
   - Mission: To identify challenges and opportunities likely to affect American security, broadly defined, and to act promptly and creatively to ensure that they are the subject of focused national examination and effective action.

4. Claremont Institute[201]:
   - Staff: 25
   - Revenue: $8.28 million (2015)
   - Donors: Weiler Foundation, Pierre F. and Enid Goodrich Foundation, Hickory Foundation, Philip M. McKenna Foundation, Aequus Institute, Sarah Scaife Foundation, Joyce and Donald Rumsfeld Foundation, Searle Freedom Trust, Roe Foundation, Deramus Foundation, Earhart Foundation, Donors Capital Fund, Paul Singer Foundation

- Founded: 1979
- Mission: The mission of The Claremont Institute is to restore the principles of the American Founding to their rightful, preeminent authority in our national life, teach these principles and their application today, to the brightest young conservative men and women who will, with our help, go on to positions of power and influence in government, the courts, academia, and the media.

5. Foreign Policy Research Institute[202]:
   - Staff: 27
   - Revenue: $1.76 million (2013)
   - Donors: Cotswold Foundation, Robert and Diane Freedman, Stanley and Arlene Ginsburg, John and Debora Haines, John and Josephine Templeton, Edward Bishop, Boeing Company, Raza Bokhari, Donald R. Kardon, Michael and Phebe Novakovic, Savitz Organization, J. Michael Barron, BNY Mellon Wealth Management, Ruth and Bob Bramson, Ahmed Charai, William Conrad, Delaware Investments, Gary Frank, James H. Gately, Susan and Woody Goldberg, Roger Hertog, S.A. Ibrahim, Marina Kats, Marshall W. Pagon, Progressive Group Foundation, Prudent Management Associates, Alan and Louise Reed, Eileen Rosenau, Ed Satell, Adele Schaeffer, Ed and Gail Snitzer
   - Founded: 1955
   - Mission: The Foreign Policy Research Institute is dedicated to bringing the insights of scholarship to bear on the foreign policy and national security challenges facing the United States by educating the public, teaching teachers, training students, and offering ideas to advance U.S. national interests based on a nonpartisan, geopolitical perspective that illuminates contemporary international affairs through the lens of history, geography, and culture.

6. Heritage Foundation[203]:
   - Staff: 275
   - Revenue: $99.9 million (2015)
   - Donors: Koch brothers, Claude R. Lambe Foundation, Donors Trust, Donors Capital Fund
   - Founded: 1973
   - Mission: The mission of The Heritage Foundation is to formulate and promote conservative public policies based on the principles of free enterprise, limited government, individual freedom, traditional American values, and a strong national defense.

7. Hoover Institution on War, Revolution and Peace[204]:
   - Staff: Unavailable
   - Revenue: $69.5 million (2015)
   - Donors: Sarah Scaife Foundation, Howard Charitable Foundation, Walton Family Foundation, John M. Olin Foundation, Lynde and Harry Bradley Foundation, Smith Richardson Foundation, Shelby Cullom Davis Foundation, William E. Simon Foundation, Carthage Foundation, Weiler Foundation, Randolph Foundation, Earhart Foundation, Bochnowski Family Foundation, Searle Freedom Trust, Jacqueline Hume Foundation, William H. Donner Foundation
   - Founded: 1919
   - Mission: the Hoover Institution seeks to improve the human condition by advancing ideas that promote economic opportunity and prosperity, while securing and safeguarding peace for America and all mankind.

8. Hudson Institute[205]:
   - Staff: 72
   - Revenue: $12.3 million (2015)

- Donors: Achelis and Bodman Foundations, Jeffrey Berenson, Lynde and Harry Bradley Foundation, William H. Donner Foundation, Hertog Foundation, Marie Josée and Henry R. Kravis Foundation, John D. and Catherine T. MacArthur Foundation, Charles Stewart Mott Foundation, Sarah Scaife Foundation, Smith Richardson Foundation, Walter P. and Elizabeth M. Stern Foundation, Margaret Whitehead, Charles H. Adler, Thomas C. Barry, Jack David, Rober A. DuPuy, Robert and Ardis James Foudnation, Leeds Family Foundation, Gilbert Scharf Family Foundation, Speyer Family Foundation, Sarah M. Stern, Tate & Lyle, and Allan Tessler
- Founded: 1961
- Mission: Promoting American leadership and global engagement for a secure, free, and prosperous future.

9. Manhattan Institute[206]:

- Staff: 58
- Revenue: $17.2 million (2014)
- Donors: Bradley Foundation, Armstrong Foundation, Bill and Melinda Gates Foundation, Castle Rock Foundation, Earhart Foundation, F.M. Kirby Foundation, Jacqueline Hume Foundation, John Templeton Foundation, John M. Olin Foundation, JM Foundation, Koch Family Foundations, Lynde and Harry Bradley Foundation, Randolph Foundation, Roe Foundation, Scaife Foundation, Shelby Cullom Davis Foundation, Smith Richardson Foundation, Walton Family Foundation, William E. Simon Foundation, William H. Donner Foundation
- Founded: 1977
- Mission: To develop and disseminate new ideas that shape American political culture, foster greater economic choice and individual responsibility.

10. Middle East Forum[207]:
    - Staff: 22
    - Revenue: $4.1 million
    - Donors: Donors Capital Fund ($2.3 m), Bradley Foundation ($305,000), Russell Berrie Foundation (($273,000), Becker Foundation ($355,000), Anchorage Fund and William Rosenwald Family Fund ($2.3 m)
    - Founded: 1990
    - Mission: The Middle East Forum promotes American interests in the Middle East and protects Western values from Middle Eastern threats such as dictatorships, radical ideologies, existential conflicts, border disagreements, corruption, political violence, and weapons of mass destruction.

11. National Center for Policy Analysis[208]:
    - Staff: 41
    - Revenue: $5.2 m (2014)
    - Donors: Armstrong Foundation, Carthage Foundation, Castle Rock Foundation, Charles Koch Charitable Foundation, Claude R. Lambe Charitable Foundation, Earhart Foundation, Exxon Mobil, JM Foundation, Jacqelin Hume Foundation, John M. Olin Foundation, Lynde and Harry Bradley Foundation, Phillip M. McKenna Foundation, roe Foundation, Samuel Roberts Noble Foundation, Sarah Scaife Foundation,
    - Founded: 1983
    - Mission: To develop and promote private, free-market alternatives to government regulation and control, solving problems by relying on the strength of the competitive, entrepreneurial private sector.

12. Pacific Research Institute[209]:
    - Staff: 28
    - Revenue: $6.85 million (2014)
    - Donors: Sarah Scaife Foundation, Searle Freedom Trust, Donors Capital Fund, Lynde and Harry Bradley Foundation, William H. Donner Foundation, Claude R. Lambe Charitable Foundation, Jaquelin Hume Foundation, William E. Simon, John M. Olin Foundation, Lovett and Ruth Peters Foundation.
    - Founded: 1979
    - Mission: To champion freedom, opportunity, and personal responsibility for all individuals by advancing free-market policy solutions

13. Project for the New American Century[210]:
    - Staff: 15
    - Revenue: N/A
    - Donors: Bradley Foundation, John M. Olin Foundation, and Scaife Foundations.
    - Founded: 1997, ceased operations in 2006
    - Mission: To promote American global leadership

Liberal Think Tanks

1. Center on Budget and Policy Priorities[211]:
    - Staff: 119
    - Revenue: $30.8 million (2014)
    - Donors: Annie E. Casey Foundation, JPB Foundation, Kresge Foundation, John D and Catherine T. MacArthur Foundation, David and Lucile Packard Foundation, Sadler Foundation, Stoneman Family Foundation, Walmart Foundation, Wyss Foundation, Robert Wood

Johnson Foundation, Charles Stewart Mott Foundation, Charles H Revson Foundation, Stephen M Silberstein, Bill & Audrey L. Wilder Foundation
- Founded: 1981
- Mission: To pursue federal and state policies designed both to reduce poverty and inequality and to restore fiscal responsibility in equitable and effective ways.

2. Center for American Progress[212]:
    - Staff: 100+
    - Revenue: $45.15 million (2014)
    - Donors: Bill and Melinda Gates Foundation, Ford Foundation, Hutchins Family Foundation, Sandler Foundation, TomKat Charitable Trust, W.K. Kellogg Foundation, William and Flora Hewitt Foundation, Crimson Lion Lavine Family Foundation, Joyce Foundation, Rockefeller Foundation, Schwab Charitable Fund, S. Donald Sussman.
    - Founded: 2003
    - Mission: To improve the lives of all Americans, through bold, progressive ideas, as well as strong leadership and concerted action and to not just change the conversation, but to change the country.

3. Center for Economic and Policy Research[213]:
    - Staff: 20
    - Revenue: $1.3 million (2014)
    - Donors: Annie E. Casey Foundation, Bauman Foundation, Ewing Marion Kauffman Foundation, Mertz Gilmore Foundation, Rauch Foundation, Rockefeller Brothers Fund, Russel Sage Foundation, Sloan Foundation, Streisand Foundation,
    - Founded: 1999

- Mission: To promote democratic debate on the most important economic and social issues that affect people's lives.

4. Center for Progressive Reform[214]:
    - Staff: 50
    - Revenue: $662,000 (2014)
    - Donors: Brenda Blom, Clifford and Joanna Britt, Jake Caldwell, Kathy & Brent Carpenter, Mary Clark, Mike Davis, Lee Flournoy, Mathew Freeman, Goodrich Quality Theaters, James Goodwin, Henry Greenspan, Michael & Rhonda Hissey, Tim Hoffman, Robert E. Kientz, Catherine Jones, Shana Jones, Diana Marmorstein, Jennifer Marshall & Neal Flieger, Mike C. Miller, Beth Newton, Cliff Rechtschaffen, Karen Kramer, Robert M. Elliot, Suzanne Reynolds, Kassie Siegel, Michael and Tina Slack, Donald Slavik, Jim Tozzi, Mikal C. Watts, William O. Whitehurst.
    - Founded: 2002
    - Mission: To protect health, safety, and the environment through analysis and commentary from a network of more than 50 well respected Member Scholars around the nation, volunteering their time and energy.

5. Demos[215]:
    - Staff: 60+
    - Revenue: $8.12 million (2013)
    - Donors: see link at endnote
    - Founded: 2000
    - Mission: To reduce both political and economic inequality and to ensure that all people in this country are given an equal say in our democracy and an equal chance in our economy.

6. Economic Policy Institute[216]:
   - Staff: 44
   - Revenue: $5.6 million (2013)
   - Donors: Berman & Company, Martin Family Foundation. little information on exact source of funding
   - Founded: 1986
   - Mission: To inform and empower individuals to seek solutions that ensure broadly shared prosperity and opportunity.
7. Institute for Policy Studies[217]:
   - Staff: 90+
   - Revenue: $4.2 million (2015)
   - Donors: see endnote for donors
   - Founded 1963
   - Mission: Dedicated to building a more equitable, ecologically sustainable, and peaceful society.
8. Public Citizen[218]:
   - Staff: 30+
   - Revenue: $9.9 million (2015)
   - Donors: David E. Breskin, Elizabeth Cabraser, Mark Chavez, Polly and Randy Cherner, Andrew Friedman, Glenn Garland, Jonathan Gertler, Sherry Gold, Neil Holtzman, Daniel F. Johnson, Ray W. Kahler, Shannon Liss-Riordan, Richard and Marilyn Mazess, Michael Rooney, Daniel Shih, Stephen Silberstein, Steve Skrovan, Shelley Powsner, Gerson Smoger, Jonathan Soros, Roger M. Townsend.
   - Founded: 1971
   - Mission: Advocates for a healthier and more equitable world by making government work for the people and by defending democracy from corporate greed.

9. The Roosevelt Institution[219]:

    - Staff: 32+
    - Revenue: $6.22 million (2014)
    - Donors: Furth Family Foundation, Henry A. Wallace Foundation
    - Founded: 1987
    - Mission: To reimagine America as a place where economic and social rules work for all, hard work is rewarded, everyone participates, and everyone enjoys a fair share of our collective prosperity.

Centrist Think Tanks

1. American Iranian Council[220]:

    - Staff: 40
    - Revenue $120,864 (2010)
    - Donors: Unavailable
    - Founded: 1990
    - Mission: The mission of the AIC provides for a sustainable dialogue and a more comprehensive understanding of US-Iran relations.

2. Aspen Institute[221]:

    - Staff: 350+
    - Revenue: $96.4 million (2014)
    - Donors: Rodel Foundation and the Budinger Family, Renée and Lester Crown/The Crown Family, Gina and Jerry Murdock, Margot and Thomas J. Pritzker Family Foundation, Resnick Family Foundation, David M. Rubenstein, Mary H and Paul Anderson, Mercedes T Bass Charitable Corporation, Bezos Family Foundation, Susan and Richard S. Braddock, Connie

and Jim Calaway, Patricia A. Crown, Jane Harman and the Harman Family Foundation, Robert and Soledad Hurst/Hurst Family Foundation, Leonard and Evelyn Lauder Foundation, William E. Mayer, John P. and Anne Welsh McNulty Foundation, David L Nevins, Mary Anne and James E. Rogers, Ricardo Salinas Foundation, Gillian and Robert Steel, Laurie M. Tisch Illumination Fund, Cheryl and Sam Wyly
   – Founded: 1949
   – Mission: To provide a nonpartisan forum for values-based leadership and the exchange of ideas to provoke, further and improve actions taken in the real world beyond the conference room.

3. Atlantic Council[222]:
   – Staff: 250+
   – Revenue: $22 million (2014)
   – Donors: Adrienne Arsht, Bahaa Hariri, UAE, Melanie Chen, Government of Sweden, Kingdom of Bahrain, MacArthur Foundation, Cheniere Energy, Raytheon, Lockheed Martin, Dentons LLP, Carnegie Corporation of NY, Airbus, MAPA Group, Smith Richardson Foundation, System Capital Management Ltd., Qualcomm Inc., Thomson Reuters, Turkish Ministry of Energy and National Resources, Ukrainian World Congress, US State Department.
   – Founded: 1961
   – Mission: To secure the future and promote constructive leadership and engagement in international affairs based on the Atlantic Community's central role in meeting global challenges.

4. Brookings Institute[223]:
   – Staff: 250+
   – Revenue: $95.3 million (2015)

- Donors: Anne T and Robert M Bass, Bill and Melinda Gates Foundation, William and Flora Hewlett Foundation, Hutchins Family Foundation, JP Morgan Chase, David M Rubenstein, John L Thornton, Cecilia Yen Koo and the Koo family, John D and Catherine T. MacArthur Foundation, Cheryl and Haim Saban
- Founded: 1916
- Mission: To conduct in-depth research that leads to new ideas for solving problems facing society at the local, national and global level.

5. Carnegie Endowment for International Peace[224]:
    - Staff: 150+
    - Revenue: $30.9 million (2015)
    - Donors: William and Flora Hewlett Foundation, Catherine James Paglia/Robert and Ardis James Foundation, Robert and Mary Carswell, John D and Catherine T MacArthur Foundation, Henry H Arnold, William and Ian Donaldson, Patricia House, Walter B Kielholz, Scott and Laura Malkin, Ken Olivier and Laura Malkin, Ken Olivier and Angela Nomellini, Peter G. Peterson Foundation, Bernard L Schwartz, George W and Pamela M. Siguler, Alfred P Sloan Foundation, Stanton Foundation.
    - Founded: 1910
    - Mission: To advance the cause of peace through analysis and development of fresh policy ideas and direct engagement and collaboration with decisionmakers in government, business, and civil society.

6. Center for Strategic and International Studies[225]:
    - Staff: 250+
    - Revenue: $44.5 million (2015)
    - Donors: Richard Armitage, Othman Benjelloun, Erskine Bowles, William E. Brock, Harold Brown,Zbigniew

Brzezinski, Carlos A. Bulgheroni, Sue M. Cobb, William S. Cohen, Lester Crozn, William M Daley, Andreas Dracopoulos, Stanley F. Druckenmiller, Martin Edelman, Jonathan Fairbanks, Henrietta H Fore, Michael P. Galvin, Helene D Gayle, Maurice R Greenberg, John Hammergreen, Linda W Hart, Benjamin W Heineman Jr., John B Hess, Carla A Hills, Elizabeth Holmes, Seok Hyun Hong, Ray L Hunt, Kazuo Inamori, E Neville Isdell, James L Jones, William T Keevan, Muhtar Kent, Fred Khosravi, Ronald Kirk, Henry A Kissinger, Kenneth G Langone, Howard Leach, W James MCNerney Jr., Sam Nunn, Joseph S. Nye Jr., Leon Panetta, Thomas J Pritzker, Charles A Sanders, Bob Schieffer, Brent Scowcroft, Andrew C. Taylor, Rex Tillerson, Frances F. Townsend, Romesh Wadhwani.
- Founded: 1962
- Mission: Dedicated to providing strategic insights and policy solutions to help decision-makers chart a course toward a better world.

7. Constitution Project[226]:

- Staff: 12
- Revenue: $1.36 million (2014)
- Donors: Bauman Foundation, Blum Kovler Foundation, Brightwater Fund, Catherine B Reynolds Foundation, Frank and Denise Quattrone Foundation, Gannett Foundation, Herb Block Foundation, John D and Catherine T MacArthur Foundation, Montpelier Foundation, Open Society Foundations, Rockefeller Brothers Foundation, Ted Stevens Foundation, Wallace Global Fund

- Founded: 1997
- Mission: To foster consensus-based solutions to the most difficult constitutional challenges of our time by bringing together policy experts and legal practitioners from across the political spectrum.

8. Corporation for Enterprise Development[227]:
   - Staff: 70+
   - Revenue: $16.4 million (2014)
   - Donors: see endnote for list of individual donors
   - Founded: 1979
   - Mission: To advance economic opportunity for all through responsive policy change at all levels of government and empower low-and moderate-income people to build wealth through innovative practical solutions.

9. Council on Foreign Relations[228]:
   - Staff: 200+
   - Revenue: $62.3 million (2015)
   - Donors: see endnote for list of donors
   - Founded: 1921
   - Mission: To be a resource for its members, government officials, business executives, journalists, educators and students, civic and religious leaders, and other interested citizens in order to help them better understand the world and the foreign policy choices facing the United States and other countries.

10. Committee for Economic Development[229]:
    - Staff: 40+
    - Revenue: $4.7 million (2014)
    - Donors: see endnote for full list of donors

- Founded: 1942
- Mission: To deliver well-researched analysis and reasoned solutions to our nation's most critical issues.

11. Information Technology and Innovation Foundation[230]:
    - Staff: 19
    - Revenue: $3.4 million (2015)
    - Donors: unavailable
    - Founded: 2006
    - Mission: To formulate, evaluate, and promote policy solutions that accelerate innovation and boost productivity to spur growth, opportunity, and progress and provide policymakers around the world with high-quality information, analysis, and recommendations they can trust.

12. New America Foundation[231]:
    - Staff: 200+
    - Revenue: $25.8 million (2015)
    - Donors: see endnote
    - Founded: 1999
    - Mission: To renew American politics, prosperity, and purpose in the digital age.

13. Resources for the Future[232]:
    - Staff: 135+
    - Revenue: $12.9 million (2015)
    - Donors: Gregory Alexander, Mark Gallogly, Heising Simons Foundation, Linden Trust for Conservation, Litterman Family Foundation, Paul G Allen Family Foundation, S.D. Bechtel Jr. Foundation, Roger and Vicki Sant, Anthony Bernhardt, W Bowman Cutter, G Unger Vetlesen Foundation, Peter Kagan, Lawrence H. Linden, Merck Family Fund, Samuel Freeman Charitable Trust.

- Founded: 1952
- Mission: Conduct rigorous economic research and analysis to help leaders make better decisions and craft smarter policies about natural resources and the environment.

14. Henry L. Stimson Center[233]:
    - Staff: 62
    - Revenue: $5.7 million
    - Donors: Refer endnote
    - Founded: 1989
    - Mission: To solve the world's greatest threats to security and prosperity through research that serves as a roadmap to address borderless threats through collective action.

15. RAND Corporation[234]:
    - Staff: 1875
    - Revenue: $293.3 million (2015)
    - Donors: Harold and Colene Brown Family Foundation, Estate of John and Carol Cazier, Marcia and Frank C Cartucci, Jacques E and Carine Dubois, Diane P and Gullford Glazer Fund, Hagopian Family Foundation Mary Ann and Kip Hagopian, Rita E Hauser, Karen Katen Foundation, Janine and Peter Lowy, Y&S Nazarian Family Foundation, Susan F and Donald B Rice, Maxine and Eugene S. Rosenfeld, Anne and James F Rosenberg, Leonard D Schaeffer, Charles J Zwick.
    - Founded: 1948
    - Mission: To help improve policy and decision making through research and analysis.

16. The Stanley Foundation[235]:
    - Staff: 19
    - Revenue: $11.2 million (2014)
    - Donors: unavailable

- Founded: 1956
- Mission: The Stanley Foundation advances multilateral action to create fair, just, and lasting solutions to critical issues of peace and security.

17. Urban Institute[236]:
    - Staff: 400
    - Revenue: $95.3 million (2015)
    - Donors: Laura and John Arnold Foundation, Annie E Casey Foundation, Bill and Melinda Gates Foundation, Robert Wood Johnson Foundation, John D and Catherine T MacArthur Foundation, Robert C Pozen and the Ashurt Foundation, Rockefeller Foundation, Peter G Peterson Foundation, Kresge Foundation.
    - Founded: 1968
    - Mission: Urban's mission is to open minds, shape decisions, and offer solutions through economic and social policy research.

18. Wilson Center[237]:
    - Staff: 100+
    - Revenue: $32.1 million (2015)
    - Donors: Alama Gildenhorn and Joseph B, Linda B Mercuro and Tobla G, Thomas R Nides, Melba Bucksbaum and Raymond Learsy, Lester Crown, Judi Flom, Leo E Zickler, Sander R Gerber, Jane W Stetson, John E Bryson, Michael Jenkins.
    - Founded: 1968
    - Mission: The Wilson Center, chartered by Congress as the official memorial to President Woodrow Wilson, is the nation's key nonpartisan policy forum for tackling global issues through independent research and open dialogue to inform actionable ideas for the policy community.

Libertarian Think Tanks

1. Ayn Rand Institute[238]:
   - Staff: 49
   - Revenue: $11 million (2015)
   - Donors: unavailable
   - Founded: 1985
   - Mission: ARI fosters a growing awareness, understanding and acceptance of Ayn Rand's philosophy, Objectivism, in order to create a culture whose guiding principles are reason, rational self-interest, individualism and laissez-faire capitalism—a culture in which individuals are free to pursue their own happiness.

2. Atlas Economic Research Foundation[239]:
   - Staff: 31+
   - Revenue: $11.3 million (2015)
   - Donors: Luis H Ball, Scott and Vanessa Barbee, Lynde and Harry Bradley Foundation, Bruni Foundation, Ravenel and Beth Curry, Arthur Dantchik, John Dobson Foundation, Peter and Cynthia Goettler, Dan Grossman, Philip Harvey, John P. Kayser, George and Inez Lengvari, Frayda and Ken Levy, Lowndes Foundation, Gerry Ohrstrom, Borut and Nadine Prah, Ronald Rankin, Chris and Melodie Rufer, Sarah Scaife Foundation, Smith Family Foundation, Thomas W Smith Foundation, John Templeton Foundation, Jeff and Janine Yass, George M. Yeager, Fred and Sandra Young.
   - Founded: 1981
   - Mission: To strengthen the worldwide freedom movement by cultivating a highly effective and expansive network that inspires and incentivizes all committed individuals and organizations to achieve lasting impact.

3. Cascade Policy Institute[240]:
   - Staff: 4+
   - Revenue: $622,288 (2014)
   - Donors: Donors Capital Fund, Donors Trust, Roe Foundation, Jacquelin Hume,
   - Founded: 1991
   - Mission: Cascade's mission is to develop and promote public policy alternatives that foster individual liberty, personal responsibility and economic opportunity.

4. CATO Institute[241]:
   - Staff: 122
   - Revenue: $28.6 million (2015)
   - Donors: Barney Family Foundation, Armstrong Foundation, Barrington Foundation, Helen W Bell Foundation, Betty & Daniel Bloomfield Fund, Lynde and Harry Bradley Foundation, Brinson Foundation, Carthage Foundation, B & E Collins Foundation, James Deering Danielson Foundation, William H Donner Foundation, George Edward Durell Foundation, Farrell Family Foundation, Gibbs Family Foundation, Gleason Family Foundation, Pierre F & Enid Goodrich Foundation, Grover Hermann Foundation, Holman Foundation, Hunt Family Foundation, John E and Sue M Jackson Charitable Trust, Robert & Ardis James Foundation, JW and Ida M Jameson Foundation, Ewing Marion Kauffman Foundation, Margaret H and James E Kelley Foundation, Kilts Family Foundation, Vernon K Krieble Foundation, Charles Koch Foundation, Marcus Foundation, Charles Maxfield and Gloria F. Parrish Foundation, John William Pope Foundation, Sarah Scaife Foundation, Searle Freedom Trust, Smith Family Foundation, Stiles Nicholson Foundation,

Suntrust Foundation, John Templeton Foundation, Triad Foundation, Walton Family Foundation.
- Founded: 1977
- Mission: The mission of the Cato Institute is to originate, disseminate, and increase understanding of public policies based on the principles of individual liberty, limited government, free markets, and peace.

5. Competitive Enterprise Institute[242]:
   - Staff: 40
   - Revenue: $7.8 million (2015)
   - Donors: Ambassador Boyden Gray, Stanford Rothschild, Stephen Modzelewski, Fred Young, Jean Claude Gruffat, Robert Luddy, Jack France, Lester Weindling, Arcadio Casilllas, James Curley, Forrest G. Hoglund, Angelo Puglisi.
   - Founded: 1984
   - Mission: To advance the principles of limited government, free enterprise, and individual liberty and promote both freedom and fairness by making good policy good politics.

6. Foundation for Economic Education[243]:
   - Staff: 26
   - Revenue: $5.2 million (2015)
   - Donors: Charles Koch Foundation, Charles Koch Institute
   - Founded: 1946
   - Mission: FEE strives to bring about a world in which the economic, ethical, and legal principles of a free society are familiar and credible to the rising generation.

7. Foundation for Rational Economics and Education[244]:
   - Staff: N/A
   - Revenue: N/A

- Donors: the Rodney Fund
- Founded: 1976
- Mission: Dedicated to public education on the principles of free-market economics, sound money and limited government.

8. Goldwater Institute[245]:

   - Staff: 31
   - Revenue: $3.9 million
   - Donors: Eric Crown, Freyda Levy, Bob Levy, James O'Connor, Carolyn Cox, Jeffrey Singer, Roy Miller, Barry Asmus, Tom Jenney,
   - Founded: 1988
   - Mission: The Goldwater Institute drives results by working daily in courts, legislatures and communities to defend and strengthen the freedom guaranteed to all Americans in the constitutions of the United States and all fifty states.

9. Heartland Institute[246]:

   - Staff: 30
   - Revenue: $4.3 million (2015)
   - Donors: Barabra and Barre Seid Foundation, Lynde and Harry Bradley Foundation, Exxon Mobil, Walton Family Foundation, Sarah Scaife Foundation, Charlotte and Walter Kohler Charitable Trust, Jacqueline Hume Foundation, Rodney Fund, JM Foundation, Castle Rock Foundation, Roe Foundation, John M. Olin Foundation, Claude R Lambe Charitable Foundation, Charles G Koch Charitable Foundation, Armstrong Foundation, Hickory Foundation, Carthage Foundation.
   - Founded: 1984

- Mission: To discover, develop, and promote free-market solutions to social and economic problems.

10. Independent Institute[247]:
    - Staff: 36
    - Revenue: $2.7 2013
    - Donors: unidentified
    - Founded: 1986
    - Mission: To boldly advance peaceful, prosperous, and free societies grounded in a commitment to human worth and dignity.

11. Mackinac Center for Public Policy[248]:
    - Staff: 100
    - Revenue: $4.9 million (2014)
    - Donors: Lynde and Harry Bradley Foundation, Castle Rock Foundation, DeVos Foundation, Herbert H and Grace A Dow Foundation, Dunn's Foundation for the Advancement of Right Thinking, Earhart Foundation, Rolin M Gerstacker Foundation, Herrick Foundation, Hickory Foundation, Jaquelin Hume Foundation, Charles G Koch Foundation, Claude R Lambe Charitable Foundation, Orville and Ruth Merillat Foundation, Ruth and Lovett Peters Foundation, Edgar and Elsa Prince Foundation, Rodney Fund, Roe Foundation, Sarah Scaife Foundation, Walton Family Foundation
    - Founded: 1987
    - Mission: The Mackinac Center for Public Policy is a nonpartisan research and educational institute dedicated to improving the quality of life for all Michigan citizens by promoting sound solutions to state and local policy questions.

12. Mercatus Center[249]:

    - Staff: 170
    - Revenue: $20.6 million (2013)
    - Donors: DonorsTrust, Donors Capital Fund, Charles G Koch Foundation, David H Koch Foundation, John Templeton Foundation, Bradley Foundation
    - Founded: 1980
    - Mission: The Mercatus Center is a university-based research center dedicated to bridging the gap between academic research and public policy problems

13. Mises Institute[250]:

    - Staff: 130+
    - Revenue: $4.1 million (2015)
    - Donors: unavailable
    - Founded: 1982
    - Mission: Teaches the scholarship of Austrian economics, freedom, and peace, in the liberal intellectual tradition of Ludwig von Mises (1881–1973) and Murray N. Rothbard (1926–1995), seeking a profound and radical shift in the intellectual climate: away from statism and toward a private property order.

14. Reason Foundation[251]:

    - Staff: 56
    - Revenue: $11.1 million (2013)
    - Donors: Unavailable
    - Founded: 1968
    - Mission: Reason Foundation advances a free society by developing, applying, and promoting libertarian principles, including individual liberty, free markets, and the rule of law.

15. Show Me Institute[252]:

- Staff: 20+
- Revenue: $2.4 million (2015)
- Donors: Cato Institute, Donors trust, Donors Capital Fund, Bradley Foundation, Roe Foundation, Claude R Lambe Charitable Foundation, Charles G Koch Charitable Foundation.
- Founded: 2005
- Mission: Dedicated to promoting free markets and individual liberty.

Average staff and revenue*

Category	Staff	Revenue $ million	# think tanks
Conservative	74.18	19.70	11
Liberal	60.55	12.44	9
Centrist	245.67	47.43	18
Libertarian	60.36	8.46	14

*In the conservative category, two think tanks were ignored for calculation of averages as the number of staff for "Hoover Institution on War, Revolution and Peace" was not available while the Revenue for "Project for the New American Century" was not available

In the Libertarian category one think tank, namely, "Foundation for Rational Economics and Education" was left out as numbers for staff and revenue were not available

Appendix E: List of Over 70 Organizations Supporting the JCPOA

The over 70 groups that signed a public statement in support of the JCPOA fell into several broad categories:

1. Jewish (4)

Americans for Peace Now
J Street
Jewish Voice for Peace
The Shalom Center

2. Arab or Iranian

Arab American Institute
NIAC Action
Public Affairs Alliance of Iranian Americans (PAAIA)

3. Religious/Spiritual/Christian (29)

Adorers of the Blood of Christ
Adrian Dominican Sisters
American Friends Service Committee
American Values Network
Catholics in Alliance for the Common Good
Church World Service
Conference of Major Superiors of Men
Franciscan Sisters of the Poor JPIC
Intercommunity Peace and Justice Center
Justice and Peace Committee of the Sisters of St. Francis of Philadelphia
Justice Team—Sisters of Mercy of the Americas
Justice, Peace and Integrity of Creation Office
Leadership Conference of Women Religious
Maryknoll Office for Global Concerns
Medical Mission Sisters
Mennonite Central Committee U.S.
National Council of Churches
NETWORK, A National Catholic Social Justice Lobby

Pax Christi International
Pax Christi USA
Sinsinawa Dominicans
Sisters of Charity, BVM
Sisters of the Holy Cross—Congregation Justice Committee
Sisters, Home Visitors of Mary
Society of Helpers—US Province
The Network of Spiritual Progressives
Unitarian Universalist Association
United Methodist Church, General Board of Church and Society

4. Media (4)

Brave New Films
Daily Kos
ReThink Media
Sojourners

5. Democrats (2)

Democrats.com
Progressive Democrats of America

6. Political advocacy groups (25)

Campaign for America's Future
CASA
Center for International Policy
Citizens for Global Solutions
CODEPINK
Congregation of Notre Dame USA Peace and Justice Office
Council for a Livable World
CREDO

Demand Progress
Global Exchange
Historians Against War
IPS, New Internationalism Project
Just Foreign Policy
MoveOn.org
National Organization for Women
National Security Network
People Demanding Action
U.S. Labor Against the War (USLAW)
United for Peace and Justice
United States Student Association
US Action
Veterans For Peace
VoteVets.org
Win Without War
Women's Action for New Directions

7. **Arms control groups (6)**

Center for Arms Control and Nonproliferation
Global Zero
Nuclear Age Peace Foundation
Peace Action
Peace Action West
Physicians for Social Responsibility

APPENDIX F: LIST OF ISLAMOPHOBIC ORGANIZATIONS

Table AF.1 Islamophobic Organizations

As identified by the Southern Poverty Law Center and the Council on American–Islamic Relations

Name	Established	After 9/11/2001	State
Abstraction Fund	2006[253]	✓	NY
ACLJ	1990[254]		DC
Act for America	2007[255]	✓	VA
Allegheny Foundation	1953[256]		PA
American Defence League[257]	2010	✓	
American Family Association	1977[258]		MS
American Freedom Defense Initiative	2010[259]	✓	TX
American Freedom Law Center	2012[260]	✓	
American Islamic Forum for Democracy	2003[261]	✓	AZ
American Islamic Leadership Coalition	2010[262]	✓	AZ
American Public Policy Alliance	2009[263]	✓	MI
Americans for Peace and Tolerance	2008[264]	✓	MA
Atlas Shrugs[265]	4/10/2005	✓	NY
Bare Naked Islam	2008[266]	✓	(Blog)
Casa D'Ice Signs[267]	NA		PA
Center for Security Policy	1988[268]		DC
Center for the Study of Political Islam	NA[269]		TN
Christian Action Network[270]	1990		VA
Christian Guardians[271]	NA		CA
Citizens for National Security	NA		FL
Citizenwarrior.com	Oct 2001	✓	TN
Clarion Project	2006[272]	✓	DC
Committee for Accuracy in Middle East Reporting	1982		MA
Concerned Women for America	1979		DC
Counter Jihad Coalition[273]	2015[274]	✓	CA
Counter Jihadist Coalition of Southern California[275]	NA		CA
Counter Terrorism Operations Center	2006[276]	✓	FL
David Horowitz Freedom Center	1988		CA
Donors Capital Fund	1999[277]		VA
Eagle Forum	1972[278]		IL

(*continued*)

(continued)

Name	Established	After 9/11/2001	State
F.M. Kirby Foundation	1931[279]		DE
Faith Freedom	Oct 2001	✓	DC
Family Security Matters[280]	2003[281]	✓	DC
Florida Family Association	1987[282]		FL
Former Muslims United	2009[283]	✓	CA
Fox News Channel	1996[284]		NY
Investigative Project on Terrorism	1995[285]		DC
Islamthreat.com[286]	2011	✓	CA
Jihad Watch	2003[287]	✓	CA
Joyce and Donald Rumsfeld Foundation	1985[288]		DC
Lynde and Harry Bradley Foundation	1942		WI
Middle East Forum	1990[289]		PA
Middle East Media Research Institute	1998[290]		DC
National Christian Foundation	1982		GA
National Review	1955[291]		NY
Oak Initiative	NA		SC
Pamelageller.com[292]	9/12/2005	✓	
Radio Jihad[293]	2008	✓	NY
Randolph Foundation	1991[294]		VA
Russell Berrie Foundation	1985[295]		NJ
Sharia Awareness Action Network[296]	2011	✓	DC
Silver bullet gun oil[297]	2006	✓	VA
Straight Way of Grace Ministry	2001[298] 2005[299]	✓	FL
Sultan Knish (blog by Daniel Greenfield)	2005	✓	NY
Tennessee Freedom Coalition[300]	2011	✓	TN
Thereligionofpeace.com	2002	✓	GA
Understanding the Threat	2012[301]	✓	
United States of America Defence League[302]	2012	✓	

(continued)

(continued)

Name	Established	After 9/11/2001	State
United States Defense League[303,304,305]	2012	✓	NC
United West	2007[306]	✓	FL
Washington Times	1982[307]		DC

Appendix G: Form 990 Information for Major Organizations

Table AG.1 Revenue and Top Salaries for Leading Nonprofit Associations Involved in the Iran Nuclear Agreement Debate

Arms Control Association

Year (ending 6/30)	Revenue	Top salary	Number making over 400K
2014	1,356,877	110,000	0
2013	1,119,926	110,000	0
2012	1,959,593	110,000	0
2011	1,501,978	106,416	0
2010	1,330,260	84,460	0
2009	880,882	83,234	0
2008	770,606	87,000	0
2007	709,041	78,000	0
2006	970,809	78,000	0
2005	984,688	78,000	0
2004	621,820	78,000	0
2003	532,032	78,000	0
2002	659,977	78,000	0
2001	610,141	75,000	0

Center for a New American Security

Year (ending 6/30)[a]	Revenue	Top salary	Number making over 400K
2015 FY ending 9/30	8,787,730	310,412	0
2014 FQ ending 9/30	1,329,249	0	0
2014 FY ending 6/30	6,014,305	248,987	0
2013	4,182,730	264,224	0
2012	5,337,335	255,218	0
2011	6,053,020	232,177	0
2010	4,398,109	234,583	0
2009	6,126,312	271,587	0
2008	6,396,744	250,001	0
2007	2,577,680	102,770	0

[a] The Org changed its FY in 2014 from ending on 6/30 of each year to ending on 9/30 hence FY 2014 has an extra 990 filed for Final Quarter (from 1 July 2014 to 30 Sep 2014) of FY 2014. The rest of the table is for FYs ending on 6/30

Friends Committee on National Legislation

Year (ending 6/30)	Revenue	Top salary	Number making over 400 K
2015	3,145,300	NA	NA
2014	2,084,362	148,052	0
2013	3,126,751	2413	0
2012	1,613,094	122,996	0
2011	1,469,149	162,746	0
2010	1,469,211	113,466	0
2009	1,619,884	100,195	0
2008	2,465,571	34,984	0
2007	1,382,177	39,915	0
2006	1,479,241	94,550	0
2005	1,326,497	101,259	0

The Israel Project

Year (ending 9/30)	Revenue	Top salary	Number making over 400 K
2014	6,601,767	425,638	1
2013	5,901,857	186,931	0
2012	2,880,352	217,297	0
2011	19,269,302	225,323	0
2010	6,958,215	229,662	0
2009	4,852,176	179,092	0
2008	8,351,312	207,809	0
2007	3,912,245	200,000	0
2006	6,088,157	200,000	0
2005	3,418,597	203,846	0
2004	4,337,622	48,462	0
2003	1,821,787	0	0

National Security Network

Year (ending 12/31)	Revenue	Top salary	Number making over 400 K
2014	1,180,332	NA	0
2013	666,968	124,793	0
2012	743,500	140,000	0
2011	1,191,240	140,000	0
2010	873,316	140,000	0
2009	1,008,638	126,000	0
2008	1,231,717	128,326	0
2007	797,319	88,542	0
2006	174,493	36,350	0

Secure America Now Foundation

Year (ending 12/31)	Revenue	Top salary	Number making over 400 K
2013	75,930	0	0
2012	30,074	0	0
2011	47,400	0	0

The income stats for Secure America Now are based on forms 990EZ

The Washington Institute

Year (ending 12/31)	Revenue	Top salary	Number making over 400 K
2007	120,573	0	0
2006	712,548	100,839	0
2005	866,212	220,802	0

According to the IRS website The Washington Institute's tax exemption was revoked on 15 May 2011

Notes

1. The provisions of this Resolution do not constitute provisions of this JCPOA.
2. Government officials' for the U.S. means senior officials of the U.S. Administration.
3. Iran will permit the IAEA to share the content of the enrichment and enrichment R&D plan, as submitted as part of the initial declaration, with the Joint Commission participants.
4. For the purpose of this Annex, non-gaseous centrifuge uranium isotope separation-related research and development or production will include laser isotope separation systems, electromagnetic isotope separation systems, chemical exchange systems, gaseous diffusion systems, vortex and aerodynamic systems, and other such processes that separate uranium isotopes.

5. For the purposes of EU legislation, "Iranian person, entity or body" means:

   1. The state of Iran or any public authority thereof;
   2. Any natural person in, or resident in, Iran;
   3. Any legal person, entity or body having its registered office in Iran;
   4. Any legal person, entity or body, inside or outside Iran, owned or controlled directly or indirectly by one or more of the above mentioned persons or bodies.

6. The headings and subheadings in this Annex are for descriptive purposes only.
7. For the purposes of this Annex, the term "associated services" means any service—including technical assistance, training, insurance, re-insurance, brokering, transportation or financial service—necessary and ordinarily incident to the underlying activity for which sanctions have been lifted pursuant to this JCPOA.
8. Unless specifically provided otherwise, the sanctions lifting described in this Section does not apply to transactions that involve persons still subject to restrictive measures and is without prejudice to sanctions that may apply under legal provisions other than those referred to in Sect. 1. Nothing in this JCPOA reflects a change in Iran's position on EU sanctions.
9. Unless specifically provided otherwise, the sanctions lifting described in this Section does not apply to transactions that involve persons still subject to restrictive measures and is without prejudice to sanctions that may apply under legal provisions other than those referred to in Sect. 1. Nothing in this JCPOA reflects a change in Iran's position on EU sanctions.
10. The sanctions that the United States will cease to apply, and subsequently terminate, or modify to effectuate the termination of, pursuant to its commitment under Sect. 4 are those

directed toward non-U.S. persons. For the purposes of Sects. 4, 6, and 7 of this JCPOA, the term "non-U.S. person" means any individual or entity, excluding (1) any United States citizen, permanent resident alien, entity organized under the laws of the United States or any jurisdiction within the United States (including foreign branches), or any person in the United States, and (2) any entity owned or controlled by a U.S. person. For the purposes of (3) of the preceding sentence, an entity is "owned or controlled" by a U.S. person if the U.S. person: (a) holds a 50 percent or greater equity interest by vote or value in the entity; (b) holds a majority of seats on the board of directors of the entity; or (c) otherwise controls the actions, policies, or personnel decisions of the entity. U.S. persons and U.S.-owned or -controlled foreign entities will continue to be generally prohibited from conducting transactions of the type permitted pursuant to this JCPOA, unless authorized to do so by the U.S. Department of the Treasury's Office of Foreign Assets Control (OFAC).

11. All citations to statutes and Executive orders included in this JCPOA refer to the statute or Executive order as amended as of the conclusion date of this JCPOA, including: the Iran Sanctions Act of 1996 (ISA), as amended by Section 102 of the Comprehensive Iran Sanctions, Accountability, and Divestment Act of 2010 (CISADA) and Sections 201–207 and 311 of the Iran Threat Reduction and Syria Human Rights Act of 2012 (TRA); CISADA, as amended by Sections 214–216, 222, 224, 311–312, 402–403 and 605 of TRA and Section 1249 of the Iran Freedom and Counter-Proliferation Act of 2012 (IFCA); the National Defense Authorization Act for Fiscal Year 2012 (NDAA), as amended by Sections 503–504 of TRA and Section 1250 of IFCA; Executive Order (E.O.) 13622, as amended by Section 15 of E.O. 13628 and Section 16 of E.O. 13645. The citations listed in Sect. 4 include authorities under which secondary sanctions will no longer apply as a result of actions described in Sect. 4.8.1.

12. Removal of NIOC from the SDN List, as provided for in Sect. 4.8.1, will include resolution of related designations and determinations.
13. See footnote 3 for the meaning of "associated services."
14. This commitment in Sect. 4.4.1 is based on the port operator(s) of Bandar Abbas no longer being controlled by a person on the SDN List.
15. To give effect to the measures described in this Sect. 5.1, the United States will license activities that do not involve any person on the SDN List and are otherwise consistent with applicable U.S. laws and regulations, including but not limited to the Export Administration Act, the Federal Food, Drug and Cosmetic Act and the Iran–Iraq Arms Nonproliferation Act.
16. Licenses issued in furtherance of Sect. 5.1.1 will include appropriate conditions to ensure that licensed activities do not involve, and no licensed aircraft, goods, or services are re-sold or re-transferred to, any person on the SDN List. Should the United States determine that licensed aircraft, goods, or services have been used for purposes other than exclusively civil aviation end-use, or have been re-sold or re-transferred to persons on the SDN List, the United States would view this as grounds to cease performing its commitments under Sect. 5.1.1 in whole or in part.
17. For the purposes of Sect. 5.1.2 of this JCPOA, a non-U.S. entity is owned or controlled by a U.S. person if the U.S. person: (1) holds a 50 per cent or greater equity interest by vote or value in the entity; (2) holds a majority of seats on the board of directors of the entity; or (3) otherwise controls the actions, policies, or personnel decisions of the entity.
18. Unless specifically provided otherwise, the sanctions lifting described in this Section does not apply to transactions that involve persons on the SDN List and is without prejudice to sanctions that may apply under legal provisions other than those cited in Sect. 4. Nothing in this JCPOA reflects a change in Iran's position on U.S. sanctions.

19. For the purposes of the cessation of application of the provisions set out in Sects. 4.1.1–4.1.7, the effects described for non-U.S. financial institutions extend to the activities outside of U.S. jurisdiction of international financial institutions.
20. Non-U.S., non-Iranian financial institutions engaging in transactions with Iranian financial institutions (including the Central Bank of Iran) not appearing on the SDN List will not be exposed to sanctions as a result of those Iranian financial institutions engaging in transactions or banking relationships involving Iranian individuals and entities, including financial institutions, on the SDN List, provided that the non-U.S., non-Iranian financial institution does not conduct or facilitate, and is not otherwise involved in, those specific transactions or banking relationships with the Iranian individuals and entities, including financial institutions, on the SDN List.
21. The effects described in Sect. 7.5 with respect to the port operator(s) of Bandar Abbas are based on the port operator(s) of Bandar Abbas no longer being controlled by a person on the SDN List.
22. *Denotes Iranian financial institutions and individuals and entities identified as GOI by the Office of Foreign Assets Control (OFAC). U.S. persons and foreign entities owned or controlled by a U.S. person will continue to be prohibited from transactions with these individuals and entities, pursuant to the Iranian Transactions and Sanctions Regulations.
23. This Annex is only for the purpose of determining the sequence of implementation of the commitments described in this JCPOA and annexes thereto and does not restrict or expand the scope of these commitments.
24. The sanctions that the United States will cease to apply are those directed toward non-U.S. persons, as described in Sect. 4 of Annex II.
25. The provisions of this Resolution do not constitute provisions of this JCPOA.

26. The Jewish Institute for National Security of America. 2015. "About." http://www.jinsa.org/about (Accessed on 6/1/2017).
27. Farhi, Paul. 2016. "Bill Kristol Knows His Predictions Have Been Bad But He's Going to Keep Making Them." *The Washington Post.* https://www.washingtonpost.com/lifestyle/style/bill-kristol-knows-his-predictions-have-been-bad-but-hes-going-to-keep-making-them/2016/02/17/3a301680-d4d4-11e5-9823-02b905009f99_story.html?utm_term=.4238040e7a22 (Accessed on 6/1/2017).
28. Kristal, William, and Dr. Michael Makovsky. 2015. "JINSA CEO Dr. Michael Makovsky and William Kristal on the Consequences of an Iran Deal in The Weekly Standard." *JINSA.* http://www.jinsa.org/jinsa-media/jinsa-ceo-dr-michael-makovsky-and-william-kristol-consequences-iran-deal-weekly-standard (Accessed on 6/1/2017).
29. Guttman, Nathan. 2012. "JINSA Leadership in Flux After Ouster." *Forward.* http://forward.com/news/149750/jinsa-leadership-in-flux-after-ouster/ (Accessed on 6/1/2017).
30. Stanton, John. 2015. "Israel's JINSA Earns Return on Investment: 190 American Admirals and Generals Appose Iran Deal." *Counterpunch.* http://www.counterpunch.org/2015/08/28/israels-jinsa-earns-return-on-investment-190-americans-admirals-and-generals-oppose-iran-deal/ (Accessed on 6/1/2017).
31. Emergency Committee for Israel. 2015. "About Emergency Committee for Israel." http://www.committeeforisrael.com/about (Accessed on 6/1/2017).
32. Ibid.
33. Pollak, Noah. 2015. "ECI Statement on Iran Framework Agreement." *Committee for Israel.* http://www.committeeforisrael.com/media (Accessed on 6/1/2017).
34. Lipton, Eric. 2015. "G.O.P.'s Israel Support Deepens s Political Contributions Shift." *The Washington Post.* https://www.nytimes.com/2015/04/05/us/politics/gops-israel-support-deepens-as-political-contributions-shift.html (Accessed on 6/1/2017).

35. Pro-Publica. 2011. "990 2010 Emergency Committee for Israel." http://www.propublica.org/documents/item/406797-990-2010-emergency-committee-for-israel (Accessed on 6/1/2017).
36. Right Web. 2015. "Emergency Committee for Israel." http://rightweb.irc-online.org/profile/emergency_committee_for_israel/ (Accessed on 6/1/2017).
37. Republican Jewish Coalition. "About RJC." http://www.rjchq.org/about (Accessed on 6/1/2017).
38. Jacobs, Ben. 2015. "Republican Contenders Visit Vegas to Woo Growing Jewish Donor Base." *The Guardian.* http://www.theguardian.com/us-news/2015/apr/27/republican-jewish-coalition-ted-cruz-jeb-bush-barack-obama-foreign-policy (Accessed on 6/1/2017).
39. Ibid.
40. Ibid.
41. Gold, Matea. 2015. "Republican Jewish Coalition Says it Sees Fundraising Boom." *The Washington Post.* http://www.washingtonpost.com/politics/republican-jewish-coalition-says-it-sees-fundraising-boom/2015/04/22/eac5634a-e873-11e4-9a6a-c1ab95a0600b_story.html (Accessed on 6/1/2017).
42. Center for Strategic and Budgetary Assessments. "Our Mission." http://csbaonline.org/ (Accessed on 6/1/2017).
43. Ibid.
44. Edelman, Eric. 2015. "Iran Nuclear Negotiations After the Second Extension: Where Are They Going?" *Center for Strategic and Budgetary Assessments.* http://csbaonline.org/research/publications/iran-nuclear-negotiations-after-the-second-extension-where-are-they-going (Accessed on 6/1/2017).
45. Kazianis, Harry J. 2015. "How America Would Wage War Against Iran." *The National Interest.* http://nationalinterest.org/blog/the-buzz/how-america-would-wage-war-against-iran-12614 (Accessed on 6/1/2017).
46. Edelman, Eric. 2015. "The Next President Can Torch Obama's Iran Deal." *Politico.* http://www.politico.com/

magazine/story/2015/05/2016-elections-obama-successor-iran-118331.html#ixzz3bSMMcsJ3 (Accessed on 6/1/2017).
47. Pro-Publica: Nonprofit Explorer. 2015. "Center for Strategic and Budgetary Assessments." https://projects.propublica.org/nonprofits/organizations/521930922 (Accessed on 6/1/2017).
48. Satloff, Robert. 2015. "Director's Message." *The Washington Institute*. http://www.washingtoninstitute.org/about/directors-message (Accessed on 6/1/2017).
49. Ibid.
50. Cortellssa, Eric. 2015. "Dennis Ross: US Must Move from Distance to Detent with Israel." *Times of Israel*. http://www.timesofisrael.com/dennis-ross-us-must-move-from-distance-to-detente-with-israel/ (Accessed on 6/1/2017).
51. The Washington Institute. 2015. "Our Experts: Leadership." http://www.washingtoninstitute.org/experts/view/clawson-patrick (Accessed on 6/1/2017).
52. Ingersoll, Geoffrey, and Michael B. Kelly. 2012. "Lobbyist Says Israel Should Create A "False Flag" to Start a War With Iran." *Business Insider*. http://www.businessinsider.com/top-researcher-suggests-israel-get-nastier-with-iran-sink-sub-illicit-false-flag-2012-9 (Accessed on 6/1/2017).
53. Stephen M. Walt. 2010. "Robert Satloff Doth Protest Too Much." *Foreign Policy*. http://foreignpolicy.com/2010/04/09/robert-satloff-doth-protest-too-much/ (Accessed on 6/1/2017).
54. Foreign Policy Initiative. 2010. "Mission Statement." http://www.foreignpolicyi.org/about (Accessed on 6/1/2017).
55. Edelman, Eric. 2014. "Iran Remains America's Biggest Challenge." *The Washington Post*. http://www.washingtonpost.com/opinions/2014/09/18/f786fd1c-3f56-11e4-9587-5dafd96295f0_story.html (Accessed on 6/1/2017).
56. Foreign Policy Initiative. "Overnight Brief." http://www.foreignpolicyi.org/ (Accessed on 6/1/2017).
57. Guidestar website. http://www.guidestar.org/ViewPdf.aspx?PdfSource=0&ein=26-4392915

58. Ibid.
59. Gray, Rosie. 2017. "A Right-Leaning Foreign-Policy Think Tank Shuts Down." *The Atlantic* (Accessed on 6/29/2017).
60. O'Connor, Patrick. 2015. "The $15 Million Ad Fight Over the Iran Nuclear Deal." *The Wall Street Journal.* http://blogs.wsj.com/washwire/2015/09/04/the-15-million-ad-blitz-over-the-iran-nuclear-deal/ (Accessed on 6/1/2017).
61. Medea, Benjamin. 2015. "Multimillion Dollar Campaign Tries to Kill Iran Nuke Deal." *Counterpunch.* http://www.counterpunch.org/2015/07/10/snuff-ads-multimillion-dollar-campaign-tries-to-kill-iran-nuke-deal (Accessed on 6/1/2017).
62. Christians United for Israel. "About Us." http://www.cufi.org/site/PageServer?pagename=about_AboutCUFI (Accessed on 6/1/2017).
63. Ibid.
64. Fetcher, Joshua. 2014. "John Hagee: Ebola is God's Punishment for Obama Dividing Jerusalem." *My San Antonio.* http://www.mysanantonio.com/news/local/article/John-Hagee-Ebola-is-God-s-punishment-for-Obama-5827110.php (Accessed on 6/1/2017).
65. Stakelbeck, Erick. 2015. "Hagee on Iran Deal: Final Blood Moon a Divine Warning." *CBN News.* http://www1.cbn.com/cbnnews/world/2015/September/Hagee-on-Iran-Deal-Blood-Moon-a-Divine-Warning (Accessed on 6/1/2017).
66. Ibid.
67. Right Web. 2017. "Christians United for Israel." http://rightweb.irc-online.org/profile/Christians_United_for_Israel (Accessed on 6/1/2017).
68. Wilson. 2013. "Glenn Pledges $100,000 Donation to Christians United for Israel During Keynote Speech." *Glenn.* http://www.glennbeck.com/2013/07/23/watch-glenn-speaks-before-christians-united-for-israel-event-in/ (Accessed on 6/1/2017).
69. Sharon, Jeremy. 2015. "United With Israel Social Media Network Celebrates Three Millionth Supporter." *The*

Jerusalem Post. http://www.jpost.com/Israel-News/United-with-Israel-social-media-network-celebrates-three-millionth-supporter-391732 (Accessed on 6/1/2017).
70. United with Israel. 2015. "About Us." http://unitedwithisrael.org/about-us/
71. Sharon, Jeremy. 2015. "United with Israel Social Media Network Celebrates Three Millionth Supporter." *The Jerusalem Post.* http://www.jpost.com/Israel-News/United-with-Israel-social-media-network-celebrates-three-millionth-supporter-391732 (Accessed on 6/1/2017).
72. Buehler, Juergen. "Mandate: The ICEJ's Scriptural Directive." *International Christian Embassy Jerusalem.* https://us.icej.org/about/mandate (Accessed on 6/1/2017).
73. Ghert-Zand, Renee. 2014. "Thousands of Christians Voice Support for Israel in Jerusalem." *The Times of Israel.* http://www.timesofisrael.com/thousands-of-christians-voice-support-for-israel-in-jerusalem/ (Accessed on 6/1/2017).
74. Right Web. 1989. "International Christian Embassy Jerusalem." http://rightweb.irc-online.org/articles/display/International_Christian_Embassy_Jerusalem#P5815_1213733 (Accessed on 6/1/2017).
75. Ibid.
76. Americans for a Safe Israel. "Mission Statement." http://www.afsi.org/about_missionstatement.aspx (Accessed on 6/1/2017).
77. Ibid.
78. Right Web. 2011. "Irving Moskowitz." http://rightweb.irc-online.org/profile/Moskowitz_Irving (Accessed on 6/1/2017).
79. National Center for Policy Analysis. "About the NCPA." http://www.ncpa.org/about/ (Accessed on 6/1/2017).
80. Ibid.
81. CNN. 2003. "U.S. Officer Fined for Harsh Interrogation Tactics." http://www.cnn.com/2003/US/12/12/sprj.nirq.west.ruling/ (Accessed on 6/1/2017).

82. Guttman, Nathan. 2014. "Sheldon Adelson is a Philanthropist Like No Other." *Forward.* http://forward.com/news/israel/208220/sheldon-adelson-is-a-philanthropist-like-no-other/ (Accessed on 6/1/2017).
83. https://emetonline.org/about-emet/
84. http://www.theisraelproject.org/board-of-directors/
85. http://zoa.org/about/
86. Right Web. 2015. "Institute for Policy Studies, Zionist Organization of America." http://rightweb.irc-online.org/profile/zionist_organization_of_america
87. http://zoa.org/category/op-ed/ (Accessed on 6/3/2017).
88. Ron Kampeas. 2012. "ZOA Loses Tax-Exempt Status." *Jewish Telegraphic Agency*, September 11. http://www.jta.org/2012/09/11/news-opinion/united-states/zoa-loses-tax-exempt-status
89. Data from GuideStar website. http://www.guidestar.org/FinDocuments/2015/135/628/2015-135628475-0d66a2c4-9.pdf
90. Ibid.
91. http://forward.com/fast-forward/372164/adelson-groups-increase-pressure-trump-embassy-issue/
92. https://www.nytimes.com/2017/06/01/world/middleeast/israel-embassy-jerusalem-trump.html?hp&action=click&pgtype=Homepage&clickSource=story-heading&module=first-column-region&region=top-news&WT.nav=top-news
93. http://www.jpost.com/Diaspora/US-senator-scolds-leader-of-Zionist-group-over-praise-for-Steve-Bannon-496427
94. Stand With Us. 2015. "About Us." https://www.standwithus.com/aboutus/ (Accessed on 6/1/2017).
95. Ibid.
96. Ibid.
97. Clifton, Eli. 2009. "Pro-Israel Group's Money Trail Veers Hard Right." *Right Web.* http://rightweb.irc-online.org/pro-israel_groups_money_trail_veers_hard_right/ (Accessed on 6/1/2017).

98. Simon Wiesenthal Center. 2015. "Understand Simon Wiesenthal Center's Mission." http://www.wiesenthal.com/site/pp.asp?c=lsKWLbPJLnF&b=4441257#.VbsXeUJViko
99. Austin, Paige. 2015. "Wiesenthal Center Leaders Condemn Nuclear Deal with Iran." *Patch.* http://patch.com/california/northhollywood/wiesenthal-center-leaders-condemn-nuclear-deal-iran (Accessed on 6/1/2017).
100. Right Web. 2016. "North Jersey Pac." http://rightweb.irc-online.org/profile/norpac (Accessed on 6/1/2017).
101. Clifton, Eli. 2015. "NORPAC Helps House Hawk Attack Iran Deal." *LobeLog Foreign Policy.* https://lobelog.com/norpac-helps-house-hawk-attack-iran-deal/ (Accessed on 6/1/2017).
102. Kampeas, Ron. 2012. "NORPAC Alerts Members to Oppose Hagel, Ex-diplomats Back Him." *JTA.* http://www.jta.org/2012/12/20/news-opinion/politics/norpac-alerts-members-to-oppose-hagel-ex-diplomats-back-him (Accessed on 6/1/2017).
103. Americans for Peace and Tolerance. "About Us." http://www.peaceandtolerance.org/about/ (Accessed on 6/1/2017).
104. Ibid.
105. Right Web. 2013. "Americans for Peace and Tolerance." http://rightweb.irc-online.org/profile/americans_for_peace_and_tolerance (Accessed on 6/1/2017).
106. Ibid.
107. Duss, Matthew, Yasmine Taeb, Ken Gude, and Ken Sofer. 2015. "Fear, Inc. 2.0." *Center for American Progress.* Page 61. https://cdn.americanprogress.org/wp-content/uploads/2015/02/FearInc-report2.11.pdf (Accessed on 6/1/2017).
108. One Israel Fund. https://oneisraelfund.org (Accessed on 6/1/2017).
109. Sliver, Charlotte. 2015. "Thirteen Palestinians Revive Lawsuit Against US "Charities" Funding Violent Israeli Settlers." *Electronic Intifada.* https://electronicintifada.net/blogs/

charlotte-silver/thirteen-palestinians-revive-lawsuit-against-us-charities-funding-violent (Accessed on 6/1/2017).
110. http://www.haaretz.com/israel-news/1.653434
111. Middle East Forum. 2015. "About the Middle East Forum." http://www.meforum.org/about.php (Accessed on 6/1/2017).
112. Duss, Matthew, Yasmine Taeb, Ken Gude, and Ken Sofer. 2015. "Fear, Inc. 2.0." *Center for American Progress.* https://cdn.americanprogress.org/wp-content/uploads/2015/02/FearInc-report2.11.pdf (Accessed on 6/1/2017).
113. Right Web. 2015. "Middle East Forum." http://www.right-web.irc-online.org/profile/Middle_East_Forum (Accessed on 6/1/2017).
114. Right Web. 2015. "Daniel Pipes." http://www.rightweb.irc-online.org/profile/pipes_daniel (Accessed on 6/1/2017).
115. Ibid.
116. American Center for Democracy. 2013. "About ACD." http://acdemocracy.org/aboutus/ (Accessed on 6/1/2017).
117. American Center for Democracy. 2013. "Directors and Advisors." http://acdemocracy.org/aboutus/ (Accessed on 6/1/2017).
118. Ibid.
119. http://rightweb.irc-online.org/profile/jerusalem_summit/
120. Israeli American Council. 2015. "About the IAC." http://www.israeliamerican.org/national/about-iac (Accessed on 6/1/2017).
121. Guttman, Nathan. 2015. "Can Israeli American Council Grow Without Kow-Towing to Big Donors Like Sheldon Adelson?" *Forward.* http://forward.com/news/217038/can-israeli-american-council-grow-without-kow-towi/ (Accessed on 6/1/2017).
122. Ibid.
123. Religious Zionists of America. "Mission Statement." http://www.rza.org/whoweare.htm (Accessed on 6/1/2017).

124. Baruch, Uzi. 2015. "RZA Chairman: Netanyahu Must Not Be Silent." *Arutz Sheva.* http://www.israelnationalnews.com/News/News.aspx/191652#.Vbz32kJViko (Accessed on 6/1/2017).
125. Scholars for Peace in the Middle East. 2015. "About SPME." http://spme.org/about-us/ (Accessed on 6/1/2017).
126. Scholars for Peace in the Middle East. 2015. http://spme.org/about-us/ (Accessed on 6/1/2017).
127. Palumbo-Liu, David. 2015. "Business of Backlash: GOP Cashes in on Koch/Adelson Anti-BDS Donations." *Salon.* http://www.salon.com/2015/04/07/business_of_backlash_gop_cashes_in_on_kochadelson_anti_bds_donations/ (Accessed on 6/1/2017).
128. The World Values Network. 2015. "About The World Values Network." https://worldvalues.us/about/ (Accessed on 6/1/2017).
129. Jacobs, Jill. 2015. "Shmuley Boteach isn't America's Rabbi." *The Washington Post.* https://www.washingtonpost.com/posteverything/wp/2015/03/04/shmuley-boteach-isnt-americas-rabbi/?utm_term=.cd4a50498a96 (Accessed on 6/1/2017).
130. JTA. 2015. "Jewish Groups Line Up to Denounce Boteach Ad on Sauce Rice." *The Jerusalem Post.* http://www.jpost.com/Diaspora/Jewish-groups-line-up-to-denounce-Boteach-ad-on-Susan-Rice-392519 (Accessed on 6/1/2017).
131. JTA. 2014. "London Times Rejects Wiesel Ad Against Hamas Child Sacrifice." http://www.jta.org/2014/08/05/news-opinion/united-states/london-times-rejects-wiesel-ad-against-hamas-child-sacrifice (Accessed on 6/1/2017).
132. Ibid.
133. Ungar-Sargon, Batya. 2014. "Celebrity Rabbi, Heal Thyself." *Tablet.* http://www.tabletmag.com/jewish-news-and-politics/179882/shmuley-boteach (Accessed on 6/1/2017).
134. Ibid.

135. Friends of Ariel. 2015 "About Ariel." http://www.friendsofariel.org/about/about-ariel/ (Accessed on 6/1/2017).
136. Morad, Tamar. 2010. "With Jewish Groups Skittish About Settlement, Ariel Looks to Evangelical Christians for Salvation." *Haaretz*. http://www.haaretz.com/beta/with-jewish-groups-skittish-about-settlement-ariel-looks-to-evangelical-christians-for-salvation-1.328512 (Accessed on 6/1/2017).
137. Lowenfeld, Jonah. 2010. "L.A. Donors Play Role in Israeli Settlement." *Jewish Journal*. http://jewishjournal.com/news/los_angeles/community/83169/ (Accessed on 6/1/2017).
138. Clifton, Eli. 2015. "Rubio's Biggest Donor Funded West Bank Settlement." *LobeLog*. http://www.lobelog.com/rubios-biggest-donor-funded-west-bank-settlement/ (Accessed on 6/1/2017).
139. Barbaro, Michael, and Steve Eder. 2015. "Billionaire Lifts Marco Rubio, Politically and Personally." *New York Times*. https://www.nytimes.com/2015/05/10/us/billionaire-lifts-marco-rubio-politically-and-personally.html?_r=0 (Accessed on 6/1/2017).
140. American Principles. 2015. http://americanprinciples.org/ (Accessed on 6/1/2017).
141. Ibid.
142. Ibid.
143. Open Secrets. 2014. "American Principles: Recipients." https://www.opensecrets.org/pacs/pacgot.php?cycle=2014&cmte=C00492579 (Accessed on 6/1/2017).
144. Open Secrets. 2016. "Vendor/Recipient: Electoral Strategies Inc." https://www.opensecrets.org/expends/vendor.php?year=2016&vendor=Electoral+Strategies+Inc (Accessed on 6/1/2017).
145. Open Secrets. 2014. "American Principles: Donors." https://www.opensecrets.org/pacs/pacgave2.php?cycle=2014&cmte=C00492579 (Accessed on 6/1/2017).
146. Human Rights Coalition Against Radical Islam. "Mission." http://hrcari.weebly.com (Accessed 6/14/17).

147. Ibid.
148. Sidman, Fern. 2010. "Responding to Islamic Extremism: An Interview with Dr. Marvin Belsky." *Jewish Press.* http://www.jewishpress.com/indepth/interviews-and-profiles/responding-to-islamic-extremism-an-interview-with-dr-marvin-belsky/2010/04/21/0/?print (Accessed on 6/1/2017).
149. Jewish National Fund. "About JNF." http://www.jnf.org/ (Accessed on 6/1/2017).
150. Ibid.
151. Jewish National Fund. 2015. "Form 990." http://www.jnf.org/assets/pdf/jnf-final-990.pdf (Accessed on 6/1/2017).
152. JPEF. 2012. "JPEF, Who We Are." http://www.jewishpoliticalchronicle.org/whoweare.htm (Accessed on 6/1/2017).
153. Benari, Elad. 2011. "U.S. Groups to Celebrate Purim at Iran's UN Mission." *Arutz Sheva.* http://www.israelnationalnews.com/News/News.aspx/142669#.VcESs0JVikp (Accessed on 6/1/2017).
154. The Investigative Project on Terrorism. 2010. "About the Investigative Project on Terrorism." http://www.investigativeproject.org/about.php (Accessed on 6/1/2017).
155. Holehouse, Matthew, and Raf Sanchez. 2015. "David Cameron: US Terror 'Expert' Steve Emerson is a 'Complete Idiot'." *The Telegraph.* http://www.telegraph.co.uk/news/uknews/terrorism-in-the-uk/11340399/David-Cameron-US-terror-expert-Steve-Emerson-is-a-complete-idiot.html (Accessed on 6/1/2017).
156. Smietana, Bob. 2010. "Anti-Muslim Crusaders Make Millions Spreading Fear." *The Tennessean.*
157. Clifton, Eli. 2010. "More Insights to Steven Emerson's Tangled Funding Web." *LobeLog.* http://lobelog.com/more-insights-into-steven-emersons-tangled-funding-web/ (Accessed on 6/1/2017).
158. Right Web. 2015. "Steve Emerson." http://rightweb.irc-online.org/profile/Emerson_Steven#_edn14 (Accessed on 6/1/2017).

159. Think Progress. 2011. "Steven Emerson: Founder and Executive Director, Investigative Project on Terrorism." http://thinkprogress.org/steven-emerson-founder-and-executive-director-investigative-project-on-terrorism/ (Accessed on 6/1/2017).
160. Southern Poverty Law Center. 2016. "A Journalist's Manual: Field Guide to Anti-Muslim Extremist." https://www.splcenter.org/20161025/journalists-manual-field-guide-anti-muslim-extremists#pipes (Accessed on 6/1/2017).
161. Republican Friends of Israel. "About Us." http://www.republicanfriendsofisrael.com/About-Us.html (Accessed on 6/1/2017).
162. The Phyllis Chesler Organization. "About Phyllis Chesler." https://phyllis-chesler.com (Accessed on 6/1/2017).
163. Esman, Abilgail R. 2015. "The Dutch Debate the Burqa—And Ban It." *Politico.* http://www.politico.eu/article/netherlands-burqa-ban/ (Accessed on 6/1/2017).
164. Resnick, Elliot. 2015. "Interview with Phyllis Chesler." *Middle East Forum.* http://www.meforum.org/5253/interview-phyllis-chesler (Accessed on 6/1/2017).
165. Scholars for Peace in the Middle East. 2015. "SPME Network." http://spme.org/spme-network/ (Accessed on 6/1/2017).
166. American Friends of Likud. 2014. "AFL, About Us." http://www.aflikud.org/#!aboutus/cjg9 (Accessed on 6/1/2017).
167. Ibid.
168. Kornbluh, Jacob. 2015. "Netanyahu to Reach Out to Jewish Americans in Live Webcast Tuesday." *Jewish Political News and Updates.* http://jpupdates.com/2015/07/30/netanyahu-to-reach-out-to-jewish-americans-in-live-webcast-tuesday/ (Accessed on 6/1/2017).
169. Frenkel, Sheera. 2015. "Three U.S. Families Fund Half of Netanyahu's Re-election Bid." *Buzzfeed News.* https://www.buzzfeed.com/sheerafrenkel/meet-the-american-families-

bankrolling-netanyahus?utm_term=.iqaodb75a4#.jc76K-woAGl (Accessed on 6/1/2017).
170. Vogel, Kenneth P. 2014. "Inside the Vast Liberal Conspiracy." *Politico.* http://www.politico.com/story/2014/06/inside-the-vast-liberal-conspiracy-108171.html (Accessed on 6/1/2017).
171. Ibid.
172. Toosi, Nahal. 2015. "Iran Deal Congress Donors Support Democrats." *Politico.* http://www.politico.com/story/2015/08/iran-deal-congress-donors-support-democrats-120938 (Accessed on 6/1/2017).
173. Center for a New American Security. "About CNAS." https://www.cnas.org/mission (Accessed on 6/1/2017).
174. Right Web. 2014. "Center for a New American Security." http://rightweb.irc-online.org/profile/center_for_a_new_american_security (Accessed on 6/1/2017).
175. Rosenberg, Elizabeth, and Ilan Rosenberg. 2015. "CNAS Press Note: What Does the Iran Nuclear Plan Achieve?" *CNAS.* http://www.cnas.org/press-note/what-does-iran-nuclear-plan-achieve#.VW90V2TBzGc (Accessed on 6/1/2017).
176. The full list can be found here: https://www.cnas.org/support-cnas/cnas-supporters This is a partial list of the most significant ones: $500,000 and Above: Department of Defense, Northrop Grumman, Smith Richardson Foundation, William and Flora Hewlett Foundation; $250,000–$499,999: Alex Soros Foundation, Carnegie Corporation, Boeing Company, Tides Foundation, Government of Japan; $100,000–$249,999: Twenty-first Century Fox, Airbus Americas, BAE Systems, North America, Boston Consulting Group, Chevron Corporation, Compton Foundation, DRS Technologies, Fortress Investment Group, Goldman Sonnenfeldt Foundation, Huntington Ingalls Industries, JPMorgan Chase & Co., Korea Foundation, Morgan Stanley, National Defense Industrial Association, Open Society

Foundations, Prudential, Raytheon Company, Roche Family Foundation, Skoll Global Threats Fund, Taipei Economic and Cultural Representative Office, The John and Patricia Rosenwald Foundation, John D. and Catherine T. MacArthur Foundation, United Arab Emirates Embassy; $50,000–$99,999: Bank of America, Bob Woodruff Foundation, BP America, CISCO, Embassy of the Republic of Lithuania, Government of Finland, General Dynamics Corporation, Google Inc., IBM, Government of Latvia, Lockheed Martin Company, Government of Norway, Ploughshares Fund, Qualcomm, Sweden Ministry of Foreign Affairs, Textron; $25,000–$49,999: Aerospace Industries Association, American Express Foundation, Bovin Family Foundation, DynCorp International, ExxonMobil, Facebook, ITOCHU Aviation, Inc., Japan Bank for International Cooperation, Mitsubishi Corporation, Morningstar Foundation, SpaceX, Spirit Aerosystems, Statoil and The May and Stanley Smith Charitable Trust.

177. WAND. "WAND Education Fund Mission Statement." https://www.wand.org (Accessed on 6/14/17).
178. Open Secrets. 2014. "Women's Action for New Directions." https://www.opensecrets.org/pacs/lookup2.php?strID=C00170316&cycle=2014 (Accessed on 6/1/2017).
179. Tides. "About." http://www.tides.org/about/ (Accessed on 6/1/2017).
180. National Security Network. 2015. "About." http://nsnetwork.org/about/ (Accessed on 6/1/2017).
181. Ibid.
182. Ibid.
183. Hsu, Spencer. 2009. "Rand Beers Tapped as Counselor to Napolitano." *The Washington Post*. http://voices.washingtonpost.com/44/2009/01/14/rand_beers_tapped_as_counselor.html (Accessed on 6/1/2017).
184. Collina, Tom Z. 2015. "Clearing the Final Hurdles in the Iran Nuclear Talks." *The National Interest*. http://nationalinter-

est.org/feature/clearing-the-final-hurdles-the-iran-nuclear-talks-12537 (Accessed on 6/1/2017).
185. Capehart, Jonathan. 2015. "Tom Cotton Picked Apart by Army General Over "Mutinous" Iran Letter." *The Washington Post.* http://www.washingtonpost.com/blogs/post-partisan/wp/2015/03/13/tom-cotton-picked-apart-by-army-general-over-mutinous-iran-letter/ (Accessed on 6/1/2017).
186. Org Council. 2015. "National Security Network Inc." http://www.orgcouncil.com/ny/new-york/national-security-network-inc-455.php (Accessed on 6/1/2017).
187. Israel Policy Forum. 2012. "About Israel Policy Forum." http://www.israelpolicyforum.org/about-israel-policy-forum (Accessed on 6/1/2017).
188. Ibid.
189. JTA. 2012. "Israel Policy Forum Revived to Rise above Partisan Fray as a Pragmatic Pro-Israel Voice." *Haaretz.* http://www.haaretz.com/news/world/israel-policy-forum-revived-to-rise-above-partisan-fray-as-a-pragmatic-pro-israel-voice-1.439722 (Accessed on 6/1/2017).
190. Forward News. 2014. "Jewish Democratic Donors Push Against Iran Sanctions." http://forward.com/news/breaking-news/193592/jewish-democratic-donors-push-against-iran-sanctio/ (Accessed on 6/1/2017).
191. Institute for Policy Studies. "About." http://www.ips-dc.org/about/ (Accessed on 6/1/2017).
192. Bennis, Phyllis. "We've Seen the Threats Against Iran Before." *Al Jazeera.* http://www.aljazeera.com/indepth/opinion/2012/02/201221510012473174.html (Accessed on 6/1/2017).
193. Institute for Policy Studies. 2014. "IPS Financial Information." http://www.ips-dc.org/wp-content/uploads/2014/12/IPS-2013-990.pdf (Accessed on 6/1/2017).
194. Institute for Policy Studies. "Support the Institute: How Does the Institute Get its Funding?" http://www.ips-dc.org/support-the-institute/ (Accessed on 6/1/2017).

195. Joffe, Alexander H. 2013. "Bad Investment: The Philanthropy of George Soros and the Arab-Israeli Conflict." NGO Monitor: Making NGOs Accountable. http://www.ngo-monitor.org/soros.pdf (Accessed on 6/1/2017).
196. Ibid.
197. Ibid.
198. Retrieved from American Enterprise Institute website https://www.aei.org/wp-content/uploads/2016/01/AEI-2015-Annual-Report.pdf (Accessed on 6/3/2017).
Retrieved from SourceWatch website http://www.sourcewatch.org/index.php/American_Enterprise_Institute#DonorsTrust_Funding (Accessed on 6/3/2017).
Retrieved from American Enterprise Inst website http://www.aei.org/about/ (Accessed on 6/3/2017).
199. Retrieved from SourceWatch website http://www.sourcewatch.org/index.php/Center_for_Immigration_Studies (Accessed on 6/3/2017).
Retrieved from Center for Immigration Studies website http://cis.org/About (Accessed on 6/3/2017).
200. Retrieved from Center for Security Policy website http://www.centerforsecuritypolicy.org/wp-content/uploads/2013/09/Center-for-Security-Policy-2012-Financial-Statements-color.pdf (Accessed on 6/3/2017).
Retrieved from Center for Security Policy website http://www.centerforsecuritypolicy.org/about-us/staff/ (Accessed on 6/3/2017).
Retrieved from website of Salon https://www.salon.com/2014/10/01/far_right_birthers_secret_funders_look_whos_backing_islamophobe_frank_gaffney/ (Accessed on 6/3/2017).
Retrieved from Center for Security Policy website https://www.centerforsecuritypolicy.org/about-us/ (Accessed on 6/3/2017).
201. Retrieved from Claremont website http://www.claremont.org/about-us/ (Accessed on 6/3/2017).

Retrieved from Charity Navigator website https://www.charitynavigator.org/index.cfm?bay=search.summary&orgid=9808 (Accessed on 6/3/2017).
Retrieved from Conservative Transparency website http://conservativetransparency.org/recipient/the-claremont-institute/ (Accessed on 6/3/2017).
Retrieved from Claremont website http://www.claremont.org/page/claremonts-mission/ (Accessed on 6/3/2017).
202. Retrieved from Foundation Center website http://990s.foundationcenter.org/990_pdf_archive/231/231731998/231731998_201312_990.pdf (Accessed on 6/3/2017).
Retrieved from Foreign Policy Research Inst website http://www.fpri.org/about/annual-reports/ (Accessed on 6/3/2017).
Retrieved from Foreign Policy Research Inst website http://www.fpri.org/about/ (Accessed on 6/3/2017).
203. Retrieved from the Heritage Foundation website https://thf-membership.s3.amazonaws.com/2015_AnnualReport.pdf (Accessed on 6/3/2017).
Retrieved from website of SourceWatch http://www.sourcewatch.org/index.php/Heritage_Foundation#Funding (Accessed on 6/3/2017).
Retrieved from the Heritage Foundation website http://www.heritage.org/about-heritage/mission (Accessed on 6/3/2017).
204. Retrieved from Hoover Institution website http://www.hoover.org/sites/default/files/2015annualreport.pdf (Accessed on 6/3/2017).
Retrieved from SourceWatch website http://www.sourcewatch.org/index.php/Hoover_Institution_on_War,_Revolution_and_Peace#Funding (Accessed on 6/3/2017).
Retrieved from Hoover Inst website http://www.hoover.org/about (Accessed on 6/3/2017).

205. Retrieved from Hudson Institute website https://s3.amazonaws.com/media.hudson.org/files/publications/2015HudsonAnnualReport.pdf (Accessed on 6/3/2017).
    Retrieved from Hudson Institute website https://www.hudson.org/about (Accessed on 6/3/2017).
206. Retrieved from Manhattan Institute website https://www.charitynavigator.org/index.cfm?bay=search.summary&orgid=4040 (Accessed on 6/3/2017).
    Retrieved from SourceWatch website http://www.sourcewatch.org/index.php/Manhattan_Institute_for_Policy_Research#Funding (Accessed on 6/3/2017).
    Retrieved from Manhattan Institute website https://www.manhattan-institute.org/about (Accessed on 6/3/2017).
207. Retrieved from Middle East Forum website http://www.meforum.org/990-form-2014.pdf (Accessed on 6/3/2017).
    Retrieved from SourceWatch website http://www.sourcewatch.org/index.php/Middle_East_Forum#Funding (Accessed on 6/3/2017).
    Retrieved from Middle East Forum website http://www.meforum.org/about.php (Accessed on 6/3/2017).
208. Retrieved from Charity Navigator website https://www.charitynavigator.org/index.cfm?bay=search.summary&orgid=6359 (Accessed on 6/3/2017).
    Retrieved from SourceWatch website http://www.sourcewatch.org/index.php/National_Center_for_Policy_Analysis (Accessed on 6/3/2017).
    Retrieved from National Center for Policy Analysis website http://www.ncpa.org/about/ (Accessed on 6/3/2017).
209. Retrieved from Charity Navigator website https://www.charitynavigator.org/index.cfm?bay=search.summary&orgid=7433 (Accessed on 6/3/2017).
    Retrieved from SourceWatch website http://www.sourcewatch.org/index.php/Pacific_Research_Institute#Funding (Accessed on 6/3/2017).
    Retrieved from Pacific Research Inst website http://www.pacificresearch.org/about/ (Accessed on 6/3/2017).

APPENDICES 451

210. Retrieved from website of SourceWatch http://www.sourcewatch.org/index.php/Project_for_the_New_American_Century (Accessed on 6/3/2017).
Retrieved from SourceWatch website http://www.sourcewatch.org/index.php/Project_for_the_New_American_Century (Accessed on 6/3/2017).
211. Retrieved from website of Center on Budget and Policy Priorities http://www.cbpp.org/sites/default/files/atoms/files/honor_roll_2015_1.21.15.pdf (Accessed on 6/3/2017).
Retrieved from website of Center on Budget and Policy Priorities http://www.cbpp.org/about/our-staff (Accessed on 6/3/2017).
Retrieved from website of Center on Budget and Policy Priorities http://www.cbpp.org/about/mission-history (Accessed on 6/3/2017).
212. Retrieved from website of Center for American Progress https://www.americanprogress.org/about/staff/ (Accessed on 6/3/2017).
Retrieved from website of Center for American Progress https://www.americanprogress.org/about/c3-our-supporters/
Retrieved from Charity Navigator website https://www.charitynavigator.org/index.cfm?bay=search.summary&orgid=12155 (Accessed on 6/3/2017).
Retrieved from website of Center for American Progress https://www.americanprogress.org/about/mission/ (Accessed on 6/3/2017).
213. Retrieved from Charity Navigator website https://www.charitynavigator.org/index.cfm?bay=search.summary&orgid=10172 (Accessed on 6/3/2017).
Retrieved from website of Center for Economic and Policy Research http://cepr.net/about-us/funders (Accessed on 6/3/2017).
Retrieved from website of Center for Economic and Policy Research http://cepr.net/about-us/about-us (Accessed on 6/3/2017).

214. Retrieved from website of Center for Progressive Reform http://www.progressivereform.org/articles/CPR10Report.pdf (Accessed on 6/3/2017).
Retrieved from Propublica website https://projects.propublica.org/nonprofits/organizations/352182224 (Accessed on 6/3/2017).
Retrieved from website of Center for Progressive Reform http://www.progressivereform.org/supportCPR.cfm (Accessed on 6/3/2017).
215. Donors http://www.demos.org/sites/default/files/imce/AnnualReport-Sept13_1.pdf (Accessed on 6/3/2017).
Retrieved from website of Demos http://www.demos.org/staff (Accessed on 6/3/2017).
Retrieved from http://www.demos.org/sites/default/files/imce/AnnualReport-Sept13_1.pdf (Accessed on 6/3/2017).
Retrieved from http://www.demos.org/about-demos (Accessed on 6/3/2017).
216. Retrieved from Charity Navigator website https://www.charitynavigator.org/index.cfm?bay=search.summary&orgid=7111 (Accessed on 6/3/2017).
Retrieved from SourceWatch website http://www.sourcewatch.org/index.php/Employment_Policies_Institute#Funding (Accessed on 6/3/2017).
Retrieved from website of Economic Policy Inst http://www.epi.org/about/ (Accessed on 6/3/2017).
217. Donors Retrieved from website of Institute for Policy Studies http://www.ips-dc.org/wp-content/uploads/2016/05/AR2015-final-6.pdf (Accessed on 6/3/2017).
Retrieved from https://www.ips-dc.org/ (Accessed on 6/3/2017).
218. Retrieved from website of Public Citizen https://www.citizen.org/documents/PC%20News%202015%20Annual%20Report.pdf (Accessed on 6/3/2017).
Retrieved from https://www.citizen.org/ (Accessed on 6/3/2017).

219. Retrieved from Charity Navigator website https://www.charitynavigator.org/index.cfm?bay=search.summary&orgid=4541 (Accessed on 6/3/2017).
Retrieved from SourceWatch website http://www.sourcewatch.org/index.php/Franklin_and_Eleanor_Roosevelt_Institute#Major_donors (Accessed on 6/3/2017).
Retrieved from website of Roosevelt Institute http://rooseveltinstitute.org/about/ (Accessed on 6/3/2017).
220. Retrieved from website of American Iranian Council http://www.us-iran.org/people/ (Accessed on 6/3/2017).
Retrieved from http://www.us-iran.org/mission-vision/ (Accessed on 6/3/2017).
221. Retrieved from Charity Navigator website https://www.charitynavigator.org/index.cfm?bay=search.summary&orgid=4528 (Accessed on 6/3/2017).
Retrieved from SCRIBD website https://www.scribd.com/doc/276060411/2015-Overview-and-2014-Annual-Report (Accessed on 6/3/2017).
Retrieved from website of Aspen Institute https://www.aspeninstitute.org/transparency/ (Accessed on 6/3/2017).
Retrieved from https://www.aspeninstitute.org/about/#our-impact (Accessed on 6/3/2017).
Retrieved from https://www.aspeninstitute.org/about/heritage/ (Accessed on 6/3/2017).
222. Retrieved from Charity Navigator website https://www.charitynavigator.org/index.cfm?bay=search.summary&orgid=5395 (Accessed on 6/3/2017).
Retrieved from website of Atlantic Council http://www.atlanticcouncil.org/support/supporters (Accessed on 6/3/2017).
Retrieved from http://www.atlanticcouncil.org/about (Accessed on 6/3/2017).
223. Retrieved from website of Brookings Institute https://www.brookings.edu/wp-content/uploads/2016/07/2015-annual-report.pdf (Accessed on 6/3/2017).

Retrieved from https://www.brookings.edu/wp-content/uploads/2016/07/2015-audited-financials-1.pdf (Accessed on 6/3/2017).
Retrieved from https://www.brookings.edu/about-us/ (Accessed on 6/3/2017).

224. Retrieved from website of Carnegie Endowment for International Peace http://carnegieendowment.org/about/pdfs/financials2015.pdf (Accessed on 6/3/2017).
Retrieved from http://carnegieendowment.org/about/annualreport/2015 (Accessed on 6/3/2017).
Retrieved from http://carnegieendowment.org/about/ (Accessed on 6/3/2017).

225. Full list of donors: Retrieved from website of Center for Strategic and International Studies https://www.csis.org/support-csis/our-donors/individual-donors (Accessed on 6/3/2017).
Retrieved from https://www.csis.org/about-us/financial-information (Accessed on 6/3/2017).
Retrieved from https://www.csis.org/about-us (Accessed on 6/3/2017).

226. Retrieved from website of Constitution Project http://www.constitutionproject.org/wp-content/uploads/2015/05/TCP-2014-Annual-Report.pdf (Accessed on 6/3/2017).
Retrieved from http://www.constitutionproject.org/about-us/ (Accessed on 6/3/2017).

227. Donor list: Retrieved from website of Corporation of Enterprise Development http://cfed.org/about/supporters/donors/ (Accessed on 6/3/2017).
Retrieved from ProPublica website https://projects.propublica.org/nonprofits/organizations/521141804 (Accessed on 6/3/2017).
Retrieved from http://cfed.org/about/ (Accessed on 6/3/2017).

228. Donor list: Retrieved from website of Council on Foreign Relations https://d1lidwm7vls1dg.cloudfront.net/content/about/annual_report/ar_2015/CFR_2015_Donor_Listing.pdf (Accessed on 6/3/2017).

Retrieved from website of Council on Foreign Relations https://d1lidwm7vls1dg.cloudfront.net/content/about/annual_report/ar_2016/AR2016_web.pdf (Accessed on 6/3/2017).
Retrieved from https://www.cfr.org/about (Accessed on 6/3/2017).
229. Full list of donors: Retrieved from website of Committee for Economic Development https://www.ced.org/people/supporters (Accessed on 6/3/2017).
Retrieved from Charity Navigator website https://www.charitynavigator.org/index.cfm?bay=search.summary&orgid=6712 (Accessed on 6/3/2017).
Retrieved from https://www.ced.org/about (Accessed on 6/3/2017).
230. Retrieved from CitizenAudit Organization website https://www.citizenaudit.org/organization/204403497/INFORMATION%20TECHNOLOGY%20ANDINNOVATION%20FOUNDATION/ (Accessed on 6/3/2017).
Retrieved from website of Information Technology and Innovation Foundation https://itif.org/about (Accessed on 6/3/2017).
231. Full list of donors: Retrieved from website of New America Foundation https://www.newamerica.org/our-funding/our-funders/ (Accessed on 6/3/2017).
Retrieved from https://www.newamerica.org/2015/ (Accessed on 6/3/2017).
Retrieved from https://www.newamerica.org/our-story/ (Accessed on 6/3/2017).
232. Retrieved from website of Resources for the Future http://www.rff.org/files/RFF-2015AnnualReport_web.pdf (Accessed on 6/3/2017).
Retrieved from http://www.rff.org/about (Accessed on 6/3/2017).
233. 2015 donor list: Retrieved from website of Henry L. Stimson Center http://www.stimson.org/sites/default/files/2015%20Funders.pdf (Accessed on 6/3/2017).

Retrieved from FindTheCompany website http://nonprofits.findthecompany.com/l/426174/Henry-L-Stimson-Center (Accessed on 6/3/2017).
Retrieved from https://www.stimson.org/content/about-us (Accessed on 6/3/2017).

234. Retrieved from website of RAND Corporation http://www.rand.org/pubs/corporate_pubs/CP1-2015.html (Accessed on 6/3/2017).
Retrieved from http://www.rand.org/about/clients_grantors.html (Accessed on 6/3/2017).
Retrieved from https://www.rand.org/about/history.html (Accessed on 6/3/2017).

235. Retrieved from CitizenAudit https://www.citizenaudit.org/organization/426071036/THE%20STANLEY%20FOUNDATION/ (Accessed on 6/3/2017).
Retrieved from website of The Stanley Foundation https://www.stanleyfoundation.org/about.cfm (Accessed on 6/3/2017).

236. Retrieved from website of Urban Institute http://www.urban.org/sites/default/files/2015-annual-report.pdf (Accessed on 6/3/2017).
Retrieved from http://www.urban.org/about (Accessed on 6/3/2017).

237. Retrieved from website of Wilson Center https://www.wilsoncenter.org/990-formsannual-reports (Accessed on 6/3/2017).
Retrieved from https://www.wilsoncenter.org/staff-directory (Accessed on 6/3/2017).
Retrieved from https://www.wilsoncenter.org/donors (Accessed on 6/3/2017).
Retrieved from https://www.wilsoncenter.org/about-the-wilson-center (Accessed on 6/3/2017).

238. Retrieved from website of Ayn Rand Institute https://ari.aynrand.org/~/media/pdf/annual-report.ashx?la=en (Accessed on 6/3/2017).

Retrieved from https://ari.aynrand.org/about-ari/mission-and-purpose (Accessed on 6/3/2017).
239. Retrieved from website of Atlas Economic Research Foundation https://www.atlasnetwork.org/assets/uploads/annual-reports/Atlas_Network_Year_in_Review_2015_Digital_Final.pdf (Accessed on 6/3/2017).
Retrieved from https://www.atlasnetwork.org/about/our-story (Accessed on 6/3/2017).
240. Retrieved from SourceWatch website http://www.sourcewatch.org/index.php/Cascade_Policy_Institute#Funding (Accessed on 6/3/2017).
Retrieved from website of Cascade Policy Institute http://cascadepolicy.org/more/about/staff/ (Accessed on 6/3/2017).
Retrieved from website of Conservative Transparency http://conservativetransparency.org/org/cascade-policy-institute/ (Accessed on 6/3/2017).
Retrieved from http://cascadepolicy.org/more/about/ (Accessed on 6/3/2017).
241. Retrieved from website of CATO Institute http://object.cato.org/sites/cato.org/files/pubs/pdf/annual-report-2015-update.pdf (Accessed on 6/3/2017).
Retrieved from SourceWatch website http://www.sourcewatch.org/index.php/Cato_Institute#Finances_and_Funding (Accessed on 6/3/2017).
Retrieved from https://www.cato.org/mission (Accessed on 6/3/2017).
242. Retrieved from website of Competitive Enterprise Institute https://cei.org/sites/default/files/CEI%20Audited%20Financials%20-%202015.PDF (Accessed on 6/3/2017).
Eilperin, Juliet. (June 20, 2013). "Anatomy of a Washington Dinner: Who Funds the Competitive Enterprise Institute?" *The Washington Post*. Retrieved from https://www.washingtonpost.com/news/the-fix/wp/2013/06/20/anatomy-of-a-washington-dinner-who-funds-the-competitive-enterprise-institute/ (Accessed on 6/3/2017).

Retrieved from https://cei.org/about-cei (Accessed on 6/3/2017).
243. Retrieved from website of Foundation for Economic Education https://fee.org/media/13457/feeannualreport-2015.pdf (Accessed on 6/3/2017).
Retrieved from website of Greenpeace http://www.greenpeace.org/usa/global-warming/climate-deniers/frontgroups/foundation-for-economic-education-fee/ (Accessed on 6/3/2017).
Retrieved from https://fee.org/about/ (Accessed on 6/3/2017).
244. Retrieved from SourceWatch website http://www.sourcewatch.org/index.php/Foundation_for_Rational_Economics_and_Education (Accessed on 6/3/2017).
Retrieved from http://www.sourcewatch.org/index.php/Foundation_for_Rational_Economics_and_Education#cite_note-nefl-1 (Accessed on 6/3/2017).
245. Retrieved from website of Goldwater Institute https://goldwater-media.s3.amazonaws.com/cms_page_media/47/GI_AR2015_FS_web.pdf (Accessed on 6/3/2017).
Retrieved from http://www.goldwaterinstitute.org/en/about/donor-spotlight/ (Accessed on 6/3/2017).
Retrieved from http://goldwaterinstitute.org/en/about/ (Accessed on 6/3/2017).
246. Retrieved from website of Heartland Institute https://www.heartland.org/_template-assets/documents/about-us/2015%20Form%20IRS%20990.pdf (Accessed on 6/3/2017).
Retrieved from SourceWatch website http://www.sourcewatch.org/index.php/Heartland_Institute#Funding (Accessed on 6/3/2017).
Retrieved from https://heartland.org/ (Accessed on 6/3/2017).
247. Retrieved from website of Independent Institute http://www.independent.org/issues/article.asp?id=8627 (Accessed on 6/3/2017).

Retrieved from http://www.independent.org/pdf/finances/2014_fy_form_990.pdf (Accessed on 6/3/2017).
Retrieved from http://www.independent.org/aboutus/ (Accessed on 6/3/2017).
248. Retrieved from CitizenAudit website https://www.citizenaudit.org/organization/382701547/MACKINAC%20CENTER/ (Accessed on 6/3/2017).
Retrieved from http://pdfs.citizenaudit.org/2015_09_EO/38-2701547_990_201412.pdf (Accessed on 6/3/2017).
Retrieved from SourceWatch website http://www.sourcewatch.org/index.php/Mackinac_Center_for_Public_Policy#Funding (Accessed on 6/3/2017).
Retrieved from website of Mackinac Center for Public Policy https://www.mackinac.org/1662 (Accessed on 6/3/2017).
249. Retrieved from ProPublica website https://projects.propublica.org/nonprofits/organizations/541436224 (Accessed on 6/3/2017).
Retrieved from SourceWatch website http://www.sourcewatch.org/index.php/Mercatus_Center#Funding (Accessed on 6/3/2017).
Retrieved from website of Mercatus Center https://www.mercatus.org/about (Accessed on 6/3/2017).
250. Retrieved from website of Mises Institute http://viewer.epageview.com/Viewer.aspx?docid=016e268a-a98c-4d13-ad8a-a5c9011de3da#?page=20 (Accessed on 6/3/2017).
Retrieved from https://mises.org/about-mises (Accessed on 6/3/2017).
251. Retrieved from website of Reason Foundation https://www.reason.org/files/2014-reason_990.pdf (Accessed on 6/3/2017).
Retrieved from http://reason.org/about/ (Accessed on 6/3/2017).
252. Retrieved from website of Show Me Institute http://showmeinstitute.org/sites/default/files/2015%20Annual%20Report_No%20Marks.pdf (Accessed on 6/3/2017).

Retrieved from http://showmeinstitute.org/about-show-me-institute (Accessed on 6/3/2017).
253. https://fconline.foundationcenter.org/grantmaker-profile/?collection=grantmakers&activity=result&key=ABST003
254. https://aclj.org/our-mission/about-aclj
255. https://www.splcenter.org/fighting-hate/extremist-files/group/act-america
256. https://fconline.foundationcenter.org/grantmaker-profile/?collection=grantmakers&activity=result&_new_search=1&location=&state=&county=&city=&metro_area=&congressional_district=&zip_code=&name=Allegheny%20foundation&ein=&type_of_grantmaker=&range=total_giving&range_start=&range_stop=&save_sort=y&sort_by=total_giving&sort_order=1&key=ALLE001&from_search=1
257. https://www.facebook.com/pg/American-Defence-League-ADL-OFFICIAL-244151382331353/about/?ref=page_internal
258. https://www.afa.net/who-we-are/our-mission/
259. http://www.latimes.com/visuals/graphics/la-na-g-afdi-overview-20150504-htmlstory.html
260. http://www.americanfreedomlawcenter.org/about/leaders/robert-j-muise-esq/
261. http://www.sourcewatch.org/index.php/American_Islamic_Forum_for_Democracy
262. https://aifdemocracy.org/american-islamic-leadership-coalition-ailc/
263. http://www.sourcewatch.org/index.php/American_Public_Policy_Alliance
264. http://www.jta.org/2013/10/24/news-opinion/united-states/pro-israel-group-calls-out-newton-schools
265. It's a website with two URLs showing up in google search: 1st one http://atlasshrugs2000.typepad.com/ and http://atlasshrugs.com/ and the 2nd one redirects to http://pamelageller.com/

266. http://www.barenakedislam.com/2016/07/08/eight-years-ago-today-bare-naked-islam-was-born/
267. This is a restaurant in North Versailles, PA. It posts signs that may be labelled as hateful. http://www.casadice.com/index.htm
268. https://www.centerforsecuritypolicy.org/about-us/frank-gaffney/
269. Founding date is not available.
270. https://www.facebook.com/pg/CANchristianactionnetwork/about/?ref=page_internal "...to protect America's religious and moral heritage through educational efforts."
271. Founded in San Francisco. https://www.facebook.com/pg/Christian-Guardians-180494276475/about/?ref=page_internal Mission "Fight injustice. Liberate the world from Islamic terror."
272. https://en.wikipedia.org/wiki/Clarion_Project
273. Counter Jihad Coalition has a website and contact address is a PO box in Huntington Beach, CA. http://counterjihad-coalition.org/
274. Website registered 2015.
275. Counter Jihad Coalition of southern California is supposed to be in Santa Monica, CA. No website or founding date.
276. https://www.bloomberg.com/profiles/companies/9996160Z:US-counter-terrorism-operations-center-llc
277. http://www.sourcewatch.org/index.php/Donors_Capital_Fund
278. http://eagleforum.org/
279. https://fconline.foundationcenter.org/grantmaker-profile?collection=grantmakers&key=KIRB001
280. **Same address as Center for Security Policy.** "The Center for Security Policy has established a partnership with the Family Security Group (FSG)." http://www.sourcewatch.org/index.php/Family_Security_Matters

281. http://www.sourcewatch.org/index.php/Family_Security_Matters
282. https://en.wikipedia.org/wiki/Florida_Family_Association
283. http://formermuslimsunited.org/about/
284. http://www.foxnews.com/us/2017/05/18/roger-ailes-former-president-fox-news-dead-at-77.html
285. https://www.investigativeproject.org/about.php
286. Website created in 2011 as per whois.net.
287. **Same mailing address as David Horowitz Freedom Center.**
288. http://www.rumsfeldfoundation.org/about/ In 2015, the Joyce and Donald Rumsfeld Foundation was transitioned to the Rumsfeld Family Fund.
289. http://www.meforum.org/about.php
290. https://www.memri.org/about
291. https://en.wikipedia.org/wiki/National_Review
292. This is Pamela Geller's website, the founder, editor and publisher of The Geller Report and President of the American Freedom Defense Initiative (AFDI) and Stop Islamization of America (SIOA).
293. It has a new website address now http://www.globalpatriotradio.com/ and an active Facebook page https://www.facebook.com/The-Radio-Jihad-Network-329740016336/ mission statement on Facebook "Our mission is to educate America on American Exceptionalism and National Security Issues."
294. https://en.wikipedia.org/wiki/Randolph_Foundation
295. https://fconline.foundationcenter.org/grantmaker-profile/?key=BERR006&view_format=standard
296. https://www.facebook.com/pg/ShariaFreeUSA/about/?ref=page_internal Has a mission statement on educating US citizens on how the Sharia Law is contrary to US constitutional Law and how it poses a threat to American way of life.
297. http://www.silverbulletgunoil.net/index.html Sells gun lubrication oil that has pig fat ... to put fear in the hearts of Islamoterrorists...

298. http://www.thestraightway.org/
299. http://www.buzzfile.com/business/Straight-Way-of-Grace-Ministry-941-223-1703 and http://www.manta.com/c/mb5hzwx/straight-way-of-grace-ministry claim it was founded in 2005.
300. https://www.facebook.com/pg/TNFreedomCoalition/about/?ref=page_internal Mission is to Educate citizens on Policy matters, education reform, tax issues and the realities of Sharia and stop the growth of radical Islam...
301. https://www.facebook.com/pg/UnderstandingtheThreat/about/?ref=page_internal
302. Twitter handle @USADL says "The United States of America Defence League (USADL) is a human rights organization seeking to halt Sharia Law in America."
303. USDL is an offshoot of English Defence League. EDL is an anti-Islam and anti-sharia org in England. EDL was formed in 2009.
304. http://www.siotw.org/news_english.item.968/the-united-states-defence-league.html
305. https://www.facebook.com/pg/United-States-Defense-League-USDL-128776677250106/about/
306. http://theunitedwest.org/about/our-mission/
307. http://www.washingtontimes.com/about/

Index[1]

NUMBERS AND SYMBOLS
9/11, 2, 15, 83, 94

A
ABC News, xxxii, 18n9
Abraham, S. Daniel, 56
Abrams, Elliot, 146
Active measures, xxx–xxxiii, liin52
Act, Legislative
  Alien and Sedition Acts, 4
  Comprehensive Iran Sanctions, Accountability, and Divestment Act, 150, 252, 352, 430n11
  Iran–Iraq Arms Nonproliferation Act, 347, 431n15
  Iran–Libya Sanctions Act, 347
  Logan Act, 3, 4, 18n13
  Nuclear Deal Review Act, 365
Adams, John, 4
Additional Protocol, 89, 200, 203, 214, 222, 230, 234, 237, 238, 329, 340, 342, 345, 348, 349, 368
Adelson, Sheldon, 51, 52, 60, 83, 91, 100n9, 100n10, 100n11, 100n12, 376, 377, 380, 381, 383, 387, 438n82, 440n121, 441n127
AEOI, *see* Atomic Energy Organization of Iran
Afghanistan, 13, 14, 85

---

[1] Note: Page number followed by 'n' refers to notes.

© The Author(s) 2018
D.C. Jett, *The Iran Nuclear Deal*,
https://doi.org/10.1007/978-3-319-59822-2

Ahmadinejad, Mahmoud, 351
AIG, *see* American International Group
AIPAC, *see* American Israel Public Affairs Committee
Airbnb, 57
Airbus, 27, 31, 168, 371, 373, 406, 445n176
Allison Graham, xxxviii
Al Qaida, 14
Alternative facts, xxiv, 41, 174, 187n16
Amano, Yukiya, 356, 358, 361, 367, 372, 373
Amendment, constitutional
  first, xvi, 4, 12
  fifth, 4
American Civil Liberties Union (ACLU), 138, 148, 149
American Enterprise Institute, xviii, 60, 84, 151, 395, 448n198
American International Group (AIG), 57, 105n48
American Israel Public Affairs Committee (AIPAC), 37, 44n28, 63, 71–80, 83, 111n98, 111n100, 112n106, 113n117, 113n119, 113n122, 114n123, 114n125, 114n126, 138, 378, 384
Americans for Prosperity, xviii, 182, 183, 190n35, 190n37
Americans for Tax Reform, xviii

Anti-Islam, 386, 463n303. *See also* Islamophobia; Islamophobic
Arafat, Yasser, 73
Araghchi, Abbas, 364
Argentina, xii, 347
Argo, 25
Arkansas Horizon, 3, 54
Arms Control Association (ACA), 34, 44n23, 88–92, 120n177, 120n179, 120n180, 120n183, 120n185, 346–375, 425, 426
Ashton, Catherine, 354, 355, 359, 362
Atlantic Council, 87, 370, 406, 453n222
Atomic Energy Organization of Iran (AEOI), 335, 346, 369
Atomstroyexport, 353
Ayres, Whit, 181

B
Bagheri, Ali, 355
Bannon, Stephen, 178, 383
Begin, Menachem, 76
Beinart, Peter, 64, 73, 74, 76, 109n83, 112n106, 113n117, 121n192, 131
Ben-Ami, Jeremy, 79, 80, 115n138
Billionaires, xvii, xix–xxi, xxiv, 2, 3, 49–70, 72, 80, 83, 84, 90, 97, 98, 135, 143, 148, 178, 182, 184, 379, 381, 387, 388

INDEX   467

Blavatnik, Leonard, 59
Blinken, Antony, 363
Bloomberg, Michael, 49, 56, 104n40
Boehner, John, 6, 20n23
Boeing, 168, 371, 396, 397, 445n176
Bolton, John, 3, 55, 82
Bradley Foundation, 61, 62, 79, 107n69, 108n76, 109n78, 386, 395, 396, 398–401, 413, 414, 416–419, 424
Braman, Norman, 54, 388
Brazil, xii, 352
Breitbart News, xxv, 134, 178
Brennan Center, xvii
Broad, Eli, 55
Brookings, Institution, xvi, 43n15, 145, 406, 453n223
Brown, Gordon, 351
Bruck, Connie, 73, 74, 103n34, 112n107
Buffett, Warren, 56
Bush
　George H.W., xlii, 27, 378
　George W., xxxvii, xlii, 3, 29, 91, 148, 182
　Jeb, 5, 19n19, 57, 65, 105n48
Business Insider, 95, 122n197, 435n52
Buzzfeed, xxvi, 391

C
Caddell, Pat, 97, 98
Cambridge Analytica, 177, 178

Campaign Finance Institute, xix
Card, Andrew, 82
Carlson, Tucker, 139, 140, 155, 161n34
Carlucci, Frank, 94
Carnegie Endowment for International Peace, 86, 118n162, 407, 454n224
Carson, Ben, 6
Carter, Jimmy, 26
Cassidy and Associates, 144
CATO Institute, xviii, 58, 105n54, 414, 415, 419, 457n241
CBS, 11, 21n35, 22n48, 23n58, 110n89, 116n148, 120n181, 188n21
Center for American Progress, 385, 402, 451n212
Center for American Progress Action Fund, xxi
Center for Arms Control and Non-Proliferation, 8
Center for Constitutional Rights, 148
Center for Media and Democracy (CMD), 61, 99n2, 107n70, 108n71, 161n34
Center for New American Security, 87
Center for Responsive Politics, xv, 184
Center for Security Policy, 62, 92–96, 121n188, 121n190, 396, 423, 448n200, 461n280

Chaffetz, Jason, 151
Chamberlain, Neville, 5, 41
Chao, Elaine, 82
Charity Navigator, 66, 67, 110n90, 449n201, 450n209, 451n212, 451n213, 452n216, 453n219, 453n221, 453n222, 455n229
Cheney, Dick, 83, 151, 175, 377
Chesky, Brian, 57
China, xliv, 17, 30, 31, 195, 196, 328, 339, 349, 369, 375
Christians United for Israel (CUFI), 51, 75, 76, 112n112, 379, 380, 383, 436n62, 436n67
ChristianTimesNewpaper.com, xxiii
Christie, Chris, 7, 58, 65
Churchill, Winston, 9, 185
CIA, xl, 29, 31, 40, 42n3, 84, 169, 386
Citizens for a Nuclear Free Iran (CNFI), 72, 73, 112n105
Citizens United decision, xv, 50, 184
Clark, Wesley, 82
Clinton
  Bill, 60
  Hillary, xxiii, 7, 8, 14, 23n54, 23n56, 52, 54, 100n13, 103n35, 132

CMD, *see* Center for Media and Democracy
Cohen, Steven, 58, 105n52, 165n73, 408
Cohen, William, 86, 408
Colombe Foundation, 92, 96
Committee on Armed Services, 86
Committee on Government Operations, 86
Committee on Intelligence, xxxi, liin53, 88, 92
Competitive Enterprise Institute, 183, 415, 457n242
Comprehensive safeguards agreement, 89, 203, 238
Congressional Research Service, 142, 170, 186n11
Connect U.S. Fund, 97
Contract With America, 142
Contra, Iran, 26, 127, 146, 153, 167, 185n2
Conway, James T., 82
Corker, Bob, 365, 374
Cotton, Tom, 1–3, 5, 17n2, 17n3, 17n4, 18n7, 21n42, 35, 40, 54, 364, 376, 394, 447n185
Council on Foreign Relations, 146, 173, 409, 454–455n228
CREDO, 138, 421
Cruz, Ted, 6, 57–59, 106n61, 377
Cuban missile crisis, xxxviii

D

Dagan, Meir, 149
Dailey, Dell, 82
Daily Caller, 139, 140, 155
Daily Caller News Foundation, 139, 161n31, 161n32
Daily Signal, 62
David Horowitz Freedom Center, 62, 423, 462n287
Dean, Howard, 82
Deep Throat, *see* Watergate
Defense Intelligence Agency, 29
Democratic National Committee (DNC), xxvi, ln39
Department of State, livn62, 33, 41n1, 42n8, 92, 347
  Bureau of Intelligence and Research in the Department of State, 92. *See also* State Department
Deputy national security adviser for strategic communications, 132
Dershowitz, Alan, 87, 119n167
Dershowitz, Toby, 83, 117n152
Desert Storm, xlii
DeVos, Betsy, xvii, xviii, xlvin7, 49, 140
Dobriansky, Paula, 82
Dole, Bob, 129, 130, 158n7, 158n8
Donors Trust, xviii, xlvin8, 49, 79, 395, 398, 414, 419

Donovan, William, xxxix
Dubowitz, Mark, 85, 86, 117n155, 118n159, 167, 168, 186n5

E

Egypt, 151
Eisenhower administration, 33
Electronic Frontier Foundation, 148
Ellison, Lawrence, 58
Equatorial Guinea, 143
European Union (EU), xliv, 31, 34, 41, 129, 173, 195, 196, 198, 205, 206, 210–214, 243, 339–342, 344, 346, 352, 354, 360, 364, 365, 368, 374, 375, 429n5, 429n8, 429n9
Exxon, xxxvii, 143, 381, 400, 446n176

F

Facebook, xxv, 73, 144, 153, 176, 188n22, 446n176, 462n293
Falwell, Jerry, 76
Federal Bureau of Investigation (FBI), 48, 77, 82
Federal Election Commission, xix
Federal Reserve, 57
Federalist Society, xviii
Federation of American Scientists, xxx

Financial Times, 147, 148, 163n52, 164n55
Fiorina, Carly, 7, 21n35
Flynn, Michael, 95, 135, 169, 374
Forbes, 49, 52, 59
Ford Foundation, 96, 402
Foreign affairs, 3, 4, 10, 81, 116n143, 127, 153, 163n50, 167, 195, 196, 214, 329, 339, 384, 446n176
Foreign Agents Registration Act, 123, 144
The Forward, 51, 52
Foundation for Defense of Democracies (FDD), 51, 53, 60, 80–88, 117n151, 118n159, 151, 167, 186n5, 382
Fox News, xxvi, 53, 64, 74, 136, 139, 390, 424
France, xliv, 17, 31, 33, 195, 196, 328, 339, 348, 349, 352
Freeh, Louis, 82
Friends Committee on National Legislation, 65, 87, 426, 427

G

Gaffney, Frank, 62, 63, 94, 95, 108n74
Gates, Bill, 57
Gatestone, 55, 102n28

General Electric, 63, 396
Germany, xliv, 17, 31, 33, 195, 196, 328, 339, 348, 349
Gerrymandering, xxvii, xxviii, xl
Gingrich, Newt, 51, 100n9, 100n11
Giuliani, Rudy, 82, 116n149
Government Accountability Office, 142
Graham, Lindsey, xxxviii, 6, 58
Greece, 148
Greenberg, Maurice Hank, 57, 105n48
GuideStar, 66, 67, 435n57, 438n89
Gulf War, 127

H

Haaretz, 37, 42n7, 44n28, 64, 74, 76, 101n20, 113n117, 163n48, 388, 394, 442n136, 447n189
Hagee, John, 75, 76, 113n114, 380, 436n64, 436n65
Hagel, Wilhelm Friedrich, 70, 122n204
Hamas, 79
Hamilton, Lee, 82
Hammond, Philip, 363
Hanks, Tom, 14, 23n53
Hannah, John, 83, 117n151, 151
Hannity, Sean, xxvii, xxix, xxxi, lin41
Harriman, Averell, xxxix

Harvey, Derek, 169
Hayden, Michael, 82
Hendricks, Diane, 58, 106n59
Heritage Action, 68, 69
Heritage Foundation, xviii, 2, 62, 67, 84, 129, 398, 449n203
Hewlett Foundation, 86, 92, 97, 407, 445n176
The Hill, 8, 21n40, 79, 92, 115n136, 120n182
Hispanic, 64, 76
Hitler, Adolf, 5, 41
Holocaust, 5, 383
Homeschool Legal Defense Association, 129
House of Lords, 31, 32
Huckabee, Mike, 5, 19n20, 380
Hudson Institute, 151, 398, 450n205
Hull, Cordell, xxxix, livn62
Human rights, 25, 26, 66, 90, 137, 168, 169, 171, 383, 384, 394
Hungary, 55
Hussein, Saddam, xl, 28, 29, 82

I
Ibsen, David, 91
Infowars, xxiv
Institute for Strategic Dialogue (ISD), 91
Intelligence community, xxii, xxvi, xxxi, 88, 89, 98, 350
Interim agreement, 7, 34, 156, 361, 362
Internal Revenue Service (IRS), 47, 48, 139, 379, 394
International Atomic Energy Agency (IAEA), 34, 38, 89, 198–202, 204–207, 209, 212, 213, 217–221, 224–241, 317, 318, 321, 323–325, 330, 335–337, 339–342, 344, 348–351, 354–362, 364–374, 394, 428n3
Iran, 425–428
 Guardian Council, 367
 Iran Air Flight 665, 27
 Iranian Revolution, 347
 Iran nuclear agreement, x, xiv, xix, xliv, xlv, 17, 37, 40, 47, 67, 68, 70, 79, 80, 88, 96, 97, 128, 167, 169, 170, 185, 377, 384
 National Council of Resistance of Iran, 81
 Revolutionary Guard Corps, 170
 Shah, 26, 33, 93
Iraq, xxxvii, xlii, 2, 28–30, 41, 87, 92, 93, 148, 151, 169, 376, 378, 379
IRS, *see* Internal Revenue Service
IR theory, xxxviii, xli, xliv, xlv
Irving Moskowitz Foundation, 94, 383

INDEX

Isaacs, John, 8
Islam, 62, 153, 463n300
Islamic State of Iraq and Syria (ISIS), 2, 81, 116n143, 116n145
Islamic State of Iraq and the Levant (ISIL), 33
Islamophobia, 62, 94, 385
Islamophobic, 53, 55, 89, 92, 385, 386, 422–425
Islamoterrorists, 462n297
Israel, 3, 5, 6, 9, 11, 14, 28, 37, 51–54, 59, 60, 63, 68, 71, 72, 74–78, 80, 84, 98, 146, 149, 151, 153, 172, 376, 378, 380–387, 389–391, 394, 427, 447n187
Israeli American Council (IAC), 51, 53, 386, 440n120, 440n121

J

Jalili, Saeed, 354, 355
Jerusalem Post, 28, 42n9, 115n139, 437n69, 437n71, 441n130
Jewish, 11, 14, 37, 42n7, 51, 52, 54–56, 60, 61, 63, 64, 72–76, 79, 97, 98, 101n21, 131, 156, 375–377, 385, 387–391, 394, 420, 433n26, 443n149, 443n151
Jews, 55, 63, 64, 75, 76, 78, 80, 128, 155, 156, 380, 382, 383

Jindal, Bobby, 8, 65
Jinping, Xi, 369
Johnson, Gary, 69
Joint Comprehensive Plan of Action (JCPOA), 33, 34, 81, 89, 195–346, 367, 371–375, 419–422, 428n1, 429n7, 429n8, 429n9, 430n10, 430n11, 431n17, 431n18, 432n23, 432n25
Joint Plan of Action (JPOA), 34, 36, 198, 359, 360, 363
Jones, Alex, xxiv, xlixn28, 55
J Street, 61, 63, 71–80, 87, 114n133, 155, 383, 389, 394, 420
Justice Department, 3, 90, 148, 149, 396

K

Kakutani, Michiko, xxix, liin51
Kamalvandi, Behrouz, 369
Kasich, John, 7, 20n33
Kennedy, Patrick, 82
Kerry, John, 170, 357, 358, 362, 365, 370, 371, 373, 393
KGB, xxx
Khamenei, *see* Supreme Leader
Khan, Abdul Qadeer, 347
Klarman, Seth, 3, 53, 60, 101n19
Klein, Ben, 59
Koch, brothers, xxi, 49, 69, 72, 79, 135, 182, 381, 395, 398

Kristol, William, 3, 376, 379
Krugman, Paul, 181, 189n31
Kurtzer, Daniel, 74
Kuwait, xlii, 85

L
Labor unions, xvi, xviii, xix, xxxiii, 59, 61
Lauder, Ronald, 54, 97, 101n21, 390
Lavrov, Sergey, 353, 363
Libya, 130, 347
Lieberman, Joseph, 91, 116n142
Likud, Party, 74, 76, 391, 392, 444n166
Lipton, Eric, 2, 18n8, 101n16, 115n140, 189n32, 433n34
Lockheed Martin, 63, 67, 68, 111n93, 396, 446n176
Loeb, Daniel, 54, 102n23
Logan, George, 4, 5

M
Manzullo, Dan, 14
Marcus, Bernard, 22n47, 53, 60, 83, 414
May, Clifford, 83, 86, 446n176
Mayer, Jane, xlviin12, 49, 57, 187n18
McBride, Anita, 82
McCain, John, 181, 392
McConnell, Mitch, 6, 82
McLaughlin, John, 97, 98

McMaster, H.R., 169
McNair, Robert, 58
MeK, *see* Mujahideen-e Khalq
Mercatus Center, 58, 418, 459n249
Mercer, Rebekah, xxv
Mercer, Robert, xxv, 57, 105n46, 178
Merkel, Angela, 44n22, 172, 186n12
The Middle East Observer, 84
Military-industrial complex, 14
Miller, Paul, 79, 115n136
Mogherini, Federica, 364, 369, 373–375
Moniz, Ernest, 365, 374
Mossad, 149
Mossadegh, Mohammad, 26, 31
MoveOn.org, 422
Mujahideen-e Khalq (MeK), 81–83, 116n144, 116n147, 347
Mukasey, Michael, 82, 386
Murdoch, Rupert, 53
Myers, Richard, 82

N
Nackaerts, Herman, 357
Najafi, Reza, 357
Nathan Cummings Foundation, 79
The Nation, 49, 55, 71, 99n4, 101n17, 101n22, 102n27, 116n145, 124, 151, 158n2

National Academy of Sciences, xxi, xlviiin21
National Council of Resistance of Iran, 81
National Intelligence Estimate (NIE), 350, 354
National Iranian American Council (NIAC), xxxv, 87, 92–96, 122n196, 168, 186n7, 420
National Public Radio (NPR), xv, 23n55, 87, 88, 163n45
National Rifle Association, xviii, 71, 130
National security advisor, 83, 95, 135, 169, 374, 383, 387
National Security Agency, 28
National Security Council (NSC), xxiv, xlixn30, xlixn31, 169, 393
NATO, 30, 127, 158n5, 171
Netanyahu, Benjamin, 34–37, 44n26, 52, 73, 74, 76, 79, 153, 165n72, 168, 356, 364, 380, 382, 387, 391, 441n124, 444n168, 444n169
New Yorker, xix, xlviin12, 57, 73, 77, 103n34, 112n107, 114n129, 187n18, 189n28
New York Times, xx, xxii, xxiv, xxix, xxxviii, xlviin16, xlviiin24, xlixn26, xlixn28, xlixn29, xlixn32, lin41, liin51, liiin59, livn60, 2, 3, 18n5, 18n8, 18n11, 21n41, 22n49, 28, 38, 40, 42n10, 45n30, 45n32, 50, 87, 91, 99n6, 100n13, 103n37, 106n60, 107n64, 107n66, 113n120, 118n158, 120n176, 132, 135, 148, 151, 159n15, 160n21, 164n57, 169, 176, 181, 183, 185n1, 185n2, 186n8, 188n21, 188n24, 189n29, 189n31, 189n32, 387
NextGen, 57
Nichols, Tom, 414
Norquist, Grover, xviii, xlviin14
North American Free Trade Agreement, 171
North Korea, xlii, 130
Northrup Grumman, 63, 396
Nuclear
  agreement, x, xiv, xix, xliv, xlv, 8–10, 17, 31, 37, 40, 54, 62, 63, 67, 68, 70, 71, 73, 79, 80, 85, 88, 91, 93, 96, 97, 128, 134, 138, 145, 167, 169, 170, 184, 185, 362, 377, 384, 391, 392, 394, 425–428
  deal, xiv, xxxiv, xli, xlii, 2, 10, 11, 16, 25, 32, 33, 35, 51, 59, 64, 75, 78, 84–87
  facilities Iranian, xli, 27, 28, 39, 68, 156; Arak, 38,

INDEX 475

202, 203, 216–223, 232, 241, 242, 320–322, 340, 341, 347, 349, 359, 360, 368, 369, 375; Bushehr, 348, 353; Fordow, 201, 227–230, 234, 322, 330, 341, 342, 351, 353, 355, 356, 374; Isfahan, 349; Natanz, 38, 200, 201, 224–226, 229, 230, 234, 237, 347, 349, 353, 356, 371
Nonproliferation Treaty, 346, 365
program, xxxiv, xli, 1, 6, 10, 25, 27, 28, 30, 33, 37, 38, 147
reactor, 202, 203, 319, 320, 346, 373
weapons, xxxiv, xli, xlii, 1, 8, 10, 29, 30, 35, 37, 39, 53, 56, 80, 88–91, 98, 197, 348, 350, 353, 354, 364, 366, 368, 369, 374, 384, 392
Nuclear Nonproliferation Treaty (NPT), 197, 198, 209, 257, 346, 365
Nuclear program, xxxiv, xli, 1, 6, 10, 25, 27, 28, 30, 33, 37, 38, 147, 155, 156, 195–197, 204, 333, 350, 351, 355–359, 361–363, 365, 367–369, 374

O

Obama, Barack, xxv, 2, 5–8, 19n18, 30, 35, 36, 40, 44n25, 52, 54, 56, 62, 68, 87, 90, 98, 101n17, 101n22, 102n26, 113n114, 115n135, 119n168, 126, 132, 138, 143, 148, 149, 152, 153, 161n29, 165n66, 172, 175, 179, 181, 351, 357, 369, 376, 377, 379, 380, 436n64
administration, xliv, xlv, 1, 5, 7, 10, 28, 32, 56, 71, 81, 134, 135, 141, 145, 147, 148, 162n44, 180, 351, 365, 374, 378, 393, 394
Obamacare, 2, 139, 161n30
Oberndorf, Bill, 56
Obiang, Teodoro, 143, 144
Open Society Foundation, 86, 394, 395, 408, 445–446n176
OpenSecrets.org, 59
Oren, Michael, 152, 153, 165n67
Organizations, x, 91, 393
Orwellian, 134
Oval Office, xxxvi

P

P5+1, 32–35, 39, 41, 85, 89, 120n179
Pace, Peter, 82

Palestine Liberation
  Organization (PLO), 73, 74
Palestinian, 37, 55, 73, 74, 79,
  113n119, 168, 378, 380,
  382, 385, 387, 439n109
PARSA Community, 95
Pataki, George, 6, 20n26, 65
Paul, Rand, livn65, 6, 20n28,
  377
Pentagon, 27, 67, 77, 78,
  113n120, 114n128, 133
Perino, Dana, 82
Perry, Rick, 8, 21n38, 377
Persian, 27, 68, 85, 93, 95,
  127, 168, 377
Peru, xi, 137
Pew Survey, xxvii
Pipes, Daniel, 62, 94, 385–387,
  390, 391, 440n114
Planned Parenthood, 138
Ploughshares, 56, 61, 80–88,
  92, 95, 96, 118n160,
  118n161, 118n163,
  118n165, 136, 446n176
Poindexter, John, 146
Politico, xlvin7, xlixn31, 21n37,
  42n12, 44n25, 44n27,
  104n44, 105n48, 105n50,
  110n88, 124, 139, 141,
  157n1, 158n7, 161n30,
  161n35, 163n49, 163n51,
  163n54, 168, 434n46,
  444n163, 445n170
Pompeo, Mike, 169
Pope Francis, 65, 110n87

Positivism, xliii
Potter, Trevor, xix
Powell, Colin, xxxviii, livn60,
  29, 78, 87, 146, 163n51,
  392
Power, Samantha, 370
Price, Ned, 133
Psychographic, 178
Push polling, 155
Putin, Vladimir, xxx, xxxi,
  xxxiii, 30

Q
Qatar, 85, 118n158
Qorvis, 144

R
Rabin, Yitzhak, 73, 74
Rajavi, Maryam, 81
Ray, James Lee, xli, xliii, xliv,
  livn64, livn66, 109n85
Raytheon, Lockheed Martin,
  63, 396, 406, 446n176
Reagan, Ronald, 26, 27, 54,
  125
  administration, 13, 28, 30,
  62, 93, 94
Reiss, Mitchell, 82
Rendell, Ed, 82
Republican Jewish Coalition
  (RJC), 51, 53, 60, 139,
  141, 376, 434n37, 434n41
Research, 383
Resnick, Lynda and Stewart, 54

Restis, Victor, 90, 148, 149
ReThink, 96–98, 122n201, 122n202, 154, 156, 165n70, 166n74, 421
Rhodes, Ben, 132–136, 145, 151, 159n15, 159n16
Richardson, Bill, 82
Rich, Seth, xxvi, xxxi, lin40
Ridge, Tom, 82
Rightweb, 97
Rockefeller Brothers Fund, 86, 95, 96, 402
Romney, Mitt, 54, 98
Roosevelt, Franklin, xxxix, livn61, 9, 175
Rosenberg, M.J., 45n32, 71, 111n99, 186n8, 411, 445n175
Rouhani, Hassan, 34, 65, 170, 356, 357, 369, 371, 373, 375
Rubio, Marco, 5, 19n18, 54, 58, 65, 102n24, 106n57, 388, 442n138, 442n139
Rumsfeld, Donald, 28, 29, 42n12, 396, 424, 462n288
Russia, xxx, xxxii, xxxiii, xliv, 17, 30, 31, 135, 172, 202, 348, 349, 352, 369, 372

S
Saban, Haim, 52, 53, 77, 100n12, 387, 407
Salehi, Ali Akbar, 358, 364, 373

SALT, 9
Samore, Gary, 81, 91, 115n141
Samuels, David, 119n168, 132–134, 136, 145, 151, 159n12, 165n64
SAN, *see* Secure America Now
Sanders, Bernie, 175, 408
Santistevan, Jorge de Noriega, 137
Santorum, Rick, 7, 65, 129
Sarkozy, Nicolas, 351
Saudi Arabia, 68, 84, 85, 151, 379
Scaife Foundation, 63, 109n78, 381, 395, 396, 398–401, 413, 414, 416, 417
Scherer, Michael, 76, 113n118
Schmid, Helga, 355, 364
Schooner Foundation, 86
Schumer, Chuck, 379
Scout magazine, 178, 189n26
Scowcroft, Brent, 146, 408
Secord, Richard, 146
Secretary of defense, 29, 62, 94, 373, 384
Secretary of state, xxxvii, xxxix, 14, 15, 29, 33, 41, 74, 78, 86, 143, 144, 162n42, 167, 170, 358, 363, 374, 375, 392
Secure America Now (SAN), 96–98, 122n203, 155, 165n71, 428
Security Council, xlii, 337, 368, 370

Senate Foreign Relations
  Committee, 81, 150, 363,
  365
Shah, 26, 33, 93, 346
Shalem Center, 52
Sharia, 94, 424, 462n296,
  463n300, 463n302
Shelton, Hugh, 82
Sherman, Wendy, 44n27, 358,
  364, 375
Shultz, George, 29, 86, 170
Silverstein, Ken, 76, 113n118
Simons, James, 58
Singer, Paul, 3, 53, 60, 83, 94,
  379
Skoll Global Threats Fund, 79,
  446n176
Snowden, Edward, 28, 42n7
Social Security, 59, 106n61,
  137
Solomon, Jay, 153, 165n68,
  394
Soros, George, 49, 52, 55, 61,
  79, 86, 102n29, 102n31,
  103n32, 392, 394, 395,
  448n195
Southern Poverty Law Center,
  94, 121n191, 390, 391,
  422, 444n160
Soviet Union, xiii, xxx, 26
Spielberg, Steven, 56
START, 9
State Department, x, xxxviii,
  xxxix, 26, 40, 81, 82, 133,
  363, 406

Steinmeier, Frank-Walter, 363
Steve Bannon, xxiv
Streyer, Tom, 57
Stuxnet, 27, 42n7, 353
Sunlight Foundation, 97
Sunni, 81
Supreme Leader, 89, 368
Sussman, Donald, 57, 402
Syria, 32, 253, 257, 343,
  430n11

T

Tax
  501, xviii, 48–50, 55, 61, 68,
    72, 73, 83, 139, 182,
    258, 377–379, 382, 383,
    386
  990, xlvin8, 62, 73, 109n80,
    118n164, 161n31,
    190n40, 376, 379, 382,
    390, 394, 425–428
  death, xix, 61
  Forms IRS, 62, 376, 394,
    428
  inheritance, xix, 61
Tea Party, 48, 64, 99n1, 139,
  179, 180, 189n29
Tehran Research Reactor
  (TRR), 202, 223, 231,
  233, 323, 329, 346, 347,
  352, 355
Tenet, George, 29, 30
Thielmann, Greg, 92,
  120n180, 120n182

Tikkun Daily, 77
Tillerson, Rex, xxxvii, xxxviii, 33, 143, 374, 375, 381, 408
Totenberg, Nina, xv, xlvin2
Townsend, Frances, 82, 404, 408
Trans-Pacific Partnership, 171
Treasury Department, 54, 369
TRR, *see* Tehran Research Reactor
Truman National Security Project, 57
Trump, Donald, xvii, xx–xxix, xxxii, 5, 37, 57, 60, 80, 82, 95, 126, 127, 140, 155, 171, 172, 174–180, 372, 375, 383, 389
  administration, xxix, xxxiii, 10, 19n15, 32, 33, 40, 41, 88, 89, 135, 168, 169, 173, 375
Turkey, 151, 352, 377
Turner, Ted, 56, 103n36
TV, 91, 112n104, 138, 178

U

UAE, *see* United Arab Emirates
UANI, *see* United Against Nuclear Iran
Uihlein, Elizabeth and Richard, 58
UN, *see* United Nations
Unions, xvi, 329
United Against Nuclear Iran (UANI), 81, 84, 90, 91, 116n142, 119n172, 147, 148, 164n59
United Arab Emirates (UAE), 15, 84, 446n176
United Kingdom (UK), 31, 32, 43n19, 44n21, 195, 328, 339, 348, 349
United Nations (UN), 3, 29, 52, 56, 91, 158n6, 197, 331, 333, 334, 336–338
  Security Council Resolution 1696, 205, 344, 349
  Security Council Resolution 1737, 205, 344, 350
  Security Council Resolution 1747, 205, 344, 350
  Security Council Resolution 1803, 205, 344, 350
  Security Council Resolution 1929, 205, 344, 352, 367, 368
University
  Ariel, 52
  George Mason, 58
  George Washington, xix
  Harvard, 87
  Maryland, 64
  Pennsylvania, 63, 67, 110n92
  Sydney, 9
  Texas, 4, 13, 22n49, 58, 63
US News, xvii, xlvin5, 54, 102n26
USS Vincennes, 27

V

Varjoranta, Tero, 367
Vidricaire, Marc, 351
Vietnam, xi, 127
Vladeck, Steve, 4

W

Walker, Scott, 5, 19n17, 59, 106n58
Wallace, Mark, 91, 405
Wall Street Journal, 18n7, 53, 84, 85, 104n41, 106n57, 111n100, 153, 186n6, 436n60
Washington Examiner, 68, 111n96, 186n10
Washington Free Beacon, 134
Washington Post, xxvi, xxxii, xxxvi, xlvin1, xlviin11, ln36, lin40, lin45, lin47, liin56, liiin58, liiin59, 17n4, 19n15, 23n54, 33, 44n26, 98, 99n8, 101n18, 103n38, 104n45, 107n68, 110n86, 110n87, 111n101, 113n121, 114n124, 114n128, 115n138, 116n146, 116n149, 121n189, 131, 135, 139, 143, 158n3, 159n10, 159n11, 161n32, 162n40, 163n46, 174–176, 187n17, 187n18, 188n19, 188n20, 188n22, 190n42, 190n43, 393, 433n27, 433n34, 434n41, 435n55, 441n129, 446n183, 447n185, 457n242
Watergate, 48
Watnick, Ezra Cohen, 169, 186n9
Weekly Standard, 3, 376, 433n28
Weinberger, Casper, 94
Welles, Sumner, xxxix
White House, 3, 4, 18n5, 18n12, 34, 36, 64, 84, 95, 133, 134, 138, 143, 151, 159n17, 160n18, 160n25, 165n63, 168, 177, 184, 186n9, 187n16, 188n22, 383
WikiLeaks, xxvi, xxxii, ln39, 14
Wilke, Wendell, 175
Wilson, Charlie, 13, 14, 16, 22n49, 22n50, 23n52, 23n53, 412
World Values Network, 51, 387, 441n128
World War, xlii, 93, 130, 175
Wounded Warrior, 66, 110n89

Y

Yemen, 32, 130, 169

Z

Zarif, Mohammad Javad, 357, 359, 362, 363, 365, 369, 370

Zinni, Anthony, 82

Zionist Organization of America (ZOA), 51, 382, 383, 438n86

Zuckerman, Mortimer, 54, 102n26

GPSR Compliance

The European Union's (EU) General Product Safety Regulation (GPSR) is a set of rules that requires consumer products to be safe and our obligations to ensure this.

If you have any concerns about our products, you can contact us on

ProductSafety@springernature.com

In case Publisher is established outside the EU, the EU authorized representative is:

Springer Nature Customer Service Center GmbH
Europaplatz 3
69115 Heidelberg, Germany

www.ingramcontent.com/pod-product-compliance
Lightning Source LLC
LaVergne TN
LVHW040729250326

834688LV00031B/221